Nutfield Rambles

STORIES FROM THE HISTORY OF
Derry, Londonderry, & Windham, New Hampshire

RICHARD HOLMES

PETER E. RANDALL PUBLISHER LLC
Portsmouth, New Hampshire 03802
2007

Library of Congress Catalog Number: 2007938613

ISBN10: 1-931807-64-7
ISBN13: 978-1-931807-64-7

Peter E. Randall Publisher LLC
Box 4726
Portsmouth, NH 03802

www.perpublisher.com

Book design: Grace Peirce

Cover photo: Broadway looking west, circa 1907

To my loving wife, Carol,
for putting up with my historic rambling
and to her loyal companions:
Holly, Moki, Inga, Xinnia and Lexa

OTHER BOOKS BY RICHARD HOLMES

A View from Meeting House Hill, 1988
Derry (with William Dugan), 1995
Chester Revisited, 1995
Derry Revisited (with William Dugan), 2005

Contents

Introduction vii
1. Our Scotch-Irish Roots   1
2. Eels, Indians, and Potatoes 11
3. The Goblet of Blood 21
4. A Neighborhood Squabble. 27
5. The Londonderry Riot 30
6. Stephen Holland, Spy Master 40
7. Nutfield's First Lawyer 55
8. The Devil and Derry. 61
9. Lafayette Was Here—Maybe Twice 71
10 The Birth of the Town. 77
11. Sally McMurphy—Thrift, Pluck, and Luck 87
12. The Barrington Beggars 90
13. Bear Hunts. 95
14. Mass Murder in Londonderry. 101
15. Love, Marriage, and Shivarees 108
16. The Yellow Day 117
17. William Pillsbury: The Man Who Made Broadway . 123
18. Leonard Pillsbury 130
19. Pillsbury versus Pillsbury 141
20. The End of the Civil War 153
21. Flora Stewart 157
22. Minstrel Days 163
23. The Great Broadway Fire of 1882. 167
24. Franklin Evans, the Derry Monster 173
25. Columbus Day in 1892 181
26. The Great Freshet of 1900. 185
27. Everett Angell 189
28. Bella Chapin Barrows: So Much in a Lifetime 194
29. The Great Derry Monster 201

30. Robert Frost and the Association Hall 207
31. The Hood Farm 215
32. The Chester and Derry Trolley 221
33. The Test 227
34. The Greatest Baseball Game Ever 233
35. Walter Adams 239
36. Louis Lewis the Cigar Maker 245
37. The Burning of Saint Thomas Aquinas Church 251
38. The Adams Mill 261
39. Hemlock Oil 267
40. Anne Frasier Norton 273
41. Daylight Saving Time 277
42. Iceboats in Derry 281
43. Ned and the Dancing Bear 285
44. The Search for Buddy Stewart 290
45. Radio Days 293
46. The Lyon and the Elephant 297
47. The Hurricane of 1938 301
48. Cigar Box John 307
49. Walter Borowski, Hero 311
50. The Great Chelmsford Fire 329
51. The Parade That Just Happened 339
52. Sin Town 347
53. The Eclipse 353
    Bibliography 357
    Index 360
    About the Author 371

Introduction

THIS BOOK IS NOT INTENDED TO BE A HISTORY OF NUTFIELD; it rather is a collection of historical rambles involving the Nutfield towns of Derry, Londonderry, and Windham. It is also not intended to be deep and dry; I hope it will be somewhat scholarly without seeming to be so. As a beginning teacher in 1967, I was told by a classroom veteran that her ways to get the students' attention was to "tell them topical stories that would get them to laugh or cry, but first and foremost you should try to avoid boring them. If you're excited about what you're teaching, the kids will be excited too. And once you get their attention, the students will learn." Her advice became my philosophy during thirty-two years of teaching sixth grade social studies, as it has been in writing this book.

To research this book I have had to peruse many, many sources. I've read the Portsmouth newspapers from 1756 to 1831; the *Exeter News-Letter* from 1831 to 1880; the *Derry News* from 1880 to the present; and sundry issues of the *Union Leader, Nutfield News*, the *Derry Serviceman*, the *Derry Star,* and the *Londonderry Times.*

I've read and reread every available book on local history and quoted, paraphrased, and stolen liberally from their pages. Many of the older stories that I borrowed from past storytellers, have had their original language reworked to make it more understandable to readers of the twenty-first century. I've aggravated my allergies by going through dusty volumes of church and town records. I've spent hours and hours enjoying fascinating conversation with our older citizens. And my computer, as a link to Google and Ancestry. com, has been a certain comfort in times of need.

Most of this book is not centered on the "big stories" in our history; there are plenty of books on General John Stark, astronaut Alan Shepard, and poet Robert Frost. I have instead concentrated on the smaller incidents in our past. I've included stories of war heroes, fires, baseball games, and local squabbles. I tried to prove that the Revolutionary War began in Derry and that the siege of Londonderry, Ireland, in 1689 led to the 1719 founding of Londonderry, New Hampshire. In one story I chronicle how we celebrated the end of the Civil War and in another I describe our parade that celebrated Alan Shepard's first flight into space. Within these pages the Great Derry Monster of 1906 stalks again and Derry is christened "Sin Town, N.H." by the *Union Leader* newspaper. I tell the sad tale of the murderer Franklin Evans, "the worse man to have ever lived in Derry." Most of my stories were once the talk of the town but are now forgotten.

Some of these stories have appeared in a somewhat different form in my weekly column in the *Derry News*; most have not. I have had no problem finding things to write about. I could, in fact, write for decades and still not come to the bottom of the well of Nutfield tales. In truth, I can't wait to get started on my next collection. Next time I'll tell the story of Ocean Born Mary, the Red Scare in Derry in the 1920s, the Adams Female Academy, our three and a half Congressional Medal of Honor winners, the actress Priscilla Lane, and Prohibition days in Nutfield. I eagerly look forward to writing about my mentor, an internationally known artist and inventor, who has made a living in Derry selling butterflies and was an active participant in the Anguilla Revolution of 1967. He presently spends much of his time building miniature medieval trebuchets.

Although I am now of the age to collect Social Security, I still feel that I have a few more years left in which I can study, learn, and write about the history of Derry, Londonderry, and Windham. And the more I delve into local history, the more I discover how much I don't know or how much I understood only imperfectly. I would appreciate hearing from anyone who has ideas for the next book or additional information or corrections about the tales in this current volume.

I wish to thank especially the Derry Heritage Commission, Pinkerton Academy, and the *Derry News* for letting me use their archives. I could not have completed this book without the help of the Derry Public Library, the Taylor Library, the New Hampshire

State Library, the New Hampshire Historical Society, and the New Hampshire State Archives. Thanks also to my worthy adviser and friend Marilyn Ham; Leslie O'Donnell; Marc Fortier; Seamus and Helen Kennedy of Derry, Ireland; Julie Huss, Barbara Bailey, Sergeant Doyle R. Betts, Richard Becker, Hercules Pappachristos, Priscilla Cox, Phyllis and George Katsakiores, Charlie Morton, Karen Anderson, Tim Brown, Barry Friedman, and Doug Rathburn. Police Chief Ed Garone, Fire Chief George Klauber, and Town Clerk Denise Neale; the Feinauer family, Patsy, Bo, Eva, Barbara, Cheri, Olga, Walter, Marina, Frank and the rest of my early morning discussion group at the Thrift Shop, Tom Lewis, Sister Margaret Auban, Charlie Morton, Margaret Bobalek King, Andrew Bell, Mike Kalil, Shelley Thompson, Roger and Theresa Beliveau, Bill Dugan, Walter and Lillian Chapman, Ralph Bonner, Janice Rioux, Rebecca Rutter, Janet Fairbanks, Marion Richardson Pounder, Bill Petch, Brian Buckley, David Narlee, and a legion of others who made the path down which I ramble much smoother and straighter.

Richard Holmes
The Old Rambler

The home of the Reverend James MacGregor was the first framed building in Nutfield. It was built in 1722 and torn down in 1863 to be replaced by a more modern house.

1.
Our Scotch-Irish Roots

THE NUTFIELD TOWNS OF DERRY, WINDHAM, AND LONDONDERRY were settled in 1719 by a pioneer band of sixteen families from the Ulster Plantation of Northern Ireland. They came here in pursuit of the religious, political and cultural freedom that was denied them in the Old World. The famous siege of Derry in 1689 did much to forge this love of liberty and fierce resistance to any perceived threat to their Scottish way of life.

By way of background, the modern city of Derry, Northern Ireland, was founded in 546 A.D. by Saint Columba. His monastery was on a small, oak-covered, hilly island by the river Foyle. The original name of the village was Doire, the Gaelic word for oak trees. In 1613 investors from London, England, built a mile-long wall around the central hill in Derry and renamed the town Londonderry. During the seventeenth century, many thousands of Scottish Presbyterians left Scotland for Northern Ireland. Much of the land they settled upon was formally the property of the native-born Irish.

During the twentieth century, sectarian struggles between Catholics and Protestants rocked the city. For decades the British army occupied much of the town and protest marches and gunfire were a daily occurrence. It has only been in the last couple of decades that a state of relative calm has enveloped the city. Today the Catholic majority prefers that the city be called by its original name—Derry. In contrast, the Protestant minority always refers to the city as Londonderry. Sometimes the town is called "Slash City" because of the politically correct designation of

Derry/Londonderry. (In this book I will use the name Derry to refer to the city.)

In 1685, James II, a Catholic, ascended to the throne of England. He soon replaced all the Protestant officers in the army with loyal Catholics. Many in England feared that Catholicism would be made the state religion and that the Protestants would become disenfranchised. In 1688 a coup forced James to flee to France. Protestant monarchs King William and Queen Mary replaced him on the throne.

In March 1689, James landed in Ireland with a French army and a call for the Irish to rise up in rebellion. Soon an estimated fifty thousand peasants heeded his call. This army, called the Jacobites, seized the cities of Ireland in the name of King James II. In time, the only Irish city still controlled by the British was Derry. Within its walls were thousands of Scottish refugees who had fled their villages and farms to escape massacre by the French-Irish army. Derry's military commander sided with the Jacobites and ordered the city gates open to admit the French. This surrender was rejected by a group of thirteen apprentice boys from Derry. These freedom-loving teenagers rushed to the Derry city wall and slammed the gate shut to keep out the enemy. Their message was "no surrender."

On April 18, 1689, King James II arrived outside the walls of Derry and demanded that the city surrender to its rightful King. The city refused his command and the siege of Derry began. The Jacobite strategy was to blockade the city and allow no food or supplies into the town. In time, starvation and the effects of daily artillery bombardments would surely force the seven thousand inhabitants to surrender.

A few miles downstream from Derry, the Jacobites constructed a floating log boom across the river Foyle. This barrier was constructed to prevent any resupplying to the city by the British navy. The French also set up artillery batteries on the nearby shores to protect the boom.

For week after week, the siege continued. Each night the defenders repaired the damage done by the artillery during the day. Each attempt at storming the walls was repelled by the men of Derry. The French army tried to tunnel under the battlements but the effort was repulsed with considerable struggle. Soon most of the buildings in the city were reduced to rubble. The inhabitants were forced to live in cellars and dig tunnels to provide ways of traveling through the town. Only the tower on the cathedral remained visible above the city walls.

There were likely more Derry men, women, and children killed by starvation and disease than by cannonballs and musket shot. Soon all the grain was eaten. All the horses were slaughtered and eaten except for nine animals that were "so lean and gaunt that it seemed useless to kill them." Salted animal hides became standard fare on the tables of Derry. The citizens grew so weak that the bodies of those who died were left unburied. The smell of death was everywhere. The leaders proclaimed that first they'd eat "the horse and hides; then the prisoners; then each other." No surrender!

According to a contemporary history of the siege, these were the actual prices charged in the food markets of Derry—a quarter of a dog, five shillings, six pence; a dog's head, two shillings, six pence; a cat, four shilling, six pence; a rat, one shilling; a mouse, six pence. Pints of blood and candle tallow were also considered suitable foodstuff. It is said that one overweight Derry man hid himself in his cellar, fearful that his neighbors would covet his flesh for their evening meal. The expression "like the fat man in Derry" used to be slang for an individual whose prosperity excites envy on the part of his less fortunate neighbors.

On July 28, 1688, on the one hundred fifth day of the siege, there were only two day's rations of food remaining in Derry. The city could not hold out much longer. Standing on the tower of the cathedral was twelve-year-old Jamie MacGregor. He had been born in Magilligan County and fled with his parents to safety inside the city walls of Londonderry. From his vantage point he could see miles downstream to where the boom was stretched across the river Foyle. As he watched, the British warships *Mountjoy* and *Phoenix* rammed the boom. With heroic efforts they finally snapped the cable and sailed toward Derry. Young Jamie MacGregor ran to the cathedral cannon and fired a volley to let the citizens know the siege had been broken. Relief was on its way! Food would soon be offloaded at the city dock and through the Shipquay gate.

Onto the dock were unloaded six thousand bushels of beef, huge wheels of cheese, kegs of butter, and so on. A diet of tallow, dog meat, and salted animal hide was replaced with a feast of delights. Soon all the bells in the city were pealing in celebration! On August 1, the Jacobite army accepted defeat and left the outskirts of Derry.

At the Battle of the Boyne, the forces of King James were routed and the sweetness of peace came again to the green land of Ireland.

Oh yes, about Jamie MacGregor, the boy who fired the cathedral cannon to signal the end of the siege. He would later attend the University of Edinburgh and became a Presbyterian minister. Probably he had seen enough of war as a boy and wanted to end his life as a man of peace. In 1701 he became a respected pastor in the small Irish village of Aghadowney. In 1710 he was allowed by the Presbyterian synod to preach in Gaelic.

In the second decade of the eighteenth century, life in Aghadowney began to turn bad for James MacGregor and his congregation. The British government decided that only members of the Anglican denomination could hold government office. This froze the Scots out of political life. A tithe was demanded to support an official state church that was not their own. Why should they be forced to contribute 10 percent of their earnings to the Church of Ireland when they were followers of the Kirk of Scotland? They were Scots who had relocated to Ireland to farm on crown land. Scots they were and Scots they would remain. Everywhere they looked they saw the improvised hovels of the native Irish. Many, perhaps all, of the Scots felt uncomfortable being surrounded by these unrepentant Catholics.

These rather stiff-necked Presbyterians were famous for the rigidity of their beliefs. They were not willing to blend in. They would remain Scots even if they were in Ireland or the New World. Their kirk was where they would worship and their dominies would be their preachers and teachers. As the poet Whittier would later write, it was a common saying that the Derry Presbyterians "would never give up a 'pint' of doctrine or a pint of rum."

Perhaps the most important problem was economic. The members of MacGregor's congregation were mainly weaver/farmers. From 1714 through 1718 there were a series of very bad harvests. Those years also saw a decline in the price of linen. After the siege of 1689, the British government had given the yeoman farmers very cheap rents in the Ulster Plantation. After 1710, there was fear that the leaseholders would see their rents doubled, or worse. It was time to leave. But to where?

In 1714 the Reverend William Holmes had left Ireland for the New World. There he met with Boston clergyman Cotton Mather, who encouraged him to find a way to increase Presbyterian migration. In 1718, the Reverent William Boyd, who had preached close to Aghadowney, successfully petitioned Governor Shute of Massachusetts for a grant of land in the New World. As a "thank you," Shute would be given a large farm in Nutfield.

By 1718, MacGregor and his congregation decided that the attractions of New England were greater than the reason to stay in Ireland. These were not young men and women off on a lark; they were mainly people of middle age who knew they were quickly approaching the end of their working life. Nor were they "your tired, your poor . . . . your huddled masses . . . the wretched refuge yearning to breath free." They were a fairly prosperous lot who didn't need to become indentured servants in order to pay for their voyage to America; they were able to pay the fare of five pounds with cash. They were also better educated than most early-eighteenth-century emigrants. They could all sign their names and read their Bibles. Some were even university graduates.

On the day before the Aghadowney pioneers left, the Reverend James MacGregor called together his flock and preached a sermon. His text was from Exodus 33:12, in which Moses prays in the wilderness: "If thy presence goes not with me, carry us not hence." He and his followers felt that they were on a holy pilgrimage but could succeed only if God was their protector. MacGregor knew that only a couple of verses back, God had said that He would not go with the children of Israel because they were a sinful "stiff-necked people." It took earnest, sincere prayer of repentance on the part of Moses to get the Lord God Jehovah to continue with them. Likewise MacGregor knew that if God was not with the pioneers from Aghadowney, they would surely fail in the American wilderness.

At the actual hour of their departure from their Irish village, there must have been many scenes of tears and sorrow. They were leaving homes they had lived in all their lives. Each knew that he would never again eat supper with elderly relatives who chose to remain behind. It would only be at the table in heaven that they would be reunited. MacGregor told his flock, "We must say farewell to friends, relations and our native land." He elaborated by giving the four reasons for their leaving: 1. "to avoid oppressive and cruel bondage"; 2. "to shun persecution and designed ruin"; 3. "to withdraw from the communion of idolaters"; and 4. "to have an opportunity of worshipping God according to the dictates of conscience and the rules of his inspired Word." In America they could build their village on a hill as a theocracy ruled by the elders, and the church sessions could forge the word of God into the law of man.

Sometime in the spring of 1718, the Reverend James Mac-Gregor set sail from Belfast bound for the New World. With him in the British brigantine *Robert* were sixteen families from his congregation. Later one elderly woman came dockside to see the pioneers off for America. On board was the pride of her life, her son William Humphrey, whom she would never see again. As the ship was leaving the quay, she yelled her parting prayer, "Go and God be wi' ye a' but Willie Humphrey—he'll take care of himself."

No one knows how long it took the ship to reach Boston, but six weeks is a good guess. The *Robert* arrived on August 4, 1718. Nor do we know the number of Aghadowney pioneers who were on this first voyage. The sixteen families would probably translate into fewer then a hundred individuals. The names of the male heads of the sixteen households were: James McKeen, John Barnett, Archibald Clendinon, John Mitchell, James Sterrett, James and Allen Anderson, Randall Alexander, James Gregg, James Clark, James Nesmith, Robert Weir, John Morrison, Samuel Allison, Thomas Steele, John Stewart, and James MacGregor.

It has now been more than ten generations since this first wave of immigrants arrived in the New World. There are doubtlessly many, many thousands of their descendants scattered across the country.

The MacGregor flock was first offered a tract of land in Casco Bay by the Pejepscot Proprietors. The good ship *Robert* took some of them to check out the site. There they wintered at the mouth of the Androscoggin River. Here they froze and starved until the colony of Massachusetts Bay sent a hundred bushel of meal and a mason to build them a fireplace. Reverend MacGregor elected to stay in Massachusetts, and he spent the winter of 1718–1719 teaching school in Dracut. Finally the governor of Massachusetts gave them a twelve-by-twelve-mile grant that was called Nutfield.

Nutfield had been named by earlier pioneers in New Hampshire. In Nutfield there were huge, long meadows that extended for miles through the forests. These grasslands were created by beavers damming streams to make ponds. In time they filled in and became grasslands. Settlers in the coastal towns would come to these meadows to cut the grass to feed their livestock. There were also forests of chestnut, walnut, butternuts, oak, and beech whose nuts could be also gathered to feed their animals. These two very desirable animal foods led to this area being named Nutfield. By the time MacGregor reached Nutfield, portions of the grant had been claimed by other towns. The original 144 square miles had been reduced to about 114.

On April 11, 1719, the first of our town's pioneers arrived in Nutfield. The men came first so they could build homes before the women and children arrived. The following day the men gathered under a large oak on the eastern shore of Beaver Lake. There Mac-Gregor preached the first sermon ever heard in the town. His text was from Isaiah 32:2 "And a man shall be as a hiding place from the wind, and a shelter from the tempest; as rivers of water in a dry place; as the shadow of a great rock in a weary land." This oak tree became a local tourist attraction. During the 1840s the tree fell to the ravages of time and was replaced by an apple tree. Around 1890, this tree was replaced by a cairn of stones. During the 1920s a farmer's son grew tired of strangers walking across his garden to see the site of the first sermon. The young man knocked down the monument and scattered the stones so that no one today knows where the sermon site was located.

To protect themselves in case of Indian attack, the men built their houses close together. On each side of West Running Brook they constructed their homes made of crudely hewn, bark-covered logs. Each house was identical and sited exactly 495 feet (thirty rods) apart from each other. Now everything was in place for the women and children to come to the wilderness of the Nutfield colony.

The men brought their families from Massachusetts by trails marked only by blazes cut into trees. It was no doubt a full day's walk from civilization to Nutfield. The horses would most certainly have been used as pack animals, with only the very old or feeble being allowed to ride. Everything they owned in the world could be carried in a relatively few bundles and sacks.

In 1881 a story was told about the first day in this tiny village. John Morrison worked hard like all the other men to build a sturdy cabin for his family. When his wife, Jane Steele Morrison, arrived after her long trek, he proudly showed off their new home. Jane did not seem thrilled with the rude building. Summoning up all of her feminine wiles, she twisted her arms lovingly around her husband's neck. Looking adorningly into his eyes, she whispered, "Well, well, dear John, if it must be a log house, do make it a log higher than the rest."

The Nutfield colony of James MacGregor grew quickly as more and more Scots from Ireland settled there. By 1721 the population of Nutfield had grown to 360 people. The next year the settlement shed its Nutfield name and became an officially charted town named Londonderry, after the city that gave them refuge back in Ireland. By 1740 only the town of Portsmouth, the capital of New Hampshire, had a larger population than that of Londonderry. In 1767 Londonderry's population had risen to 2,389. In addition to this resident population there were thousands of first-, second-, or third-generation Scotch Irish who emigrated from Londonderry, New Hampshire, to found towns through out the east coast of America and Canada.

In reference books, MacGregor is sometimes called the Moses of the Scotch Irish in America. The church he started—the First Parish Church in East Derry—is this year celebrating its two hundred eighty-eighth birthday. James MacGregor went to his eternal rest in 1729 at the age of fifty-two. He left a grieving widow and seven children. Five men who had been his comrades at the siege of Derry carried his body from his church to nearby Forest Hill Cemetery. He would likely have been comforted to know that in time his wife would marry the Reverend Matthew Clark, his replacement as pastor in Derry. Mr. Clark was also a veteran of the siege and his temple proudly bore a battle wound that never healed. No doubt there are thousands of his descendants in America today. James MacGregor's great- great-great-great-great-great-grandson is Senator John Kerry, who ran for president in 2004.

There were a number of farms in colonial Derry, Londonderry, and Windham that were exempt from paying property taxes because the owners had fought in the siege of Derry, Ireland. The telling and retelling of the story of the siege would go on for decades. Each new generation heard afresh how their ancestors bravely stood up against an enemy determined to destroy their Highlander way of life. Fifty-eight years after the original settlement of Nutfield, the Scotch Irish of Derry, Londonderry, and Windham would be among the leaders in the American Revolution. These heroes of 1776 would certainly have remembered the resolve of their forefathers in 1689. The memory of the courage of their ancestors may well have led General John Stark of Derry, New Hampshire, to pen the phrase "live free or die."

In 1874 a meeting of the Derry/Londonderry Historical Society heard a newly written poem by Miss Lucinda Gregg entitled "The Heroes of Londonderry." One stanza contained this emotional appeal:

> Their holy altar and their homes—for these
>   they periled all;
> And still the banner waved on high; still stood
>   the firm old wall;
> Still "no surrender" thrilled each heart and
>   nerved each dying hand,
> And every home was hallowed by the heroism
>   grand!
>
> ******
>
> Right onward toward the joyful town, the
>   conquering vessels passed;
> 'Twas life! Sweet life! 'Twas home! Dear home!
> 'Twas victory at last!

It was reported that the poem that night "elicited the plaudits of the whole assembly."

If I was arguing the need to encourage the study of history, I'd offer the following sentiment: Today, in 2007, our country is fretful as the jackals of anarchy howl outside our door. We are increasingly anxious as the vipers of self-doubt have entered our homes and marketplaces. Perhaps now is the right day and time to recall the bravery of James MacGregor and the heroes of the siege of Derry in 1689. We should not forget the courage it took for them to leave everything and come to a new world to pursue the dream of freedom for themselves and their progeny. We should take the time to pause and remember the watchword of old Derry: *"No surrender."*

The National Potato Shrine in Derry Village was erected in 1962.

2.
Eels, Indians and Potatoes

IN DISTANT TIMES, NEW HAMPSHIRE WAS THE DOMAIN OF NATIVE Americans. It was unlikely, however that there was ever a permanent Indian village here in Derry. We were instead annually visited by a few nomadic tribesmen and -women who wandered through the area in their seasonal quest for food. We were rather off the beaten path. The only Indian trail that cut through Derry was on our southern border near Island Pond. Because we were not connected to the extensive Indian trail system, we were only infrequently visited by these People of the Dawn.

Before settlement by the white man in New Hampshire, there may have been twelve thousand Indians living in the territory. Those who lived around Derry belonged to the Penacook tribe, a subgroup of the Algonquian-speaking Indians and a part of the great Abenaki Confederation. European diseases and attacks by the British and Iroquois greatly reduced the Native American population. In 1677, the last 139 Penacook left the state and moved to Canada. There may have been a few Indians living around Concord in the 1720s but for the most part, the southern part of New Hampshire was pretty much devoid of Indian settlements.

There are a few Indian links to Derry. In 1629 the Reverend John Wheelwright supposedly purchased the land that makes up our town from Chief Passaconaway (1580–1666), the legendary leader of the Penacook. In 1719 our town's founders bought the title from Parson Wheelwright's grandson. Many, however, now believe that the 1629 deed is a forgery.

A century ago, our two chief lakes were sometimes called by their reported Indian names. Beaver Lake was referred to as Lake Tsienneto and Island Pond as Escumbuit Pond. There is still today, a Tsienneto Road and the Escumbuit Island. A pamphlet published in 1907 said that Tsienneto was actually the name of a local fairy or wood nymph.

Only rarely was there any direct contact between the Native Americans and our earliest settlers. In 1724, Indians captured Thomas Smith and John Carr near the Derry–Chester town line. After a couple of days as prisoners, they managed to escape from their captors. Recently discovered information suggests that those men were illegally selling liquor to the Indians. Derry native John Stark (1723–1822) was taken prisoner by the Indians in 1752. Major Robert Rogers, who lived here during the 1730s, is credited with ending the danger of Indian attacks in New England by his massacre of the St. Francis Indians in 1759.

Derry/Londonderry/Windham never suffered an attack or a massacre as had the towns of Kingston, Dover, Rye, and Nashua. Some early historians believed that this fortunate condition was because the Reverend James MacGregor, the town's founder, had gone to college with the viceroy of Canada. Others claim we weren't attacked because we bought the land (indirectly) from Passaconaway and had not ripped it off like other towns. They believed that this somehow indemnified us from the ire of the Indians. Still others believed that the Indians viewed the Scotch-Irish as much too formidable an enemy to attack. It is more likely that the Nutfield colony was not attacked because it was not on any Indian trails or canoe-ways. This made it too difficult for Indian raiding parties who were coming down from New France to covertly get here and safely make their escape. Just to take no chance, the men of the town carried their muskets whenever they left home.

By state law, in 1718, the royal government of New Hampshire required that each town maintain stocks of one barrel of gunpowder, two hundred pounds of lead bullets, and three hundred flints for every sixty men who were able to serve as solders in the event of an Indian attack. It is said the powder was stored in the attic of the East Derry Meeting House. If a lightning strike had hit the building during church service, the effects would certainly have been mindblowing. In 1745 the town purchased two barrels of gunpowder, which were divided and kept in the east and west meeting houses.

The town had several stockade houses where families could find sanctuary. One of these was the home of the Reverend James MacGregor located off Island Pond Road. This was the first framed house in town. It was surrounded by a palisade of logs called flankers, which were driven into the ground. The home was razed in 1863. The other house of refuge was a stone structure in Derry Village that had been built in 1723 by mill owner James Gregg. The stonemason was Archibald Stark, the father of Revolutionary War General John Stark. The structure was torn down in 1810.

INDIANS IN THE CELLAR

In 1881 there appeared a story in the *Derry News* about a 1731 Indian attack in town. The author reported that the story was of "questionable tradition" and couldn't be "recited as strictly reliable history." There are no personal names included with the account, so its credibility is impossible to ascertain. As Derry auctioneer Otis "Topper" Hamblett used to say, "Here it is for what it is."

On the northern bank of the West Running Brook there was the small log house of Jonathan D. and his wife, Jane. Early one autumn morning Jonathan left his wife alone when he went to drive out some Haverhill men who were trying to claim some of our land. During his absence, his home was visited by three Indians, who for some unknown reason "entertained a vindictive spirit toward him."

When Jane opened the door, she must have been terrified. There were the three "blood thirsty savages, wildly flourishing their tomahawks and recklessly brandishing their scalping-knives, while hairy trophies suggestively dangled at their sides." They demanded to speak to her husband and wouldn't accept her reply that he was not at home.

The trio of Native Americans entered the house in pursuit of the settler. Just before they gave up their search, they spotted a trapdoor leading to the cellar. Lighting a candle, the three men climbed down the ladder, feeling sure they had trapped Jonathan hiding in the dark storeroom. As soon as the last head disappeared below floor level, Jane slammed shut the trapdoor and locked it tight. Quickly she ran for help.

Later the Indians were tied up by the men of the village and brought to the stone garrison that once stood at the corner of Thornton Street and Hampstead Road. There in front of a "jubilant gathering of settlers" the Indians had their backs scourged by whips. It was reported as fact that the Indians never returned to Derry looking for Jonathan D.

THE FEARFUL MOTHER

Archibald McMurphy was a weaver and leatherworker who came to Nutfield around 1719 and lived with his wife, Elizabeth, in today's northern Londonderry. On Sunday the couple were walking to church having left their children at home. About two miles into their journey, they passed a band of eight Indians on their way to fish at the Amoskeag Falls. This made Elizabeth very nervous, as she knew these Native Americans would have to pass right by her home. In her mind, all Indians were a threat and she had horrifying visions of her children being massacred and scalped.

Immediately she told her husband she was going home to protect her helpless family. Archibald tried hard to persuade her to continue on to church. He argued that the eight Indians were too powerful to fight. She said that if he wouldn't come with her, she'd go back alone. What could she do against eight Indians? he asked. She replied, "I'll die with the weans [children] if I can't do better." Archibald knew that if his wife was that adamant, he had better go with her. On the way back to their cabin, they found the entrails of a deer along the side of the road. At home they saw the Indians camped out near their doorstep. On their campfire was roasting the deer and they were giving the McMurphy children a fine meal of venison.

OLD EZEKIEL AND THE EELS

The most important Native American in the story of Nutfield was Old Ezekiel, who lived in the southern part of town. Unlike the trio of Indians in the first story, Ezekiel was almost certainly an actual historic figure. He lived alone on the shore of a small body of water that is today bordered by Route 128 and Windham Depot Road. The pond has since 1722 been called Ezekiel's Pond. The state reports that it is twelve acres in area and home to frogs, migratory birds, and pan fish such as largemouth bass, pickerel, and horned pout. The old bachelor Indian had reportedly constructed a three-hundred-foot long dugways to nearby Wilson's Meadow so he could paddle his canoe around the area.

In 1719, the first Scotch-Irish pioneers settled in the area called Nutfield. The men came first and built a row of cabins on Ryan's Hill. With that task completed, they returned to the settled coast to get their wives and children and take them to their new frontier home. The nearest roads were likely in Dracut, Massachusetts and Kingston, New Hampshire. All we had here were narrow paths cut through the thick, dark forests. This was real isolation.

Soon the Nutfield pioneers had consumed what food they had brought by packhorses and on their backs. Their larders were bare. Their attempt at deer hunting had been less than a resounding success. It would be months before their kitchen gardens were ready to harvest. To get a supply of food from the coastal towns would require days of travel through paths marked only by blazed trees. This task would also call for an exchange of money for food, and these settlers were not blessed with deep pockets and were too proud to beg. Many of the English settlers were antagonistic to the Scots, and not likely to extend much charity their way.

Everyone in the Nutfield colony was discouraged. There was talk of having to give up their dream of this village on a hill where they could find religious and cultural freedom. Without food, they could not survive.

Ezekiel, the old Indian, heard this talk of gloom and doom. He interrupted the conversation and according to the story said, "Oomph—Why don't you eat fish?" The Scots said there wasn't enough fish in Beaver Lake to feed the sixteen families who made up the Nutfield settlement. The Indian pointed to a tall pine far in the distance and said, "White man, go straight to that tree, then keep on same line. You get plenty fish."

There didn't seem to be any alternative but to follow the Indian's suggestion. The leaders selected a team of men to follow Ezekiel's directions. Using a crude compass to keep their bearings, they set out to the west toward that lone tree far in the distance. As they trekked, they cut blazes in the trees to help them find their way home. After a three days journey, they came to what was called the Ammosceaq (Amoskeag) Falls on the swift-moving Merrimack River.

At the site of the future city of Manchester, they found the rushing water teeming with salmon, shad, and eels. After an hour or so they were able to hand-catch enough fish to fill up the packs on their horses. They went back to their settlement in Derry and soon returned to the falls with more men and more horses. With scoop nets on long poles, they caught enough fish to feed the sixteen families until their gardens were ready to harvest that autumn. Thanks to Ezekiel, calamity had been averted.

Several Indian artifacts have been discovered by the Winifred Brown and Gladys Burdick families in the area around Ezekiel's Pond. These include a gouge, whetstone, and several projectile points. Relics collected by Alex Proctor are in the collection of Dartmouth College. During 1996-2006, preliminary archaeological test pits have been excavated by Patricia W. Hume, of Londonderry. Her report is included in the spring 2007 edition of the newsletter of the New Hampshire Archeological Society.

The boneless lamprey eel became the staple food of the children of the Nutfield colony. These snakelike animals were sometime called Derryfield beef. In the mid-nineteenth century it was said that the settlers' children ate so many of the slimy critters that they physically began to evolve and had faces with sloping foreheads that somewhat resembled eels. Some claimed our babies didn't learn to crawl—instead they first moved across the cabin floor by wiggling and squirming. Other said that the men of eighteenth-century Nutfield, because of their diet from childhood, had boney fins down their backs and had a devil of a time taking their shirts off.

In 1851, William Stark wrote a poem in honor of the centennial of Derryfield (now Manchester) separating from old Londonderry. Stark was the great-grandson of General John Stark. The poem is eminently forgettable except for a couple of stanzas that speak about the feisty character of the Scotch-Irish and their fondness for the squirming lamprey eel.

Our fathers treasured the slimy prize:
They loved the eel as their very eyes:
And of one 'tis said, with a slender rife,
For a sting of eels, he sold his wife!

* * * * * *

Such a mighty power did the squirmers wield
O'er the goody men of old Derryfield,
It was often said that their only care,
And their only wish, and their only prayer,
For the present world and the world to come,
Was a string of eels and a jug of rum!

The Nutfield colony survived that first season on eels. This gave the pioneers of 1719 the time and energy to clear a plot of land they called the common field. Here the first crops could be planted and its bounty shared by all. They watered this first garden from a nearby stream. This river was considered odd because it didn't flow easterly to the sea as did all the other rivers in the area. These pioneers named this contrary stream the West-Running Brook. It was later immortalized by Robert Frost in a 1928 volume of poetry. The common field is now the site of an apartment complex of 850 units. Nearby is the West Running Brook School.

POTATOES

The most famous crop planted in the common field of colonial Derry was potatoes. They are believed to be the first potatoes ever grown in North America. The claim that Derry is the home of the potato is supported by many diverse sources including the U.S. Department of Agriculture, the Ontario Pork Producers, and the Potato Institute of America.

The potato has its origins in the misty Andes Mountains of South America. There as far back as 500 B.C. the native peoples of Chile and Peru were cultivating the tubers. In 1565, the Spanish conquistadors brought the potatoes home to Spain. Within a couple of decades, potatoes were being grown all over Europe. According to legend, in 1588 potatoes first appeared in Ireland when they floated in from the wrecked ships of the Spanish Armada.

The potato soon became the staple food of both the native Irish and the Scotch-Irish. Praddies were easy to grow, tasty, and very nutritious. The potato became so associated with the Emerald Isle that they are frequently called "the Irish white potato." In 1718, when the Reverend James MacGregor sailed to the British province of New Hampshire, he brought with him a sack of seed potatoes. These he planted in 1719 in the common field of colonial Derry. This, most believe, was the genesis of the massive potato industry in America.

There are, unfortunately, other claimants to the honor of being the birthplace of the potato in America. The most publicized has been that of the state of Virginia. It is said by some that in 1621 the potato was brought from Bermuda to Virginia and thus preempts us by nearly a century. Derry has, of course, always disputed this claim. We have long said that Virginia's potatoes were probably just yams and even if they were white potatoes, they were brought to Virginia to be eaten, not to be cultivated.

In 1962, Perley I. Fitts, the New Hampshire commissioner of agriculture, received a letter from Parke Brinkley, the Virginia commissioner of agriculture. The southern gentleman wrote, "According to the best information that we can find, Irish Potatoes did not come to Virginia until after your 1719 incorporation. We therefore concede to the great state of New Hampshire, the honor of introducing to this country one of the great food crops." Although the rival claim by Virginia has been successfully parried, there are other attacks on our preeminence. New Jersey, Pennsylvania, South Carolinas, and Canada all claim they raised potatoes sometime before 1700. The potato war goes on!

In 1722, the Nutfield colony applied to Royal Governor Shute to be incorporated as a town called Londonderry. In many town charters in New Hampshire, a token yearly rent was included in the incorporating document. In the town of Chester, each year the selectmen were supposed to pay the governor a quitrent of one pound of good-quality hemp. It is just as well that this debt has gone unpaid for a couple of centuries; the growing of hemp is now illegal by both federal and state law.

The token rent required by Londonderry was much easier to procure. We were to pay the governor "one peck of potatoes, on the first day of October, yearly, forever." In 1863, a panic spread through Londonderry over the peck of potatoes. Some malicious fellow had circulated the false rumor that because the town hadn't paid its rent in potatoes in years, Londonderry was going to be unincorporated! I believe that the last time the rent was actually paid was in 1872, when Robert Mack delivered a peck to Governor Weston in Manchester.

In 1954 there was a drive to erect a monument to commemorate Derry's place as "the birthplace of America's great potato industry." The National Potato Shrine Committee was formed in Boston. Its chairman was George Moore, the director of public relations for the First National Stores; the treasurer was the New Hampshire commissioner of agriculture. Other participants were members of Maine's and New Hampshire's potato councils and commissions. The only local on the shrine committee was Republican activist Mrs. Carolyn Murdock White. Her inclusion made sense, as she owned the former "common field" on which the proposed potato monument was to be erected.

The pamphlet published by the shrine committee said that the size of the monument "will depend on contributions received." Concord artist Alice Cosgrove (1909–1971) was commissioned to design the memorial. She is perhaps best remembered as the artist who in 1955 drew "Chippa Granite" a little boy who was the symbol of the New Hampshire ski industry. She is also the designer of the twelve-foot tall New Hampshire Marine Memorial at Hampton Beach. Here in Derry she envisioned a forested park surrounding a large boulder placed on a raised fieldstone bed. On the rock would be a bronze panel portraying the first planting in 1719. A notice was put in *Yankee Magazine* advising its readers that Derry was on the lookout for a "potato-shaped boulder."

All this effort was to no avail; the National Potato Shrine Committee apparently was never able to raise the funds necessary to construct the memorial. After eight years of waiting for the potato shrine to be erected, members of the Nutfield Grange, Patrons of the Husbandry, decided to take matters into their own hands. For a few bucks, they bought a six-foot sheet of plywood. The nearby Benjamin Chase Mill cut it into the shape of a flattened potato. A quart of potato-colored brown paint completed the transformation from plywood to spud. Neatly painted white lettering was added announcing that the Patten-Murdock-White farm was the North American birthplace of the potato. The sign was fastened to a pair of two-by-fours and placed on the west side of Main Street on the slope of a hill just before Carrie White's home.

The plywood National Potato Shrine was dedicated on May 20, 1962. Dignitaries who attended include the state commissioner of agriculture and members of the Maine and New Hampshire Potato Growers Association. Following the dedication speeches and prayers, the throng adjourned to the Upper Village Hall, which was the home of the Nutfield Grange. Here a luncheon was enjoyed, catered by the Granite State Potato Chip Company of Salem Depot.

The Potato Shrine of Derry remained standing for the next thirty years. Eventually it fell over and it was never righted. It has since been lost. At present the only monument to cite Derry's role in the history of the potato is a brief mention on a state historical marker in East Derry.

Today the only monument devoted to just the potato is in the former Soviet Union. The tater was brought to Russia in the eighteenth century by Czar Peter the Great. Soon the "ground apple" was a staple food in most peasant families and was sometimes called "the second bread." During the World Wars, it saved millions from starvation. Its versatility as a food was much appreciated and potato vodka is a common beverage in the country. The monument at Novgorod is attached to a potato-shaped rock. Its inscription says, "Thank you, Columbus; thank you, Peter the Great, for our beloved vegetable."

I'm sure there is no shortage of potato-shaped boulders in the Derry area. Erecting a monument in honor of the American birthplace of the spud would likely be a significant tourist draw. Each year we could have a potato festival and a reenactment of the Reverend James MacGregor planting the first crop in 1719. Perhaps we could combine the festival with a tribute to Ezekiel and how he saved the Nutfield colony by telling us to "go fish." Maybe the town could sponsor a parade with prizes for the best float in honor of the lamprey eel, or the cooks in Derry could take part in an eel bake-off.

3.
The Goblet of Blood

As ONE DRIVES FROM THE DANFORTH TRAFFIC CIRCLE HEADING toward the village of East Derry, the road suddenly begins to climb a long, steep hill. This hill is the reason why East Derry is often called the Upper Village. In earlier times, this rise was even steeper. Municipal road crews have over the years cut down its slope to make it more manageable for climbing by both horses and automobiles.

Today most of us call it East Derry Hill, but formerly the knoll was known as Horse Hill. This name has two possible origins and I don't honestly know which is correct.

During the eighteenth century, the meetinghouse, school, and tavern were all in East Derry but the population was scattered throughout the rest of town. When locals made the trek to the Upper Village, they found the hill too steep for their horses. Tradition tells us that they would tie up their steeds at the bottom of the hill and walk up the rest of the way. That act of kindness toward their animals is perhaps why the rise was named Horse Hill.

Another possible origin of the name also goes back to the early days of the town. It is said that a couple of men on a warm summer's day had tied up their horses at the base of the hill and walked up to the Upper Village. In their absence, the horses got loose from their hitch. Being a hot day, the wandering steeds headed toward nearby Upper Meadow. This is a wide bog that almost touches the road to the Upper Village and extends a half mile east to the shores of Beaver Lake.

To get their drink, the horses walked deep into the swamp's black water. Soon they were stuck in the mud up to their bellies. There the horses remained for hours, unable to move. When their owners finally returned, they tried without success to extricate their animals. Failing in their efforts, they called for help. Gangs of men with ropes could not break the suction of the mud that held fast the trapped horses. Nothing could be done. It took a long time for the poor beasts to die. For many, many months thereafter, the lifeless bodies of the horses remained standing upright in the swamp. In time the flesh decayed; what remained was just the hide-covered bones standing motionless in the water. Because of this long remembered tragedy, the nearby stone dam was named the Skin Dam and the hill was called Horse Hill. Because of the death of the horses, local legend also claims that the area is haunted by phantom horses standing in the dark water of the Upper Meadow.

On the top of Horse Hill was the village of East Derry. It was here in 1719 that the Nutfield pioneers established their town center. Here in 1722, the town built its meetinghouse as a place to worship and hold town meetings. This two-storied building was forty-five feet square and stood just about where the Civil War monument sits now. The town's first school was constructed nearby in 1726. This small rude log structure was not much larger than a modern one-stall garage. There were likely no other buildings on the hill until 1762 when Stephen Holland (1731–1797) built a tavern directly across from the school and meetinghouse.

Most of the people did not live in the village; most lived in farmhouses scattered throughout the 114-square-mile Nutfield grant. The woods that covered the sides of Horse Hill were criss-crossed by meandering trails that served as shortcuts from the scattered homes to the meetinghouse, school, and tavern. It was not until after the Revolutionary War that East Derry acquired its neat row of stately homes.

The tavern of Colonel Stephen Holland was a popular gathering place in the years immediately before the Revolutionary War. Holland was the local royal magistrate and was viewed by most as the perfect example of what a gentleman should be. His tavern provided lodging for the occasional traveler coming through town. The taproom was always filled with men who spent hours drinking rum toddies or flips and arguing the politics of the day. Holland was a very skilled bartender and the eighteenth-century version of the "hail fellow, well met." Irish born, he was blessed with a touch of the blarney. To the patriot, he was a zealous supporter of liberty, the rights of man, and "no taxation without representation." To a Tory, he could eagerly offer up a toast to have "God save the king." Later it was proved that Stephen Holland was really a British spy. When the British were forced out of Boston, Holland fled with them. He would spend the remainder of his life in Ireland. His property, including the tavern, was confiscated by the town in 1778. His estate was estimated to be valued at ten thousand British pounds, which made him one of the wealthiest men in New Hampshire.

The frame of the story that I am about to relate was written in 1840. It was not originally presented as a piece of fiction but instead was offered as a news story, a true reporting of the past. Perhaps it is in truth just a fable, designed to scare the kids at night while they're sitting in front of the fireplace. Perhaps not. Any appraisal of its accuracy and truth, I'll leave to the judgment of my readers.

To help him run his busy public house, Colonel Holland owned a number of slaves. In addition of his three female slaves, he had two males. The oldest of these was an African named Scipio; the younger called Caesar, was quiet and sincere and the very soul of innocence. In this way, he was the exact opposite of the older Black man.

Scipio enjoyed being at the center of things. He was a natural-born showman with the gift of gab and a flair for the dramatic. Physically, he was strikingly handsome with very dark skin, which made him quite an exotic figure in this frontier community. He could amaze the tavern regulars with magic and sleight-of-hand. To the young women he claimed to be able to see into the future and predict the course of impending romances. He could even craft magic charms to heal the sick or improve luck. One deacon was sure Scipio was in league with the devil. If this had been Salem, Massachusetts in the 1690s, the black man would no doubt have been put on trial for practicing the black arts.

Scipio was also known throughout the region for his athletic prowess. He would walk through the village on his hands as fast as most people could walk upright. At other times, he could be seen standing on the ridgepole of Holland's tavern. He would proceed to walk on the peak of the roof as easily as if he was on the ground and then to everyone's amazement, he would do a double somer-sault. Suddenly Scipio would disappear from sight, and then almost instantly, reappear on the top of the chimney, where he would do a pirouette on one toe. In response to the applause of the crowd, he would take a courtly bow.

One night Colonel Holland took sick and Dr. Matthew Thornton was rushed to the tavern. Doubtlessly Thornton used every trick in his eighteenth-century bag of medicine to speed the man's recovery. Holland was an important man in this isolated town and his passing would be detrimental to both the community and his own medical reputation. Finally Dr. Thornton decided on a drastic course of treatment. He would bleed the publican!

Bleeding or scarification was a common medical practice until fairly recent times. The principle behind bleeding was the belief that bad humors in the blood were often the cause of illness. If that was true then the obvious cure was to bleed the patient to remove the bad humors. This procedure was, of course, inherently dangerous. A patient who was critically ill easily might die from the effect of the bleeding. In 1799, George Washington died soon after his doctor scarified the immortal father of our nation. Truly the cure could be far worse than the disease.

The actually process of scarification was simple and rather low-tech even by eighteenth-century standards. Cuts were made by a lance into the flesh of the patient (aka victim). Usually the arm or leg was the site for the procedure. After blood began to flow, a heated cup known in medical terminology as a cupa was inverted onto the site of the cuts. As the cup began to cool, a vacuum was created and blood would flow freely. After a few minutes, the blood-filled cupa was dumped into another container, reheated, and reapplied. Probably the sickroom's bed and floor would be awash with the crimson blood that had spilled from the cupa during scarification.

As the blood was drawn from Colonel Holland's body, it was collected into one of the tavern's goblets. When the procedure was finished, Scipio was given the responsibility of bringing the half-filled beaker downstairs to be thrown away. As he performed this task, the other black servant caught a glimpse of the black man putting the goblet to his mouth. In horror he watched Scipio drinking his master's still warm blood. Even in the subdued light, Caesar could see that the older slave's lips were now stained red—blood red! Quickly the news of Scipio's action spread through the household. Of all the servants, young Caesar seemed the most horrified by this act of cannibalism.

By sunrise the next morning, both Scipio and Caesar had disappeared. A search of the house and the neighborhood turned up no sign of either man. They apparently had just vanished off the face of the earth. The next night the sounds began. They were as loud as thunder and seemed to be carried on the wings of the wind. Some thought it sounded like two men fighting or maybe the screaming of souls who were in deep distress and despair. Others thought it more closely resembled the wail of a baby. It seemed to come from everywhere, from out of the trees that surrounded Horse Hill, from the sky above, even from the ground itself.

The horrible sounds in the dark of night seemed to go on for hours. Then suddenly they stopped, only to start up again a few nights later. The cries continued at random intervals for weeks and months. Riders on horseback would find their steeds would freeze in place the instant the sounds began, and remain as motionless as Lot's wife until the night air grew silent once again. Amazingly, the sounds were never heard by anyone who was geographically not standing on Horse Hill.

For years after, the screams revisited the village, but in time the intervals between their return grew longer and longer. Sometimes it would be years before the sound of Scipio and Caesar would be heard again. The last recorded incident of the night sounds occurred in 1815. By the 1840s most Derry residents had never heard the noises and many doubted the truthfulness of the story of their existence. The sounds had become more legend and myth than accepted historical fact. Newcomers to Derry theorized that the sounds were just the howls of wolves and that they were now silent because they had been hunted to extinction.

In time, the only ones who could really remember the sounds were a few gray-haired men. They would tell open-mouthed youngsters how when they were just boys their fathers had awoken them in the middle of the night. With a blanket wrapped around their bedclothes, they had been led into a forest clearing far away from their homes. There in the silence of the moonlit night, their fathers had put a finger to their mouths to keep them quite. Then, without warning, the sounds would begin.

With each passing minute the sounds grew louder and louder, until they filled every space in each of the listeners heads. Sometimes the noises sounded like recognizable words and at other times all that could be heard were just strange wails. Then, just as suddenly as they began, the sounds would stop and all that was left was the stillness of a peaceful East Derry night. On the way back to their warm beds, the fathers would tell the story of Scipio and Caesar and the goblet of blood.

It has now been nearly two centuries since the last report of the night sounds on Horse Hill. Perhaps they will never return again. But some summer's night, when you're walking alone through East Derry, you might want to pause and be very quiet. Maybe if you try very hard you'll hear the sounds of Scipio and Caesar, locked for all eternity in their fight in the woods of East Derry. And as you drive down Horse Hill toward the Lower Village, watch out for the phantom horses that are trapped forever standing in the black waters of the Upper Meadow.

4.
A Neighborhood Squabble

TODAY WE LOOK BACK AT THE PIONEER DAYS IN OLD NUTFIELD AND imagine it to be a time of harmony and peace. Those were the good old days. Our town's eighteenth-century ancestors spent their lives taming the wilderness and attending services in the meetinghouse. They went to bed at sundown and awoke at sunup. Dad farmed, hunted, and fished. Mom sewed, cooked, churned butter, raised the kids, and cleaned the cabin. These saints of old Nutfield didn't have the time or the inclination to partake of the petty squabbles and bickering that fill up so much of our life in 2007.

Wrong!

This idyllic view of Nutfield nearly three centuries ago, while pleasant to imagine, is most certainly more myth than reality. The Scotch-Irish pioneers of our town could be just as petty, mean-spirited and unforgiving as we are in the twenty-first century. The records of the Nutfield saints are filled with litigation and protracted skirmishes.

Consider two men of early Nutfield—Thomas Steele (1683–1748) and William Humphrey (1686–1767). Both were among the very first settlers of Nutfield and in 1722 both were listed as proprietors of the newly chartered town of Londonderry (modern-day Derry, Windham, and Londonderry). Both were elected to town office in the first town meeting: Thomas as auditor and William as hog reeve. Both lived in the southeast section of town in the vicinity of Kilrea Road. Both were married and had children. And both hated each other. Here is their story as it has come down to us.

The root cause of their mutual dislike is unrecorded. Always keep in mind that these were tough-minded Scots who were inclined neither to forgive nor to forget. The two men should perhaps be best thought of as being like poles of a magnet that for eternity must always repel each other. Possibly the disagreement began with a minor matter such as the Steeles' cows wandering into the Humphreys' garden, a boundary dispute, or Tom's boy hitting Bill's girl. Regardless of the cause, the feud was mean enough to be remembered and written about more than a century after both men had gone to their graves.

Despite attempts at mediation by friends and neighbors, nothing could pacify the men's anger. After long years of bickering, William Humphrey became deathly ill and Pastor James MacGregor (1677–1729) saw this as an opportunity to bring reconciliation to the antagonists. The cleric went to each man separately. He convinced each of the need to make things right because any day he might be made to stand before his maker at the throne of judgment.

Thomas Steele was brought to the bedside of his sick neighbor. In the presence of their families and the saintly parson, Steele and Humphrey agreed to end their years of fighting and put their quarrel into the past. They shook hands as their bond. Just as Steele was going out the door, William Humphrey, using all of his strength, raised himself up in the bed. Looking directly at the face of Tom Steele, he said, "Mind you, neighbor Steele, if I get well, the old grudge holds gude and continues." Farmer Humphrey did recover and true to his word, the old grudge did indeed still hold "gude" and continued.

Later, Tom Steele approached Judge James McKeen (1665–1756), who was the town's first magistrate, with a request. He told the judge that his section of town was in chaos. All the neighbors were fighting with each other and the area was reverting to a state of lawlessness. What the southeast section needed was the appointment of some reasonable and honorable man to be the constable for the Kilrea area. Whenever there was a disagreement, the constable could mediate and settle it in an impartial manner. When Judge McKeen asked who Steele thought would be a good candidate for this sensitive job, Steele said he would be willing to accept the responsibility. He, after all, had been a tithing man in 1724.

Judge McKeen thought it over for a few minutes before giving his response. Finally he turned to Steele and said, "If things are as bad as you say, I guess we have to do something. All those neighbors fighting—it's terrible for sure. I'll give it some thought." A few minutes later, as the conversation turned to other matters, the judge caught William off guard by remarking, "I am somewhat surprised to hear that your section of town has grown so much in population. There used to be hardly anyone living out there." To this Steele said, "Ach, it still hasn't changed any. It's still just Willie Humphrey and me who live in Kilrea."

Another time Steele, in a fit of anger, publicly denounced William Humphrey as a liar. This was too much for the proud Humphrey to ignore. He demanded that Steele be brought up before sessions, the ecclesiastical court of the local Presbyterian church. There Steele was ordered by the elders to apologize for his angry words or he would be excommunicated from the church. Standing before Pastor MacGregor, the elders, and members of the church he made this apology: "I called Brother Humphrey a liar. For this I am sorry but it is a failing I've had from my youth of always speaking the truth."

The heat of the anger between Thomas Steele and William Humphrey is now cooled forever by their deaths. Both today are buried in Forest Hill Cemetery and rest for eternity only a few yards from each other. It is not recorded whether they ever resolved their problems and became good neighbors. Probably not. They were, after all, burly Scots who were inclined neither to forgive nor to forget. I do know, however, that here in old Nutfield neither has spoken to the other for the last 240 years.

5.

The Londonderry Riot

WE HAVE ALL GROWN UP BELIEVING THE AMERICAN REVOLUTIONARY War started on the eighteenth of April in 1775. It was the events of that date that precipitated the battle at Lexington Green, where the "embattled farmers stood and fired the shot heard round the world." This would lead to the Battle of Bunker Hill, the Declaration of Independence, Valley Forge, Saratoga, and the surrender at Yorktown. All this is pretty straightforward.

I would like to add one minor adjustment to that old, old story. Despite what every schoolboy (or -girl) knows, I am about to present my argument that the first attack on British troops didn't happen in that fine state to the south of us. Nor did it occur in 1774 at Fort William and Mary over by Portsmouth. Here I will hypothesize that Derry is the site of the first armed resistance against the king's army—and that it happened fully six years before Paul Revere's ride. The incident to which I refer was not a battle in the classic sense, with one army attacking another army; rather, it was a spontaneous armed insurrection against an isolated segment of the British army.

So here, my children, you shall read of Jimmy Aikin and his heroic deed: how on a cold winter's day in '69, we first attacked the redcoat's line.

This article is the result of more than two decades of research. Back in 1984, when I was doing research for another book, I found a two-sentence reference to the Londonderry attack in Jere Daniell's *Colonial New Hampshire*. I mentally filed away the information, hoping to find out more later.

In 1995, I was doing background for another book and discovered a paragraph about the incident in the Reverend Edward Parker's *History of Londonderry* (1851). This historian tells the basic story of what happened but there was only a single name mentioned—that of Captain James Aiken. To add to the frustration, Parker offers just an approximate date for when the incident occurred. He said it happened "while the British were quartered in Boston and before the encounter at Lexington." This would mean somewhere between 1768 and 1775. This writer does increase his credibility by adding that his source was "an aged veteran who was prominent in the adventure." Parker's account was slavishly retold in *Willey's Book of Nutfield* in 1895. The author; George Franklyn Willey, concludes that the Londonderry attack was the "first act of open resistance to British authority and arms in the colonies."

Another reference to the attack was printed in *Historical New Hampshire* in 1947. Dr. Kenneth Scott in his excellent article "Colonel Stephen Holland of Londonderry" retells the basic facts of the incident as reported by Parker and Willey. Though he doesn't date the incident, he links it to one in "June or July of 1774" when he mentions Superior Court Judge Meshech Weare promising 303 acres of land to any of the soldiers in General Gage's army in Boston who chose to desert. Scott further quotes a deposition made in 1782 that Holland was the spy who told the authorities of the deserters' presence in Londonderry. This deposition, however, does not talk about any prisoners being liberated, so it is likely referring to another incident that may well have occurred in mid-1774.

A couple of years ago, I was looking through the back issues of the *Exeter News-Letter* for a new history of Derry. In the September 20, 1849 edition was a long article on the incident at Londonderry. The author, who signed his story with only the initial *G*, dated the incident to "a short time before the actual outbreak of the Revolutionary War." The writer identifies the patriot leaders as "Major G. and Captain A." Much of this article, unfortunately, seems more like a short story than an objective history. The "G" recounting is also filled with a number of anti-Irish barbs that further hurt its credibility.

The alleged attack took on the certainty of truth in 2006 when I discovered a set of letters in the New Hampshire State Archives. In a file set up by the venerable state archivist Dr. Frank Meevers, I stuck gold! Dr. Meevers had found an unpublished copybook that contained the manuscript of letters written by Royal Governor John Wentworth of New Hampshire. Here at last was confirmation of the story that had been written about by Parker, "G," Scott, and Willey. The correspondence also added much flesh to the skeleton of their story and established a definite date for the event. It happened in January 1769.

This telling of the Londonderry event will have to be pieced together like a patchwork quilt using Parker's paragraph, the "G" article, and a dozen letters written by Governor Wentworth. It must be understood that the first two sources were written nearly ninety years after the events and that the Wentworth letters give only one side of a two-way correspondence. With such limitations, I cannot guarantee the absolute accuracy or completeness of this story. A dozen years from now I may turn up a whole bunch of new material on the incident. This article is, however, I believe, the first attempt at systematically presenting the story.

The events of the Londonderry attack begin in January 1769. Those were definitely the times that tried men's souls. All over the thirteen colonies, anti-British sentiment was reaching the boiling stage. In Portsmouth a mob had forced the resignation of a British stamp tax collector. The newly imposed Townsend Acts, which allowed the quartering of soldiers in private home, were being debated through out the colony. Tavern talk centered on James Otis's invective that "taxation without representation is tyranny."

Local pro-British sentiment was centered primarily on the Portsmouth area. The farther inland you traveled, the more opposition you encountered to the royal government. Those who were for a change of government were usually called Whigs, radicals, Revolutionaries, or patriots. Those who were for keeping the status quo were called Tories, conservatives, or loyalists.

Within our town the overwhelming majority were Whigs. They would later side with George Washington and be passionately for independence. We did, however, have those residents who remained loyal to Mother England. Most of these pro-British families lived near the English Range Road section of town. One decidedly non-patriot was Anne Cummings (1684–1770), who is remembered for saying that she "wished that the English Range, from its head to Beaver Pond, ran ankle deep in Whig blood."

New Hampshire was a royal colony with a population that numbered around fifty-five thousand. In the census of 1775, the colony's largest town was Portsmouth, with a population of 4,590. Londonderry, which then consisted of the present-day towns of Derry and Londonderry, was in second place with about 2,590 inhabitants. By comparison, the three largest cities of today—Manchester, Nashua, and Concord—back then had a population of only 924, 705, and 1,052 respectively.

The royal governor of the colony of New Hampshire was John Wentworth (1737–1820), who lived in Portsmouth. His family went back many generations in our state. He was in the same Harvard graduating class with future patriot leader John Adams. John Wentworth was appointed governor in 1767, succeeding his uncle Benning Wentworth.

One of the major problems for the British rulers of America was the ever-increasing number of cases of desertion from the ranks of their army. Many a young man decided that life as a New World yeoman farmer would be far better than a career in the military. Army pay was low and discipline was harsh. It wouldn't take much planning or smarts to successfully go AWOL in America. It would be relatively easy to establish a new life concealed in the great American wilderness. There one could marry a farmer's daughter and never again be under the army's rule. Once a former soldier was away from the coastal cities, a deserter could live with little fear of capture.

Early in January 1769, a group of deserters were living in Londonderry. Parker says there were a total of four such defectors here. The writer "G" says there was only one and the Wentworth letters refer to two escapees. The first two writers believed that a local Tory had secretly reported their presence to the royal authorities. It is now known with certainty that our local judge and taverner Stephen Holland was a British spy and was in communication with General Howe. Many local residents suspected that Holland was a loyalist but lacked proof. The three authors are in agreement that a detachment of British regulars was quickly dispatched to our town and that the AWOL soldier(s) was (were) quickly rounded up. Even in those pre-telephone days, it didn't take long for news of the apprehension to spread through town.

The squad of British regulars quickly marched their prisoners out of town. Their route was probably east on Hampstead Road and then south onto today's Route 121 toward Haverhill. "G" reports that the lone deserter was an Irishman named Phelim O'Shaughnessey.

This frightened son of Erin was told by his captors that the standard punishment for desertion from the British army was hanging—"and nothing else."

As soon as the word got out, a group of Londonderry men left their homes and farms to attempt to free the prisoners. "G" identifies the leaders of the rescue party as "Major G." and "Captain A." He wrote that both men were veterans of the French and Indian War. Parker identifies only one individual in the mob—its leader, "Captain James Aiken (1739–1830). Governor Wentworth identifies the brothers Thomas and James Atkin as the leaders but writes that a third brother, Edward Atkin, was not involved. It is almost certain that Wentworth was actually referring to members of the Aiken family and not the Atkin's family. Wentworth also wrote that there were eleven Londonderry men involved in the incident.

The men from Londonderry overtook the British about an hour's march outside of town. The location of the conflict was in the town of Atkinson on a steep slope called Providence Hill. The eleven Londonderry men concealed themselves just back from the British. The energetic James Aiken managed stealthily to run around the side of the column of marching soldiers and cut them off from the front. With his pistols drawn, James leaped out in front of the surprised redcoats. With authority, he ordered the squad to halt. He kept his weapons pointed at the head of their leader, "Sergeant Henderson." The British were ordered to throw their guns onto the dirt road and not pick them up on penalty of having Henderson's "brains scattered." The Londonderry men now surrounded the soldiers and freed their prisoners. Captain Aiken kept his pistols trained on the sergeant until he, his men, and the rescued deserters were safely on their way back to East Derry.

The entire episode couldn't have lasted more than a few minutes and must have been an incredible shock to the British soldiers. They thought of themselves as being a part of the world's greatest fighting force. They prided themselves on being highly disciplined, well trained, and impressively uniformed. To the British, the Americans were just a collection of provincial farmers—and yet these simple, country bumpkins had just hijacked their prisoners. The redcoated British soldiers were left to stand in the middle of a dirt road with their mouths open in amazement and their weapons scattered over the ground. It was truly the world turned upside down.

Word of the events at Londonderry quickly spread to the highest levels in the British army. Governor Wentworth, however, was in Vermont and didn't get the news until January 20, 1769. In his reply to a letter from Brigadier General John Pomeroy, the commander of His Majesty's Sixth Regiment in Boston, he argued that the incident probably happened in Massachusetts so it was not his responsibility. By way of consolation, Wentworth does offer sympathy over "this reprehensible violence, which is universally disapproved and resented throughout the whole province."

Two days after writing this letter, Wentworth received a response from Major General Thomas Gage, commander of all the British troops in North America. In his fawning reply, Governor Wentworth conceded that the incident did actually occur in New Hampshire. He informed the general that on February 2, he called two magistrates from Londonderry to his office in Portsmouth. These two local officials said that the freeing of the deserters had been done without their knowledge and "it was disapproved by the whole town." The pair also couldn't give any "useful information" to aid in the case. One of these officials might well have been British spy Colonel Stephen Holland.

The governor must have been very shocked that such antigovernment unrest should have occurred in Londonderry. He must have felt a personal sense of betrayal. In 1767, when he became the colony's chief executive, he had received a proclamation of love and support from the town's selectmen and thanked his family for the support they had given in the past. (Note: The Wentworth dynasty had ruled New Hampshire since 1717.) When other colonies had discouraged settlement by the Scotch-Irish, the Wentworths had taken them in as "strangers in a strange land." The proclamation of 1767 from our town leaders had even expressed a hope that the Wentworth family be made the hereditary governors of New Hampshire.

Wentworth began to send letters to individuals all over his domain. On Feb 4 he wrote to his friend Edward Goldstone Lutwyche, of Merrimack, that the Boston generals were angry at New Hampshire. They felt the deserters had been "harbored and concealed by our citizens who are making it easy for the soldiers" to be "seduced away from their duty." Wentworth further wrote that having these escaped soldiers in New Hampshire might lead to a region-wide crime spree. He feared that unless they were caught, they would "scatter every kind of mischief, villainy and rapine thru all our towns."

The governor also let Lutwyche know that there were other "extensive benefits" to be realized by the successful hunting down of the escapees. In this, he likely meant that he would be allowed to keep his royal appointment as governor as well as getting Generals Gage and Pomeroy off his back. He closed his letter with a warning to the Merrimack official to inform the residents of his town that it was against the law to harbor deserters and that a "considerable" penalty would be imposed on those who did conceal them. Similar letters were sent by Wentworth to thirteen other local leaders in remote frontier towns such as Keene and New Ipswich.

Most royal governors during the colonial period didn't stray far outside the settled areas of the coastal cities and towns. John Wentworth was the exception. In his capacity as surveyor of the King's Woods in America, he had ventured far into the New Hampshire wilderness, traveling by wagon, boat, horse, and foot. He had visited many of the isolated frontier communities and was well known to many of their leaders. He may have been the most popular governor in all the colonies. John Wentworth was not some stranger politico who had been sent to the New World by the English government and would retire in London after his tour of duty was completed. Wentworth was New Hampshire born and New England educated.

Soon Wentworth discovered that James Evans, a farmer in Londonderry, was harboring one of the deserters and that a shoemaker in Suncook was hiding another. There is, however, no evidence that Evans or the shoemaker was ever charged with a crime. A couple of days later, on February 19, Governor Wentworth reported that Private Sherwood, one of the freed deserters, had been brought before him the previous night and was now secured in a Portsmouth jail.

In a February 20, 1769, letter to Brigadier-General Pomeroy, Wentworth remarked on how cooperative the prisoner proved to be. He predicted that Sherwood would continue to be a helpful witness in any trial against the "rescuers." The governor further wrote that the only reason the deserter was being locked up was that General Gage demanded such treatment. Wentworth himself believed Sherwood was no longer a threat to desert again.

Wentworth advised the brigadier-general that the British should avoid being publicly perceived as being overly harsh on Sherwood. He felt it would be far better to show a measure of leniency toward the deserter. The governor wrote of his own "intimate knowledge of the genius and prejudices of the people of New England." His citizens, with their "sense of humanity" and "misguided compassion" could never be expected to turn in a deserter. If the soldiers were allowed to return to the army without punishment, he believed New Hampshire's citizens would cease to provide them with safe harbor.

A month later, the governor reported to Pomeroy that Sherwood had given credible evidence against Thomas and James Atkin. He wrote that the Londonderry town fathers had assured him that all the deserters had now fled from their town to "remote and more thinly settled districts." Wentworth added that he actually disbelieved their claim of a deserter-free Londonderry. He calculated that there was "double the number [of deserters] you've been informed of in Londonderry." Wentworth wrote that he recently sent "three of as good sheriffs as there are on the continent" to ferret out the guilty. Regardless of the success of these sheriffs, he predicted that the royal government could never prevail in a local court of law. Wentworth said that in a trial by their peers, jury members would show very "little vigor" in finding the Londonderry eleven guilty.

Wentworth once again asked Pomeroy to show compassion to lessen the inclination of the locals to side with the underdogs. He wrote that he was sure that the Americans "can not be prevailed upon to discover or give information to an officer" if there is cruel punishment given to deserters. If the British army shows mercy, they just might succeed in winning the hearts and minds of the people and get their missing soldiers back.

The British hierarchy remained most disturbed over the issue of their soldiers taking French leave. Governor Wentworth would have logically felt that he had to publicly demonstrate his support for the rule of law. On March 23, 1769, he issued an official proclamation that was distributed to every town in New Hampshire. It told how Generals Gage and Pomeroy had made him aware that "sundry private soldiers" had deserted, escaped, and been concealed "particularly in and about Londonderry." The governor wanted all his citizens to know that "harboring or entertaining them" was a violation of royal law and that the British parliament had severe punishments in store for those who were found guilty of such a crime. The proclamation ended with the usual phrase, "God save the King."

In April, Wentworth informed Pomeroy that "shortly" every deserter in New Hampshire would be caught. He also reported that he had no success in bringing the Londonderry rioters to justice. He optimistically claimed, however, that the only way they would ultimately escape justice was by fleeing the country. That month he recommended to the general that any deserter snagged in New Hampshire be quietly brought to the Massachusetts border and from there transferred into custody of the British army. Wentworth wrote that such a course of action would save having the royal army travel all the way from Boston to Portsmouth. It would free them from much "marching, fatigue and absence." It is more likely that Wentworth was just trying to prevent another riot from occurring in his colony. If the Whigs saw another detachment of British soldiers marching with prisoners in tow there was no way of predicting what would happen.

Four months after the incident at Londonderry, Wentworth announced that all the deserters in New Hampshire had now fled to other colonies or were so well "concealed and disguised" that they could never be found. The case was closed!

There does not seem to be any evidence that the Londonderry eleven were ever brought to justice. The writer "G" relates that "Major G." and "Captain A." hid in the town of Londonderry and were never caught. He said that both men would later serve as members of the local Committee of Safety during the Revolutionary War. He further wrote that they "both died peacefully in their own beds—one at the advanced age of ninety-two years."

What became of the rescued deserter Phelim O'Shaughnessey? "G" uses this rhetorical question as an opportunity to exhibit his anti-Irish prejudice. He ends his story by saying, "Being an Irishman I don't know if anything became of him." Parker says only that the liberated deserters became residents of the town.

Governor Wentworth was forced to flee New Hampshire in 1775. He would later serve for fourteen years as royal governor of Nova Scotia. He reportedly always enjoyed hearing news about his native state, to which he was never allowed to return. If the Revolution hadn't occurred, he would no doubt have remained a popular political leader in New Hampshire.

In 1776, the new state of New Hampshire circulated a document called the Association Test. All citizens over the age of twenty-one were required to sign this form to demonstrate their support for the patriot cause. This was intended as a way to ascertain who was to be trusted and who was to be watched as a suspected British sympathizer. The oath at the top of the Association Test said that it was signed "at the risk of our lives and fortunes." The only ones who were exempt from declaring their allegiance to the United States were lunatics, idiots, Negroes, and women. In Londonderry there were 374 who signed and only sixteen who refused. Our town was thus officially 96 percent for American independence. However, some of the individuals who signed the Association Test would later violate their oath and side with the British. Others who chose not to sign would later become patriots.

During the Revolutionary War we would contribute about six dozen men to the patriot army. More than two centuries ago, our town's fathers, husbands, brothers, and friends would fight bravely in such battles as Bunker Hill, Saratoga, and Yorktown. We were also the hometown to Generals John Stark and George Reid. Doctor Matthew Thornton of Derry Village, signed the Declaration of Independence. General John Sullivan went to school on East Derry Hill. The courage we showed in 1769 when our townsmen surrounded the British soldiers was thus further validated by the honors we earned in the war of 1776.

Let Massachusetts glory in her tea party and the "shot heard round the world"; may Valley Forge be forever a memorial to the determination of General Washington; may Philadelphia be a hallowed shrine to the signers of the Declaration of Independence. Here in Derry we have among our heroes that small, brave band of eleven nameless men: those patriots, who in 1769, helped start our country on its trek down the road to independence.

6.

Stephen Holland, Spy Master

It has now been more than 230 years since the start of the Revolutionary War. In our twenty-first-century minds, the justice of the patriots' cause seems to be just common sense. Wasn't England ruled by the freedom-hating King George III? And every schoolboy knows that the colonies were unanimous in their support of the godlike George Washington. We were right; they were wrong. The American Revolutionary War was the classic battle of justice, liberty, and truth against the forces of tyranny and oppression.

As with most things in life, the Revolutionary War cannot be understood in black and white terms. Not every American subscribed to the legitimacy of the patriot cause. The commonly accepted formula is that in the thirteen colonies, one-third favored the British, one-third was pro-patriots, and a final third was neutral. Although it is impossible to ascertain if this division was true in Nutfield, it is safe to say we were not all patriots. Some very good Nutfield residents remained loyal to king, country, and the Union Jack.

The story that follows could easily be rewritten into a modern spy thriller by Robert Ludlum or Tom Clancy. It involves many of the most significant figures in American history, including George Washington, John and William Stark, Ethan Allen, Robert Rogers, Matthew Thornton, John Wentworth, John Langdon and several British generals. It would be a simple matter to transport the tale to twenty-first-century America. Think of the main character as a respected businessman and elected politician who is really a Taliban mole.

Arguably the most important loyalist in the Revolutionary War period of New Hampshire was Colonel Stephen Holland of Londonderry. Most sources report that he was born in 1733 in the vicinity of Coleraine, Northern Ireland. He emigrated to America as a young man. On July 24, 1756, he enlisted as a sergeant in the legendary Roger's Rangers. He rose through the ranks to ensign by February 1757 and was promoted to second lieutenant in 1759. In 1761 he purchased the rank of second lieutenant in Gorham's battalion for two hundred seventy-five pounds sterling. He left the military in 1762 after being wounded first at the battle of Fort William Henry and then at the battle for the city of Quebec. Because of his service and wounds, he received a pension of half pay.

In 1761 he moved to Londonderry and purchased a lot on Horse Hill, directly across from the meetinghouse in East Derry. His land extended all the way east to the shores of Beaver Lake. The next year the selectmen examined his character and found him "a proper person to keep a tavern in this town." His tavern was at a prime location in the frontier town. East Derry was at the time the educational, political, and religious center of the region.

Do not confuse the village of East Derry today with that of 1762. In the mid-eighteenth century, the settlement on Horse Hill consisted of just the meetinghouse, a cemetery, and a one-room school. Even the pastor lived a mile away. Stephen Holland's tavern was only the third building ever built in the immediate area. The present First Parish Church was built in 1769 to replace the original meetinghouse. Most of the buildings there now were built in the late eighteenth and nineteenth centuries. In 1762 the population of Londonderry was scattered haphazardly throughout the town in isolated farmhouses.

Holland's tavern was a welcome addition to the tiny community. During recesses at the town meetings, the men could adjourn to his taproom for libations and strategy sessions. Here the town fathers held meetings and received taxes. It would also serve as the town's defacto post office, as weekly post riders would leave mail and newspapers there to await pickup by their owners. On Sunday the worship service at the meeting house would begin in the morning and continue into the afternoon. During the "nooning" (lunch break) the tavern was a definite destination. This was certainly true during the winter months, as the meeting house was unheated. Rooms were available for the occasional visitor and a store sold staple items such as tobacco, spirits, notions, and crockery. It was at "Squire" Holland's tavern on December 8, 1768 that the plans for the building of the present First Parish Church were drawn up.

At Holland's tavern the great issues of the day were debated. In its rooms there were discussions on all the political and economic issues that were fueling the call for revolution within the colonies. It was here that "taxation without representation is tyranny" was argued. Within its taproom, patriot leaders such as Matthew Thornton, George Reid, and John Bell would likely have planned their next course of action. Luminaries like Robert Rogers, John Stark, and Josiah Bartlett would have been frequent visitors. In the decade before the Revolutionary War, Londonderry was no longer the small, isolated frontier community it had been in the 1720s. Now only the coastal town of Portsmouth had a greater population.

Regrettably, we do not know what Stephen Holland's tavern looked like, as it was torn down in the 1870s. It was probably a spacious, Georgian-style building similar to the present Pinkerton Tavern Restaurant. A legal advertisement in 1780 describes it as "a large mansion house . . . .well calculated for any sort of public business in its situation, together with eighty or ninety acres of choice land, three barns, a store, out houses and stables; said land is well proportioned with mowing, tillage, pasture, wood and watering, well fenced with stone walls."

There are also no existing portraits of Stephen Holland, but newspaper notices from 1777 and 1778 give us a partial description of the man. He was reported to be "a well looking man" of about forty-five years of age, five foot, eight inches tall, "rather fleshy"(stout) "of a ruddy, comely countenance" with a face "pitted with small pox" and "given to wearing a wig." So he was of about average height, handsome, with a red, pockmarked face, somewhat pudgy and wearing a wig. This head covering may have been a stylish affectation or merely used to hide a bald pate. Because of his wealth and social standing, he probably dressed in a manner appropriate for a country squire.

He married Betsey (Jane) Stinson sometime around 1751. She was the daughter of John Stinson and Mary Hogg. They had nine children, two of whom are known to be buried at Forest Hill Cemetery in East Derry, as are his parents-in-law. His oldest son he named John Wentworth Holland, after the governor of New

Hampshire. A member of the family of General George Reid named one of his children Stephen Holland Reid.

Holland soon became a very wealthy citizen. He owned a pew in the First Parish Church and was one of the few here who could afford a gold pocket watch. He quickly became the banker for the area, always willing to loan money and hold mortgages at an interest rate of 10 percent per annum. In 1763 he loaned a Londonderry resident nearly six thousand pounds to purchase land from the legendary Ranger Robert Rogers.

Tavern keeper Holland also invested in local land. By 1778, in addition to his own estate he owned the McNeal farm with a large house, barn and approximately sixty acres of land; the Wiar farm, with a large stone house, a barn, a cider mill, an orchard, and about eighty-five acres; the Gregg farm with a house and barn in need of repair and sixty acres of land; the Nesmith lot, of thirty-five acres consisting of orchard, mowing, pasture, and woodland; the Barr lot, of about seventy acres which was covered with a forest of oaks. In addition he owned land near Beaver Lake, including three meadow lots which produced hay and were good for hunting ducks and geese. He also owned sundry smaller lots, making him the holder of about four hundred acres in town.

During the French and Indian War he was given two thousand acres near the town of Thornton, New Hampshire as a reward for his military service. This land was the unincorporated town of Holland's Location which had a settled population and an ordained clergyman. In time Holland's Location would become the town of Livermore. In addition he owned eight hundred acres in Hill, a thousand acres in Tamworth, and other tracts in about sixty-five other New Hampshire towns stretching across the state. He also owned "$1/3$ of $1/8$ of $1/15$ part" of the Mason patent, which claimed much of the southern half of the state. In total he held title to about ten thousand acres of land worth in excess of eight thousand British pounds sterling. In addition to this he owned about 8000 acres in Vermont. Although most of his land was unsettled wilderness, it had the potential for substantial profit as more and more pioneers moved north, leaving the crowded southern tier of the state in pursuit of elbow room.

Soon after he arrived in town, Holland was appointed a justice of the peace for the province, which gave him judicial authority. Probably through the intervention of his Portsmouth friends, he was appointed clerk of the Court of Common Pleas and clerk of the court in Hillsborough County. These two political plums gave him an annual salary of 190 pounds. This income alone was considerably more than most locals earned in a year. Mr. Holland was indeed a very wealthy man.

Because of his military experience, Stephen Holland was a commissioned colonel in the local militia. Among his brother officers were ardent patriots George Reid, Matthew Thornton, and John Bell. Several times a year there was a training day when all adult men were drilled in the fundamentals of military maneuvers. Holland also was elected to serve in several local offices. He was surveyor of highways for the portion of the town east of Beaver Brook in 1771 as well a member of the board of selectmen. He was elected a member of the colonial legislature to represent Londonderry and Windham a total of five times between 1771 and 1775. His election as representative in 1771 did not sit well with many citizens. On January 1, 1772, a petition signed by 186 residents of Londonderry, Derry, and Windham was delivered to the legislature to request a new election. A tie vote in the assembly allowed Holland to retain his seat. The reason for this anti-Holland sentiment is not known.

By the early 1760s, the political climate was becoming more and more hostile toward remaining a colony of Britain. Deserters from the English army were known to be harbored in Londonderry. In February 1769, our local militia freed some of these deserters from a squad of redcoats who had been sent to retrieve them. There were the 1766 Stamp Act riots in Portsmouth and the anti-British resolves published by several New Hampshire towns in 1768. In June 1774, Governor John Wentworth narrowly averted having a shipload of tea thrown into the Piscataqua River.

On April 29, 1773, the inhabitants of Londonderry presented Governor Wentworth with an extremely fawning proclamation. It praised the king for appointing Wentworth, "a gentleman whose birth and education has been in the province over which he presides." The proclamation further stated that the governor's "ear have been ever open to their voice, the easy access they have gained and the polite and courteous reception they have ever met with from you has offered them the means of communicating and your Excellency receiving all necessary of their wishes and wants." The document ends by declaring that its purpose was to reassure the governor of their loyalty to the king and to offer their prayer for

Wentworth to "live long." It is likely that Holland had a hand in the composition of this proclamation. Despite the avowed popularity of Governor John Wentworth, the dislike of the British government in Whitehall was too strong to be stilled.

On April 2, 1774, a town meeting was called by Stephen Holland and four other men, who decreed the eastern part of the town to be a separate town. A petition by 137 of the leading townsmen demanded that the legislature declare the April 2 Town Meeting of the "pretended east town" null and void. The reason for this Holland-led coup is unknown but it probably had something to do with preventing anti-British feelings from controlling the political agenda. The meeting and the election were declared void by the legislature and five new selectmen were elected. It was further decided that Holland's election as representative was "illegal in every respect."

In mid-1774, word spread throughout New Hampshire that a provincial congress was being called to meet at Exeter on July 21 to discuss the gathering political storm. This Exeter meeting was quickly declared illegal by Royal Governor Wentworth. In Londonderry, a town meeting was called to elect delegates to the Exeter Congress and to authorize forming a company of local minutemen should hostilities break out. Before anything could be done, Justice of the Peace Stephen Holland ordered the meeting to be broken up as illegal. He, in effect, read them the riot act and threatened to arrest anyone who failed to leave the meetinghouse. Because of this action, the town was officially unrepresented at the state's first political convention.

Stephen Holland was becoming a very unpopular man, as the overwhelming majority in his town were firmly on the patriot side. One of Holland's allies was Constable William Vance, of Londonderry, who in 1774 had arrested some deserters from General Gage's army who were being hidden in town. Vance would frequently, while staying at Stephen Holland's tavern, have to post guards at night. On at least one occasion, the tavern was surrounded by a mob and Vance, Holland, and their friends had to use force to drive off the assailants.

On December 14, 1774, British Fort William and Mary at Portsmouth was attacked and briefly seized by an army of New Hampshire men. War was now inevitable. On April 1, 1775, Paul Revere made his fabled ride and the next day, at Lexington green, the shot was fired that "was heard round the world." The Revolutionary War had begun.

There was suspicion in town that tavern keeper Holland was a Tory and couldn't be trusted. There were even some who suspected that he was a clandestine British spy.

Fearing for his life and the erosion of his position in local society, Stephen Holland had to come up with a way to restore his credibility. On April 23, 1775, a town meeting was held at the First Parish meetinghouse with Matthew Thornton as moderator. Most of the issues on the warrant dealt with war matters such as pay for the local soldiers who were fighting in Massachusetts and the local supply of gunpowder. The meeting was adjourned to Saturday, April 29.

At the start of this reconvened meeting, Stephen Holland stood up and asked to be allowed to address the hall. He mustered all of his considerable eloquence to win over his fellow citizens. With obvious sincerity he proclaimed:

> Whereas by mistake, misunderstanding, misrepresentation, or for reasons unknown to me, I am represented an enemy to my country, to satisfy the public, I solemnly declare I never aided or assisted any enemy to my country in anything whatsoever and I make this declaration not out of fear of any thing I may suffer but because it gives me great uneasiness to think that the true sons of liberty and real friends to their country, from any of the first mention reasons, should believe me capable so much as in thought of injuring or betraying my country, when the truth is I am ready to assist my countrymen in the glorious cause of liberty at the risk of my life and fortune.

This speech did it. The town meeting unanimously voted that it was "satisfactory for his conduct." The meeting continued and appointed a committee "to look into the conduct of those men thought to be friends to their country." Holland, however, was not chosen to serve on this board. The meeting voted to raise thirty minute men and purchase three hundred pounds of gunpowder and lead for bullets.

As a further expression of its trust, the town meeting in June 22, 1775, elected Holland as moderator. He replaced Matthew

Thornton, who was serving as president of New Hampshire's Provincial Congress. The town meeting later voted that every man who was able, had a gun, twenty bullets and six flints, and was "willing to go against the enemy" would be given a share of the town stock of powder to be used "only on self defense." The town meeting on November 7 even petitioned the state government to have Holland and Matthew Thornton continue in the rank of colonel in the militia. Holland was later offered the command of a battalion with the rank of brigadier general but he declined with disdain.

Stephen Holland's speech at the town meeting had worked; he was now viewed as a patriot and worthy of trust by the townspeople. His April 29 speech was even published in the state's only newspaper. In reality, Holland was lying through his teeth! He was, in fact, a British spy who was secretly sending information to Royal Governor Wentworth in Portsmouth, who would in turn forward the data to British General Gage in Boston. Holland was so trusted that on June 19, 1775, patriot General John Stark sent him a private communication with details of the Battle of Bunker Hill, which had occurred just two days earlier.

What General Stark didn't know was that on June 18, Holland had gone to coastal New Hampshire to recruit an army to assist the British in the defense of Boston. He was able to get more than two hundred men to swear an oath of allegiance to England and to march with him to Massachusetts. Holland's army got as far as Somerville but was barred from reaching General Gage because the patriots had blockaded all the roads in and out of Boston. Governor Wentworth would later beg Holland not to defect to the British because he would be of more service if he remained in Londonderry as a secret British agent.

In April 1776, the Continental Congress decided it was time to take a census to identify the supporters of the patriots. Every person was invited to sign "the Association Test." The subscribers, by adding their name to the list, were showing that they were willing "to join our American brethren in defending the lives, liberties, properties of the inhabitants of the united colonies . . . at the risk of our lives and fortunes, with arms, oppose the hostile proceedings of the British fleets and armies." The only ones who were not required to sign were those below the age of twenty-one as well as "lunatic, idiots, negroes"; and, of course, women. The names of those who would not sign were sent to the patriot authorities in Exeter.

In Londonderry, there were 376 men who were willing to acknowledge that they supported George Washington and thus renounced all allegiance to King George III. On June 24, 1776, the town clerk reported that there were only fourteen men who would not sign. Among the first to sign was Stephen Holland. Once again the gentleman tavern keeper publicly lied so he could remain a spy.

Holland later said that the only reason he stayed in New Hampshire was that in April 1775 he had made a promise to Governor Wentworth. John Wentworth was preparing to flee the state. Holland had told him that he personally "considered it dangerous to remain in the province." The Governor convinced him to stay and "use his utmost efforts to repress the military exertions . . . and to use every art and address to circumvent and disappoint their views, and keep me informed." And like the good soldier he was, Holland agreed to stay in New Hampshire and lie for king and country.

An example of his spying can be found in a letter from Major General Sir Archibald Campbell (1739–1791). In 1776–1777, Campbell was a prisoner of the American Army. During those years, Holland would frequently travel the forty miles from Londonderry to Reading, Massachusetts, to meet with Campbell in his jail cell. Holland would smuggle private letters from Campbell to the British authorities. Campbell later recalled that this relaying of intelligence was performed at great risk to Holland, whose "personal liberty and life was in danger." In 1778, Campbell was exchanged for Ethan Allen.

For two more years Holland remained in New Hampshire as a very effective British secret agent. His cover was finally accidentally blown in a way worthy of a modern spy novel. Brothers John and Robert Moor, of Londonderry, were employed hauling loads of flax from Connecticut to New Hampshire. During the January 1777 trip, John Moor took sick with smallpox and subsequently died. A farm boy went into his barn in search of chicken eggs. He put his hand into a crevice in the coop and found a flat rock where no flat rock should be. His curiosity was piqued. Under the stone he found a bundle of letters. In time these pages were turned over to Governor Trumbell, of Connecticut, who forwarded them to the Committee of Safety in New Hampshire.

Among the letters were two that were addressed to "Colonel Stephen Ash of Nutfield." One of these said that Ash should flee to safety behind the British lines in New York. It was quickly determined that "Ash" was actually Stephen Holland. The writer signed himself William Strong. The identity of Mr. Strong was determined to be William Stark—the brother of patriot general John Stark. William was born in 1724 in what is now the town of Derry. In 1776 he had felt ill-used by not being given a command commission in the New Hampshire militia. In retaliation for this slight he joined the British army as a lieutenant colonel of Loyalist troops. William Stark died after falling off a horse—possibly during a polo match—the date of his death is disputed, but it did occur in New York prior to 1781. Stark was related through marriage to Stephen Holland.

On March 11, 1777, the Committee of Safety ordered Holland and Robert Moor arrested "on suspicion of their being enemies to the liberties of America." Holland again managed to use his Gaelic charm to talk his way out of the charges. Moor was released only after posting a bond but Holland was freed "with honor." Despite his release, he would now be monitored constantly by the local watch and ward.

His freedom didn't last long. He was soon arrested for being a part of a Tory counterfeiting ring. His gang was printing huge amounts of New Hampshire money with the purpose of ruining the state's economy. In Londonderry, authorities wrote to the state that one local had so much counterfeit money that he offered "$30 for a gill of rum." Holland and five of his co-conspirators was soon imprisoned in the state prison at Exeter. Holland would later call the lockup a "noisome vault of a jail." On May 2, 1777, Holland was found guilty of treason and sentenced to death. That night he managed to break out of the prison. His description was published in the *Portsmouth Gazette* and a reward of one hundred dollars was posted for his apprehension.

All over New England, authorities were trying to apprehend Holland, who many considered to be New Hampshire's arch Tory. Guards were placed at ferries and bridges "from Andover to the Amoskeag Falls to prevent him getting over." His mansion and farms in Londonderry were searched and a guard posted should Holland be foolish enough to return home.

On May 5, Londonderry's town fathers received an order from the state to seize and take an inventory of Holland's property. The five selectmen and seven members of the town's Committee of Safety were selected to undertake this task. They billed the state three pounds, twelve shillings plus the cost of a dinner and a gallon of rum for their efforts.

A month later, Stephen Holland was captured hiding in Boston and was thrown into the city's jail. For four nights he was confined to a dark, windowless, dank dungeon cell that measured only four by six feet. He was not given any food—not even the traditional ration of bread and water. He had to sleep on the cold floor without any bedding or straw to give him comfort. A prisoner in an adjoining cell was able to use a pipe to give a little water to Holland. It was reported by a prison trustee that the jailors had been ordered to starve the Londonderry man to death.

Finally, on June 10, Stephen Holland was released from the hell of the Boston jail. He probably couldn't have survived much longer. The New Hampshire authorities arrived in the nick of time to return him to Exeter. He was surrounded by a "strong guard of soldiers" despite the fact that he appeared too weak to attempt an escape. He was made to ride horseback with his arms restrained with handcuffs and his legs shackled by a chain that ran from ankle to ankle under the horse's stomach. He was so heavily bound that he could walk only with the support of two guards to hold him up.

In Exeter he was thrown into the lockup with eight soldiers guarding him at all times. To further keep him confined, the jailor requested that he be chained to the cell's floor. A guard was always at his cell door expressly to keep him from talking to anyone. Holland was so weak and sick that finally, after repeated requests, a doctor was allowed to see him. The physician reported there was little he could do and predicted the feverish prisoner would soon die.

Holland was not the only local Tory in jail. Also in Exeter was Robert Fulton, of Londonderry, who was charged with being an enemy sympathizer and accusing the patriots of being "bloodthirsty." On September 9, 1777, Fulton wrote to the Londonderry Committee of Safety that he was an "unhappy prisoner." He claimed his wife was sick and living in a remote wilderness area of Londonderry. She had no man or boy to help her on the farm, only an "old woman." He requested that he be allowed to go home until his wife got better. He further asked that he be allowed to be exiled "to any part of the globe your honors shall see fit . . . without delay in any way and manner." It appears that most of the witnesses chose not to testify against Fulton and he was soon released.

Holland still had a number of supporters in his hometown. Many locals felt sorry that their former town father was suffering "in a loathsome jail replete with the noxious fumes of an infectious vault." In September, Abraham Reid circulated a petition in Windham and Londonderry requesting that the ailing prisoner be set free until he could recover his health. The signers offered their homes and farms as security should Holland fail to return to prison after his health improved. It was reported that 133 men signed this request for mercy. The petition was rejected and the authorities publicly denounced the signers as "enemies of the people" and demanded that the citizens of the state, 'have no communication with them."

Although the Reid petition has not survived, a similar one was circulated by Holland's father-in-law, John Stinson. It requested that Holland be set free because of the illness he contracted while in jail. It argued that unless he was given an "alteration of diet, fresh air, and exercise, his strength almost totally exhausted, will totally fail." The petitioners argued that the confinement without the possibility of parole was in effect imposing a punishment without having been found guilty. This, they charged, was "incompatible with justice and the principles of a free government."

The British government also tried to get Holland released from jail. On September 12, patriot leader John Langdon received a note from his brother, the merchant Woodbury Langdon. He had been captured and was being held prisoner by the British army in New York City. He wrote that former governor John Wentworth had brokered a deal; he would be released in exchange for Stephen Holland. The Committee of Safety refused to make the exchange because the charge of counterfeiting still had to be put to trial. In time, Langdon managed to escape to New Hampshire. Later his brother, Governor John Langdon, said he hoped someday to have Holland hanged, as "he has done more damage than ten thousand men could have done."

Holland was finally put on trial in October and was found guilty of producing funny money. The sentence was relatively light: three months in jail and a fine of two thousand pounds. He was also no longer to be shackled in irons. He was likely given this mild punishment because they knew a capital trial for treason would soon take place and then he would certainly receive the death sentence.

In January 1778, a jury of twelve men in the Superior Court found Holland guilty of high treason. The punishment was death by hanging. That night Holland did the impossible. By some unknown means, Holland once again escaped from the Exeter jail. His description was again printed in the newspaper and a hundred pounds was

offered for his apprehension. Holland probably was hidden in loyalist "safe houses" in Massachusetts and Connecticut. Perhaps he
rode hidden underneath hay in a farmer's wagon or dressed himself
in a woman's gown. We will never know how he managed to elude
the authorities, who were very eager to see him back in prison. All
we know is that soon after his escape, Holland and his son John
arrived safely behind British lines in Long Island, New York. They
would never again return to New Hampshire.

Now that Stephen Holland was legally declared an enemy of
the people, his property could be sold. Any money realized from
its sale would be turned over to the state treasury to pay his fines.
The rules of the auction written in Exeter were sent to "Londerry"
(sic). Everything was to go to the highest bidder and had tot be
paid for in a month. The Londonderry property was sold in March
1780. The hundreds of tracts of land that were scattered throughout
the state were sold in January 1781.Included in this sales were Stephen Holland's gold watch and his pew in the First Parish Meeting
House. The estate was finally settled in 1787, when his brother-in-
law paid to the town of Londonderry one thousand dollars for what
was left of Holland's "personnel estate."

Jane Holland and three of her children were given permis-
sion to join her husband in exile. An armed mob in Londonderry
took all of her belongings and left the family with just the clothing
on their backs. The selectmen reported that as she was leaving
Londonderry for the last time, she attacked the town fathers with
insults "too gross to mention." She told anyone who would listen
that her husband "will return in a few weeks in greater honor and
glory than ever and tread on the neck of his enemies."

Once Stephen Holland was safe behind British lines, he began
to seek ways to help the king. A letter of recommendation was sent
to the British commander in chief, General Sir Henry Clinton from
General Sir Archibald Campbell. As a result of this letter, Holland
was appointed captain in the Prince of Wales's American Regiment
in Newport, Rhode Island. According to all records, Holland performed his duties well and brought credit to himself. His son John
Wentworth Holland served as his ensign.

On May 17, 1781, while in British service, Stephen Holland
sent a letter to his old friend General John Sullivan of New Hampshire. Holland proposed that the patriots start negotiations with the
British to see if reconciliation was possible. He said he knew that

the terms offered by Whitehall would be quite acceptable by the patriots. America would be "forever exempt from the British taxation, that every freedom of trade is to be extended, that our charters and established forms of government are to be secured and that every satisfaction and security is to be given forever in the subject of military establishment." This would put America and Britain into a political marriage similar to that enjoyed by Canada after confederation in 1867. Holland said the letter had been approved by General Clinton and should be kept an "inviolable secret" until later. This peace overture was never acted on by the colonists.

With the surrender of the British army at Yorktown on October 19, 1781, any possibility of victory by the English had passed. In December 1782, Stephen Holland left New York for England. He took with him his son John Wentworth Holland. His wife and three other children remained behind within British lines. Four of their children stayed in New Hampshire.

Jane Holland requested that she be allowed to return to Londonderry to collect her children and straighten out her personal affairs. General Washington agreed to General John Sullivan's request that she be permitted to travel under a flag of truce. The New Hampshire Legislature even agreed that she could return to her old hometown.

Jane's return may have been okay with Washington, Sullivan and the state legislature, but it was decidedly not acceptable to the men of Londonderry. On December 18, 1782, they submitted to the state a petition signed by eighty-six citizens protesting her return. The signers argued that she would be a spy and "a channel of intelligence and correspondence between our enemies at New York and those here among us, and your petitioners dread the consequence." This local protest was enough to make the legislature reconsider its vote. Jane could not return to her home. Was she unhappy? I reckon she was.

The Londonderry town meeting in May 1783 voted unanimously that no Tory ever be allowed to return to town. In the resolve, members wrote that these traitors have "murdered our brethren; in cold blood they have burnt our towns, robbed and plundered our citizens, ravished our daughters and been guilty of every sort of rapine and carnage." In closing, the gentle people of Londonderry wanted New Hampshire to provide "a gallows' halter and a hangman" for any loyalists who should dare "show their vile countenances among us."

In time, Jane Holland and most of her children were able to reunite with Stephen Holland in London. In 1797, he was back in his hometown of Coleraine in county Londonderry, Northern Ireland. He was receiving an army pension of sixty pounds annually. In that year he was suing an estate in Londonderry, New Hampshire to recover a debt of $150. I have not been able to determine when either Stephen or Jane Holland died. By 1797, they were both in their sixties and considered fairly elderly by eighteenth-century standards.

Of the Holland children, little is known. The records indicate that several daughters stayed in America after their parents sailed for London. I suspect they were older children who were already married. The only one whom I have been able to track down is Margaret (1758–1840) who married James MacGregor and lived in Londonderry for the rest of her life. The couple named their first son Stephen Holland MacGregor. At Forest Hill Cemetery is the grave of Jean Holland, who died in infancy in 1768. John Wentworth Holland, the oldest son of Jane and Stephen Holland, had a long career in the British army. He was the respected captain of the H.M.S. Phoebe during the Napoleonic wars. He is also remembered as being an excellent violinist. He died in the city of Bath, England, in 1841.

Perhaps the next time that I'm in Northern Ireland, I'll travel over to Coleraine to find out more about the last days of Stephen Holland. He was certainly one of our most interesting figures. He was one of Londonderry's wealthiest and most distinguished citizens, a man who was willing to sacrifice his fortune, health, family, and honor for his king and his country. Unfortunately, Holland was on the wrong side of history. Perhaps if the British had won, some quotation of his would have been inscribed on New Hampshire's license plates instead of "Live free or die," said by General John Stark of Derry. As things actually did turn out, however, Holland will be forever cast as our state's greatest traitor and most unrepentant liar.

❧❧

For additional information I recommend Dr. Kenneth Scott's excellent article in *Historical New Hampshire*, spring 1947.

7.
Nutfield's First Lawyer

TODAY IN DERRY, WINDHAM, AND LONDONDERRY THERE ARE somewhere around two dozen lawyers. Some of these are in general practice; others specialize in bankruptcy or corporate law. If you were in our towns in the years around the Revolutionary War, your choice of attorneys would number exactly one: the Honorable John Prentice—and his legal specialty was doing whatever his client asked him to do.

John Prentice was born in Cambridge, Massachusetts in 1747. His father was a barrel maker and had to struggle to support his large family. To make ends meet, his mother, Susanna, had to work outside the home. She labored as a "sweeper" at Harvard College to pay for her son's tuition at the school. His class at Harvard consisted of the sons of New England's wealthiest families including the future baronet William Pepperell. It must have been difficult for the teenage boy to move in such a high social environment while his mother was in public view as the school's janitor.

For the rest of his life, he would always acknowledge that any success he achieved was the result of his mother's sacrifices. He is remembered as saying, "She was one of the best of mothers, and I loved her tenderly. No woman ever possessed a sweeter disposition or discharged the duties of her station with prudence or greater fidelity." When he received word of her passing, he stayed in bed for many days in deepest depression over his loss.

After college, he studied law under the royal governor's Attorney General Samuel Livermore, who lived in the section of Londonderry that would in 1827 become Derry. For a while, he

The home of attorney John Prentice on Lane road was erected in the 1770s and destroyed in a 1926 fire.

practiced law in Marblehead, Massachusetts, where in May 1774 he signed a public letter of support for the royal governor. For such actions, he always remained under suspicion by the supporters of the patriot cause. He would later twice recant his brief espousal of the Tory governor. Five months later in October 1774, he publicly ate crow by posting a letter that announced: "Whereas I the subscriber, signed an address to the late Governor Hutchinson, I wish the devil had had the address before I had seen it."

In June 1775, Prentice moved to Derry, where he again had to give a public retraction of the pro-Tory letter. According to tradition, his presence in Derry was not met with a great deal of support. Many townsfolk didn't want their community's reputation to be sullied by the presence of a lawyer. He was warned not to start a practice here. This was at the beginning of the Revolutionary War and it was likely that many saw the legal profession as in direct opposition to the natural rights of man.

Standing up to his critics, Prentice proposed that his right to stay be decided by a trial by combat. The local Scots thought this reasonable. They put up as their champion "a mighty bruiser." The young lawyer took a real pummeling but gave back nearly as good as he got. Because Prentice took the beating in a manly manner, he earned local acceptance. Derry now had its first full-time lawyer. In deference to my East Derry cousin, Attorney Rebecca Rutter, I will not call for such a trial of honor to be codified as the standard screening for new lawyers in Derry.

John Prentice married well. His first wife was Ruth Lemon, the daughter of a wealthy Marblehead physician. Suddenly he was no longer the poor charwoman's son. He used part of her dowry to purchased 234 acres of land on Lane Road from his teacher Samuel Livermore. There in East Derry, he built a huge mansion with a ballroom and a third floor cupola that was the size of a small house. The house would eventually contain some ten thousand square feet of floor space, making it the largest house ever built in Derry. The mansion was destroyed by fire in 1926.

He represented the town in the state legislature for thirteen years, starting in 1785. He was Speaker of the House in 1794, 1795, 1798–1805. This makes him the longest serving Speaker in our state's history. In 1805, the Democratic Party won the majority in the House and Prentice elected to return to private life rather than become minority leader. He also served as the New Hampshire's Attorneys General from 1787 to 1793. In 1798 he was appointed to the Superior Court but declined the honor.

He never earned a reputation as a highly educated legal mind, instead, he seems to have preferred winning cases by passion rather than book learning. Once at the start of a trial the opposing lawyer tried to have the case dismissed because Prentice's client had recently died. The Derry lawyer protested to the judge that Jenny McPherson was still alive. The judge lectured him that "the records of the court cannot lie." "Can't they?" Prentice fired back. "I tell Your Honor that my client is alive and well and if Your Honor's records say that she is dead, they do lie like hell!"

Once a fellow lawyer was testifying for the prosecution in a case in which Prentice was the counsel for the defense. As he began his questioning, he leaned forward to admonish the man in the witness stand. In a very audible stage whisper he said, "Brother Lawyer, if you are determined to fill up all the chinks in the case, do it as handsomely as you can, but don't commit any *unnecessary* perjury."

In the earliest days of our town, most travel was done by walking. It was not uncommon for our citizens to make a two-day trek to Boston by foot. In the years around the Revolutionary War, horses became more common. On Sundays, it was a natural sight to see a horse carrying a man in front and his wife sitting on the pillion behind with a baby in her arms. John Prentice brought the first carriage to Derry around 1800. This vehicle caused great excitement throughout town. To most however, the two-wheeled chaise was viewed as "an unjustifiable extravagance." The first horse-drawn wagon wouldn't come to town until 1814. The first automobile sputtered through in 1899.

Prentice was deemed by his neighbors to be an "honest man and a good citizen." He was also known for his exaggerated speech. Once he was complaining about the poor-quality workmanship in a new stone wall he had paid to be built. He said it couldn't "stand a heavy dew." He further reported that half of it had already fallen over and that he had just seen a robin sitting on it "and when she flew away, she threw down 300 feet of it at one kick." Another time he complained that the firewood he had just purchased contained too much pitch. This, he claimed, caused his stove to smoke so badly that when he came home, "Old Rose [his black servant] was the whitest in the home"!

Like all real farmers, he took a great pride in his skills as a yeoman farmer. He boasted to his neighbors that he raised a melon "as big as a barrel." He also told of clearing a field and digging out a pine stump that had yielded him "25 cord of wood."

One year, he and his help had just finished cutting the hay in his fields when it began to rain. He reluctantly had to wait days before the hay was suitably dried out. Just before he brought it into the barn, it rained again. Getting progressively angrier, he waited another week to let the hay dry out. Once more, the sky grew gray and opened up with a torrent that drenched his crop of cow fodder. John Prentice was not a man who would let this happen a fourth time! The frustrated man decided now was the time to act. He would stand up to Mother Nature. He ordered his gang of men to set the entire hay crop on fire and burn it where it lay in the field.

After the death of his first wife, in 1791, he married Tabitha, the daughter of Judge Nathaniel Sargent of Haverhill, Massachusetts. By each of these wives he had eight children. A number of his offspring did not survive to reach maturity. I once did an analysis of mortality in this area and found that during the eighteenth century 56 percent of the population would die before reaching adulthood.

Only 12 percent would live to age sixty. At Forest Hill Cemetery there are buried ten of his family in addition to his two wives, who died at ages forty-two and thirty-seven, respectively. There in the family plot are six of his children who died as infants, one who succumbed as a teenager and three who survived only into their twenties. In this last set is Hannah Prentice, who died in 1793 at age twenty. A writer remembering her nearly fifty years later commented that she was of "surpassing beauty." Three of Prentice's sons he named "John" after himself, but all died young.

Death came to John Prentice on May 18, 1808, at age sixty-one. He now rests in a marble box-vault at Forest Hill Cemetery. His grave is pretty much ignored by passersby. Time, acid rain, and lichen have done their best to make the inscription virtually illegible and its granite base needs repointing. The cleaning and restoration of his memorial might be a suitable project for the members of Derry's legal community. Perhaps on the anniversary of his passing a wreath could be placed on his grave to honor the town's first lawyer and his fight to earn respect here in Derry, 232 years ago.

Doctor Matthew Thornton (1714-1802) of Derry Village was a signer of the Declaration of Independence.

8.

The Devil and Derry

HERE IS A SELECTION OF STORIES I FOUND TUCKED AWAY IN MY notes. I make no claim that they're true; only that they're old. The "newest" of these tales was told in 1895. The stories are brief, so I'm going to lump them together as one chapter. Some of these events took place in eighteenth-century Derry while others occurred in the nineteenth century. All, however, have a common theme. Each is typical of the stories and yarns that were swapped by men as they sat by the potbellied stove in the town's country stores. I doubt very much whether a teller would ever let the truth get in the way of a good yarn. I further suspect that each time a story was told, it was "improved" by the narrator.

THORNTON IN HELL

Matthew Thornton (1714–1803) lived in Derry Village and practiced medicine from his house on Thornton Square. He was a selectmen, a colonel in the local militia, and a member of the Committee of Safety. On November 4, 1776, he signed the Declaration of Independence. He was also a natural storyteller with an easy charm, and was considered a master of repartee.

One day Dr. Thornton was riding his horse on the outskirts of Derry when a "ruffianly-looking" man leaped out of the bushes and stood in front of his steed. The shabbily dressed man recognized the Derry Village doctor and thought he would have a little sport at his expense. Calling to Thornton in a loud, angry voice, he bellowed:

"You don't know me, sir; but I know all about you, sir! All about you!"

"Well," said the doctor, "if you are so well informed, will you please tell me who I am, where I'm from, and where I'm going?"

"Your name is Dr. Matthew Thornton from Derry Village and you're going straight to the devil!"

"Aha!" said the doctor. "If that's the case, from the appearance of the land and the looks of the people, I must be pretty near my journey's end."

BROADWAY AND HELL

This story was told by Leonard H. Pillsbury (1835–1933). He was a Broadway merchant, a veteran of the Civil War, a district court judge, and a founder of the local Baptist church. He was very, very outspoken in his opposition to the sale of alcohol in Derry. In a 1916 letter to the *Derry News* he voiced his plea for voters to elect only candidates who supported a nationwide prohibition. Pillsbury recalled how in the recent past Derry was a wide-open town with very active saloons. To the pious, Broadway bore a fair resemblance to the ancient Sodom and Gomorrah. Judge Pillsbury used this story to illustrate Derry in the bad old days.

Awhile back there had been a very proper and staid conductor on the Boston and Maine Railroad line that ran from Manchester to the cities in Massachusetts. This passenger train was just coming in to make its usual ten-minute stop at the passenger and freight station on Broadway. On board was a loud and vocal drunk who was attracting considerable attention from the other passengers. He had been irritating the poor conductor ever since he had stumbled on board back in Manchester. In frustration, the railroad official asked the old souse where he was going—hoping that he was going to get off at the next stop. The drunk by this time had entered into a fit of melancholy and was sobbing about his life and misfortunes.

Just as the train began to roll to a stop at the Broadway station, the frustrated conductor again interrupted him. "Where are you going, sir?" he asked.

The man through his tears said, "I'm going to Hell!" Without a pause, the conductor got the man to his feet and escorted him to the exit. While walking, he firmly told the drunk, "Well, that place is only a little ways from the depot at Derry, so you better get off now and walk."

WHIZ TOM

In the earliest days of the town, the roads at night were dark and lonely. A man on horseback could ride for miles without encountering the warm, comforting lights of a farmhouse. After dark, the trees flanking the narrow roads could look like hands and talons positioned to grab and snatch away an unsuspecting traveler.

A couple of centuries ago, there was a Derry farmer named Tom—his last name has been forgotten—who was riding back to his home near Island Pond. He had just sold a pair of oxen to a farmer who lived on the shores of Lake Massabesic in Auburn. In his saddlebags, he carried a purse with a pretty good poke of money. He was a happy man and felt proud of the profit he had made on the deal.

As he passed Devil's Den in Auburn, he sped up his horse; after all, that cave was rumored to be the dwelling place of Old Scratch himself. On the road to Beaver Lake his anxiety grew as he went by Boyd's Rock, which was considered by some to be another hiding place for highwaymen. As he approached the Derry town line, the sun began to sink behind the trees; soon it was dusk and then dark. As he rode passed Jenny Dickie Brook his fear of unseen terrors lurking in the thick forest made him a "leetle bit shaken."

He felt much braver when he rode up Horse Hill and into the lights of the village of East Derry. He was very relieved when he tied up his horse in front of Thom's Tavern. Soon Tom was bellying up to the bar. Here he brought his courage to the sticking place by ordering a few "spine stiffeners." After he threw back these measures of rum, he felt much braver and man enough to finish his ride to Island Pond.

His courage quickly faded when he left the village and rode into the moonless night. As he traveled along, he kept a "careful lookout for any enemy who might be lurking in the darkness." Steadily he inched closer and closer to home. For most of the way the only sounds to break the stillness of the night were the rhythmic clopping of his horse's hooves and the jingling of the money in his saddlebags. Every so often a wind would stir up the leaves on the quaking aspens and make a rattling sound. Sometimes the melancholy hoot of an owl and the irritating call of a whip-poor-will could be heard coming from somewhere deep in the dark East Derry woods.

As he began to climb Allison's Hill, he entered into an area of cultivated farmland. Tom looked over to the side of the lane and saw the gigantic, towering figure of a dark man. In the starlight the giant was "furiously flourishing his arms in a fearful, menacing manner." Tom froze as the man tried to grab him. His "heart was in his throat" and his hair literally stood on end, "nearly lifting his hat from his head."

At the top of his lungs he screamed at the villain, "Spare me. Take my money, but spare me." In terror, he reached into the saddle-bags and grabbed his sack of money. With all his strength, he tossed the purse as hard as he could toward the giant highwayman.

Tom grabbed the reins and started to whip his horse to make it break into a gallop. The thundering sound of swiftly moving hooves filled the night air as horse and man whizzed down the deserted road at breakneck speed. As he rode, Tom was too intent to look either right or left. He was too scared to look behind him lest he see the giant gaining on him. His only concern was finding sanctuary and safety with other people of Derry. There would be strength in numbers!

Finally he came to the village blacksmith shop. Here a group of men had gathered to discuss politics and life. Tom was safe, his life was spared. A jug of good New England rum was as usual snaking its way from man to man. "Gasping for breath," Tom did his best to tell the crowd about the cause of his terror.

After hearing Tom's story, the men grabbed whatever weapons they could find in the smithy. Some carried axes, others picks, scythes, or hammers. Down the road they hiked to confront the giant. As they approached the site of the holdup, the crowd grew quiet. Immediately they found the source of Tom's night terror. In his cornfield a farmer had erected a "remarkably life-like scarecrow." It had long cloth arms that were flailing about in the swift-moving wind. It was not until after daylight that a search party finally found the missing bag of money.

For years the story of the scarecrow highwayman was told and retold around the cracker barrels and campfires of Derry. For decades, the poor embarrassed night rider was called by the nick-name "Whiz Tom."

NEVER SHAME THE DEVIL

Around the time of the War of 1812, many in the town were suspicious of the loyalty of a local clergyman. Though the old man had been born in British-controlled Ireland, he had lived in America for many decades. Unlike other preachers, this Scotch-Irish cleric was not filling his Sunday sermons with anti-British themes; his prayers didn't invoke fiery coals and brimstone on the head of the English king. He didn't quote chapter and verse from scripture to prove the righteousness of the American cause and the ungodliness of everything British.

A delegation of town fathers showed up unannounced at the cleric's front door. They demanded that he clarify his position and publicly proclaim his views. The minister thought for a minute and then gave his answer in the form of a parable combining Scottish caution and Irish humor.

> "I once knew a widow lady in Scotland who had only one son," he said. "He had been absent from home for a long time attending school. On the night of his return, just before retiring for the night, the good old mother turned kindly toward her boy and said,
>
> 'I know ye are a good and learned lad, Johnny, and I want to hear ye pray.' John readily complied with his mother's request.
>
> "When he arose from his knees, he quietly asked his mother how she liked his prayer.
>
> 'Pretty well, pretty well, Johnny, but why didn't ye give the Devil a good hard slap and thumping in your prayer?'
>
> 'Oh!' replied Johnny with a knowing wink and a nod. 'Not I—not I, I would not do it, Mother, for you never know whose hands we may sometime fall into.'"

PAY FOR THE POT

The hill on the road leading up to East Derry from Derry Village is correctly called Horse Hill. At its base, the road passes close by a swampy arm of Beaver Lake. It was believed by many that this dark bog was bottomless and the home to the spirit of a long-dead horse that had become stuck in the mud.

One dark night, as Timothy D. rode his horse up the hill, he let his imagination get the best of him. Just as he passed the haunted spot, he turned around and thought he saw his horse's tail glowing with a "strangely tinted light." In panic, he dug in his spurs and rode up the hill as fast as his horse could gallop.

When Tim arrived in East Derry, he ran into the country store to tell his adventure to the crowd sitting by the potbellied stove. Just as he got through the door, he tripped and fell headfirst into a small cast-iron pot. He instantly stood up and found that his head was firmly encased in the pot.

A throng crowded around Tim as he tried to get his head free. It was said that because of his extremely large nose, he was unable to extricate his head from its iron prison. Several men tried to bull his head free but to no avail. Finally it was decided by the spectators that the only way to save this pot-head was to use a hammer and crack open the helmet. With a crash, Tim was free and the pot was in pieces.

Immediately a debate broke out between the storekeeper and Tim over paying for the broken pot. Tim argued quite reasonably that the whole incident was unintentional on his part and he was only a victim of circumstances. Besides, he reasoned, he hadn't wielded the mallet that broke the pot. The merchant countered that the incident was the result of Tim's clumsiness. He further argued that "Tim had no right to be poking his nose into other people's business." For hours the argument between the two went round and round but no resolution could be reached.

The storekeeper was determined to exact his revenge. During a lull in the argument, he went into a storeroom and found a pair of "long faced pumpkins." With his pocketknife he carved each into a jack-o-lantern with a rather horse-shaped face. In time, Tim left the store and headed down Horse Hill on the way back home. He had a wee bit of trouble staying in the saddle due to his enthusiastic appreciation for the quality of the store's brand of rum.

As soon as Tim went out the door, the merchant persuaded two long-legged customers to play a little trick on their departed friend. Staying out of sight by cutting through the field, the men carried their pumpkins to the bottom of the hill. Here they put lit candles into the jack-o-lanterns and waited in the bushes by the side of the road.

In a few minutes, the drunken rider came trotting by. Immediately the two friends sprung into action and held the horse-faced pumpkins over their heads. They "loudly called out, in tones like bull frogs . . . pay for the pot—pay for the pot!"

In terror, poor Timothy reacted immediately. He threw his money purse toward the banshees and with a scream flew down the road "like a phantom" on horseback. The "banshees" quickly spirited the money back to the store. There, the excess funds were used to purchase liquid refreshment for the thirsty customers sitting around the potbelly stove.

In time, Timothy found out about the trick that had been played on him. The records say he was more than a little "disgusted."

MOTHER WATKINS

In olden times, Derry folk were more likely to believe in superstitions than are we in the twenty-first century. Today, science rules; belief in headless horses and the evil eye has been pretty much relegated to the realm of fairy tales. However, during the nineteenth century, tales of the supernatural were standard fare as men sat around the cheerful wood fire in the country stove.

To many in those days, it was important to determine just who was and who was not a witch. Such knowledge was an aspect of self-protection. You didn't want a curse placed on you by a witch you had inadvertently made angry. One tried-and-true method of identifying a witch was to use a piece of steel to make a cross within her footprint in the dirt. If a woman really was a witch, she would instantly halt and turn around.

One Fourth of July a gang of boys was playing in a Derry Village road when Mother Watkins walked by. She was rather an evil-looking "old crone" who wandered through the area begging and telling fortunes. This "Yankee Gypsy" seemed to enjoy her reputation as a witch. It was good for business.

These preteen boys put their heads together and decided to find out, once and for all, if Mother Watkins was a witch. Jerry H. had just bought a new jackknife and led his gang as they quietly followed the old woman. From a position only a few feet from Mother Watkins, he bent over and used the blade to make a cross inside her footprint.

"By a ludicrous coincidence" the old woman halted and turned around the instant the mystical symbol was made. Immediately the boys began to run as fast as their legs would take them. From then on, these Derry youngsters believed in witchcraft and always showed exaggerated politeness when coming near Mother Watkins.

WITCH HAZEL

Witch hazel is a common shrub in Derry. In July 1889, Albert Gould came to town and built a three-story factory in which to manufacture Gould's Witch Hazel. His four-thousand-square-foot distillery and bottling plant was in the southern part of town near Hubbard's Railroad Station. His supply of the plant was nearly endless; most farmers were quite happy to have Gould cut down the weed that grew wild in their pastures. His product was a popular astringent that could be used as an aftershave or to heal bruises. Witch Hazel's name is derived from a pair of old English words: *witch* meaning bendable and *hazel,* which refers to its use in finding water as a dowsing rod. Despite the etymology, the people of old Derry firmly believed the plant was enchanted and that it was somehow the herbaceous personification of those in league with the devil.

In the southern part of Derry there lived a farmer and his wife. Nearby up a bridle path lived an old lady whom many considered to be a witch. The farmer never trusted his ancient neighbor and the old woman didn't much care for him either. Around 1790, the farmer was hauling some logs to Haverhill with a yoke of oxen. On the way home, he drove his team up a long hill. The climb was so steep that he frequently had to use his goad stick to get the draft animals to keep moving.

Just as he got to the crest of the hill, the clevis pin that cinched the connection between the yoke and the wagon's spire slipped out and fell onto the road. Immediately the loaded wagon began to roll backward. All the man could do was stand by his oxen as he watched it roll faster and faster down the half-mile hill. As he watched, he felt sure the wagon would be smashed and the load of logs lost. Then something miraculous happened: The wagon's tongue fell and began to drag on the ground. Acting like a ship's rudder, it kept the fast-moving wagon rolling straight until it reached the base of the hill. There it sat, waiting for the farmer to come and get it.

Such an accident had never before happened to the man. It was almost like witchcraft. Although he was not happy, he was at least thankful that his wagon was still in one piece. Reluctantly, he made the long walk down to the bottom of the hill and rehitched his oxen to the wagon. Slowly the man and his wagon made the trek up the long slope with much use of the goad stick. It was when he finally got to the top of the hill that he heard again that dreaded sound; the clevis pin had popped out again! The whole scene began to replay. Straight down the hill rolled the wagon and again it did not stop until it got to the bottom. Was the farmer angry? You bet he was—but there was nothing he could do other than accept his fate.

Frustrated, the farmer ruminated over what had just happened. Spotting some witch hazel at the side of the road, the man came up with a plan. He cut down some of the pliant plant and twisted it around and around the spire like a rope. This twisting, handmade rope secured the clevis pin in place so it couldn't pop out. With that jerry-rigged solution, the farmer again started up the hill, now very pleased with his cleverness. The third time was a charm. In a couple of hours he was leading his oxen into a lumberyard in Haverhill. The return trip was uneventful.

By the time he reached his own farm yard, it was nearly dusk and he was tired and hungry. He didn't even unhitch his oxen but just brought them into the barn to eat their fodder. In the meantime, his wife came running out excitedly to greet him. She said their old lady neighbor had taken sick and appeared near death. The woman was pleading for the farmer to visit her as soon as he returned from Haverhill.

The farmer still pondering the events of the day, told his wife to go to the neighbor but to keep an eye on the clock. He would join her after he had finished his supper. She did as she was told and when she came to her neighbor's bedside she found that the woman's condition had worsened. Now she was "groaning and grasping for breath in great agony." She appeared near death.

After his evening meal, the farmer walked out into his barn. At exactly seven o'clock, he untied the witch hazel from the spire of his hitch. He then walked over to be with his wife. There he found out that at exactly seven o'clock, the old lady had became "perfectly quiet and free from pain." This confirmed to the farmer what he had long suspected. The elderly lady was really a witch!

In very clear words, he let his neighbor know that he knew her to be in league with the devil and that it had only been because of his wife's pleading that he had helped her this time. If another trick was ever played on him or his wagon, he would again twist the witch hazel and this time he wouldn't untie it to prevent her death from strangulation.

9.
Lafayette Was Here— Maybe Twice

RECENTLY, WHILE GOING THROUGH THE MANUSCRIPT ARCHIVES OF the Taylor Library, I came upon an account of Lafayette's visit to Derry. The memories of the 1825 event were transcribed in 1876 and sent to Philadelphia as an exhibit at America's first World's Fair.

In 1825, Marie Joseph Paul Yves Roch Gilbert du Motier, the Marquis de Lafayette (1757–1834), was one of the last surviving soldiers of the American Revolutionary War. When General Lafayette was a young man, he had served on George Washington's military staff. Nearly a half-century after the war, the national heroes of 1776—Washington, Jefferson, Adams, Franklin, and Stark—were now in Valhalla. Only Lafayette remained alive and could be honored in the flesh by the young republic.

Lafayette arrived in Boston on August 15, 1824, for his fourth and final farewell tour of America. He would remain in this country for over a year and visit twenty-four states. Wherever his retinue went, he was mobbed by crowds anxious to see this last leaf on the tree of liberty. He was as popular as a rock star or a movie star is today. Across America, many boys were named Mark by parents who believed Marquis to be Lafayette's first name and wrote the name phonetically.

According to an undocumented story, Lafayette first came to Derry on September 1, 1824, on the way from Portsmouth to Boston. He stayed overnight in the mansion of General Elias Haskett Derby

The Adams Female Academy.

Jr. on Lane Road in East Derry. Derby was a member of the legendary family of merchant princes of Salem, Massachusetts. Their clipper ships were the first to open up the Far East to American mercantile interests. During the war, Derby had become a close friend of Lafayette. General Derby had moved to Derry (then part of Londonderry) around 1809 and established a three-hundred acre farm. He was the first to introduce merino sheep to America. He died in Derry in 1826 of the gout and is buried in nearby Forest Hill Cemetery. His palatial ten-thousand-square-foot mansion was destroyed in a 1926 fire. (Attorney Rebecca Rutter's law office is now on the site of the Derby house.) Later during the visit, the Frenchman dined at Redfield's Tavern. (This public house was later the Derry Village home of milk czar H. P. Hood. It is now Chen's Restaurant on East Broadway.)

As the marquis was leaving Derry, he stopped for a drink at a mineral spring on Windham Road. He was so impressed by the water that he requested two barrels of it to be sent to Boston for his personal use. He later sent a cask of whiskey back to Derry as payment. For the next 150 years, this spring was known as Lafayette Spring. Around 1900, a local company utilized the water to make Lafayette Mineral Springs Soda. Its best-selling drink was Lafayette

Ginger Ale. In the 1980s, a developer who was working the Tyler Road area decided to bulldoze this landmark spring.

Lafayette returned to Derry on June 21, 1825, en route from Boston, where he had just laid the cornerstone of the Bunker Hill Monument. He was scheduled to arrive in town at eleven in the morning. He would be greeted in East Derry by General Derby and brought to the Adams Female Academy on Lane Road. He was to be accompanied by his son George Washington Lafayette.

The Adams Female Academy was just beginning to enjoy a national reputation. It claimed to be the first endowed girls school in America to offer a real curriculum. Among the schools over-seers would be essayist Ralph Waldo Emerson and future president Franklin Pierce. Mary Lyon (1797–1849), its principal teacher, would later go on to create the curriculum at Wheaton College. In 1837 she founded Mount Holyoke College, which was America's first women's college. Mary Lyon is honored at both the U.S. Hall of Fame and the National Women's Hall of Fame. In 1987, the U. S. Post Office issued a stamp in her honor.

That June morning, little learning took place at the school. All the girls and young women were much too excited to do their lessons. To pass the time, Headmaster Zilpah Polly Grant Bannister (1794–1874) and teacher Mary Lyon read to the classes a biography of Lafayette. At exactly eleven, all the students went onto the front lawn to join the crowd awaiting the marquis's arrival. Each girl wore a flowing, white, Grecian-style dress that extended down to her ankles. Around her waist every student wore a pink sash and in her arms each carried a bouquet of wildflowers. None of the girls and young women wore a bonnet or placed flowers in her hair; each let the beauty of her long locks go proudly unadorned.

For hours, the 101 girls of the Adams Female Academy waited. Their hero never appeared. Slowly the crowd of Derry Village residents began to disperse. Soon only the girls of the school remained. The sky grew dark with clouds and it began to rain. The girls had to run for cover back to their classroom. Next the thunder boomed and the lightning flashed so violently that many of the children were terrified. Despite this, the young ladies would not go home or give up hope. They alone in East Derry believed the great Lafayette would not let them down.

Finally, at five in the afternoon, a rider galloped by the school to say Lafayette was approaching! Suddenly down Lane Road roared his retinue, which consisted of a stagecoach, a two-horse wagon, and a magnificent barouche carriage pulled by four horses. In this latter vehicle sat Lafayette. His carriage was driven by a man sitting in a seat high above the ground. The general sat lower so that his head was no higher than people on the ground. This made it convenient for Lafayette to shake hands with spectators without having to rise from his seat.

Lafayette came into the schoolhouse, where he was greeted by the Reverend Daniel Dana who was pastor of the Presbyterian church in western Londonderry and a former president of Dartmouth College. He told the guest that the Adams Female Academy was the first girl's school in America to educate women in the same way that males were taught in college. In closing, Dana turned to the Frenchman and said, "You will not refuse these young ladies . . . the gratification of welcoming to our country the friend of man and the friend of America." Lafayette in response said a few words of appreciation to the teachers and then addressed the students. At the end of his brief speech, Principal Polly Grant asked the marquis if each girl and young lady could be presented to him individually. The Frenchman graciously gave his consent to this bold request.

Each academy student curtseyed as she was presented to the tall, red-haired man with the piercing green eyes. Lafayette shook every girl's hand and gave to each a few words of greeting. Then he climbed into his regal barouche. Just before he left, he expressed satisfaction with his visit to East Derry. Then he bowed to his admirers and said, "Farewell—forever." As he drove away, the rain let up and then stopped, and the sun cut through the clouds. Suddenly a rainbow appeared in the east.

As Lafayette headed toward Derry Village, the bell on the First Parish church pealed. Passing over the brow of the hill, he came within sight of the lower village. As soon as he was spotted, a cannon was fired, the tower-bell at Pinkerton Academy was rung, and a band began to play. The village was awash with residents from all over the region. One contemporary observer reported that "the sounds of many voices were heard in shouts of welcome. Ringing voices betokening healthy lungs and the shouts were overwhelming." Everyone wanted to see the man whom the great Washington considered to be almost a son.

The French general had a meal at Redfield's Tavern. Long tables were set in the dining room so that the local gentry could share in the occasion. Several times the meal was interrupted by the cheering of the crowd that surrounded the tavern. In response, an appreciative Lafayette would come onto the porch to acknowledge their homage with a flourish and a bow. In reply, impromptu speeches were offered by yeoman farmers.

As night started to fall, Lafayette left Derry and went on to Pembroke, where he spent the night with Major Caleb Stark, the son of Derry native General John Stark, who had died three years earlier. The next day in Concord he was mobbed by crowds and feted at a banquet for seven hundred. In the state capital, he dined with U.S. Senator Samuel Bell who had been born in what is now the town of Derry.

Later that week, Lafayette would visit several other New Hampshire towns. On June 27, 1825, he left our state and entered Vermont. In September he returned to his home in France. The Marquis de Lafayette, the last great hero of the Revolutionary War, died nine years later.

Here in Derry in 1825 we were incredibly blessed. We had a chance to thank the great Lafayette for his selfless contributions to our nation and to hear him say to us, "Farewell—forever."

The First Parish Church was the site of the 1827 split between Derry and Londonderry.

10.

The Birth of the Town

HISTORIANS HATE BEING UNABLE TO ANSWER LEGITIMATE QUERIES IN areas in which they are the supposed experts. A common question over the years has been "Why did Derry and Londonderry split in 1827?" I have read the manuscripts of the town records several times without coming up with a good answer. The official record by the town clerk in 1827 says almost nothing about the reason for the separation. In fact the records look like they have been "cleaned" to keep us from understanding what really happen.

The Reverend Edward Parker wrote our first town history in 1850. He devoted little space to the 1827 breakup. This omission is rather surprising, as he was an actual witness to the events that led to the Derry-Londonderry divorce. All Parker writes is, "In 1828 [sic] the number of inhabitants, the extent of the territory, the inconvenience of attending the town meeting, together with many local and rival interests, which frequently agitated the community induced those residing in the eastern part, to apply to the legislature for a division of the town." Possibly he didn't write more for fear of aggravating old wounds and upsetting local leaders.

To flesh out the story, I've made many trips to Concord to reread town records, sift through legislative petitions, and explore contemporary newspapers. Because of this research, I now believe I've come close to understanding the dynamics of the events of 1827. This is the first systematic exploration into what happened 180 years ago that caused the towns to separate.

Hold on tight. This is going to be quite a ride, full of twists and turns. Pay careful attention, as it does get a mite confusing. You have been fair warned.

As stated earlier, in 1719, when our town's pioneer ancestors came here from Ireland, they were able to secure a grant of land called Nutfield. In 1722 it was incorporated into a town they named Londonderry, after their former home in Northern Ireland. During the next century, this 114-square-mile town saw pieces break off to form new towns. The clearest example of this is in 1741 when Southern Londonderry became the town of Windham.

In 1740, Londonderry had been divided, by the Royal Governor, into the east and west parishes of Londonderry. Each parish had its own Presbyterian meetinghouse and taxed itself to pay for its own pastor. The original dividing line of the two parishes ran about north and south from approximately where the traffic circle is today and followed the route of modern day Route 28 from Salem and 28 bypass to Auburn.

The eastern parish of Londonderry was soon calling itself Derry and the western parish was known popularly as Londonderry. This was the genesis of the rift that led to the Londonderry and Derry split-up in 1827. The two Presbyterian parishes were more then simply fellow workers in the garden of the Lord; they appeared to be rivals that wanted little to do with the other. The Derry church was considered to be stiff-necked, traditional Calvinist, while the Londonderry parish represented a more evangelical, born-again fellowship.

The west and east parishes were officially, of course, part of a single town, which consisted of an area of seventy-eight square miles. The town of Londonderry held an annual town meeting in which the citizens set the tax rate by voting for a town budget and elected their town officers. Starting in 1790, it was official policy to alternate the location of the town meeting between the meetinghouses of the two parishes. The two divisions had approximately the same populations and tax values. The western parish of Londonderry was larger in size at approximately fifty square miles, but had a smaller population density.

The east parish was home to most of the town's doctors, lawyers, and merchants. It was also the site of the Adams Female Academy. Pinkerton Academy was just over the line into the Londonderry parish. The town's major highway was the Londonderry Turnpike (today's Route 28 and 28 bypass), which had made Derry Village the commercial center of the town. The west parish was much more rural and agricultural. It could logically be assumed that those in the eastern parish viewed their fellow townspeople in the western parish as country bumpkins and themselves as sophisticates. Remember that in 1827, the Broadway section of town was legally a part of the west parish and the exact opposite of what it is today. Broadway was then only an unnamed cart path that ran through open farms. It wouldn't become urbanized until after the railroad came through in 1848-1849.

In most years, the majority of the three-man board of selectmen were residents of east Londonderry, aka the parish of Derry. Starting in the mid 1820s, the Londonderry parish voters began to vote as a bloc. At the town meeting of 1826, farmers of the west parish managed to capture control of the board of selectman. This break with tradition upset many of the former ruling elite of east Londonderry. A cabal led by members of the Tucker, Thom, and Porter families of the east parish hatched a plot that would allow them next year to slither their way back into power.

On February 23, 1827, Constable Billy R. Gage posted the warrant for the annual town meeting, which was to convene in the meetinghouse of the east parish. Most of the articles dealt with mundane town business such as the election of officers, the boundaries of school districts, and road construction. The document this year, however, contained a real shocker. Way down inside the warrant were articles 15 and 16, which had been submitted by petition. They called for the splitting off of the eastern part of Londonderry into a new town.

There were probably few in either of the two parishes who would have lost much sleep over the thought of a potential breakup of the town. After all, pieces of the original Nutfield grant had been breaking off for years. Parts of the old grant were now incorporated into the towns of Windham, Salem, Chester, Hudson, Manchester, and Pelham. There were probably many in west Londonderry who would be pleased to see east Londonderry leave. Good riddance to those effete east side snobs. However, this warrant article called for separation by drawing a new boundary line. That was a major bone of contention! This is what made Robert Mack angry and his face turn as red as the apples in his orchard.

The east Londonderry people wanted to disregard the old parish line and draw a new border nearly a mile farther to the west. The petition for the new town of east Londonderry was proposing to grab land that had been a part of the parish of west Londonderry since 1740. The present Broadway section of town had been a part of the west parish for nearly a century. Now these eastern rebels wanted to rip it off and make it part of the new town in the east. This was just too much to accept lying down!

On Tuesday, March 13, 1827, at 9 in the morning, the town meeting began in the meetinghouse of the First Parish Church. It was a splendid turnout. An estimated 463 men crowded into the sanctuary and its balcony. William Choate Jr. was elected moderator; Samuel Adams was chosen as clerk. (Both of these men were from the east parish.) The first order of business was to vote for state governor. Democrat Benjamin Pierce swept over his Republican challenger with 90 percent of the vote. For long hours, the voting for other officers continued. Finally, by late afternoon, came the first of the important votes—the election of three representatives to the state legislature. The victors would represent the town in Concord. This vote was critical. Any plan for splitting Londonderry into two towns required legislative approval. Both factions wanted their own men in Concord.

Voting in those days was performed by writing the name of a candidate on a little piece of paper and putting it in the voting box. Londonderry was allowed by law to send up to three representatives to the state legislature. Moderator Choate allowed voters to cast their votes for all three representatives at the same time. The three men with the highest number of votes would be the winners.

The west Londonderry voters were in the majority but scattered their votes among a dozen candidates; the east Londonderry people were better organized and this time voted as a bloc. John Miltimore, John Porter, and Alanson Tucker were duly elected to represent Londonderry in Concord. This was perceived as a triumph for the secessionists as Tucker and Porter were the leaders in the pro-split faction.

The west Londonderry voters were distressed to see that two east Londonderry politicos would represent the town in Concord. Quickly a motion was made to send only one representative to the legislature that year rather than the three the law allowed. With only a single representative, there was a strong chance that his influence would be insufficient to sway the other members of the legislature to vote to allow east Londonderry to split from the west.

The motion passed. John Miltimore, because he had received the most votes on the original tally, was declared to be the one and only representative from Londonderry. This was a triumph for the anti-split voters. Miltimore had never publicly favored the division of Londonderry. He was not expected to submit a bill calling for a split of the town. Without such a legislative bill, Londonderry could not be split in two.

By now it was getting dark. It was time to adjourn the town meeting until another day. Next week the meeting would reconvene in the meeting house to finish up town business. This, of course, included voting on the actual articles to break up the town. Within moments, over a hundred of the west Londonderry voters left the meetinghouse to begin their long trek home. Most believed the meeting had been voted as adjourned until next Monday. The Londonderry parish men had to travel miles on foot or horseback. There were evening chores to take care of and nobody wanted to be walking an hour or two in the dark. They went home feeling happy and were doubtlessly eager to tell their wives how they had saved Londonderry from being split by Thom, Tucker, and Porter.

The few extant records allow us to only somewhat reconstruct the final moments of the town meeting of Match 13, 1827. It's a pity that the camcorder had not yet been invented because what followed was worthy of broadcasting on a segment of the Jerry Springer television show.

As soon as it was clear that most of the west Londonderry voters were out of earshot, the town meeting sprung back to life. A motion was made to reconvene the meeting and reconsider the last vote. This reconsideration was not challenged by the moderator and thus prevailed. It was moved, seconded, and approved by voice vote to have Londonderry send three representatives to the state legislature.

The few west Londonderry voters that were still in the hall tried calling for a point of order to have the vote declared illegal. One can easily imagine the angry scene as the moderator ignored their frantic cry of "Point of order! Mr. Moderator, please. Point of order!" The westerners were yelling at the top of their lungs that the meeting had been adjourned but were ignored by moderator Choate who was pro-split.

The sun had now gone down and the hall was getting dark. Candles were lit to allow the votes to be counted. Joseph Dickey and David Tenney, of west Londonderry, went out to their wagons and got long ox whips. With great skill, they went through the hall whipping out the flames. They figured that if the hall was dark, the votes couldn't be counted. The east Londonderry men followed the two men and rekindled the candles. Other Londonderry men snuck around the hall like ferrets, and just like it was someone's birthday, blew out candles with their breath,. This spectacle of men dueling with whips and matches continued for quite a while. In the end, however, the ballots were counted. John Porter and Alanson Tucker were elected to the legislature. The eastsiders had stolen the election! With that victory achieved, Moderator Choate adjourned the meeting until March 19, when the town meeting would reconvene in west Londonderry.

The week's break between sessions of the town meeting gave the west Londonderry forces time to plan their counterattack. They knew that Moderator Choate wouldn't allow a second reconsideration; all they could do was try to find ways to restrain the power of the eastsiders.

The session of March 19 was a clear victory for the westsiders. The voting for selectmen saw the election of three men from the west. Soon came the moment everybody was waiting for—Articles 15 and 16, which called for the splitting of the town.

When the two articles were brought up for consideration, the westsiders voted as a bloc to defeat the motion. The final vote was 303 NO–253 YES. The Londonderry men voted to stay together as one town. The town further voted for Colonel William Adams and Colonel Robert Patterson as agents of the town in Concord. They were given the task of finding ways "expedient to oppose the division of the town" by the legislature. They were also charged with persuading the legislature not to allow Tucker, Porter, and Miltimore to be sworn in as members of the House of Representatives. Town Meeting also voted to press charges against Town Clerk Samuel Adams for not recording a true account of the meeting of March 13.

Agents Adams and Patterson published a four-page "Remonstrance" to the members of the House of Representatives and the Senate that stated the arguments for why Londonderry should not be divided. It began by affirming that while Londonderry was a large town in area, there were other towns in New Hampshire that were even larger. Also, the distance needed to travel to Town Meetings did not place a serious hardship on voters. In fact, "those residing in the remote sections of the town are among the most punctual in their attendance" at Town Meetings.

Adams and Patterson wrote that among the major problems facing Londonderry as a result of a split would be the repaying of the debt incurred to build Mammoth Road; the whole town had voted for it but now west Londonderry would have to pay for it. There was also the problem of the poor farm which was situated in east Londonderry. After a split, who would own it? Giving it to east Londonderry wouldn't be fair to the taxpayers of west Londonderry, who helped buy it in 1820. The proposed new town line would also divide three school districts and three militia companies. In addition there would be many farms that would see their acreage divided between the towns. A west Londonderry resident in that situation would have to pay nonresident property tax in east Londonderry but not be able to vote at the town meeting in which the tax rate on his farm was set.

The authors of the Remonstrance accused the secessionists of being just a few angry individuals who were "smarting under the reproof of a recent removal from public trust . . . .determined to divide what they are unable to control." These mean-spirited few tried to get their way at the last town meeting by "flattery addressed to the indifferent and threats to those who were opposed," but still they lost the the critical vote on division by a "most decided majority."

James Aiken, Thomas Patterson, William Adams, Ebenezer Fisher, and John Pinkerton wrote a second Remonstrance to the Senate and House. This appeal was different from the first in that it dealt only with the illegality of the March 13, 1827, town meeting. The authors claimed that after the election of John Miltimore to the legislature, it was moved, seconded and voted to adjourn the meeting for the day. The vote was claimed to be 219 to 208 in favor of adjournment. Aiken and the others charged that as soon as a sufficient number of west Londonderry residents had left the building, Moderator Choate reconvened the meeting and put into motion the rump election of two more representatives.

The two remonstrances were submitted with a petition signed by three hundred men of West Londonderry. It's main point was that the town was already exactly the right size and should not be divided. Likewise a petition was submitted to the legislature by John Morrison, Alanson Tucker, John Burnham, James Thom, and John

Porter and 311 others. It refuted all of Londonderry's claims and, in brief, said the town was too big and should be divided.

The two remonstrances from Londonderry appear to have had little effect on the legislature. There were several hearings centering on where the new boundary line should be but in each case the east Londonderry plan prevailed.

On Monday, July 2, 1827 the House and Senate voted to create a new town in east Londonderry. Governor Benjamin Pierce signed the bill into law that same day. The new town's boundary would not be the 1740 parish line that ran through today's Derry Village but instead a north-south line that was about a mile farther to the west. The law also spelled out the payment of old debts and future taxes. A committee from the two towns was to be appointed by the town meetings to settle such matters as who would get the gravediggers' shovels and the old record books. The first town meeting in the new town voted three thousand dollars to pay for the expense of getting the town incorporated. This sum may have been used to influence the members of the legislature to approve the split from Londonderry.

As soon as the divorce was legal, the towns hired Captain John Clark to draw the north-south line between Derry and Londonderry. The distance surveyed measured 36,493 feet, or 6.9 miles, long. On the north, the line would start at a point at the middle of the Londonderry Turnpike at the Chester town line. It would continue south until it hit the Windham town line. Clark stopped for the night after sighting a tree farther to the south that he believed to be on the Windham line.

It snowed the next day so the survey was never completed. Later, a stone marker was erected on the spot. Eventually it was discovered that the stone was about seventy feet north of the Windham line and 690 feet to the east. This mistake gave Londonderry more land than it was entitled to. Derry protested but Judge William Richardson of Chester declared the crocked line had been agreed to by the two towns so it would remain the boundary of Derry and Londonderry. The original Clark map is on display in the assessor's office in Derry.

There was a valiant attempt by Alanson Tucker and James Thom to officially give the new town the name of Londonderry, which meant the western section would have to take a new name. Their reasoning was based on the fact that the town's oldest settlement had been in the eastern part of town. This name grab was foiled through the efforts of Robert Mack. The Londonderry people likely countered with the argument that because the eastern part of town had opted to separate, it gave up all rights to the old name.

East Londonderry was forced to come up with a new name. The people chose to be called Derry. This is what their half of the town had been called for years anyway. The name Derry comes from the Gaelic word *Doire* which means "oak woods." Derry was the original name of the town of Londonderry, Ireland. This was the city their Scotch-Irish ancestors had left in 1719 to settle in the New World.

The new town of Derry, New Hampshire in 1827 had a population of about twenty-one hundred and measured about thirty-six square miles. The town of Londonderry that year had about fourteen hundred inhabitants inside its forty-two square miles. Today, 180 years later, Derry has a population of nearly thirty-five thousand and Londonderry has about twenty-three thousand residents. In 2002 there was a short-lived attempt to have East Derry secede from the rest of the town. This time the legislature voted overwhelmingly to keep the town intact.

Across the Atlantic, the city of Derry, Ireland, is often times referred to as "slash city" because the press often calls it Derry/Londonderry. The Protestants always call it Londonderry; the Catholics refer to their hometown as Derry. The city's two leading newspapers are the *Londonderry Sentinel* and the *Derry Journal*.

Last fall I received a telephone call from Radio Ireland requesting an interview. They had heard about the Mack Plaque rivalry between the high schools of Derry and Londonderry, New Hampshire. They wanted me to give them the names of the players and their religious affiliations. They were sure that every citizen in the two New Hampshire towns was waiting breathlessly to see which town won the plaque. The Irish commentator was also certain that the two towns hated each other and that Derry was all Catholic and Londonderry inhabited only by Protestants. I don't believe that I was really able to persuade the reporter that despite our divorce in 1827, the two towns are quite similar in demographics and frequently cooperate on issues of common concern such as exit 4A. I told him if towns were people, then Londonderry and Derry would be considered very good friends despite the events of 1827.

The McMurphy home is shown in this 1897 photograph to be near the tracks of the Boston and Maine Railroad.

11.

Sally McMurphy: Thrift, Pluck and Luck.

ACCORDING TO ECONOMISTS, AMERICA IS NO LONGER A NATION of savers. One month last year, our saving percent rate was negative 0.2 percent—in other words, we spent more than we earned! We are now socking away less than at any other time since the Great Depression. The citizens of Canada, Japan, and France save three times as much as do we Americans.

I am offering the story of Sarah (Sally) Reid McMurphy as an example of the benefits of hard work, frugality, listening to sound advice, and careful investments. Her story is also about overcoming adversity and helping others. Her life reads like a rags-to-riches novel by Horatio Alger. You might want to read this article to your children when they ask for a raise in their allowance.

Sarah Reid was born in Londonderry (now Derry) in 1809 and was orphaned as an infant. She was brought up in the home of David Gilcreast and later by her uncle David Reid. Both households were already crowded with children, so at a young age Sally moved out to be on her own. It was likely she didn't want to be a bother.

At the age of seventeen, she found full-time employment in the house of Deacon James Pinkerton, who lived at what is now the Pinkerton Tavern Restaurant. Deacon James owned a number of farms, and many of his laborers lived with him in his home. In addition, the house was a combination general store and tavern. Sally's wage as a housekeeper was fifty cents a week plus room and board.

Despite such a meager salary, she was happy to be in a safe, Christian home.

Sally lived very frugally and asked Elder Pinkerton to hold her earnings in trust for her. If she needed anything, she would ask him for the money. She was such a hardworking, cheerful housekeeper that Pinkerton thought of her as almost a daughter. He even gave her clothing from his store without charge so she could more easily live on her salary. It is almost unbelievable but at the end of two years, she had saved fifty dollars. In 102 weeks, she had spent just two dollars on herself!

Pinkerton advised her to find a way to invest her money. He lectured her on the wisdom of letting your money work for you. He thought that maybe her old benefactor, David Gilcreast, might be persuaded to borrow her fifty dollars and pay her interest.

After serving supper, she walked two miles to the Gilchrest home but David said he didn't need any money at the moment. As it was late in the day, he allowed her to sleep there overnight. With tears in her eyes, she went into the kitchen to help Mrs. Gilchrest. The next morning, after Sally had helped with the breakfast chores, David decided he should help the hardworking girl. He took her money and gave her a promissory note in exchange. Sally didn't want to take the receipt, saying she trusted him, but he insisted that everything be done properly. In parting, he told her that the interest would allow her to buy a new pair of shoes every year.

In around 1838, Sally Reid joined many other local girls working in the mills in Lowell. As a factory girl, she lived very carefully with "plain food and cheap lodging." Within a few years she was able to return to Derry with a savings of $250. She accepted the advice of storekeeper Richard Melvin and bought five shares of stock in the Concord Railroad. She returned to Lowell and soon earned enough money to buy even more shares. This turned out to be a good investment, as the company annually paid a dividend of over ten percent. In addition, the value of the stock rose and a stock split would eventually increase the number of shares she controlled.

In 1841 she returned to Derry and taught in a one- room schoolhouse. The next year, at the age of thirty-one, she married forty-four- year old James McMurphy. He was a farmer who had recently bought from his father a large house on Franklin Street Extension. In time they would become the parents of two children. Their son, Henry, attended Dartmouth College on a scholarship and became a schoolteacher. He died of tuberculosis at the age of twenty-five. Their daughter, Abbie, graduated from the Pinkerton Academy and became a teacher in Lawrence. She died at age twenty-eight.

For the next six years, Sally and Jim lived all alone in their big house, mourning the loss of their children; the house had become "very desolate and cheerless." James McMurphy died in 1881 when he was eighty-two. Sally would remain in the house "meditating upon the best means of doing good with her money and perpetuating the memory of her children."

In 1888, widow Sally McMurphy sought the advice of experts in law and public service to assist her in drawing up her will. She had stock investments worth about seven thousand dollars. This was the money she had saved and invested from the time she earned fifty cents a week at Deacon Pinkerton's to her years as a mill girl in Lowell and a teacher in Derry. This sum would be equal to several hundred thousand dollars today.

Remembering her years as an orphan, she bequeathed one-thousand dollars to the orphans home in Concord. The remainder of the estate was left to Dartmouth College to provide three scholarships for students of limited means.

She died on Christmas Eve in 1894 in her eighty-fifth year. Her funeral was held at her Franklin Street home. Pastor Samuel French, of the Londonderry Presbyterian church, spoke of Sally's piety, Christian character, and renunciation of her own interests in favor of helping others. She is buried at Forest Hill cemetery along with her husband and two children. Her home was torn down in the 1960s to make way for an apartment complex.

12.

The Barrington Beggars

BARRINGTON IS BY ALL ACCOUNTS A NICE LITTLE TOWN WHICH IS LESS than an hour's drive from Derry. It was settled in 1722, the same year Nutfield was incorporated as the town of Londonderry. Its early settlers raised flax as did our first inhabitants.

Although the Nutfield towns have always had a sterling reputation for honesty, such was not the case with Barrington. During the first half of the nineteenth century, that town was known as the home to a wandering tribe of vagabonds called the Barrington Beggars. Most of these vagrants bore the surname Leathers. Their existence is even the topic of a short story by John Greenleaf Whittier.

No one really knows the origin of the Barrington Beggars. They were described as having "dark, piercing eyes and Asiatic countenances," indicating to some that they were of Gypsy origin. This ethnic background seems unlikely as the Leathers family first appeared in America in 1667. The family was and is a credit to the New World producing generation after generation of hardworking, honest citizens.

There was, though, the black sheep branch of Leatherses who settled in the Granite State during the mid-seventeenth century. Regrettably, this is the side of the family that has gained the most notoriety and soiled the window through which we view all members of the Leathers family.

In our state they settled in Barrington, where they lived on a sandy plain by a lake in the center of a desolate pine barren. Most locals called this area Leathers City. Here they dwelled in a cluster of about thirty small shacks, having little contact with the rest of this farming community. They all appeared to be related in some way and all shared the family name Leathers somewhere in their family tree. They were probably a matriarchal society, with their leader being an old hag named Patricia Leathers.

It was believed by most outsiders that all members of the Leathers tribe in Barrington shared an aversion to work and instead preferred to avail themselves of the fruits of other people's labor. They reportedly had in common a love of the outdoor life and of singing. In their defense, it must be said that many Barrington Leatherses lived off honest labor. A number of the family members went door-to-door selling hand-made split-ash baskets or skillfully woven coverlets. There were Leatherses who were itinerate preachers who religiously never failed to pass the hat after their exhortations. Other Leatherses were into fortune-telling.

Regretfully, the best-remembered family members were the dishonest Leathers who were beggars specializing in faking debilitating conditions. They also had a reputation for stealing and other similar crimes. No man's chickens were considered truly safe while the Barrington Beggars were in town! These merchants of hokum would range through southern New Hampshire and northern Massachusetts soliciting charity at isolated farmhouses. Whittier in a short story describes a dark, rainy evening when he was surprised by a visit from Stephen Leathers. "I rise and open the door. A tall shambling, loose-jointed figure; a pinched, shrewd face, sun-brown and wind-dried; small, quick-winking black eyes—there he stands, the water dripping from his pulpy hat and ragged elbows."

The silent night visitors gave Whittier a legal-looking document signed by the Italian council in Boston. It purported that the man was "Pietro Frugoni, a mute who had been shipwrecked off New England's coast" and needed the "alms of all charitable Christian persons." Whittier immediately told the man his name was actually Stephen Leathers and then asked him "the news from old Barrington." With that, the startled beggar knew his cover was blown and admitted his true identity. Leathers confided to the poet that he was just trying to help the real Pietro Frugoni get some money so the man could get by. He further explained that the "poor furriner . . . couldn't make himself understood any more than a wild goose." With that fanciful tale, Mr. Leathers left the Whittier home in search of an easier piece of change.

Whittier knew well the identity of Stephen Leathers because of his past attempts to separate the poet from his hard-earned money. Sometimes the beggar wrapped himself in a blanket and claimed to be a Penobscot Indian who had lost the use of his hands while trapping to gather food in the frozen north for his starving family. Other times he appeared in the guise of a "forlorn father" of six small children whom a doctor had "pisened and crippled." Frequently he played an unfortunate man who was suffering from the palsy. His hands shook so hard, he could hardly take the charity offered to him.

A regular visitor to Derry in the 1840s was Hopping Pat Leathers, "the wise woman of her tribe." She frequently traveled with her grandson. That boy had a "gift for preaching as well as for many other things not exactly compatible with holy orders." For a few coins he would exhort the sacred word but only after he wrapped a white handkerchief around his neck to appear more ecclesiastical. He often had on his shoulder a trained talking crow that Whittier described as a "shrewd, knavish-looking bird."

The grandmother was called "Hopping" Pat because of the peculiar gait with which she walked. She was never thought of as a thing of beauty. In truth she seemed to fit the classic description of an ugly old hag straight out of one of Grimms' fairy tales. "Have an apple, my pretty!"

On one of her visits to Derry, she cased one of our village homes. Believing the man of the house was absent, she saw the chance to an easy charity handout from the wife and children. An easy mark!

As she approached the house, Hopping Pat distorted her features by appearing to be in unbelievable pain. She fell to the ground in convulsions. She moaned. She groaned. She rolled and tumbled around the front lawn. In the history of Derry, has there ever been a woman in this much agony? The children were terrified and crying hysterically. The mother was near panic for fear that the woman would die on her front lawn. This poor old saint had to be helped! In an act of Christian charity, the wife brought Pat Leathers into the comfort of her house.

The husband walked in just as Hopping Pat was nearing the climax of her performance. Instantly he recognized her to be the leader of the Barrington Beggars. Quickly he thought of a plan to drive her away.

The man called to friend who was walking by and loudly addressed him as "Doctor." He inquired of the faux physician as to the best way to treat such a sick woman. His friend caught on to what was going on and played along. The "doctor" gave an immediate diagnosis and said she must be "blistered" with his "largest cupa."

Blistering was a way of ridding the body of bad humors by drawing blood from the afflicted patient. Cuts were made on the skin and then covered with a heated glass cup (cupa). As the cup cooled, a vacuum was created. Blood filled the cup and a blister formed. The "doctor further prescribed a purgative agent be given her to drink." The ingredients of the cure she was to chug-a-lug were "salt, senna, and rhubarb." Immediately upon hearing this prescription, Hopping Pat miraculously regained control of her faculties. "Looking neither right nor left," she ran out of the house, shaking her fist at the two men and "hurling at them her loudest curses with all the glibness her voluble tongue was capable of projecting."

After the mid-nineteenth century, nothing more was reported of the Barrington Beggars. Did they give up their wicked, wicked ways? Did they just move out of New Hampshire—maybe to that white-marble city on the Virginia-Maryland border? It is recorded that on June 18, 1844, a dozen of the Leathers family of Barrington changed their names. The various tribe members answered to the names Wilson, Tyler, or Banks. By 1900, the Leathers family had become extinct in Barrington.

While researching this article, I accidentally stumbled upon the possibility of a connection between the Leathers family and a distinguished American politician. A Manchester, N.H. newspaper in 1867 said Henry Wilson was "true to his gypsy origin" and referred to him as "Henry Leathers." Such a Leathers-Wilson link is unrecorded in any known biography of Henry Wilson.

Henry Wilson (1812–1875) was vice president of the United States under President Grant. He had been born in Farmington, NH as Jeremiah Jones Colbath. This eastern New Hampshire town is a near neighbor to Barrington. In 1833, he changed his name to Henry Wilson. There has never been a commonly agreed upon explanation as to why he switched names. Is it possible that the Colbaths were related to the Leathers clan? Did Henry change his name to distance himself from the reputations of his disreputable cousins? Much more research needs to be done on the origins of Henry Wilson's name.

There were bands of true Gypsies who occasionally visited the Derry area. Their appearances are recorded during the nineteenth and twentieth centuries. As late as 1950, the police would escort them out of town as soon as their presence became known. Their local unsavory reputation was probably based more on a fear of the unknown than on their being an actual threat to the safety, morals, and well-being of the community.

In July 1902 a Gypsy caravan drove into Derry and remained here for three days. Their wagon-homes were very ornate and colorful and hard not to notice in our staid New Hampshire town. They camped overnight in East Derry before moving to Derry Village. While they were here, their camp was visited by large numbers of locals during the day. Some came to the Gypsies to buy small baskets of sweet grass, others to have their fortune told, but most visited because they were curious about their vagabond way of life. Several farmers bought or swapped horses with the Gypsy men. The Gypsies would however, not do any business on Sunday because of their religious considerations. Although there was no crime wave in Derry because of their visit, the Derry selectmen ordered them to leave town. The local newspaper characterized the Gypsies as a "ragged, desperate lot."

13.

Bear Hunts

THE FIRST SETTLERS CAME TO THIS SECTION OF NEW HAMPSHIRE in 1719. These Nutfield pioneers found a virgin wilderness unmarred by a single road or cleared field. The only non-forested area in the entire one hundred fourteen-square-mile-tract consisted of the ponds and meadows that had been flooded by beavers.

The land teemed with wildlife. This was home to eagles, wolves, and moose. A squirrel could possibly travel from here to the Mississippi without having to leave the trees and scurry onto land. Among the largest of the local land animals was the black bear.

The black bear can be as tall as a man, weigh up to 250 pounds, and able to walk on the soles of its feet like a human. Reverend Jeremy Belknap, in his 1792 history of New Hampshire, cites two cases in which bears have killed children. One of those incidents occurred in 1731 only a dozen or so miles from Derry. That historian called the bear "one of the most noxious animals of our forest." The state Fish and Game Commission says that the last fatal attack by a bear in New Hampshire occurred in 1784.

At the beginning of the nineteenth century, the landscape of Londonderry had greatly changed. In order to support an agriculture-based economy, the forests had been cut down. By this time we were about 85 percent open fields. The deep woods were now pastures for cows and fields of corn. In those days, grand vistas were the rule. Our town today is much more tree covered than it was two hundred years ago.

With its deforestation, Derry was no longer a suitable environment for many species of mammals. The ideal bear range is a densely forested area thick with undergrowth. There was a definite cause and effect in play; fewer forests means fewer bears. With each year's passing during the eighteenth century, there were fewer and fewer bear sightings. It is probable that most residents in those days viewed the extermination of the bear population as a good thing.

THE BEAR HUNT

In mid-eighteenth-century Londonderry, most of the people were of Scottish ancestry and there were only a relatively few last names. To add to the confusion, many individuals had similar first names. To keep straight all the Wallaces, Pinkertons, MacGregors, and Wilsons, they added military ranks, church titles, or nicknames to the personal names so everybody could understand to which person they were referring. The town was filled with individuals whose first names were always preceded by the word *major, elder, deacon, old, young,* and so on. To differentiate the two Mary Wilsons, one was called "Mary over the Brook" Wilson because she lived on the east side of Aikens Brook. Her cousin was "Ocean-Born" Mary Wilson, so called because her birth had occurred on the voyage from Ireland. In the town clerk's records, one man is called by the incredible name of "John-the-Man-Cochran." The two James Wilsons were called "Curley" Jim and "Black" Jim Wilson.

Black Jim and Curley Jim Wilson operated a sawmill on the Aikens Brook. One day the cousins spotted a bear and decided to go on a bruin hunt. They grabbed a couple of axes and chased the animal into the woods. Finally they cornered the bear in his den, which consisted of a cave set in a pile of boulders and tree roots. One of the Jim Wilsons waited with his ax on top of the den while the other Jim Wilson went to get help and a gun.

At the home of Mr. Josselyn, Jim asked the man if he would return to the den with his rifle and kill the trapped bear. Josselyn declined, saying his "common fowling piece" was too small for the task and would put their lives in danger. Jim finally persuaded the man to let him borrow the gun. Wilson returned to the den with the rifle, with Josselyn following at a safe distance.

The bear was killed with a single shot. While the Wilson cousins crawled into the den, the far-removed Mr. Josselyn kept on yelling "Is he dead?" and "Is the bear killed?" Finally the Wilsons dragged the bloody body out of the cave. Only then did Josselyn approach the carcass. The bear weighed about four hundred pounds and the meat was distributed among the neighbors, with Josselyn getting a very large share. For a long time thereafter, whenever Josselyn met one of the neighbors, he would give a very animated account of how "we killed the bear."

THE SAWMILL AND THE BEAR

There is a second story of the two Jim Wilsons and a bear. This time the men were sitting on a log at their sawmill eating their lunch when a bear suddenly approached. Not enthusiastic about getting into a confrontation without a gun, the men hid in the rafters of the mill.

The bear sniffed the air and decided that the Wilsons' lunch would make a better lunch than would the Wilsons' flesh. The bear sat down on the log to enjoy his alfresco meal. What the bruin didn't know was that the log he was sitting on was being sliced in half by an automatic up-and-down saw blade. There the animal sat happily filling his jowls while behind his back the saw was slicing closer and closer.

Suddenly the bear felt a little nip on the end of his tail. It didn't cause any real pain so the animal didn't turn around. All he did was let out an angry snarl and sit up a little straighter. He quickly returned to his meal. Soon the saw moved again and this time cut a savage gash in his back. This was enough to get the bear's full attention. The animal stood up and turned around. In a rage, it started to do battle with whatever had caused it pain. With his powerful paws and jaws, he attacked the teeth of the saw. Within seconds the battle was over. Curley Jim and Black Jim Wilson would have roast of bear on their dinner table for weeks to come. I'm sure it would only be a short time before their kids were complaining, "Not bear for supper again."

THE LAST BEAR HUNT

This is a story that was passed on by word of mouth for decades before it was finally set down in print in 1851. Many versions have been published since then. I'm basing my story from a 1931 retelling of the events by Rosecrans Pillsbury. He heard it from his father, who heard it from Peter Crowell, who, as a boy of fifteen, took part in the great bear hunt of 1807.

One morning in March 1807, two Londonderry men went hunting in the northwest section of town—near where the town lines of Hudson, Litchfield, and Londonderry meet. They were startled to find fresh bear tracks and decided to go in pursuit of Sir Bruin. As they advanced, the bear could be spotted only a few hundred yards ahead of them. The night before there had been a light snow, so it was easy to follow the tracks of the fast-moving animal.

The fleeing bear took off in a southerly direction and always remained just out of the range of their muzzle-loading rifles. They pursued the beast at a "double-quick" pace for about four miles through the woods and fields. After many hours, the exhausted pair of hunters willingly relinquished the chase to a group of four or five men, who took over the pursuit.

The bear continued to elude the huntsmen and by nightfall had hidden himself in a swamp near the meetinghouse at the center of Pelham. All through the night the news of the bear hunt swept the area. By the first light of dawn there was a large group of hunters assembled, eager to continue the chase. Townsmen and boys from all over the region were excited over the prospect of participating in this contest of man versus bear. It was like a story out of their grandfather's youth. This was an adventure!

Sensing danger, the panicking bear began to retrace his path of the previous day. The animal headed north and by nightfall was hiding in the swamp near the present-day library in Windham. The hunters reluctantly returned to their homes, pledging to resume the chase at daybreak.

On the third day of the hunt, the bear continued to flee in a northerly direction. Its path took pursuers near the line that now separates the towns of Derry and Londonderry. By this time the beast was "followed by men, boys, and dogs, too numerous to mention." An estimate of the number of hunters was about fifty individuals. Around the middle of the day, the bear began to tire out. Hoping to evade his pursuers, he climbed a large pine tree by Londonderry's Valley Cemetery on Pillsbury Road.

The hunters eventually found the animal perched high up in the pine. A single shot from the rifle of Deacon/Selectman John Fisher brought the bear tumbling to the ground—dead. The carcass was hauled to the nearby house of Daniel Gilcreast where the men would decide what to do with the spoils of their adventure.

At the Gilcreast home a nose-count revealed that there were fifty-two men who had been involved in the three-day hunt. After the bear was butchered, the flesh was found to weigh two hundred pounds. Each hunter received about four pounds of meat as a reward for his participation in the chase. The pelt was taken to the store of Deacon James Pinkerton, which is now the Pinkerton Tavern Restaurant. The bearskin was traded for a barrel of whiskey.

The liquor was brought back to the Gilcreast house; there, water was heated in a kettle to mix with the liquor. There was ample firewater for all. A chronicler in 1880 related that "the company celebrated the occasion by jollification in general and a 'whiskey skin' in particular."

Since the great hunt of 1807, the bear population of New Hampshire has rebounded. The hunting season now begins on the first day of September; those who hunt with dogs have to wait until September 9. The season ends when the Fish and Game people reckon enough bears have been killed. In 2005, there were 527 killed but none was dispatched in our little corner of the world. The fee for a bear-hunting license is five dollars. There is an outfit in Rochester that will take hunters for a two-day bear-hunting expedition for $925.

There are now an estimated fifty-three hundred bears in our state. Most of them live far to the north, around Coos County. Today we view the animal as more of a nuisance than a danger. Bears regularly raid bird feeders and garbage cans of the homes that are built in their traditional range. There may actually be more bears in southern New Hampshire today than there were at the time of the Civil War. When farming was king, there were few forests to provide suitable habitat for bears, moose, and wildcats. Now those fields and pastures have morphed into timberland . . . and the large animals are returning. When I was a very young boy, my dad took me into the deep woods of our home town, Sandown, to show me bear paw prints in the snow. These were the first evidence of bears he had seen in town since he was a boy.

Sightings of bears are now much more common. In June 2005, a hundred-pound bear was spotted in a tree in the Copper Beach Road area of Salem. Another bear was seen a week later around Crystal Lake in Manchester. A local police officer described such sightings as "not uncommon."

The Chrispeen farm, Londonderry in 1895. In front is eighty-six-year-old George Washington Chrispeen.

14.
Mass Murder in Londonderry

THE STORY OF THE CHRISPEEN MASS MURDER, WHILE AMAZING, IS quite true. It was reported in the *Exeter News-Letter* in 1831 only a few weeks after the events transpired. Fact is indeed sometimes more fantastical than fiction. All I have done is to fill in elaborative details and background to flesh out the facts of this tragedy.

The setting for this crime story is in the area that borders the towns of Derry and Londonderry. This is the section that extends north from Ash Street to the shores of Scobey Pond and is presently one of the more rural areas of the two towns. A couple of centuries ago, this section was divided into a number of small farms. In those years perhaps three-quarters was cleared for pasture and the rest was either forest or marsh. The geography of the area can be characterized as a twisted tangle of hills with soil that is only moderately fertile. The more-prominent landholders were the Pinkertons, Eayes, Scobeys, Craigs, Reids and Chrispeens. Many of these landowners chose to live their lives in their own remote world, isolated from all but their family and immediate neighbors.

Among the most reclusive families was the Craig clan, who had lived there since the earliest days of the town. They wanted to be left alone. The Craig men were tough but the Craig girls were considered even more intimidating. One day Tax Collector Alexander McMurphy was riding through on horseback when he noticed a flock of sheep in the Craigs' pasture. The official decided that now was a good time to count the flock to see if old Bob Craig was paying his full share of taxes. Some of the animals had huddled against a fence that separated the rider from the field. To bring the animals fully into view, he reached over the fence and hit them with his long leather riding whip. He continued to do this as he rode down the wall, when suddenly up jumped Hannah Craig from behind the fence. McMurphy was so startled by her unexpected appearance that he couldn't think of a thing to say. Hannah just stared at him with such intensity and hate that he turned his horse and rode away at a gallop.

During the 1820s, Robert Craig sold a certain number of cords of oak timber to Benjamin Eastman of East Derry. The wood was destined to be made into ship's elbows. After a while, Craig got it into his head that Eastman was taking too much timber. To keep any more oak from leaving his woodlot, Bob Craig put poles as a barrier across the bar gap. When Eastman's cutters came to work, they found the three middle-aged Craig girls leaning against the barrier, "saying nothing but looking defiant." Eastman ordered his men to move the pole but the maiden ladies would not release their hold. The barrier was lifted off the bar gap with the Craig girls still holding on to it. Their legs were a-twitching into empty air while they screamed that they were being bruised.

No one was really hurt in the incident but Bob Craig decided to retaliate by embarrassing Eastman. He persuaded Pastor Edward Parker, of the First Parish Church, to request from the pulpit that the congregation pray for the Misses Craig's speedy recovery from serious injuries that had been caused by Benjamin Eastman and his men. The last of the old maid Craig girls died in 1847.

The farm of Hannah and Richard Chrispeen was just to the west of the Craig farm. It was located in the Eayes Range of eastern Londonderry between what is now called the Seven Hills and Trolley Car Lane. In 1830 the Chrispeens were about fifty-five years of age and the parents of two children, George W., thirty-one and Ruby, twenty-two. Their hill land farm was not large and its kitchen garden produced a fine new crop of rocks each spring. The cape style house was small and consisted of a large kitchen, a couple bedrooms and a loft. A central fireplace provided the only heat for the house. The gray clapboard that covered the house had never seen a drop of paint. A couple small barns, a wood shed, and a few out-buildings completed the farm. To the passerby, the whole Chrispeen homestead, appeared nearer to poverty then prosperity.

The farm was isolated and surrounded by open fields and thick forests. The land outside their clearing was extremely hilly and forbidding. In years past, the area had a particularly evil reputation and was believed to be the abode of families of sheep stealers.

At night, from the Chrispeen's front door, it was impossible to see the light of any neighbor's home.

It was likely that this lonely setting in the Londonderry woods was what caused bouts of depression in young Ruby Chrispeen. She could only dream of the excitement of the city, its stores, and theaters while her days were filled with the monotony of house and farm work. Any talk about moving to Lowell would certainly have met with no support from her parents; her labor on the farm was too important for maintaining the family's economic wellbeing.

In 1831, Ruby Chrispeen began to think more and more about leaving Londonderry. If she could just get to Lowell, she could find a job in the mills. There she would be with people of her own age. With her pay, she could buy new clothes, ribbons, and sweets. Maybe there, she could even meet a man, with whom she could fall in love. All she needed was the money to buy a stagecoach ticket to Lowell.

Early one summer's morning, Ruby snuck her hand into her father's desk. From a drawer, she took a bank note and carefully forged his signature. Immediately she started to walk the three miles to East Derry. In her hand would be a bag crammed with a few of her treasures. She tried to appear calm and nonchalant as she sauntered into the brick bank building. As she walked up to the teller's desk, she rehearsed the speech she'd give to explain why she was cashing the note. If all went as planned, in a couple of hours she could board the stagecoach at Thom's Tavern and be on the way to her new life.

As soon as Ruby gave the bank note to cashier John Noyes, her plan quickly fell apart. Mr. Noyes knew Richard Chrispeen personally. He knew that the reclusive farmer was too miserly to trust his daughter or any one else with his money. The local constable was called in and Ruby was taken to the town's poor farm. There, locked in a small room with oak bars across the window, she had time to meditate on her situation. Soon her father would be here and she would leave in disgrace to go back to her home or to the state prison in Concord. To escape that fate, she had to come up with a scheme.

The crying Ruby called through the door that she wanted to confess to authorities. As they sat in amazement, she told them a story that made her attempted cashing of a forged check shrink into a very, very minor transgression. As Ruby got into the heart of her tale, her sobbing ceased. Her previously barely audible voice became stronger and more expressive.

Ruby began her story with the events of an afternoon in 1826. A visitor had appeared without warning on the doorstep of her Londonderry home. He was a pack peddler of the kind who wandered from one isolated farmhouse to another in pursuit of a sale. He would carry sewing needles, nutmegs, and ribbons—considerable temptations to a farm wife and her daughters. Remember that in those pre-railroad days, the town had only a single store and it was more than an hour's walk away. The mercantile's stock in trade was whatever the storekeeper thought you needed, and not what you wanted. If a farm woman didn't have the money for a purchase, the pack peddler would accept in trade old silver spoons, eyeglass frames, or old books.

Being too far from the village to make the tavern before nightfall, the weary and worn peddler asked Dick Chrispeen if he could sleep there overnight. The farmer agreed and even offered him supper—for a price. Later that night, the two men began to imbibe in what the temperance people called "the devil's tea." Soon the two men were quite drunk and had become the best of friends. To repay his host for his hospitality, the traveling salesman offered to show him the special treasurers he had stowed away in his backpack.

Onto the kitchen table the traveler spread out a staggering array of brightly colored gems and pieces of jewelry—all shining with an uncommon luster in the light from the fireplace. Dick sat there transfixed and staring at the tabletop. In his mind he thought for a moment he had been transported to Arabia and was surrounded by the riches of Baghdad. He was Ali Baba and by saying "Open sesame" had entered into the cave of the forty thieves.

Without thinking, the farmer let his lust control his mind and body. He grabbed a stick from the wood box and began to beat the head of the defenseless peddler. Within seconds the unfortunate man was on the floor in a pool of blood—dead. His unblinking, sightless eyes stared fixedly at his murderer.

In a panic, the assailant aroused his sleeping wife and children. Soon the four members of the Chrispeen family were standing over the lifeless body. After a few moments of explanations and tears, the family huddled to formulate a plan. Together they lifted the lifeless man onto the kitchen table. With the knife they used to butcher sheep, they cut up the peddler into small, manageable pieces. As a family, they brought the bloody carrion down the stairs and into the dirt floored cellar. They buried the victim in a shallow grave and pledged to each other never to speak of the crime again.

The summer's heat soon made the smell from the cellar too strong to ignore. Finally the family was forced to exhume the decaying body. In the dead of night, they carried the body, piece by piece, to the edge of their farmyard. Without ceremony, they dumped the chunks into an unused tanning pit. Now at last they felt they could forget about their terrible crime.

Ruby Chrispeen offered to take the spellbound magistrates to the burial site. A posse was formed as all over the village the news of the Chrispeen murder spread via the town's grapevine. Quickly Richard, George, and Hannah Chrispeen were arrested, though loudly proclaiming their innocence. A large crowd soon arrived at the Londonderry farm. Ruby was as good as her word and showed the authorities the location of the burial pit. With that disclosure, Ruby faded into the crowd and was last seen walking toward the dark forests that surrounded the farm.

A score of shovels went digging through the rocky Londonderry soil. Within a few minutes the first bone was found. Soon it was followed by dozens. The magistrates now began to think that Ruby was actually covering up for her dad. Here was evidence of mass murder! There were just too many bones to be the burial site for a single homicide. There were skulls, leg bones, and ribs everywhere. The Chrispeens must have dispatched an army of peddlers!

Standing on the edge of the burial pit was a large circle of men. One of the more observant spectators was also a wag. He shouted down to the sweaty diggers that old Dick Chrispeen had murdered the devil because that last skull they found had horns growing from its forehead! "If Satan was dead, then the second coming had come. Praise the Lord!"

Now the diggers began to really look at the bones they had been working so hard to excavate. Sure enough, there were horns on several of the skulls. They had been digging up a burial pit of butchered sheep! Everyone was now caught up in the foolishness of the situation and the hills of Londonderry rang with laughter. The farmer was released from custody with a formal apology. About that time, the missing pack peddler wandered in to join the crowd in the jollification.

After a while, one member of the ex-posse call out that he recognized one of the sheep's skulls. He pointed out a peculiarly shaped set of horns. He told anyone who would listen that it definitely and without question belonged to a ram that had been stolen from him several years ago. Other farmers began to recognize horn marks from their own beasts that had disappeared under mysterious circumstances.

In recent years, local farmers had been finding that their flock was missing an animal or two every few months. Most believed the animals had been taken by ranging wolves or wandering vagabonds. Here was proof that the animals had been spirited away by a local thief—Richard Chrispeen.

The farmer was put back into custody with the charge reduced from mass murder to sheep stealing. With Chrispeen's arrest, the crime wave of animal theft was over.

The records are silent on the rest of the story. What punishment was handed out to Dick Chrispeen? Was Ruby ever recaptured and punished for lying to the authorities? Did she ever find her dream life in Lowell? All I have discovered with certainty is that in 1840, Hannah was still living at the homestead with her son George. Her husband, Richard, was nowhere to be seen. The last of the clan to live in Londonderry was the son, George Washington Chrispeen, who died on September 20, 1900, at the age of ninety-one years, three months, sixteen days.

The years that followed the Chrispeen "mass murder" were not kind to this border section of Londonderry and Derry. Each year the area's population decreased as more and more farms closed. The soil was at best only marginally productive and the hilly landscape was prone to erosion. Far better farmland could be had out west in Washington, Idaho, and Oregon for only a dollar twenty-five an acre. In addition, many farmers' children opted to work in the mills of Lawrence, Lowell, and Derry.

The fields and pastures were quickly overgrown with brush and scrub. The farmhouses and barns fell into disrepair and in time all that was left was cellar holes. Fences rotted and fall over and tracts blended together, with individual ownership difficult to determine. Taxes went unpaid and even the town frequently couldn't find anyone who would take the land by paying the back taxes. Hundreds of acres became literally "no man's land." Some of the land was taken over by families of squatters, who lived the best way they could by means both fair and foul.

Large tracts were rented for a trifling consideration by farmers who lived in other parts of Derry and Londonderry. They used the land as sheep stations, where the animals were allowed to run free from early spring though late fall. Each autumn, when the owner took a census, it was expected that the herd's number would have increased because of the birth of spring lambs.

Too frequently, however, the number of sheep in a farmer's free range actually decreased from one year to another. Incidents of sheep rustling were suspected to be very common. The scene was similar to that of medieval Scotland, where Highlanders were always raiding the sheep herds of the lowland farmers. The prevailing thought there was that although "the offenders were well known and the theft easily proven, it was not prudent nor profitable nor even safe to resort to the law for redress and punishment of the offender." Letting the neighbors have some stolen mutton for the family table was far cheaper than having their whole herd mysteriously disappear and end up in the Brighton livestock market.

The methods of the local pre-Civil War sheep-stealer were included in an 1896 article in the *Derry News*. "Two or more rogues visited the pasture at the same time; frequently these excursions were in broad daylight. The sheep had paths through the tangled bushes that were about breast high and along these paths they would rush in a single file if alarmed. One of the gang would lay down in the bushes by the path within reach of the passing flock, the others drove the sheep together and corralled them toward the path, selecting the fattest and keeping an eye upon that sheep as it filed along the path. At the proper moment, a shrill whistle announced to the man in the bushes that he should seize the passing sheep by the leg."

Usually one sheep was enough for a day. The terrified animal would be quickly killed, skinned, and cut into quarters. The unwanted parts of the critter were buried nearby. The meat was taken home and a creative myth was fabricated to explain to their families about the origins of this leg of lamb. At the end of the nineteenth century, Edward Ballou bought a piece of a former sheep farm in this area and began to clear the land of brush and trees. When he cut down one large hollow tree, he found in the center seventeen pelts that had been hidden by sheep thieves.

15.

Love, Marriage, and Shivarees

I SUPPOSE THAT EVERY COUPLE THINKS THEY WERE THE FIRST TO discover love. When spring comes, the minds of our young people, suddenly and without warning, turn to romance. As soon as the snows melt and the trees bud, love floats like a zephyr in the Derry air. Every June, churches become wedding chapels and melodies by Wagner and Mendelssohn remind the older folk of their own young love. Unfortunately for the historian, the sweet words, lovers' quarrels, and pillow talk are usually kept private and almost never passed on to later generations. The following stories of love and weddings are the exceptions, and are made all the sweeter by their being so rare.

REJECTED LOVE

One of the oldest love stories was first put into print in 1831 by an elderly lady who had known the main characters. The scene is a parlor in the Woodburn home in Londonderry, New Hampshire, around 1764. Sitting in a chair is the very attractive Mary (Molly) Woodburn (1735–1823). She is the high-spirited daughter of the local squire. Into the room enters a young man. He is Lieutenant John Cochran (1729–1795) who had served with General Wolfe during the French and Indian War and was wounded at the Battle of the Plains of Abraham in 1759. He has faced down the French muskets at Quebec but is very shy around this woman with whom he is smitten.

Both of our characters are the children of Scottish immigrants and speak in the burr of their ancestral home. There would remain a few Gaelic speakers for two or three generations after the town was settled in 1719. Although most of the first Londonderry residents spoke only English, they kept the pronunciations of the lowland Scots until the beginning of the nineteenth century. Irish-born patriot Matthew Thornton was nationally famous for his brogue. The Forest Hill Cemetery grave of Thomas Steele (1683–1748) has an epitaph that rhymes the personal pronoun *me* with the word *die*. This is because the Scottish pronunciation of the word for "death" was "dee."

Building up his courage, Cochran turns to the woman: "Mary, if I were you, I'd ha' me."

Mary seemed not to hear him and takes no notice of his words.

Again he says: "I say, Mary, if I were you, I'd ha' me and not ha' that George Reid. He had been na'e where; he's nathing at all and ne'er been out of the sight of his mither in his life, and I ha'e been all over the country. I've traveled and been to war. I've been to the Plains of Abram and faut there and bled there. Now Mary, ha' me."

Mary turns and looks squarely into the red face of her suitor. Firmly she tells him: "I'll na' ha'e ye, John, ye mus gang hamme, your mither wants ye, and I'll ha'e Georgie Reid, dead or alive."

In 1765 she did marry George Reid (1733–1815). He may well have been the only patriot officer to be at both the beginning of the war at the Battle of Bunker Hill and at its finish—as a member of Washington's staff at the Battle of Yorktown.

During General Reid's six-year absence, he trusted his wife to run the farm, oversee the construction of their new house, and raise their young children. In the male-dominated world of the nineteenth century, Molly Reid was looked on as the equal of any man. General John Stark said, "If ever there is a woman in New Hampshire fit to be governor, 'tis Molly Reid."

A FAMILY QUARREL

Frequently parents were against a proposed marriage and would do anything to stop the course of true love. Such was the case with lovers Thomas Burnside and Susan MacGregor. Thomas, a storekeeper, was born in Ireland and Susan was the daughter of

Alexander MacGregor, who was the son of Reverend James Mac-Gregor, the founder of Londonderry, and the brother of David MacGregor, the first pastor in what is now the modern town of Londonderry. The engaged couple knew that her parents would oppose their marriage, so they eloped in broad daylight thanks to careful planning, a fast horse, and a willing parson.

After they had been legally hitched, they set up housekeeping in Londonderry. The MacGregors would not visit the couple, who had defied their parental wishes. On the first Sunday, Susan persuaded her husband to attend worship service at her uncle David MacGregor's church. The newlyweds walked down the aisle to sit in the pew of her uncle James MacGregor Jr. Uncle James opened the box pew door to allow in his niece but quickly closed it to fence Thomas Burnside out.

Not a man to be easily put off, Burnside vaulted over the three-foot-high pew wall and sat down in triumph beside his new wife. Uncle James stood up and grabbed the interloper and was prepared to pitch him back into the aisle when from the pulpit came the booming voice of Pastor David MacGregor: "Brother James, do not disturb the house of the Lord!" With that admonishment, order was restored.

Despite the pastorally imposed peace, the Burnsides and Mac-Gregors did not talk to each other until after Susan Burnside had her first child.

During the French and Indian War, Thomas Burnside served with the legendary Rogers's Rangers. On January 20, 1757, he took part in a battle near Lake Champlain in which he and several of his men were wounded. The nearest medical help was forty miles away. Despite his injuries, Burnside and John Stark volunteered to go for help. On snow shoes they traveled for twelve hours through deep snow to reach help and by the next day the wounded were being treated.

In 1767, Susan and Thomas Burnside with their three young sons became the first permanent settlers of Northumberland, New Hampshire. Awhile later Thomas traveled by horse to the colonial capital at Portsmouth in order to secure an appointment as the local justice of the peace. To help his case, he brought with him a "firkin of butter and a roll of linen" as a gift to Royal Governor John Wentworth. When the governor asked how many people lived in the town, Burnside told Wentworth that there was just him and another

man but "he is no more fit for the job of justice of peace than a chestnut burr is for an eye stone." With that colorful description, the Governor appointed Burnside a magistrate.

Before leaving the governor's office, Thomas Burnside asked Wentworth, "When I get home to my folks, what shall I tell them that the governor gave me that was good to drink?"

The amused Wentworth replied "Some brandy," and went to his sideboard to get a decanter of that liquor.

Just before he returned to Northumberland, Thomas revisited the governor to say his good-byes. Wentworth asked Thomas now what would he tell his neighbors about their governor's generosity. Burnside thought for a moment and replied, "I shall tell them that I had two drinks of brandy with him."

The governor looked confused and said, "But you only had one."

Thomas quickly replied, "Yes, but I expect another." And he got it!

THE LONGEST COURTSHIP

In the natural order of things, love leads to courtship and in due season to marriage. This was not the case with Rachel Wilson and Gabriel Barr of old Londonderry. They were certainly in love and had dreams of a life together in a double hitch. Their love, however, was never consummated.

The problem was not that their union would be over the objections of their parents or friends. Everyone agreed that their marriage would be a good match. The reason for their failure to unite was their respective churches. Rachel belonged to David Mac-Gregor's church in what is now the town of Londonderry; Gabriel was a member of the Reverend Davidson's meetinghouse in what is now the village of East Derry. The couple could not agree in which of these Presbyterian churches they should worship as man and wife.

Because they could not agree, they could never marry.

They remained betrothed during the rest of the eighteenth century. After a forty-year engagement, they died unwed and each went to their graves to sleep forever alone as spinster and bachelor.

THE RUN FOR THE BOTTLE

According to the Reverend Edward Parker in his *History of Londonderry* (1851), the earliest courtship and wedding customs in the Nutfield colony were brought over from Ireland. Before a wedding, the groom and the bride's father would visit the parson to have the banns published. It was usually required that the couple's intentions be read in church for several weeks before the wedding. Weddings were usually performed at home, not in the church, as it was a civil ceremony that required jumping through bureaucratic hoops put in place by the royal governor and town clerk.

The morning of the wedding there was a volley of rifle fire from the neighborhoods of the happy couple. This, according to Parker, was a tradition instituted by the Protestants of Ireland to show their superiority to the local Catholics, who weren't allowed to have guns. At an agreed-upon time, the groom and his friends would leave his home and ride toward the bride's residence. Midway they would be met by a party of the bride's friends. They would stop their travels and each would choose one man from each group to "run for the bottle." The two men would race to the bride's home, where the winner would be awarded a bottle of liquor as his trophy. This would be brought back to the horsemen and women where the champion would offer up a toast to the bride.

THE SHIVAREE

Back in 1975, my father and I were spending an evening watching television together. The *TV Guide* said that an upcoming episode of *The Waltons* was called "The Shivaree." I didn't have a clue as to what that word meant. Dad patiently explained to me that shivarees were common in his younger days in Sandown.

After a wedding, the men of town would find where the honeymooning couple were spending their first night together as man and wife. The gang would conspire to descend on the love nest with the earnest intent of interrupting any possibility of connubial bliss. Sometimes the men sang songs, beat the top of trash barrels, or fired shotguns over the top of the honeymoon cottage. The mob would demand that the couple come to the door and join in the revelry. The celebration frequently didn't end until daybreak and the couple were given no time to be alone. Sometimes the men took even more dramatic steps. The conspirators would break into the

house and kidnap the groom. He would be taken away in his night-clothes and dropped off on a deserted road many miles away. It would usually take all night for the barefoot man to walk home to his bride. Great fun, eh?

Dad recalled fondly the last shivaree in which he took an active part. One midnight in June 1935, the men of Sandown approached the house across from the Old Meeting House where newlyweds Harold and Nellie Lovering were spending their special night. Their avowed intent was to kidnap Harold. The couple, from the comfort of their wedding bed, could hear the hooting and hollering as the revelers came up Fremont Road. When the men burst through the front door, the couple ran out the back door carrying a quilt and wearing only their pajamas and nightgown. The lovers ran down a wood path and spent the first night of their honeymoon sleeping under the stars in Ray Bassett's pasture.

Londonderry historian Marilyn Ham was told that in 1928, when her parents were married, shivarees were still in vogue. Marilyn's dad handcuffed his bride to his wrist to prevent either one of them being kidnapped by high-spirited friends. If they were to be taken, they wanted to go together.

The word *shivaree* is a corruption of the French word *charivari,* which means "a noisy mock serenade for newlyweds," and may have come from a Latin word for headache. By the early nineteenth century shivarees were common all over rural America. They were, however, seldom mentioned in newspapers or chronicled in town histories. This is probably because shivarees were considered rather low class and ribald and usually involved the consumption of lots of spirituous liquor.

On April 16, 1890, the Reverend Irad Taggart, of the Londonderry Methodist church, conducted the service that united William Washington Gage, age twenty-five to Miss Harriet E. Roach, age seventeen. He was a carpenter and she was a member of the socially prominent Tenney and Peabody families. The couple soon took up housekeeping in an apartment in the northern part of Londonderry.

All was peaceful until Friday, April 25, when the young men of Londonderry got it into their heads that the newlyweds were badly in need of a "serenade." Many of the witnesses believed the revelers were overly lubricated. One critic of this shivaree classified the group as "drunken ruffians and a gang of idiots." One of the

participants would later refute the statement that they were all inebriates. The charge that they were "idiots and ruffians" was apparently undeniable. The participant claimed that, with only one exception, everyone was cold sober that night. He further proclaimed, "Nor are they in the habit of drinking nor are they regarded as drinking young men."

This group of sober (?) young Londonderry men sang outside the couple's window for quite a while but their efforts were seemingly ignored. The lovebirds kept their window shut tight, their kerosene lamps unlit, and their marital privacy was left inviolate.

The serenaders would not to be put off by window curtains drawn shut. Being young "laboring men" without great personal fortune, they regretted not being able to hire a marching band with seventy-six trombones like the legendary Patrick Gilmore's Band. The group was forced to resort to creating its own orchestra, which consisted of "blowing horns and whistles and thumping tin pans," but still they were ignored! The house stayed dark.

Much later that evening a delegation of the men went up onto the front porch of the honeymoon house and the stairs collapsed from their weight. The door was barred and they were denied entrance to the love nest. The bridegroom stationed himself behind the door with a shotgun ready to repel any home invasion. Despite their best efforts, the gang never did get the newlyweds even to acknowledge their presence, nor did the traditional kidnapping of the groom occur that April night in Londonderry.

The marriage of Hattie and Washington Gage did not last too long. Sadly, several pregnancies ended with stillborn babies. After only fifteen years together, they divorced. In 1906 Hattie married farmer and state highway worker Nathan Watts, who was about three years her senior. They would remain childless. That same year, Mr. Gage, age forty-five married Carrie Raymond, age twenty-one. Within three years they were the parents of three children.

On July 7, 1897, schoolteacher Lillian Merrill married *Derry News* printer Charles Sefton. They were both twenty-five years old. On the day of their wedding, they settled into their Derry Village home looking forward to married life. After dark, without warning, a mob of strangers appeared at their door and demanded admission. The Seftons refused to unlock their door, hoping the mob would leave.

The "well wishers" refused to be deterred by this lack of hospitality. They trampled a flower bed and broke two windows and screens to gain access to the living room. They stayed for an hour "shrieking, howling and raving like wild Indians." Outside the house they disturbed the neighborhood by setting off volley after volley of rockets and firecrackers. As they left, they walked toward West Derry, threatening to return later. A writer to the *Derry News* wondered if in the future "bridegroom's outfits must in part consist of a Winchester rifle and a pair or revolvers and must a wedding be followed by a funeral or two in order that peaceful citizens may enjoy their (conjugal) rights."

Today it is pretty much standard operating procedure to decorate the newlyweds' automobile with crepe streamers, signs, paint, and tin cans. The earliest such activity I have so far discovered occurred in September 1909. Frank Smith, of Londonderry, married Miss Cora Lurvey, of Goffstown, at the home of the groom's parents. The couple were driven from the wedding to their luncheon in an automobile "decorated but not according to the tastes of the bridal party."

TWO HUSBANDS

This story was found in *Willey's Book of Nutfield* and so far no independent confirmation of its authenticity has been discovered. According to the story, sometime during the 1750s Benjamin Downs married Mary Downs. Though both had grown up in old Londonderry and they had the same surname, they were not related. Theirs was a happy marriage and soon they were blessed with the birth of their son, Benjamin Junior. Within the year, however, the French and Indian War broke out. The frontier had to be protected. Benjamin enlisted in this fight to protect hearth and home.

For months, no word was received back home about Benjamin. All Mary could do was worry and hope for the best. In time, some returning soldiers gave "vague rumors of his death" but there was nothing to confirm such a tragedy. Around 1765, after eight years of widowhood, Mary accepted the marriage proposal of her suitor James Clark. In time they became parents of a daughter, Elice.

Years later, when Benjamin was twelve, he was playing outside when he saw a stranger coming up the dirt road. The man inquired for Mary Downs. Quickly the visitor was revealed to be the long missing Benjamin Downs Senior. Amid the tears and shock, the story was told how for a dozen years he had been held prisoner by the Indians in Canada.

Mary Downs Clark now had two husbands and was very confused as to what to do. Whichever husband she chose, a traumatic situation was in store for one of her two husbands, the children, and herself. Finally after a period of adjustment, the returning soldier decided not to exercise his right to claim his wife and son. One morning, without a word, he shouldered his sack and wandered again down the dirt road.

He was never heard of again by anyone in his family or in the town of Londonderry.

16.

The Yellow Day

I WAS RECENTLY CHECKING OUT WHAT HAPPENED IN HISTORY ON September 6. On this date in 1620 the good ship *Mayflower* set sail for New England and in 1757 Lafayette was born. September 6 is also the date in 1901 when President McKinley was assassinated. On that date in 1910, the first primary was held in New Hampshire. Locally, September 6 is remembered (at least in my home) as the date in 1945 when I was born in East Derry in the original Alexander-Eastman Hospital. Besides my birthday, it is the anniversary in Derry of the "Yellow Day" of 1881. This article will explain the latter event and I'll try to ignore the former.

The morning of September 6, 1881, began like any other late-summer day in Derry. It was warm and the sky was nearly cloudless. In Portsmouth the weather was described as "warm, sultry and disagreeable."

Many in Derry were anxious because of a recent assassination attempt on the president. On July 2, President James Garfield had been shot at a railroad station in Washington, D.C. On September 6 the gravely ill president was being taken by train to the New Jersey seashore. There he could recuperate in a cooler climate. New Hampshire Governor Charles Bell (his father was born in Derry) called for a statewide day of "humiliation and supplication" for the recovery of the president. This request didn't please Nathaniel Bartlett, the editor of the *Derry News*. The Harvard-educated editor advised his readers that such prayers would have no effect on the recovery of the president. Bartlett said we were no longer in the "age of miracles" and should not return to the "age of superstition."

Prayer, according to Bartlett, had power over the heart and soul but not the physical body. Garfield died on September 19, 1881.

For several days, many towns in southern New Hampshire had complained of a strong smoky smell that filled the air. This odor, however, was not reported in Derry, Windham, or Londonderry. Early in the morning of September 6, the sky and the sun took on a reddish hue. By noon the air took on "a yellow cast." Some described it as "a strange ghastly sulfurous look." No matter where you looked, your vision was being filtered through a brassy yellow haze. The world began to look as though King Midas had turned it into gold.

The *Derry News* editor reported that "lamps burning in this light gave a flame that looked white. Things that are green appeared of an unnatural brightness and looked tinged with deep blue." Yellow flowers looked gray and the grass on the lawns seemed blue. The sun became a red ball surrounded by yellow clouds. Day turned to night and no one could read without the use of lamps or candles. The darkness that enveloped Derry appeared to have come without an obvious reason; there was no fog or eclipse. To add to the eeriness, not a breath of air was "stirring during the day."

Those local residents who had nerves that were always "kind of twittery" saw the darkness as an omen of dire days a-coming. Did the yellow day foretell the death of the president or was it a premonition of the "day of judgment"? Would Gabriel soon be blowing his horn? This had been the common reaction on May 19, 1780. That date is known as New England's "Dark Day."

The manuscript records of the Londonderry/Derry town clerk reported that "May ye 19th, 1780 was a day of darkness that no man could read at noontime without the help of a candle. A day that ought to be remembered forever by all the spectators and in the night of said day was as dark as Egypt Darkness for the space of three hours notwithstanding it was near the full of the noon. The next day was a good day. Blessed be God forever for its great deliverance."

The year 1780 had, by all accounts, been very, very, strange. Many nights saw the sky streaked with red and gold streamers. The winter had been particularly harsh, with snow staying on the ground from early November, 1779 to mid-April, 1780. In December the snow measured four feet on the level and drifts were ten feet high. New York's Long Island Sound was frozen so solid that it was crossed by a company of heavy artillery soldiers, canons and all. In

early May, much of New England experienced a "vapor" that filled the air and left the smell of sulfur everywhere.

May 19, 1780 had begun clear but then, around nine in the morning, the clouds became "lowery and then black and ominous." Soon thunder roared and lightning flashed. By ten, the sky became an "unearthly brassy color" and then by eleven, dark clouds made the day as black as night. It appeared as though the sun had gone into an unscheduled total eclipse. Throughout New England the religious fell on their knees to ask for God's mercy and forgiveness. It wouldn't be until midnight that the black clouds in the sky disappeared.

In some places in New England, it was too dark to read at midday. Candles were lit in many homes and the chickens went into their nests to roost. In Connecticut, the legislature debated if they should adjourn because they couldn't read their papers and possibly the end of the world was at hand. Colonel Abraham Davenport voted in the negative saying: "I am against an adjournment. The day of judgment is either approaching, or it is not. If it is not, there is no cause of an adjournment: if it is, I choose to be found doing my duty. I wish therefore that candles may be brought." John Greenleaf Whittier later wrote a poem about the Colonel Davenport protest. In New Hampshire a poem on the Dark Day was widely distributed in 1780. Its first stanza is:

Let us adore and bow before,
The sovereign Lord of might;
Who turns away the shinning day,
Into the shades of night.

One hundred and one years later, during the Yellow Day of 1881, the members of the Adventist church in Worchester, Massachusetts, went to their meeting hall in a local school. There the congregation waited prayerfully for what they believed was "the end of the world."

All through the area in 1881, the reaction was one of mystification. In Londonderry, it was reported that the birds fell silent but that crickets continued to chirp. The children of the town's Sunday schools had been looking forward to their annual Union Sabbath School picnic. This was the last group activity before the fall school term began. There would be baseball, tug-of-war, and swimming. All the mothers had prepared their best culinary delights to reward the children for their hard work at church school. The Londonderry church leaders looked at the yellow sky and sent the kids home. There was no telling what would happen next on that "strange day." The picnic was rescheduled for later that week.

In Hampton, New Hampshire, the air during the Yellow Day was reported to sting the eyes. It was said that no one could read ordinary print without the use of a lamp. One seacoast resident reported that one couldn't even read the dial of a clock from across the room. The light at noontime was no brighter than it was at midnight when there was a full moon overhead.

In Hanover, New Hampshire, an observer wrote that white-painted houses appeared yellow. Overhead the sky was a "pale-olive shadow" and at the horizon there was "a line of green." Some locals reported that they felt dizzy looking at all the yellow. I recall a similar experience back in 1978, when I took a tour of the Lawrence *Eagle Tribune*. There was one room in the production area that for some reason had to be lit only with yellow light bulbs; everything in that room was bathed in yellow light. Within only a couple of minutes I felt very nauseated.

In Framingham, it was chronicled that the light from a burning match was as strong as that from an electric light bulb. Home-owners were reluctant to turn on gaslight because it was too bright and hurt their eyes. Professor Charles F. Emerson, of Dartmouth College, postulated that "there was something in the atmosphere which absorbs the shorter and longer wave length, leaving only those which give of the colors yellow and green."

The cause of the Yellow Day is believed to lie a thousand miles to the west. A massive forest fire was ravaging northern Michigan and the province of Ontario. In the area around Lake Huron, the fire burned hundreds of square miles of forest and did millions of dollars in damage. There were twenty villages destroyed and an estimated five hundred people died. The smoke from this major conflagration wafted east and may have caused the Yellow Day in New England.

Editor Bartlett of the *Derry News* later attempted to explain the yellowness to his readers: "We conceive that gases were exhaled with the common smoke from the Canadian fires, that these gases rose into the light air above, and were themselves light enough to float on the denser air beneath. Now every gas tends of itself to expand without limit when free to do so. This gas was free to expand laterally in the strata of atmosphere in which it lay. It lay above our lower atmosphere, and it spread out like a film of oil upon water. As there was no wind to blow it away, and no rain to absorb it, there it lay through the day till the wind and the rain of the night dispelled it."

It has now been 126 years since the Yellow Day and 227 years since the Dark Day. I would just as soon that those historical curiosities not revisit our town. The weather lately has been strange enough.

The residence of Col. William Pillsbury on Pillsbury Road, Londonderry.

17.

William Pillsbury: The Man Who Made Broadway

I SUPPOSE MOST PEOPLE DRIVE ON BROADWAY AND NEVER GIVE a moment's thought as to how it came to be the cultural, commercial, and political center of town. Once upon a time it was the tiniest part of a small town. Downtown Derry, as it is today, owes its existence to one man—Colonel William S. Pillsbury.

He was born in Sutton, New Hampshire, in 1833, the son of Baptist minister Stephen and Lavinia Pillsbury. (His cousin John S. Pillsbury [1828–1901] would later leave Sutton to found the Pillsbury Flour Company in Minneapolis.) Reverend Pillsbury was called to Londonderry in 1836. His parish was small and poor. There was little money left after buying the necessities for a family with nine children. William was forced to leave school when he was only fourteen years of age.

The young teenager got a job as a shoemaker in Manchester and later was employed in several shops in Massachusetts at a dollar twenty-five a day. Until he was twenty-one years old, all of his earnings after paying his room and board were given to support his now-widowed mother. In 1856 he was hired to manage the Currier and Boyd shoe factory on Broadway. This small company was never very successful and was closed about as frequently as it was open. After about a year, he joined a number of his family members farming in Kansas. There he was part of the brave band of three thousand abolitionists who were there to keep the territory from joining the list of slave states. Bloody Kansas was a dangerous place to be with the proslavery "Border Ruffians" killing and intimidating as many as they could.

Around 1860, William returned home with a small nest egg. Soon he opened a small, ten-foot by ten-foot shoe shop in Londonderry. The Civil War soon disrupted his career. He had been raised in a family active in the abolitionist movement. The twenty-eight-year-old Pillsbury would enlist proudly in this war that he viewed as a moral crusade.

On September 5, 1861, he joined the fourth New Hampshire Infantry as a private. His leadership skills were soon apparent and he was commissioned a first lieutenant. He rode with his men by train as far as Annapolis, Maryland, when an injury forced him to resign his commission and return home. After a few months of recuperation, he and his brother Leonard were appointed recruiting officers for the Ninth New Hampshire Infantry. Once again William left New Hampshire and headed for war.

Lieutenant Pillsbury proved to be an outstanding military leader. At the Battle of South Mountain (September 14, 1862), his quick thinking was credited with saving his company from mass casualties during an attack on an entrenched Confederate detachment. He also took part in the Battle of Antietam only three days later. With twenty-three thousand killed, this was the bloodiest single-day battle in American history. There were more killed at Antietam than died in the Revolutionary War, the War of 1812, the Mexican War, and the Spanish-American War combined. During this one battle there were nine times the number who were killed on D-Day in 1944.

After the battle, Pillsbury came down with pneumonia and again had to resign his commission. While recuperating, he managed a shoe factory in Virginia. He later enlisted in the First New Hampshire Heavy Artillery as ordinance officer. He was mustered out of the Army on June 15, 1865.

Within a month, he was back working in his little shoe shop in Londonderry. In December 1870 he decided to expand his operation and move closer to the railroad. He saw opportunity in what was then called Derry Depot. The area around Broadway was at the time in a deep economic depression. Its only shoe factory, which opened in 1852, had been closed for several years. Only a few dozen people lived in the area. The other commercial activity on Broadway consisted of the railroad depot, a single store, a hotel, a stable, a small brick bank, and a combination lumber and grist-mill. There were just nineteen buildings and homes in the entire village. There were few roads. Birch Street and Crystal Avenues were yet to be built. Fordway was so named because in 1870 all wagons and horses that went on that dirt path had to "ford" the unbridged Beaver Brook.

Pillsbury linked up with Colonel Jesse Clement and George Colburn, of Boston's Clement, Colburn Shoe Company, and purchased the old Currier and Boyd factory on Broadway. The Boston company would own the building, provide the capital, and sell the shoes; Pillsbury would manage the business, hire the workers, buy the leather, and oversee production. William Pillsbury was given the title of superintendent but in fact he was viceroy. In Derry, he alone called the shots. The factory sign may have said *Clement, Colburn* (later it was renamed Colburn & Fuller and still later it was called Clement, Erskine & Co.), but everyone in Derry knew it was Colonel Pillsbury's factory. Within nine months the new shop went from employing thirty workers to one hundred twenty-five. In 1899, Pillsbury and his son Rosecrans bought the company and created the W. S. & R. S. Pillsbury Shoe Company.

During his years as superintendent, the company kept growing. Soon there were separate buildings to dye leather, sew buttonholes, and manufacture boxes. Under his management the factory went twenty-three years without being shut down for lack of orders. In 1899, the business was so busy that to fill orders, the employees worked eleven hours a day, six days a week.

The main factory extended 220 feet along the side of Broadway and went 135 feet down Central Street. Its basic shape rather resembled the letter *H*. In 1881 the factory covered fifty-thousand square feet of work space on four floors. It was claimed to be the largest shoe factory in the state. All of the structure was of wood-frame construction except for the brick office, which had formerly been the Derry Bank and later a district school. Some of the buildings were connected by elevated skywalks. In that year, the company's shoes and boots were sold in Brazil, Mexico, Peru, Chile, New Zealand, Australia, South Africa, Denmark, Norway, Russia, India, and every state and territory within the United States. They were manufacturing about five hundred different styles of shoes. The company employed four salesmen who traveled throughout the world taking orders.

Although in 1881 Pillsbury was prosperous, he was not the town's wealthiest man. That honor fell to H. P. Hood; Pillsbury in fact tied for twenty-first place among Derry's taxpayers. He was, however, the town's largest employer and likely its most popular citizen. In that year he and his wife, Martha Stowell Pillsbury were the focus of a twenty-fifth wedding-anniversary celebration that was attended by hundreds of their neighbors and employees. They were escorted from his brother Leonard's house to the Opera House by Lambert's Military Brass Band. Such a village-wide celebration was repeated in 1906 on the couple's fiftieth anniversary.

Over the next few decades, Pillsbury invested lots of Colburn & Fuller's money to modernize the factory. A huge boiler was installed to produce steam to generate 125-horsepower of energy. His first boiler had yielded a steam force of only fifteen horsepower. The roof was originally made of wood shingles; he had them replaced with fireproof slate. This saved the factory from certain destruction in the great fire of 1882. Electric light replaced the old kerosene lamps. Shoes were now glued or sewn together and not pegged.

One of the keys to the company's success was William's management style. He hired good foremen who earned the respect of the workers. There was never a strike in the Pillsbury Shoe Factory during the years when Pillsbury was totally in charge. In 1890 he even allowed a trade union to manage one of his new factories. By 1895 he was employing nearly seven hundred workers. Of these, 40 percent were women and girls. The men earned a dollar eighty a day and the females averaged thirty-five cents an hour less. When the Boston owners tried to reduce costs by cutting wages, Colonel Pillsbury stood up for the workers. He pleaded successfully their need for a fair, living wage.

Were there children employed in the Pillsbury shoe factories? Certainly. Child labor laws were still a generation in the future and it must also be recalled that Colonel Pillsbury was himself put to work when he was just fourteen. Several nineteenth-century photographs in the collection of the Derry Museum of History show young teenage boys and girls standing alongside the adult workers.

The Derry factory by 1881 was producing about forty thousand pairs of shoes a year. In 1886 this figure rose to a million pairs per year and the output was two million by 1900. These shoes were being sold on five different continents. By that time Pillsbury was producing nearly four hundred styles of women's shoes alone. In

Derry the salaries paid to workers were probably in excess of three hundred thousand dollars a year up, all of this going to local workers who bought their food and clothes in local stores.

In addition to the shoe factory, Pillsbury owned several blocks of stores and at least ten tenements. In 1885 he formed the Citizens Building Association to plan and control the course of Derry's growth. This group saw a definite need for affordable housing for the shoe workers and their families. The association built rows and rows of neat, small homes that could be rented or bought for small sums. Familiar examples are the houses that line Birch Street in the vicinity of Peabody's Funeral Home. As they were originally constructed, they looked like little Monopoly game pieces with each house the same as every other house on the street. In the last hundred years, however, the home owners have added personalizing touches. Now each house is unique. By 1900, West Derry had grown in thirty years from just nineteen buildings to more than four hundred homes, factories, churches, halls, and stores.

Members of the Citizens Building Association decided that more shoe factories would mean more prosperity. In 1890 they built the Woodbury Shoe Factory; in 1902 they had constructed the Derry Shoe Building off South Avenue. This structure claimed to be the largest wooden factory in the world. Between 1901 and 1909 they constructed a complex of shoe factories on Maple Street. All these buildings would be rented to other shoe manufacturers but cooperation with the Pillsbury juggernaut was expected. By 1910, Derry was pretty much a one-industry town, with about three-quarters of its men and women employed in the shoe industry. In 1915 the five largest factories of West Derry were turning out a combined production of twenty thousand pair of shoes each workday.

William Pillsbury believed in civic responsibility. For nineteen years he was Londonderry's town moderator. He had also been elected County Commissioner, state Representative, state Senator, Justice of the Peace, Leach Library Trustee, and a member of the Governor's Council. In 1877 he was appointed military aide-de-camp to the governor with the rank of colonel. In 1883, Company F, New Hampshire National Guard, was named the Pillsbury Guard in his honor. In 1909 the local Sons of the Union Veterans club was named after him. He was a lifelong Republican.

From 1870 to 1900 he rode his carriage every day from his Pillsbury Road home to his office on Broadway. On New Year's Day

1901 he decided to do the math on those trips. He figured he had traveled back and forth a distance of 49,600 miles or the equivalent of around the world twice. Some of those trips were by carriage, others in a sleigh. In checking his diaries, he found that the largest number of days he used a sleigh in a single winter was 126; the smallest number was just eight.

Locally, he had served as commander of the local chapter of the Grand Army of the Republic, a Civil War veterans group, and was later elected its state commander and served as a national board member. Fraternally, he was a Mason and a Shriner. He attended the Presbyterian church in Londonderry.

He was generous to the town of Derry. His name was always in the *Derry News* for gifts to various charities. In 1902 he and his son Rosecrans gave the land upon which the Adams Memorial Building would be built in 1903–1905. They also gave a thousand dollars to start the town's library in that building. On the back end of this lot, the two shoe factory owners had Pillsbury Street constructed and lined it with tenements for their workers.

William Pillsbury retired in 1908 at age sixty-five and turned over the reigns to his son Rosecrans. He died at his home in Londonderry in 1911. He was survived by Martha his wife of fifty-five years; as well as two sons, a daughter, thirteen grandchildren, and his brother Judge Leonard Pillsbury of Derry.

His obituary in the *Derry News* called him "the man who made Derry." Those who lived during those years knew this was not just a reporter's exaggeration. By this phrase, the newsman was referring to the Broadway section of Derry. When William Pillsbury came to town in 1870, West Derry (Broadway) was the smallest of the three villages in town. Its only factory had shut down and there seemed no plan for reopening it. The only reason you would come to West Derry is if you were passing through on the way to somewhere else.

Because of William Pillsbury's vision, organizational skill, and zeal, the Broadway area of town was transformed from a sleepy crossroad into a bustling industrial complex. Immediately after his arrival the area began its industrial awakening. West Derry became Derry's place to be as sprawling shoe factories revitalized the area's economy. New streets were built across the former cow pastures, and rows of homes and tenements were springing up like mushrooms. Within a decade, Broadway would be lined with stores, churches, social clubs, schools, restaurants, and saloons. The night of payday, the streets were awash with thousands of workers and their families eager to spend the contents of their pay envelopes in the Broadway stores. The growth in the prosperity of Derry in the half-century from 1870 to 1920 was the direct result of William Pillsbury.

During the decades after Colonel Pillsbury's passing, the shoe industry began its decline. In 1915 the Broadway factory closed and was converted by Rosecrans Pillsbury, Wallace Mack, and Charles S. Emerson into thirty-one kitchenette apartments. Another part of the complex was made into a movie theater. A row of one-story brick stores was added to the front of the former factory on Broadway. In 1979 a fire destroyed the eastern end of the block, which also contained the American House Apartments. The remainder of the block was razed in 1981. On this lot was built a brick apartment building for seniors. Into its facade was placed a granite block that had been originally located over the entrance to the old kitchenettes. Carved in the stone in very large letters is the name Pillsbury. Sadly this stone is our town's only public memorial to William S. Pillsbury—the man who made Broadway.

18.

Leonard Pillsbury

THERE IS AN ANCIENT JEWISH FOLKTALE CALLED THE "TZADDIKIM Nistarim," which says that in the world there are just thirty-six righteous men scattered across the seven continents. It is only for their sake that the world escapes destruction by God, who is disgusted with the sins of mankind. These men by virtue of their saintliness justify to God the purpose of man on earth. These thirty-six righteous men do not know each other and none is ever aware of his special role in the world. When one of the thirty-six dies, another is born to take his place.

I thought about this tale while researching the remarkable life of Leonard Pillsbury. If the folktale is true, he just might have been one of these thirty-six righteous men.

Leonard Hobart Pillsbury was born in Dunbarton, New Hampshire on Christmas Day 1835. He was the ninth child of Baptist minister Stephen and his wife Lavinia Hobart Pillsbury. From childhood, he was always called Hobart by members of his family. He came from very good stock. His grandfather Micajah was a veteran of the Revolutionary War. Among his near cousins were the Pillsburys, who left Sutton, New Hampshire, before the Civil War and in Minneapolis founded the Pillsbury Flour Company. Another cousin was Parker Pillsbury, who grew up in Henniker, New Hampshire. He was one of the giants in the national campaign for the abolition of slavery and for women's rights.

The Reverend Stephen Pillsbury had pastorates in the New Hampshire towns of Hebron, Sutton, and Dunbarton. He was a pioneer in the state in the crusade against alcohol. Originally a

Democrat, he switched over to the Free Soil Party around 1848. Its slogan was "Free Soil, Free Speech, Free Labor and Free Men." This radical reforming party was the immediate precursor to the Republican Party. In 1836 Stephen Pillsbury accepted the call to preach in Londonderry.

The cleric was recognized by all as a good man. One source called him "the most correct exemplary Christian gentleman . . . prudent, amiable and unselfish." On the day of his death, in 1855, he attended a wedding and a funeral. His wife, Lavinia, was a composer of Christian prose, poems, and hymns. She was called to her reward in 1871.

Leonard Pillsbury moved to Londonderry with his parents when he was just a baby. Here he attended the one-room district school. It is not known what he did to earn a living immediately after leaving school. His older brother, William, began to learn the shoemaker's craft at age fourteen. It is likely that Leonard also worked in a shop or store at about that same age. The genteel poverty of a Baptist preacher's home, especially one with nine children, would have precluded any thought of Leonard remaining in school once he was old enough to work.

The passage of the Kansas-Nebraska Act in 1854 would forever change Leonard's life. By this law, the citizens of Kansas would vote on whether or not they wanted the state to allow slavery within its boarders. Soon the "Border Ruffians" were streaming in from Missouri to attack the antislavery farmers of Kansas. What was being called "Bleeding Kansas" horrified the abolitionists of the East. One of the leading abolitionists was the Reverend Henry Ward Beecher, of New York, who with the Lawrence family of Lawrence, Massachusetts, organized the New England Emigrant Aid Society. Its purpose was to encourage anti-slavery northerners to move to Kansas and vote to make it a free state. The town of Lawrence, Kansas, is named after Amos Lawrence, a major supporter of John Brown, who led the 1859 insurrection at Harper's Ferry.

About twenty-six hundred men and women answered Beecher's call and went to the contested territory. In the words of Haverhill's poet James Greenleaf Whittier:

To rear a wall of men on Freedom's southern line
And plant beside the cotton tree, the rugged northern pine.

The residence of Judge Leonard Pillsbury on Manchester Road, 1897.

Among those who responded were seven members of the Pillsbury family, including Leonard and his sister Ann. The family had always been strongly opposed to slavery and the children had learned about its evils on their father's knee and through their mother's hymns.

On March 12, 1855, the Pillsburys left the safety of their homes and put their lives in the hands of the New England Emigration Aid Society. They went by railroad to Alton, Illinois, then by boat down the Missouri River to St. Louis and Kansas City. The remainder of the trip was by ox cart on their trek to Lawrence, Kansas.

Leonard Pillsbury was soon guided through the process of claiming a homestead of 160 acres on the prairie. For the next few years he was a farmer trying to survive attacks by chinch bugs, drought, grasshoppers, and border ruffians. He was forced by circumstances to always carry a rifle. These guns were known euphemistically as"Beecher's Bibles." The fiery preacher had been quoted as saying that the "rifle was a truly moral agent." His followers shipped to Kansas guns in crates that were marked "Bibles" so they wouldn't be confiscated by embargo inspectors. In recent years the Pillsbury descendents have given about three thousand family letters from this period to the University of Kansas at Lawrence.

After about four years on the frontier farming his 160 acres of prairie, Leonard Pillsbury returned to New Hampshire and entered Exeter Academy. There he happily immersed himself in the study of "Euclid and the roots of Greek verbs." Just before he was supposed to graduate came the attack on Fort Sumter. Immediately he enlisted as a private in the Ninth New Hampshire Volunteer Infantry. During much of that summer, he was in charge of the recruiting office in Exeter. He was sworn in on August 22, 1862, and the next day married Evelyn Sanborn. On August 25, 1862, the Ninth marched down Concord's main street past cheering crowds on their way to war. At the head of Company A, the Rockingham County Company, was its newly commissioned officer, Captain Leonard H. Pillsbury.

Those who were acquainted with Pillsbury knew he was a man who hated violence and loved peace. To him, however, slavery was worse than war. Holding people in bondage was a war against freedom and humanity. It must be stopped! He could easily have stayed home by hiring a substitute to serve in his place. Few would have criticized him because of his deeply held beliefs in the holiness of peace. His conscience, however, would not let him remain safely in New Hampshire while others fought, bled, and died for this righteous cause. He was a member of the church militant, a soldier, off on a holy mission.

Within three weeks of leaving Concord, the Ninth New Hampshire was involved in the battle at South Mountain. Later Pillsbury led Company A in hard-fought combat at Antietam, Fredericksburg, and Vicksburg. By the time of that last engagement, the company, which had so proudly left New Hampshire with ninety-eight men, had seen its numbers reduced to only seven. Pillsbury had himself been hit by a bombshell at Antietam. He was given leave to go home and resigned his commission on August 7, 1863.

For the remainder of the war he was a customs officer at the port of New York. His biggest coup was discovering a contraband shipment of thousands of cases of cavalry boots destined for the confederate army. The crates in the English ship were labeled women's grain leather peg shoes. Having grown up around shoemakers and cobblers, he knew the crates were much too heavy to be what they claimed. Because of Pillsbury's sharp eye and mind, the government confiscated the boat and its cargo. This seizure yielded the government more than a hundred thousand dollars in profit.

After the war, Leonard Pillsbury taught for a short time in New York City at a private academy. In 1866 he moved to Kansas, where he and his brother Josiah published a newspaper called the *Manhattan Independent*. After eight years he moved to Memphis, Tennessee, where for the next five years he was a clerk of the United States Circuit Court during Reconstruction. In this judicial position he saw firsthand the effects Jim Crow laws and the Ku Klux Klan had on the newly emancipated Blacks.

In 1878 he was raising cattle with Josiah, but that venture proved unsuccessful when the price of cattle fell dramatically. Around this time he was also stricken with malaria so he returned to New Hampshire to recover physically and financially. He then decided to throw in his lot with his older brother William, who predicted great prosperity for the area in Derry around Broadway. Together they opened a general store near the site of today's D & J Automotives at Martin Street and Broadway. Leonard and his family lived on the second floor; the top floor being rented as the Odd Fellows lodge.

The great Broadway fire of 1882 wiped out all of Leonard's investments. His apartment, store, and the lodge went up in flames. The loss of building and stock was estimated at seven thousand dollars but was insured for only five thousand. He had no insurance coverage on his furniture and personal belongings. Within three days however, the brothers had erected a temporary twenty-four-by-thirty foot building to sell dry goods, groceries, grain, and furniture. Within months, this was replaced by a modern, elegant, Queen Anne style three-story store. The post office rented some of the ground floor until 1886. In imitation of their Minneapolis cousins, the brothers sold their own flour, manufactured by the Pillsbury Improved Flour Co. of Derry Depot, New Hampshire. One of their sacks is on display at the Derry Museum of History.

In August 1888, Leonard Pillsbury decided to go it alone. He opened a furniture store in a new block on Broadway—at about the site of today's Abbott House at 10 West Broadway. He promised his customers that he would visit Boston weekly and buy whatever they wanted—"from a cambric needle to an ensilage cutter"—and supply them at satisfactory prices. The store was 104 feet deep with a full basement and had several storage buildings.

He was obviously successful in attracting customers because the L.H. Pillsbury & Son store would continue in operation for the next ninety-one years. In time it would be run by his son Ambrose Burnside Pillsbury and later by his grandson Everett (1908–2007). The store was sold on January 1, 1967, to Raymond and Rita Buckley. It continued in business until 1979.The building was razed in 1981.The sign from the original store is on permanent display at the Derry Museum of History.

Around 1873 Leonard Pillsbury began to take an active role in the American Peace Society. This national group was opposed to war in principle. Its members by and large did not oppose the Civil War because it was viewed as an internal revolt that had to be put down in order to preserve the Union. Its membership was also in agreement with the war's abolitionist overtones. The society's sentiments were completely shared without reservation by Mr. Pillsbury. It was not the horrors that he saw in battle that first taught him to hate war. He did not suddenly get converted, like Paul on the road to Damascus. Around 1860, he was teaching in a district school in New London, New Hampshire. The local lyceum challenged him to debate future Massachusetts governor John Q. A. Brackett on the topic of "resolved, that all military establishments ought to be abolished." Pillsbury took the affirmative side and was voted the victor by the debate's judges.

For over twenty-five years Pillsbury was national vice president of the American Peace Society. He knew from first-hand experience the horror of war and had been wounded in battle. In the peace movement, he was the peer of luminaries such as Robert Treat Paine and President Charles Elliot of Harvard. In 1914, Leonard admitted that he had never played a game of baseball in his life and had previously thought of the sport as a waste of time. Rethinking this position, he reasoned that sports could be a replacement for war. Manly contests on the ball field would be a fine substitute for conflict on the battlefield.

Leonard Pillsbury was outspoken in his opposition to the Spanish-American War. His criticism of this war was shared by many, including Mark Twain and Andrew Carnegie. In November 1898 he wrote a peace resolution that was read on the floors of the U. S. Senate and House. Pillsbury argued in his resolve that it was wrong to get our country involved in a war that would require us to maintain a peacekeeping force garrisoned in the pacified areas years after the war had ended. Such a course of action, he felt, was both immoral and a major drain on the taxpayers of our country.

His opposition to U.S. involvement in the Philippine Insurrection was the subject of a number of letters that were printed in the *Derry News*. One Derry citizen, using the pen name "Violet," questioned Pillsbury for daring to criticize the president. At the time our army was trying to put down a popular uprising by Filipino nationalists. Violet asked, "If a mob of rough people should go through the streets of Derry stealing from the rich and killing their families and burning their property would he [Pillsbury] be a 'man of peace' then?" Pillsbury was also told that it wasn't Christian to second-guess the president and that our national leader was "doing what he thinks is right."

In response to such criticism, Pillsbury wrote to the newspaper a letter that quoted a bellicose Philadelphia cleric who said, "Every [American] cannon discharged, every musket fired and every flag waved in the Philippines is in the cause of righteousness." Pillsbury called such chauvinistic sentiments "sad and impossible to understand." He concluded the letter by saying that "there are Christians—and there are others."

During the 1880s, Pillsbury was elected to the State Legislature. He was viewed in the House as being pro labor and anti-big business. He consistently voted against giving the railroads and the rich any special treatment. He was considered a member of the progressive wing of the G.O.P. and beholden to no man or special interest. He was also Derry's postmaster from 1879 to 1885 and served as commander of the local veterans club.

In 1880 Leonard Pillsbury and thirteen other area residents organized the First Baptist Church. This was the first church to be formed in the Broadway area. He was the society's first clerk. For the rest of his life, Pillsbury would remain a member of that denomination. For the next twenty-five years he served as the church's Sunday school superintendent but ardently refused an ecclesiastical title. No one knows the reason why he wouldn't agree to sit on the board of deacons but we do know he was very definite about the subject.

One Sunday morning, on the front stairs of the church, a local doctor mistakenly addressed him as "Deacon Pillsbury." Quickly he drew the man aside to explain he would accept being called Judge, Mister, or Captain Pillsbury but not Deacon Pillsbury. He further told the startled doctor that he had taken a vow that "any man who addressed me as deacon shall not live to do so a second time." On another occasion he told a lady in Iowa that it was a law in New

Hampshire that all "deacons" have gardens that could yield at least twenty bushels of corn. His farm on Manchester Road in Derry was so poor that all he could raise was eighteen bushels—and that is why he could never be a deacon.

Upon the retirement of District Judge Charles Abbott in 1902, Leonard Pillsbury was appointed assistant justice of Derry's police court. The next year he was elevated to serve as judge. He was then sixty-six years of age.

During his time as judge, he was an ardent foe of the consumption of alcohol. Derry was at the time a fairly wide-open town. Citizens were always complaining of drunks staggering out of saloons like the Hotel Bradford and the Rat's Nest on Railroad Avenue. Many women wouldn't walk alone on Broadway for fear of being molested. While serving on the bench, Judge Pillsbury was a member of the executive board of New Hampshire's Anti-Saloon League. He organized the voters and wrote frequent letters to the *Derry News* in his crusade to close all barrooms in Derry. In May 1904, the town voted to go dry. In November, the Derry District Court went an entire month without the arrest of anyone for public drunkenness. Derry was now being viewed as a decent place for decent people to live.

In 1963 John Pillsbury was a candidate for governor of the state. He was the great-grandson of the judge. While in Derry, he passed on a family legend. It seems that in 1904 Rosecrans Pillsbury—the judge's nephew—was organizing his supporters in anticipation of his campaign for governor the next year. Liquor was being served at this private strategy meeting. Somehow the judge found out about the libations and he called in the police. Everyone was arrested and had to appear before the bench of the police court and pay a fine. This story may be apocryphal but it does speak to why people saw this judge as evenhanded in his application of justice.

On Christmas Day 1905, the judge turned seventy years old and was forced to retire from the bench. He would remain very active for nearly thirty more years and started a new profession as a civil engineer, operating from his sixty-acre Elmwood Farm in northern Derry. It was said that by the 1920s he had written more deeds than anyone else alive in western Rockingham County.

He continued to write letters to the *Derry News*. Usually they were on the subject of stopping the sale of alcohol but occasionally they supported cleaner streets or the need for more public parks. In

1916 the movie *Birth of a Nation* played at a local theater and raised the judge's ire. This popular movie was very critical of southern blacks and praised their suppression by the Ku Klux Klan during the Reconstruction era. Pillsbury wrote about when he was a "carpetbagger" in the South during this time. He had the personal experience in the 1870s of hearing the testimony of witnesses to blacks being subject to mass murder. He says this movie was filled with falsehoods and he could easily put readers "on the trail of truth."

He was very proud of his service in the war to help free the blacks. He would often tell visitors about his friendship with Lincoln, Grant, Sherman, and Burnside. Members of his family remembered that well into his old age he could still fire off a good imitation of the rebel yell he heard in combat half a century before. While in his nineties, he was still called on each Memorial Day to give the oration at the local ceremonies.

Until his ninety-seventh birthday the judge would walk a mile into town each morning. He was for a number of years the holder of the Boston Post Cane, which was presented to the oldest man in town. In 1932, declining health and blindness required that he move in with his daughter on Oak Street. His beloved wife had passed away a dozen years earlier. He died on December 26, 1933—a day after his ninety-eighth birthday. He was at that time the oldest alumnus of Exeter Academy, the oldest member of the American Peace Society, and the last surviving founder of the local Baptist church. Four children, eleven grandchildren and eight great-grandchildren survived him. After a service at the Baptist Church, he was laid to rest at the Foresthill Cemetery. One of his grandsons, Walter A. Pillsbury (1905–1985) would later serve as judge of the Derry court. He, too, would have to retire on his seventieth birthday.

Leonard Hobart Pillsbury led a most interesting life. He was universally recognized as a good man who led by example. Some may view his zeal as morally excessive. I'm sure Judge Pillsbury would eagerly accept that criticism and consider it a compliment. He would have probably agreed with Barry Goldwater's phrase that "extremism in the defense of liberty is no vice; moderation in the pursuit of justice is no virtue." During his long life he gave his all, whether as a military leader, a teacher, an editor, a farmer, a church leader, a merchant, a legislator, a jurist, an activist for peace, a protector of the rights of the poor, or a civil engineer.

On Easter Sunday 1896, he wrote a poem that I believe defines the life of Judge Pillsbury. It speaks from his heart about his hope for the future and calls out for personal action in bringing about a better world. It says in part:

There's a good time coming and it hastens on
    Apace
When salvation shall be spoken to every tribe and
    Race
When peace like a flowing river gently gliding to
    The sea
Shall lave with living waters all the lands and
    Make them free.
When nations shall be free from war and men be
    Free from rum
The earth shall yield her fruit with joy; enough
    In every land
The rich with surfeit shall not cloy; with what the
    Poor demand.

The good time coming, who shall bring and who
    Fling out the banner?
Who follows where the master leads and shout the
    Loud hosanna?
Who stem the tide of war and rum and selfishness
    And sorrow?
God calls you children to bring in the good time
    Of tomorrow.
You hear his call in every note that birds and
    Bees are singing
You hear his voice in every breeze from Easter
    Bells while ringing.
He bids you by the deeds of men whose voices
    Bring them sorrow
That you shall help him usher in the good times of
    Tomorrow.

Broadway, circa 1905. Leonard Pillsbury's furniture store is located in the center of the middle block.

19.
Pillsbury versus Pillsbury

I HOPE YOU HAVE ALREADY READ THE TWO PREVIOUS CHAPTERS ON William and Leonard Pillsbury. If so, you've discovered that they were both very good men. Each quit school at a young age, each served with distinction as a combat officer in the Civil War. Both were respected family men who held many town and state offices. William and Leonard were both highly regarded businessmen who, during their long careers, were never the subject of scandal or fraud or charged with anything dishonest. These two men, by all accounts, enjoyed solid reputations and when they died they were sincerely mourned by the entire community.

There are, however, signifying differences between the Pillsbury brothers. Although they shared parents, physically they did not look at all alike. William was a big, robust man who was full-bodied and sported a large impressive mustache. His posture was erect and he had the bearing of a military officer. He gave the appearance of being an honest, respectable businessman who would seal a deal with a firm handshake. One source called him "deliberate and dignified." Leonard, in contrast, was thin, wore a rather limp mustache, was rawboned, and possessed a delicate appearance. One report said that he was" nervous and incessantly active," and he had a reputation for participating in "political intrigues and shrewd dealings." If they belonged to the canine species and not to the Pillsbury clan, I would say William was a boxer and Leonard a greyhound.

Both men were strong in their faith. Each held church posts for decades. William belonged to the Presbyterian church in Londonderry Center. This was an orthodox fellowship that was very

141

staid and respectable. It had a history that went back to 1739 and was the establishment's church. Leonard was a founding member of the First Baptist Church on Broadway in Derry. This was the new church in town and it was evangelical in bringing salvation to the masses, loud in its hymn sings, and often perceived as the church for the common man.

Economically, the Pillsbury brothers were also rather different. According to the *Boston Post* in September, 1899, the two sides of the family were differentiated in Derry by the name the "rich Pillsburys" and the "poor Pillsburys." William had made tons of money with his far-flung shoe empire and investments. He lived in a large, fine house in Londonderry with "help" to keep things going. Each day he drove a fancy carriage to his office. Leonard, on the other hand, lived in a farmhouse with no servants, just farm hands. Every morning, in all four seasons, he'd walk a mile to open up his furniture store on Broadway.

All these difference were fairly unimportant, and both men conceded that they were "no big thing." The "poor Pillsburys" had a very comfortable life and the "rich Pillsburys" didn't live all that ostentatiously. The real division centered on their philosophy about drinking. Leonard was the town's leading advocate for prohibition. For decades he crusaded to make Derry a dry community. He was the saloon keeper's worst nightmare. He was the ultimate "cold water Baptist" and Adam's ale was his drink of choice. Each year dozens of his letters to the editor were printed in area newspapers. Usually his well-constructed epistles dealt with his two favorite subjects: alcohol (he was against it); peace (he was in favor of it). Locally Leonard Pillsbury was Derry's "Old Man Morality."

William Pillsbury, however, was a businessman accustomed to working with a wide variety of people. He believed in live and let live. If a workman wanted a beer or two after work, that was fine with him. In his mind there were worse sins than bellying up to the bar for a shot of red-eye and some congenial conversation. Leonard spent a lot of time trying to find legal ways to prosecute the rum seller; William and his lawyer son Rosecrans devoted much of their efforts to protecting the drinking rights of the Derry working man. It was this fraternal split that caused a near riot and lynching on Broadway in 1899.

To better understand the causes of the problems that year, it is important to know a little more about Rosecrans Pillsbury. He was a most impressive figure in Derry and by 1899 had gained a state-wide reputation as a populist. He was born in 1863, the oldest son of William Pillsbury. By his family he was always called Rose. He was tall, stout and rather baby-faced. After graduating from Pinkerton Academy, in 1880, he attended Dartmouth College to study law. He opened a practice in Derry and Londonderry and was his father's partner in the shoe industry. His three-hundred-acre Londonderry farm and orchard were the first in town to raise Macintosh apples.

Politically, he belonged to the progressive Republican camp and represented Londonderry in the legislature in 1897–99, 1905, and 1911. He was elected moderator in Londonderry for more than twenty years. He was an unsuccessful candidate for the nomination of governor in 1905 and 1914 and Congress in 1920. He was a powerful speaker and debater who had a fine command of both the spoken and written word and knew how to control his audience. In 1906 he purchased the *Manchester Union* and continued as its publisher for over two decades. In 1899, he was also a director of a copper mining company in Mexico that was producing six million pounds of copper per month.

He belonged to the Masons, Shriners, Elks, Knights of Pythias, Grange, and Derryfield Club. He was a captain in the National Guard company named after his father and donated the land on which Derry built the Adams Memorial Building. In 1904 he gave the funds to establish the Derry Public Library. He was a member of the official American delegation to the Paris Exposition of 1899–1901. In 1929, after retiring from public service, he was employed by the federal government to eradicate the Mediterranean fruit fly in Florida. He died in 1932 and is buried in the Valley Cemetery in Londonderry.

Despite Rose Pillsbury's life of public service, his reputation has been somewhat soiled by stories of self-serving political she-nanigans. These accounts were all chronicled by his rivals, so it is difficult to determine their truthfulness. It was claimed that in 1985 on the night before a town election, he and his father opened the package of ballots and pasted a friend's name over his opponent's name. The friend won. Twice when he failed to secure the Republican nomination for the state senate, it is said he campaigned for the Democratic candidate. In at least two Republican state conventions, it is claimed he switched candidates despite having pledged to "stick to the last ballot" with his original choice. One writer in a

Manchester newspaper around 1920 called him a traitor in the same mold as "Cataline, Judas and Benedict Arnold."

He also developed the reputation for being somewhat of a male chauvinist. In 1902 the state's Constitutional Convention was debating the issue of allowing women to vote. Rose Pillsbury was opposed to such a radical reform. His speech on women has been republished several times. On the floor of the convention he said, "We all admire the motherly woman and the woman who raises her family, directs the feet of her children in the direction they should go, takes an interest in their pleasures and tasks, educates them and watches over them. That is the kind of woman that we admire, the kind of a wife that any man of New Hampshire should aspire to. In the past we have had those women in New Hampshire, and I hope the women of our state will remain on the pedestal where we have always worshipped them." The male voters of the state agreed with Rose Pillsbury. They cast their ballots to continue restricting the franchise to men by a tally of 21,788–13,809.

Uncle Leonard Pillsbury was not fond of his nephew. Rose, the populist lawyer, frequently committed the sin of being the attorney for drinkers and rum sellers. As a skilled lawyer, he could usually find ways to get the guilty found innocent by judge or jury. Uncle Leonard also knew that nephew Rose drank. His beverage of choice on a hot Derry day was beer, not lemonade. It would also appear that the sons of Colonel William Pillsbury and storekeeper Leonard Hobart Pillsbury did not like their cousins. Attorney Rosecrans Pillsbury was frequently in opposition to two of Uncle Leonard's sons: William, who was a horse trader by profession; and Frederick, the local justice of the peace.

The first reported public squabble between the two Pillsbury families occurred back in 1892, when Leonard ran in the Republican primary against his nephew Rose in the race for the nomination for the state Senate. Rosecrans won in Derry and felt that his political star was in the ascendancy. In a magnificent carriage pulled by six dapple gray horses, he rode in triumph to the Republican caucus in Nashua. He brought with him a retinue of vocal supporters. There he suffered the embarrassment of losing to George Stevens of Nashua, who was himself born in Derry.

Uncle Leonard quickly found out via telegraph of his nephew's defeat. He gleefully ran across the street and posted the election results on the wall opposite the railroad depot. When the disappointed Rose came back to town, Leonard's son William set off "six dynamite cartridges" to celebrate his cousin's defeat. It is said that the "rich Pillsburys" were so angry that they temporarily left the Republican Party and tried to defeat Stevens. In 1898 Leonard used his influence to scuttle Rosecrans Pillsbury's attempt to be elected Speaker of the New Hampshire Legislature.

The political feud between the Pillsburys turned into a battle royal in the winter of 1895. The local police, who were supporters of Colonel William Pillsbury, heard talk of wild goings-on in a rented room in the Association Hall in Derry Village. Derry was a dry town and public drinking was illegal. And more important, here was a chance to embarrass Leonard Pillsbury. Colonel Pillsbury, being a Mason was able to get the police into the third-floor lodge room which was directly above the hired ballroom where the party was going on. Using a drill, they bored a hole through the floor. Now they could spy on the party and take down the names of those who were drinking.

Everyone in the room was arrested. Among those caught in this net was Leonard Pillsbury's son Will. The police prosecutor was his old antagonist and first cousin Rosecrans Pillsbury. The next day, just before the trial, Will and Rose passed each other on Broadway. Will knocked onto the dirt street all the law books Rose was carrying in his arms. Immediately, one of Will's friends started to punch out one of Rose's friends. According to one observer, "Pretty soon half the men in town were in the fight. Each side claimed victory after it was over, so I guess it was about a draw."

Just because the town laws said no booze, it doesn't mean that Derry was really dry. Residents could drink in their own homes, just not in public. There were a number of places where booze could be procured in defiance of the law. The Rockingham Lodge on Island Pond, the Klondike in Londonderry, the Rat Trap on Rail Road Avenue, and numerous Broadway stores would sell liquor if the customer was known to the owner. Usually the constable and the selectmen would face the other way rather than close down these places just to enforce the temperance laws.

In 1898, things began to change. Leonard Pillsbury helped get two prohibitionists elected to the three-member board of selectman. Finally there would be no shilly-shallying and the temperance laws would be enforced.

To combat these clandestine alcohol sales, the anti-liquor men and women formed the Law and Order Society of Derry. The three leaders were the Reverend Hiram Putnam, of Central Congregational Church; Professor George Bingham, the headmaster of Pinkerton Academy; and Leonard Pillsbury. The society employed "spotters" who would ferret out where booze was being sold. Once an illicit seller was identified, the Law and Order Society would raid the place with dozens of its members and the town constable. Each member wore a white ribbon on his or her coat to show publicly their belief in temperance.

The churches were a bastion in the crusade against alcohol. Typical of the prohibitionist sermons was one given in 1899 at St. Luke's Methodist Church. The Reverend S. H. Trow lectured: "Intemperance is a mighty whirlpool into its awful vortex thousands of young men go down every year to ruin and death and no man can tell whose son may be numbered among the dead nor whose daughter may live a living death. It is awful to contemplate these results of intemperance ... restrict the sale of liquor and immediately the number of arrests and crimes become less; open the saloons and disorder and crime multiply; and so goes down to the grave many of our brightest and our prominent young men and brings brutality into the finest natures."

For many years, Derry's chief violator of the liquor laws was the Hotel Bradford, which still stands at the corner of Martin Street and Broadway. It was built in 1882 primarily to provide lodging for commercial travelers who came to town on the railroad. In addition to a restaurant and stable, it had a large barroom. When the board of selectman was tolerant of drinking, the bar operated openly. During the administration of temperance-leaning selectmen, the bar would be closed by the police. With no bar, the hotel would lose money and soon go into bankruptcy. From 1882 to 1899, there had been five different owners or leaseholder's who had gone economically belly-up because drinking men couldn't belly-up to their bar.

A number of the men who ran the hotel tried to find ways to operate secretly as a non-temperance hotel. There were hidden trapdoors everywhere that would allow liquor to be brought clandestinely to individual guest rooms. Secret passages extended from the garret down to the hotel's storehouse in the basement. The story goes that cocktails could be made from gin hidden inside oil lamps and that in some rooms librations would flow by simply turning on a certain valve in the steam-heat radiators.

In July 1899, a grand banquet was held at the Hotel Bradford, sponsored by the Derry Businessman's Association in honor of the twenty-nine-year-old Ralph Thyng. He had just rented the hotel and was reopening it after it had been closed for the previous four months. With the help of his Scottish wife, Adie, as cook and an Irish clerk and a German porter, he hoped to succeed where so many others had failed. Of the thirty-eight merchants in town, only Leonard Pillsbury elected not to come to the celebration. By his federal license, Thyng was allowed to sell liquor but only to out-of-town visitors; locals would have to remain thirsty.

On Wednesday, September 6, 1899, the selectmen, with the approval of Justice of the Peace Frederick Pillsbury, authorized a raid on the hotel. Constable Frank Bradford and Patrolman Nelson Payne led the charge into the building, and bringing up the rear were the stalwart men and women of the Law and Order Society. They went through the building's rooms and halls without finding any illicit materials. The hotel appeared to be so dry that Ralph Thyng could spit cotton. The raiders were about to give up when they came to a locked door on the second floor.

Tavern keeper Thyng refused to open the door to the mysterious room number six. He explained that it was Rose Pillsbury's private room and that he rented the chamber as a place where he "dines and entertains his friends." In the absence of a key, the police tried unsuccessfully to break down the door. Finally a cop was lifted through the transom and opened the door from the inside. In the room were a table, a few chairs, and an ice chest-type refrigerator. Inside the ice box was a case of nicely chilled lager beer.

The cold beer was in effect the smoking gun for which the local police were looking. The bottles were seized by Constable Bradford and hotel owner Thyng was arrested. That afternoon the now dry Rose Pillsbury drafted a "writ of replevin," which is a legal command that material taken illegally must be returned to its rightful owner. Sheriff Abbott took charge of the case of lager until everything could be straightened out. In addition, Rose had Sheriff Abbott arrest Constable Bradford, who was charged with the theft of one case of beer. The constable quickly made bail and went free.

A court hearing was held the next day, with lawyers for the hotel and the town disputing the facts of the case. Rosecrans

Pillsbury, representing himself, said the beer was his private stash and that the police had no legal reason to enter his private room and confiscate his private property. The case had become so politically charged that no local magistrate would rule on the case of Pillsbury and Thyng vs. the Town of Derry. In desperation, the litigation was sent on to the October term of the New Hampshire Supreme Court. The now-warm lager was retained as evidence.

The incident at the Bradford greatly upset the wealthier branch of the Pillsbury family. Rose announced that he was considering closing his West Derry shoe factories. He would take the fifty thousand dollars that he was going to spend in Derry and invest it in a friendlier town. This could spell economic disaster. Almost every Derry man, woman, and child was economically tied to the Pillsbury shoe industry. As a general fact, you either worked in his factory or provided services to his shoe workers.

Soon hundreds of green handbills began to flood downtown Derry. They had almost certainly been clandestinely printed by the Magnet Printing Company, which was owned by Rose Pillsbury. They said:

NOTICE

All persons who are in favor of retaining the business interests of Derry, and protecting private property of whatever name and nature, are requested to meet near the office of **W. S. Pillsbury** at 7 o'clock this P.M.

—Business

At the appointed time, a crowd estimated to number eight hundred filled Broadway. A packing crate was provided for Colonel William Pillsbury to stand on as he addressed the gathering. He reminded the throng that he had "labored thirty years on the interests of Derry." He said his son Rose was about to open another shoe factory in Derry but that he was tired of "being persecuted." Rose was going to find a more appreciative town in which to invest his money.

The elder Pillsbury was followed on the shoe crate by Rose. The younger man had a powerful voice that could be heard for blocks. He retold the story of how his case of beer had been stolen by Constable Bradford and "no man's private property was safe if such action was allowed." Father and son asked the crowd to petition the selectmen to make things right. They also asked the throng to vote for a better board of selectmen at the next election.

The spirited crowd now moved east about fifty feet to stand in front of the furniture store of Leonard Pillsbury and Son. The throng became extremely agitated when Leonard and his son Frederick came out to address them. A lecture on temperance was not what they wanted. The two prohibitionists were shouted down. There were cries from the crowd of "Lynch them" and "String them up." To preserve their lives, Leonard and Fred had to retreat and barricade themselves in their store. Patrolman Nelson Payne read the angry mob the riot act and told the agitated eight hundred to return to their homes. Peace and quiet were restored to Broadway.

On October 3, 1899, the case of Constable Bradford and the Town of Derry versus Rosecrans Pillsbury and Fred Thyng of the Hotel Bradford was heard in the state Supreme Court. The facts were presented to a jury of twelve men. The verdict was rendered in a very speedy manner. Thyng was found not guilty. The raid was illegal and Rose Pillsbury could now reclaim his case of very warm lager.

On December 28, 1899, the businessmen of Derry gave a thank-you banquet at the hotel in honor of the shoe manufacturers of Derry. They wanted to show their gratitude to the rich Pillsburys for supplying so many jobs and for "all the work they have done for the good of the town, that tends to their prosperity." The Pillsbury Company had just announced they were opening a new shoe factory and would be hiring two hundred more workers. Sheriff Abbott was the toastmaster; Rose and Colonel William Pillsbury were beaming during the tribute. There is no mention of Leonard Pillsbury being in attendance. Nor is there any mention of the beverage that was served that night in the hotel.

The next town meeting was held on Tuesday, March 13, 1900, at the town hall in East Derry. More than half the men of the town turned out to vote. The new Chester and Derry trolley made getting to the meeting very easy. For the first time in history, the selectmen ordered that there would be no smoking at Town Meeting and the Nutfield Grange served supper. The meeting started at ten in the morning and was adjourned at 5:45 in the evening.

The near riot on Broadway the previous September was still on the minds of many of the voters. The Republican Party was the dominant political group in town but it was now badly split between two factions. The anti-alcohol group, led by Leonard Pillsbury, was refusing to work with the laissez-faire faction led by Rosecrans Pillsbury. The Democrats took advantage of this split by voting as a bloc. After six hours of balloting, the Democratic Party now controlled the board of selectmen. The wets were in charge.

Two warrant articles were proposed by the dry leaders. They wanted the town to elect three liquor agents who would serve as a watch and ward to ferret out illegal drinking or the selling of liquor. The other article proposed the installation of an eight o'clock curfew, which would affect young people who were hanging around the streets of West Derry. Both articles went down to defeat.

⊗⊗

One of the first things the new board of selectmen did was to appoint a new group of patrolmen. No longer was Nelson Payne on the police force. It was likely he was viewed as being too strongly aligned with Leonard Pillsbury. In a March 1900 letter to the *Derry News*, Leonard revealed that he had asked personally for Payne's reappointment to the Derry police. "He is my personal friend as are all members of his father's family. The way he dispersed last summer, the only mob with which Derry was ever disgraced shows that he is worthy of wearing the blue coat and brass buttons."

Because of the 1899 near riot and the 1900 town meeting, Rose Pillsbury was castigated by some as the cause of much of the town's problems. The *Derry News* said that "now it would be next to impossible for a decent man to get liquor in case of a sickness or accident, there will probably be no difficulty whatever for 'common drinkers' getting all they want, as in the past." Rose Pillsbury quickly fired back: "If I was responsible for one half the acts with which I am charged by my enemies and detractors, I should find no time to devote to a business which is paying in labor alone over $20,000 per month."

District Court Judge William W. Poor had a practical way to deal with the liquor-selling problem in 1900. He said that stores and hotels could stay open plying their trade but every two months they would have to pay a fifty-dollar fine "if they stay in business." In 1904, the temperance people regained control of local government. The town would remain officially dry for the next thirty years. Despite this, none of the old-timers to whom I have talked, remembers any problem finding a drink in Derry during those "dry" years.

Main Street, Derry Village in the early twentieth century. This was the route of the parade in 1865 which celebrated the end of the Civil War.

20.

The End of the Civil War

THE CIVIL WAR WAS A CONFLICT BOTH POLITICAL AND philosophical. Some saw it as a moral crusade to end the sin of slavery; others viewed it as a conflict centering on states rights and the restoration of the Union. By the time of the war's end, in 1865, everyone would recognize the Civil War to be a tragedy beyond belief. It cost the lives of more than six hundred thousand Americans.

The little town of Derry, with a population of about two thousand souls, sent 152 of its sons to fight on southern soil. Of that number, two dozen would not return home alive. Many of these heroes now rest under the green grass of Forest Hill Cemetery in East Derry. Most of their graves are forgotten now except once each year, when a small American flag is placed on each plot on Memorial Day.

The carnage of the Civil War can be better understood by comparing the Derry of 1865 to the much larger Derry of today. The impact of the twenty-four local fatalities in the Civil War would be proportionately equal to the horror that would be felt if more than three hundred Derry men and women were killed in the present war in Iraq.

The Civil War dragged on for four long years. Each week brought news of battles won and lost, of young men from Derry, Londonderry, and Windham being wounded, killed, or taken prisoner. By the spring of 1865, the tide had turned so that a Union victory was seen as a certainty. It was now only a matter of time before the cannons were silenced and all our Johnnys were marching home again. We were weary of war and wanted peace.

On April 9, 1865, the news of the war's end came to Derry Village via the Boston newspapers. The press reported that the surrender would take place that day. At noon, General Ulysses S. Grant was scheduled to accept the surrender from General Robert E. Lee at a place called Appomattox Court House, Virginia, at the home of Wilmer McLean.

A young Pinkerton Academy student was at the post office that morning when the newspapers arrived. Keeping the story to himself, he ran up to the school. He hid himself in the first-floor closet where the rope from the steeple bell hung. Sitting in a crouched position, he kept one hand on the bell's cord and one eye peering through the keyhole. From that awkward position, he could look up the stairs and see the clock on the wall on the second floor. The boy waited anxiously until the time when the newspaper said the surrender was to occur. When the exact minute arrived, he used all his strength to start the steeple bell swinging. To those in Derry Village that noon, the sound of the bell could mean only one thing—victory! The war was over! Peace!

The sexton of the Central Congregational Church, on Crescent Street, heard the bell. In echo to the Pinkerton Academy bell, he rang joyfully his own church's bell. The noise of jubilee was heard up the hill in East Derry. Within minutes, the deep voice of the bell at the First Parish Church was sending glad tidings throughout town. Such a carillon of bells must have been heard in Londonderry, Hampstead, and Chester. Farmers would pause in their plowing, housewives would put down their mending, and children would stop their games to listen to the bells of Derry. So many prayers of thanksgiving must have been offered up when the news of the surrender swept like wildfire through the area.

The students at Pinkerton Academy decided that this was not an appropriate time to be in the classroom. It was a turning point in history and the walls of their classrooms could not contain their excitement. Out onto the academy grounds they streamed. With the end of the war, the school had much to celebrate. There were 121 "Old Boys" from the school in the Army. By war's end, twenty-three academy graduates had died in service to their country. Among the fatalities were Dr. Luther V. Bell (class of 1816) and his kid brother General Louis Bell (class of 1850).

The academy's boys, on their own, decided that such an occasion demanded a parade. The school principal, John P. Newell, agreed that such a momentous event justified a jollification. All the students lined up but quickly decided that something was missing. They didn't have a drum! What's a parade without a drum to measure out the cadence? Even if they could find a drum in Derry Village, none of the boys knew how to play it in a manner fitting such a grand occasion.

To the boy's rescue came sixteen-year-old Helen Adams, a student at the academy and assistant postmaster. She said she could play the martial instrument. She ran into her house and emerged with her brother's drum. She strapped it on over her shoulders and took up her position at the head of the column. Each class formed a separate division behind her in the line of march. All the girls would have been in ankle-length dresses; the boys in knickerbocker pants held up by suspenders.

With Helen as their leader, the academy students marched down the hill toward the present Danforth Circle. Helen was reported to be a "fine drummer and efficient captain." All of the village certainly would have turned out to cheer the marchers in this spontaneous parade. Past the two stores, post office, law office, hotel, and homes they paraded with military precision. With the proud young woman in the lead, they marched up Thornton Street and back up the hill to the school.

When the parade returned to the school grounds, Principal Newell acknowledged their need for celebration and praised the students for their efforts. With that, he ordered everyone back to class. Victory or not, education must go on.

I'm sure that Concord and Manchester that day had a mammoth parade with equestrians and fine brass bands. At the city parks there would likely have been cannons fired and stirring speeches from local politicians. In Washington, D.C., the war-weary hearts would be moved by long rows of Union soldiers parading down Pennsylvania Avenue to be reviewed by President Lincoln. All over the northern states, the streets were festooned with red, white, and blue banners and the evening skies were alight with fireworks. The celebrations in the cities must have been truly grand that day as young and old danced in the streets to celebrate peace.

I wonder, however, if any of these big-city celebrations came close to equaling the excitement in Derry Village that day in April when we rang the bells and Helen Adams led the Pinkerton parade.

Mrs. Flora Stewart in 1867 when she was at a reported age of 117.

21.
Flora Stewart

ACCORDING TO STATISTICS, THE CHANCES OF LIVING TO THE AGE OF 116 are two billion to one. In Londonderry in 1867 there was Flora Stewart, who was reported to have lived past her 117th birthday. The oldest person in the world at present is only 114 years old. Recently, Londonderry saw the passing of John Madden at the venerable age of 103, which made him the oldest man in New Hampshire. Because of her age, Flora was a legend in her own time! Was her tale true? Read on. I'll give you the rest of the story.

Please understand that it is very difficult to research the life of a former slave. Usually census returns didn't list slaves by name. Seldom did a town clerk believe that these servants were significant enough to record their births, marriages, or deaths. They were, after all, just property in the minds of most people in the eighteenth century.

That there were slaves in town is supported by a few documents. In 1773, Derry/Londonderry was credited by the state with twelve male and thirteen female slaves. In 1782, the census recorded locally only three female slaves with no male slaves. It was likely that the black men were off fighting in the American Revolution—a war that was fought over freedom and the rights of man. The last record of slaves here was in 1790, when Robert Fulton, Joseph Hogg, Lemuel Jackson, Robert Moore, and James MacGregor were each listed as owning a single slave.

The 1774 meetinghouse in the neighboring town of Sandown had slave pens, in which the people of color sat during church services. It is almost certain that the East Derry Meeting House—now the First Parish Church—originally had a similarly segregated seating arrangement. This belief is born out by the fact that the East Derry pastor, William Davidson (1720–1797), owned a mother-and-daughter pair of slaves named Poll and Moll.

In what is now the town of Londonderry, a male slave named Toney was owned by Thomas Wallace (1672–1754). This servant must have been a very capable young man because he had been bought for the incredibly large sum of one hundred dollars. His purchase price was a point of pride for Toney. It probably allowed him to lord it over all the other slaves. The story goes that during a spring flood, Toney built himself a raft and went for a sail down the Fourteen Acre Meadow Brook. During his adventure, his craft began to break up and he feared for his life. Toney saw his master watching him from the shore. In panic he screamed to Mr. Wallace to "come and save your hundred dollars."

The pages of the *New Hampshire Gazette,* published in Portsmouth, occasionally contained advertisements by masters seeking the return of their runaway slaves. These notices allow us to better visualize slaves in our state ten generations ago. An ad paid for by William Cotton of Portsmouth on April 22, 1780, seeks the return of his slave Garrack:

STOP THE RUNAWAY

Runaway the ninth of this instant April from his master William Cotton of Portsmouth, tanner, a Negro man about 5 feet 10 inches high, about 25 years of age, a stout, spry fellow, upon the yellow order, a stripe upon his cheeks, left-hand little finger broken off; two stripes from his nipple round to his nipple, has on a yellow colored pea jacket lined with a woolen check and a blue jacket, buck leather breaches, a dark brown cap milled . . . Whoever will take up said negro and convey him to his master shall have 45 pounds reward and necessary charges paid by me.

The same slave was captured but ran away again in August, and is further described as speaking broken English in a deep voice.

A *Gazette* advertisement in 1779 offered fifty dollars for the return of Caesar, a thirty-year-old slave who was "very fond of singing." On November 9, 1779, there were nearly identical advertisements for the sale of two women.

TO BE SOLD, A LIKELY NEGRO

woman about 28 years old, born in America, will suit town or country service. Enquire of the printer.

TO BE GIVEN AWAY, A NEGRO WOMAN

with a sum of money. Enquire of the printer.

It is likely that the latter slave was either elderly or in some way unable to do much work so, her owner was willing to pay someone to take her away. Sad!

According to the story, Flora Stewart was been born in Boston around 1750 and grew up as a slave on a plantation. (Slavery would not be abolished in Massachusetts until 1783 and was not technically illegal in New Hampshire until 1857.) While young, Flora was sold and taken to Windham, New Hampshire. where she was "brought up" by a member of the Simpson family. In 1775 there were thirteen slaves in that town. Around 1784, it is believed that she was emancipated and moved to Derry a free woman.

For many years, she was employed by Dr. Isaac Thom, who lived on East Derry Hill. In addition to his medical practice, he was the town's postmaster and ran a tavern at the site of today's Shepard Park. With nine children in the Thom family, it was certain that Flora was kept very busy as a housekeeper.

Around 1799, she married Isaiah Stewart, who lived in the Western part of the state. The wedding was held at the Thom home and the Doctor's daughters pitched in to make it a properly festive occasion. The newlyweds moved to Litchfield, New Hampshire, where they had three children: Isaiah born in 1801; George in 1807; Salona in 1809. In time Flora separated from her husband, due to his chronic drunkenness. She returned to Derry and was employed as a housekeeper at the home of Attorney James Thom, the son of her former employer.

In the 1830s, there was a great religious revival in Derry, sparked by members of the Methodist church of Derry Village. Flora was caught up in the spirit and found religion. An 1883 *Derry News* article reported that "prior to this she was fractious and irritable; had no patience with the children; now she is quite the reverse." After this conversion, she became an example to the whole town as a prayer warrior and as a righteous member of the Methodist Church on Nesmith Street.

Around 1840, Flora Stewart bought a little piece of land in Londonderry where she and her daughter Salona built a small house of their very own. Here for the next quarter-century, the two of them would live. Flora was employed at the home of George Pinkerton and could easily walk to work. Salona was also employed as a housekeeper and was reported to have earned a dollar seventy-five a week.

The two sons by contrast, are remembered as being rather adverse to work of any kind; they instead, preferred to sit for hours in the sun, employed in idleness. For a donation of two cents, they would wiggle their ears to the amusement of one and all. It is said that they shared a fondness for drink. In the1850 census, George was listed as a forty-three year old laborer in Manchester. After this, he seems to have disappeared from the area. It is said that Isaiah Jr. went to sea as a young man. In 1870 he was listed in Londonderry as a seventy-year-old laborer and then disappeared from the records. It was said that he was the strongest man to ever have lived in Londonderry. Reportedly he could hoist a barrel of flour on his shoulder and carry it up two flights of stairs. At the age of eighty he could still do handsprings. There is no evidence that any of the three Stewart children married or left descendants.

When the Manchester and Lawrence Railroad was built in 1849, the track passed only a few feet from Flora's house. She allowed the workers—but not their horses—to freely draw water from her well. One day Isaiah came home and was told by his mother that the railroad workers had been "saucy" to her. He was furious. He grabbed a club and went to the workers' camp. "In very short order there were 17 railroad workers stretched all over the ground." This area where the tracks crossed the Manchester Road was known locally as N****r's Crossing. Fortunately, that place-name is now seldom used and soon, I hope, will be disposed of into the dustbin of historical anachronisms.

After the Civil War, Flora Stewart's age had made her a local figure of prominence. On November 5, 1867, she was invited to have dinner with Manchester's mayor Frederick Smyth. To save the 117-year-old woman from the fatigue of traveling the one and a half miles to the Broadway depot, it was arranged to have the train pick her up right at her door. Such a courtesy was never offered by the railroad to anyone before or since.

Flora was met at the Manchester train station by the mayor's fancy carriage. After dinner at the mayor's North Elm Street mansion, a public reception was held. The Kimball Photography Company was engaged to take a picture of the old lady so the curious could see what a 117-year-old woman looked like. A Manchester newspaper reported that Flora was the oldest person in New England and assured his readers that the photograph would be "colored." Upon her return to Londonderry, Flora herself announced that she "didn't see a prettier lady on the streets of the city than she was herself."

To many in Derry and Londonderry, Flora was viewed as a saintly women and helping her in her last years was a blessing in itself. She was after all, the Methuselah of the town! Flora was also the area's leading foe of intemperance. She refused, even on her death bed, to take a dram of whiskey as medicine.

Many locals would make pilgrimages to her tiny home to hear stories about the old days. She was, to them, the last leaf holding onto the oak tree in winter. She remembered Major Pinkerton, patriot Matthew Thornton, and even Lafayette. She had been alive during the Revolutionary War and witnessed the birth of America. She could remember, with incredible clarity, every detail of the time she served dinner to General George Washington.

Flora Stewart died on August 17, 1868, and was mourned by all who knew her. She was buried in the Valley Cemetery, Londonderry. Next to her lies her daughter, Salona, who died in 1887 at the age of seventy-eight.

All my life I have known the story of the saintly Flora Stewart. I have paused by her gravestone many times. Recently I began to rethink her story and the numbers just don't work. I don't know if I'm the first to question the story. I really do hate to be the debunker of a local legend but . . . .

According to the documents, her oldest child would have been born when Flora was about fifty-one years old and her youngest when she was nearly sixty. Such an advanced age for motherhood is rather incredible—especially in the nineteenth century. In 1850 she was recorded in the federal census as seventy-six years old and so was born in 1774. Ten years later, in 1860, she was listed as 102 years old and thus must have been born in 1758. Seven years, later in 1867, she was claiming to be 117 years old; this would make her birth year as 1750. In just twenty years, according to the official records, Flora Stewart had aged forty-one years!

I know that few slaves knew their age with any degree of certainty. However this discrepancy in the reported age of Flora Stewart is significantly more than being just a few years off. We are separated from Flora Stewart by about fourteen decades, which makes it difficult to arrive at absolute truth—but here is my scenario, based on my analysis of the available facts.

Flora Stewart was likely born around 1774 and was taken as a small child to Windham, where she lived with the Simpson family. She probably came to Derry as a teenager and supported herself as a house servant. She married Isaiah in 1799 when she was twenty-five years old and they had their last child in 1809, when she was about thirty-five. During the last decade of her life, Flora was feeble and unable to work. Perhaps to gain status and respect, she began to add extra years to her age. In 1868, at her passing, she was probably ninety-three years of age. While this was certainly a respectable longevity for a woman of the nineteenth century, it was nowhere near her self-claimed age of five score and seventeen years. Am I absolutely sure my facts and analysis are right? No—but I think they make sense and will stand up to impartial scrutiny.

22.
Minstrel Days

DURING THE NINETEENTH CENTURY, THE MINSTREL SHOW WAS A popular form of entertainment. The performers—both black and white—put burnt cork on their faces and outlined their mouths with white greasepaint to produce an exaggerated African racial appearance. Touring troops visited big cities and small towns, bringing their form of entertainment to the masses. Performers affected an over-the-top southern drawl and wore gaudy costumes. The slapstick humor was usually based on stereotyped views of blacks. This racially insensitive form of entertainment began to decline at the end of the nineteenth century when vaudeville replaced it. By the 1930s, radio and movies had eclipsed vaudeville.

A minstrel show was normally presented in three acts. At the start of a performance, the black-faced stars would rush onto the stage and sit in a semicircle facing the audience. The well-dressed man in the center was called the interlocutor and functioned as the master of ceremonies. On either side of him were the end men, who sported names like Mr. Bones, Jimbo, Sambo, and Rastus. They would engage in snappy dialogue and tell jokes. Dance routines called "walk arounds" and tambourine shaking were the usual showstopping tours de force. The second act was more like a variety show, with cast members playing bones, doing acrobatic stunts, singing, or performing magic. The third act was often a play, usually a take-off on a serious drama, such as by Shakespeare or Gilbert and Sullivan. A shortened version of *Uncle Tom's Cabin* was standard fare.

Bell's Opera House on West Broadway in 1897.

On January 10, 1890, George F. Rollins, the manager of the Derry Opera House, announced some exciting news. On the evening of Saturday, January 18, his hall would host a performance by the world-famous Haverley's Minstrels. The opera house had been built in 1888 but was heavily damaged in a fire the next year. It was, however, immediately rebuilt. Its second-floor auditorium had a seating capacity of just over four hundred spectators when you added in its "sharply sloping balcony." The three-story building was torn down in 1953 and replaced by the modern buildings now at 31-35 East Broadway.

Haverley's Minstrels was one of America's four largest touring shows. Impresario Jack Haverley had been leading his United Mastodon Minstrels since 1864. He had brought his brand of entertainment from coast to coast in America and had performed before the crowned heads of Europe. One poster shows his uniformed band marching up the stairs of the U.S. Capitol in 1881 to perform at President Garfield's inaugural. Among the songs that had been written for his show were "Oh, Dem Golden Slippers" and "Good Night Irene."

Soon the performance was being advertised in posters around Derry. The show was promised to be "the acme of refinement" and "the world's mirth provoker." There would be twenty-five performers plus a uniformed brass band. The performers would present "beautiful music and delightful dancing and a grand reproduction of life on an old plantation." There was also to be a performance by Lou

Ayr, who was billed as the world's strongest man; performances on mandolins and guitars, jubilee (gospel) singing; and a comedian. Billy Bryant would sing the hit song of 1890: "Down Went McGinty to the Bottom of the Sea." The main performer was to be Sam Lucas (1850–1916), who was America's most famous black performer. This talented singer, actor, and composer would later be called the "grand old man of the negro stage." Lucas stared in *Uncle Tom's Cabin* on both stage and screen.

Manager Rollins paid the Minstrels one hundred dollars for their one-show visit to Derry. This was a huge sum in 1890 and corresponds to many thousands of dollars today. To increase ticket sales, the brass band would march down Broadway and give a free concert in front of the opera house. The price of admission was: floor seats, fifty cents; first-row seats in the balcony, thirty-five cents; gallery seats, twenty-five cents. Rollins said he would meet all of his expenses only if he sold every seat in the house. Having a world-class show by Haverley's Minstrels would yield instant prestige for the Derry Opera House.

The advance publicity did the trick. The show was a sell-out! The audience showed up early in anticipation of a night to remember. The crowd hushed as onto the stage walked four men who sang "We Are All Here, Do Thyself No Harm." They were followed by minstrel manager Fletcher Smith, who announced with regret that seven of his stars were sick with "the grippe." The entire first act would have to be skipped. There would be no walk around, no snappy patter between Sambo and Rastus, and no Sam Lucas. Even Jack Haverley was AWOL.

The rest of the show was less than memorable! Each performer as he came on stage was introduced as "the champion of the world" or "world renowned." The audience was not convinced. Typical was the performer who walked on stage with a harmonica in hand ("the champion harmonica player of the world"). He announced he would pay one hundred dollars to any one in Derry who was better than he was. There was apparently no one in the audience who had a mouth organ in his frock coat that night. The world champion played "Home Sweet Home" for his audience and then rendered the same song on a guitar, a mandolin, and a banjo. According to the critics, each musical rendering sounded more like a "rehearsal" than a finished performance. The artist left the stage to the sound of hissing, catcalls, and boos from an "insulted, indignant audience."

As soon as the curtain came down, the performers snuck out the back door. As they made their way to the railroad depot, they were met by a barrage of eggs and rocks thrown by Derry theater critics. The next week opera house manager George Rollins published an apology in the *Derry News*. He claimed that he didn't have any prior knowledge about the minstrel troupe. He had taken it on face value that it really was Haverley Minstrels. Only after the show did he discover the group consisted of half a dozen shoe factory workers from Haverhill, Massachusetts, who thought they could make a few bucks by putting one over on the rural rubes of Derry. They hired a brass band for the day, fashioned a few costumes, put together a few musical acts, and voila—a minstrel show by the Haverhill, ah, I mean Haverley's Minstrels.

The Derry audience was reported to have felt that they were "duped, defrauded and cheated." out of their fifty-cent admission. Rollins wrote that he trusted that the "public will not blame me in this matter." In the future he promised to hire only "first class" acts.

By 1905, the Adams Memorial Building had become Derry's opera house of choice and the old hall was converted into apartments and a lodge room. Within another decade, live performances were replaced by motion pictures at the Scenic or the Broadway movie theater.

By 1910 minstrel shows were passé. The only performers who continued to appear on stage in black face were Al Jolson and George Jessel. The radio and TV show *Amos n' Andy,* though popular for decades, was in time judged to be offensive to our African-American neighbors. Minstrel shows continued to be performed in Derry by local civic and fraternal groups right up to the 1960s. Now the minstrel show has been almost universally thought of as an embarrassing part of our history. The civil rights movement of recent decades has educated us all to disdain humor based on racial stereotyping. Archie Bunker deserves much of the credit for teaching us the foolishness of bigotry.

23.

The Great Broadway Fire of 1882

FOR THE FIRST 175 YEARS OF THE HISTORY OF DERRY, THERE wasn't much offered in the way of fire protection. In 1828 the voters at Town Meeting authorized the appointment of six fire wards. Their responsibility was to direct bucket brigades and to ring the church bells to bring out the neighbors. The voters rejected paying for fire hooks and other such equipment for the wards.

On August 1, 1882, the Goodwin family barn in western Derry was razed by fire. In reaction to this calamity, an anonymous resident wrote to the *Derry News* on August 4 to propose that the town provide fire protection in West Derry. The writer also suggested careful inspection of the shoe factory to make sure the doors opened outward, as law required. The next week, editor Charles Bartlett, of the *Derry News*, responded with the suggestion that the town buy hand-tub fire engines for Derry Village and Derry Depot. Bartlett prophetically told his readers that "it is better to be prepared for fire even if we don't anticipate any immediate danger—for it is likely to come when we least expect it."

Derry at that time consisted of three villages—East Derry, Derry Village, and West Derry. The latter was also known as Derry Depot. The town's population was about twenty-three hundred residents. (This is about 7 percent of the population in 2007.) Derry Village and West Derry were economic rivals, with each claiming to be the commercial center of town. West Derry was the newest part of town, having been established only after the railroad came through in 1849.

Broadway in 1877.

West Derry was by every definition a classic self-contained village. Economically, it could stand by itself and was surrounded by large tracts of farmland and forest. If you left the village and walked east toward the present traffic circle, you would have to hike nearly a mile before you could cross a road or see another house. Broadway was a dirt road—as were all the other roads in town. It would be another eighteen years before the first automobile visited Derry.

The village was centered on the depot of the Manchester and Lawrence Railroad. In the Broadway area there was the Colburn, Fuller shoe factory, run by Colonel William Pillsbury; three blocks of stores; hotel, post office, and livery stable; a one-room schoolhouse; a sawmill at Horne's Pond; and the H. P. Hood icehouse. There were probably a dozen homes in the neighborhood. The lodge of the Odd Fellows met on the third floor of one building and the newly formed Baptist church met in the auditorium of Smith Hall. During the summer of 1882, Miss Bradford's Ice Cream Parlor at the Railroad House hotel used three thousand pounds of ice, two hundred gallons of cream, and five hundred eggs.

It was 3:30 on a warm Saturday afternoon, August 19, 1882, when workmen noticed smoke coming from the stable of the hotel. (This was where Benson's Hardware is today.) By the time the men could shout for help, the embers had spread to the adjoining hotel.

Within minutes, the three-story structure was doomed. So fast was the destruction that hardly anything could be saved, and guests were forced to flee for their lives.

Immediately, a brisk northwest breeze sent the sparks high into the sky and "the tongues of flames stretched out toward adjoining buildings." The fire was now spreading south across Broadway and attacked more buildings.

Area residents attempted the hopeless task of saving their houses. They soaked their clothes and covered their heads with towels, blankets, and doormats. Colonel William Pillsbury stationed his shoe workers on the roof of his factory to douse any flames. Fortunately, this roof was made of fireproof slate and was spared. It was a close call, however. The shoe factory's tenement immediately to the south was destroyed.

Soon the citizens realized that their only chance of saving what was left of the village was to make a stand at the Bly house. This large structure was immediately west of the hotel. If this home burned, the flames would certainly jump to the shoe factory. And if that was allowed to happen, the rest of the village would follow down the fiery path to destruction.

Pillsbury had his superintendent R. R. Merrick direct the fight to save the Bly house. A few brave men climbed onto its roof and used buckets of water to drench the wood shingles and cool the building so the windows wouldn't shatter. The men kept to their post even while part of the house was enveloped in flames. It was because of their courage that much of the village was spared.

With each passing minute, the fire grew hotter. The flying sparks ignited acres of underbrush to the south of the village. The Carmi Norton home half a mile away was set afire by blowing embers.

Soon the flames approached the depot, and in an instant the passenger station was gone. The intense heat even caused the heavy iron train rails to be ripped from their ties. The hellish temperatures twisted the metal into grotesque shapes rising out of the railroad bed.

Flames were consuming more and more of the economic and social life of Derry. Soon the post office was no more. The Odd Fellows lodge, Pillsbury's store, the Baptist chapel, and the pool hall quickly joined it in ruins. George A. Colby had just built a home in West Derry and only the day before moved in the furniture. Soon the home was reduced to a glowing pile of embers.

Derry, for all practical purposes, was at the mercy of the fire. There was no fire-fighting equipment. There were no rain clouds on the horizon. All citizens could do was pray and try to save what few belongings they could from their homes, factories, and shops. The people of Derry were resigned to just waiting until the fire slowly burned itself out.

The engineer on a railroad train that was approaching the station quickly saw that West Derry was in deep trouble. He jumped from the locomotive and ran to the telegraph office. From there he sent a frantic request for help to the railroad's headquarters in Manchester. At 3:40, the railroad alerted the Manchester City Fire Department of Derry's peril. The city's fire chief reacted immediately. He ordered his men to rush to Derry's rescue. They hooked up their mighty Amoskeag steam fire engine called, the Fire King, to a team of four horses. Through the streets of the city they galloped at breakneck speed to reach the Manchester Railroad freight depot. They put Fire King, a relief steam pumper, and a hose reel onto a flatbed railroad car. The fire chief commandeered a boxcar to carry the team of four horses and a passenger car for a crew of twenty firemen. At four o'clock the train was speeding along the twelve miles of iron tracks toward Derry. At 4:19 the Manchester firemen were on Broadway. The amount of time that elapsed from the first notification in Manchester to their arrival in Manchester was just thirty-nine minutes!

Quickly the Manchester professionals realized that the first problem was to secure a supply of water. The nearest source was the diminutive Aiken Brook, which flowed southward from Horne's Pond and crossed Broadway to the west of the fire. Teams of men with shovels were sent to dredge the streambed and build a dam to create a reservoir. The firemen were forced to lay out 1,558 feet of hose to provide the water to quench the fire. The Fire King would continue to pump water nearly continuously for the next twenty-four hours.

The owner of Jones's Hotel doled out coffee and doughnuts to those fighting the fire. The next morning he offered a free breakfast to all victims and firemen. He served up a hundred pounds of beefsteak, platters of ham, and many, many dozens of eggs.

Within less than four hours, all that remained of most of downtown Derry was "blackened chimneys and smoldering ruins." Now it was time to start over. Immediately crews from the railroad began to replace the fire-twisted tracks. By 7:10 in the evening, the first passenger car passed over the restored tracks.

The next morning, the *Derry News* distributed a single-page "extra" to the hundreds of spectators who came to see the destruction. The Bartlett & Shepard Fire Insurance Company of Derry sponsored the "extra."

The losses were staggering. In total, some twenty-four stores, offices, homes, and other buildings were destroyed. Much of the loss was not covered by insurance. Destroyed were the Railroad House Hotel, the W.S. Pillsbury Store building, W.S. Pillsbury's tenement, the L.H. & W. S. Pillsbury store, Rollins & Smith's store, and the Caleb Colby residence.

Also, Norton's butcher shop, the Colburn, Fuller leather storehouse, Bessie's Millinery, the H.P. Hood icehouse and storage building, Sutton's Barber Shop, W. O. Ladd's Jewelry store, Hammond's Harness Shop, and the Echo Lodge, Odd Fellows.

Also, the post office, Plummer's Pool Hall, the Telegraph office, Smith's Hall, Pattee's law office, the Boley residence, the railroad passenger station, the railroad water station, the railroad freight depot, and the railroad section house.

There were many other buildings damaged by fire, heat, and smoke. The Baptist church lost what sacramental items it had at Smith's Hall. Lambert's Coronet Band saw the destruction of all its instruments and uniforms.

It was certainly regarded as a miracle that there was no loss of human life. Thirteen hogs in the hotel's stable were killed. Among this sea of tragedies was also the death of Floss, the beloved white-haired dog belonging to Henry May, a teamster for the Rollins & Smith's general store. Floss used to ride throughout town next to his master in the grocery store's delivery wagon. To the notice of the animal's passing, Editor Bartlett added "Requiescat in Pace."

While the ruined buildings were still smoldering, the citizens of Derry were planning how to begin again. Soon West Derry would begin to rise, phoenix-like, from its ashes. By Monday, James Sutton had erected a large tent on Broadway to serve as a temporary barbershop. Rollins & Smith's general store had leased a barn and moved in some of its stock from its Derry Village store. All this happened while Broadway was lined with furniture rescued from burning buildings.

Leonard and William Pillsbury took only three days to put up a twenty-four-by-thirty-foot building to sell dry goods, groceries, grain, and furniture. The post office opened in a nearby store. The Baptists held services at the nearby one-room school. The railroad ticket office operated from stationmaster Priest's living room. Makeshift passenger and freight depots were up within days. A bigger station (the present Depot Steakhouse) was erected and opened by the end of October—less than seventy days after the fire.

Within the year, Alden Bradford Smith replaced his ruined Railroad House hotel with a three-story, sixty-by-fifty-foot building. It was built in the popular French style with a mansard roof, an ornamental tower, and several piazzas. It was painted light green with an elephant green trim. Smith named the new forty-room building the Hotel Bradford. This building still stands at the corner of Martin Street and Broadway. The piazzas have long since been converted into stores.

The Pillsbury brothers soon began to build a new store. They chose the popular Queen Anne style of architecture for their cash-only emporium. It was to be bigger and better than their old store. The color was "elephant green with a narrow red stripe and clapboards of old gold." It also had a mansard roof. This building would be destroyed in a 1934 fire.

The Odd Fellows built a new lodge in 1884 but it was destroyed in an 1897 blaze. The third Odd Fellows Hall burned in 1963. The lot is now the site of Cumberland Farms and Cutter's Hallmark Stores. Smith's Hall was also rebuilt, but was destroyed in a 1979 fire.

There was some definite good that arose out of the tragedy of the great fire of 1882. The citizens were forced to confront the need for a fire department. Only two days after the fire, a meeting was held at Association Hall in Derry Village to decide on a course of action. A letter to the *Derry News* a week after the fire counseled, "You have been warned . . . penny wise and pound foolish is a poor currency for such a town as Derry to deal in." At the annual town meeting in March 1883, the citizens voted to spend three thousand dollars to establish three separate village fire departments. The taxpayers authorized the spending of fifteen hundred dollars for Derry Depot, nine hundred for Derry Villages and six hundred for East Derry. The first engine house for West Derry was near the site of the present municipal center on Manning Street. In 1899, the brick firehouse (now the Fire Hall Restaurant) opened.

24.

Franklin Evans, the Derry Monster

PROBABLY THE WORST MAN TO EVER LIVE IN DERRY WAS FRANKLIN Benjamin Evans. He was born in 1810 in the little town of Strafford, which is about thirty miles to the northeast of Nutfield. He was raised the son of a poor dirt farmer. Early in his life, Franklin decided that the classroom was not where he wanted to spend his days. He dropped out of the district school before his teenage years. He remained semiliterate and his known manuscripts show that he could write only in ill-formed capital letters. Around 1839 he married Mrs. Hannah Peavey and became the stepfather of her children by a previous marriage. A daughter, Vienna, was born in 1835 and a son, Benjamin Franklin Evans, in1840. During the next decade the family expanded with the birth of two more daughters. In time they would leave Strafford and live variously in Salem and Lawrence, Massachusetts, and in Manchester, New Hampshire.

Around 1845, Franklin found religion. He attended some Adventist church services in Manchester and felt the call to preach. He was an apt student and soon could quote chapter and verse of the Bible as "proofs" of the road to salvation. Among the ill educated and un-churched, he developed quite a following. When preaching, he would accept anything into the collection basket, including produce and old clothes. The religious leaders in the city rejected him as an uneducated buffoon and an opportunist. It was said that he frequently kept all his neighbors awake at night with his loud prayers and exhortations to his congregation, which usually consisted of just himself and his family.

Franklin Evans, (1810-1874), the Derry monster.

To support himself, Evans sold his services as a procurer of medicinal herbs. Most towns had a man like him. In Chester, "Doctor" John Dunlap (1780–1867) would wander the fields and forests gathering roots, twigs, bark, and plants. These herbs he would sell to local doctors, storekeepers, and pharmacists. Soon Franklin was being called "Doctor" Evans. Now, for a fee, he would offer his medical services to members of the lower classes. He sported a long, dignified beard and possessed an easy, glib way of speaking that made him believable to his patients. His high, whining voice and his demeanor marked him as a true New Hampshire "swamp Yankee." To his many skeptics, he was only an irritating town character. His ignorance of most things medical was obvious to everybody—except to those few who were even more ignorant than "Doctor" Evans.

Around 1850, Franklin and Hannah Evans ceased to live together. She kept the children in Salem and he became a wanderer. Being penniless and having nowhere else to go, he moved to Derry, which was home to a number of his near relations. He moved in with his stepson Gardner Peavey on Brandy Rock Road. Here in Derry he continued to be a forest stalker, always in pursuit of elusive healing plants in nature's medicine cabinet.

On Hall's Village Road in northern Derry, there was the little home of Stephen and Eliza Mills. He was a day laborer and she did what she could. Within their single-story fifteen-by-thirty-foot home they raised five children, ranging from a newborn girl to a six-year-old boy and including four-year-old twins, Mary and Nancy Mills. The twenty-seven-year-old mother was a cousin of Franklin Evans.

On the evening of October 15, 1850, Mrs. Mills locked her children in the house and made the mile-long walk to where her husband was working in Hampstead. During her absence, Evans made an unannounced visit. Finding the house dark and all locked up, he put his ear to the door and heard the sound of a child moaning. His curiosity got the better of him and he snuck into the house through an unlocked window. There, in the dim light, he found four children fast asleep. Sitting up awake, however, was four-year-old Nancy, who appeared to be sick. "Doctor" Evans examined the child and determined she "could not live until morning."

Franklin Evans picked up the child in his arms and walked out of the house. He "resolved to kill her" and dissect the child's body "for surgical purposes." In his perverted mind, he justified the murder in the interest of medical science. He would be a better doctor if he better understood human physiology. After walking a distance into the dark woods, he put Nancy down on the ground and strangled her with his bare hands.

After removing her clothes, he examined the lifeless body of Nancy Mills. Evans soon discovered that the child's hip and spine were deformed. He now decided not to cut up the child to explore her internal organs. In his confession, he explained he did this partly because the cadaver wasn't "perfect" but also out of "a feeling of remorse and terror." By the junction of two little streams, Evans found the rotten stump of an old chestnut tree. He used his strength to lift up the stump. Into the cavity created by the tree's roots he threw the body of Nancy Mills. Immediately he replaced the rotting chestnut stump to cover the body of the innocent child. There she has rested since 1850; her exact burial spot has never been found.

Stephen and Eliza Mills arrived home that night around nine o'clock and discovered little Nancy was missing. They checked at a nearby house to see if she had wandered there. Not finding their daughter, unbelievably the parents went to bed, and did not continue their search until the next morning. The family arose at their normal hour and at his usual time Dad went off to work. About mid-morning, the mother told a couple of neighbors about the missing child. These people immediately began to search the area for the four-year-old girl. Soon the Derry selectmen were informed about the situation.

For the next few days, about forty of the town's men went looking for Nancy. The selectmen offered a one-hundred-dollar reward for her recovery. The only clue to her possible whereabouts was that six-year-old Stephen Mills Jr. told the authorities that he saw a man wearing blue overalls climb into the house via the window and carry Nancy away. The Mills family were moved to the town's poor farm. Here they remained as town charges until 1847. During the 1850s, Mary, the other twin, would die and two other daughters would be born into the Mills family.

The day after the murder, Franklin Evans tried to act normally. He wandered around Derry looking for ways to make a buck. He called on at least five homes. At the General Derby mansion on Lane Road, he borrowed a pick and shovel so he could go into the woods to find medicinal roots. Over the next year, he tried a number of times, unsuccessfully, to find the spot where he had buried the child. Many times he was scared off by groups of people hunting for chestnuts.

Evans remained in Derry for more than a year after the murder. Every day it was said he talked about the missing girl, speculating on her whereabouts or fate. The local authorities suspected Evans of abducting the child but never charged him because of lack of any evidence. He lived for a while with his brother James, who operated a blacksmith shop on the corner of Hampstead and Adams Pond Roads. In the fall of 1851, Franklin Evans left Derry and moved out of state.

The Derry murderer next surfaced locally in Manchester in 1856, when he moved in with his stepdaughter. Here he continued his career as an herb doctor and held Adventist church services. After a while he moved to Concord with a new wife, who took in washing to support the family. In 1862, his son Benjamin enlisted in the army to fight in the Civil War. During the war, Franklin divided his time between Boston and Concord. He was now making his living as a procurer of liquor and prostitutes for soldiers and sailors. Benjamin was seriously wounded in October 1863 in the Battle of Raccoon Ford, Virginia. During his recovery in Candia, his father moved in with him and went around the county collecting funds for his son's support. All money collected, however, was used to support Franklin Benjamin Evans and not Benjamin Franklin Evans. After his recovery, the disabled Benjamin reenlisted in the Army. As a member of the Veterans Brigade, he would have served as an aide in a military hospital. After the war, Benjamin settled in Derry.

The remainder of the decade of the 1860s was not kind to Franklin Evans. More and more acquaintances began to view him as a lowlife and a pariah. He hired a hall in Manchester to hold Adventist services but failed to win any followers. His "remarks were so foolish and he aced so rash, like a lunatic" that the local Adventist church refused him fellowship. Most viewed him as a "mean sneaking hypocrite" who even if he had money still begged for money for food. It was said that once Evans claimed to be hungry and the charitable Adventists gave him twenty dollars. Later they found that he used the money to purchase a fancy meerschaum smoking pipe.

In 1872, the sixty-two-year-old Franklin Evans migrated to Northwood, New Hampshire. This new home was only a few miles from his birthplace in Strafford. By now his second wife had left him and his children were avoiding his company. He moved in with his sister, Deborah Day. Also in the farmhouse was his niece, the Civil War widow Susan Lovering, age thirty, and her daughter Georgianna (Georgie) age twelve. According to his confessions, Franklin Evans was soon sleeping with his niece, his preteen grandniece, and his grandniece's best friend.

Evans claimed that after a few months, Georgie threatened to turn him in to the authorities on the charges of counterfeiting and pornography. Not wanting to be put in the county lockup, Franklin Evans had to find a way to silence the young girl. He later clamed that he was led on the road to murder by an evil spirit that "seemed to bear a human form." At other times he said voices in his head directed his actions.

On October 25, 1872, Evans lured young Georgie into the woods on the pretext of trapping pigeons. There in the dark forest, he strangled his grandniece. With his pocketknife, he cut her into pieces "to gain some knowledge of the human system that might be of use to me as a doctor" He scattered the parts in a swamp.

Within days, local police had trained their efforts into the disappearance of Georgie Lovering onto her great-uncle Franklin. He was their only suspect. During the interrogation, the police used stealthy, trickery, and threats to wrest a confession from the murderer. For days Evans denied knowledge of any crime. He told the police he thought she had probably run off with a man. Without a body, there was no way to convict Evans of anything. Finally, in desperation, the sheriff sent out for a couple of bottles of whiskey. In a few hours the now drunk Franklin Evans finally confessed to the murder. In return for the truth, the police told him that once he showed them where the body was, they would help him escape to Canada. Evans took a search party to Georgie's multiple graves and immediately discovered that the police had lied. He was not to be allowed to escape to Quebec. He was handcuffed and thrown back into jail. The body parts were collected and given a Christian burial.

The murder trial was held at the county seat in Exeter. The presiding judge was Charles Doe (1830–1896), who had been born at the General Derby mansion in Derry. The trial lasted just three days and the jury took only twelve minutes to find Evans guilty of murder in the first degree. His punishment was to hang by the neck until dead.

While in the Exeter jail, he had plenty of down-time. He took advantage of the free time to write in his journal. He complained that the lockup was "dark and lonsom." Most of his writings were about the visions he was experiencing. One entry said that: "I saw the Blessed saviour standing at the foot of my bead with a gold vessel in his hands with all manner fruit that I never saw before in all My life . . . I then trid to ris I then woak Praising god I felt so happy and have not lost much time in surving god Night and day, for it is all my theme." He later wrote that God told him facts about the future. "I do believe the World will have its final end in 1888 . . . Jesus will come and set up his everlasting kingdom glory to god for what he has shon me and what he had don for me sence I have ben to this Plaice. He also wrote poetry. The last lines in a hymn of eleven stanzas are:

O glories day o blessed hope my hart leaps
Forward at the though when, in that
Happey, happey land we no more
Take the parting hand.

Immediately after the trial, he was taken to the state prison in Concord. State law then required a year and a day between the pronouncement of the death sentence and an actual execution. While confined to his cell, Evans spent much of his waking hours reading his Bible and denying his guilt. Just before the date of his hanging, the prison warden and the chaplain convinced him that he couldn't get into heaven without confessing his sins. For hours he dictated to the warden his autobiography, which included the murders of both Nancy Mills and Georgie Lovering. One of his last acts was to sell his body for fifty dollars to the Dartmouth Medical School. Before accepting the money, he checked the notes very carefully to make sure they weren't counterfeit. The money was believed to have been sent to his son in Derry.

At exactly 11:01 A.M. on February 18, 1874, Franklin Evans was walked out into the prison courtyard after a night spent in confession and prayer. Spectators from the general public were admitted to the execution upon presenting a ticket obtained from the warden. The gallows was freshly painted a bright blue for the occasion. Together the high sheriff, chaplain, guards, and Evans climbed the thirteen steps up to the twelve-foot-high scaffold. Evans did not tremble or show any emotion. When everything was in place, the high sheriff placed a black hood over Evans's head. Franklin Evans was then handcuffed and his legs bound. A three-quarter-inch hemp rope of thirteen strands, tied in a hangman's noose, was positioned over his head; the knot positioned just behind his left ear.

When given the opportunity, Evans chose to make no last speech or apologize for his deeds. In this macabre theater, the last act came when High Sheriff Odlin read the warrant for the execution. The final words Franklin Evans would ever hear was the phrase "and may God have mercy upon your soul." Immediately, Odlin put his foot on the spring and Franklin Evans's body fell ten feet through the trapdoor. He plunged to his death "as a log would have fallen" if it had been attached to a rope. A doctor was immediately dispatched to determine if the murderer was dead. He was not. It would take fully nineteen minutes before his breathing ceased and his heart stopped beating. The monster that was Franklin Evans was then no more.

Souvenir photographs of the body of Franklin Evans on the dissecting table at Dartmouth were later sold throughout the state.

Perhaps this was a way for the medical school to recoup the fifty dollars it spent to purchase the cadaver.

∽∽

The murderer of little Nancy Mills and Georgie Lovering was the fourteenth person to be executed in the state of New Hampshire; there would, in time, be ten more. The last person to go to the gallows was rapist-murderer Howard Long in 1939. At present there is no one on "death row" in our state. The current form of execution is by lethal injection or by hanging. In a recent poll, only an estimated 35 percent of the state's residents are in favor of retaining the death penalty. The last time Derry citizens were officially queried on the subject was at the 1844 town meeting. We voted 28–162 to retain capital punishment in the state.

The road that used to lead to the Mills family home in Derry has long been closed and is now relegated to just a pleasant overgrown path in the thick, dark woods. There is a very pretty little meadow near the cellar hole of Nancy's old home. In the spring, the edge of a small pond is awash with wildflowers and it is home to dozens of birds. I'm sure that during her young life, Nancy Mills played right here in this piney spot. Right now the marsh has no name. I don't think anyone will object to my naming it "Nancy's Meadow" on the official Derry town map.

This autumn will mark the 157th anniversary of the murder and burial of little Nancy Mills. Perhaps one day soon I will try to find her burial place. It's somewhere near the junction of two streams near the old Halls Village Road. There I'll say a few words of prayer and pile up some stones as a mitzvah to mark her resting place and to be a monument to this Derry tragedy. If anyone would like to join me, I'd appreciate the company. You come, too.

25.
Columbus Day in 1892

I HAVE A CONFESSION: THIS YEAR I DIDN'T REMEMBER IT WAS Columbus Day until after it was over. I suspect that most of you were like me and didn't do much partying to celebrate the discovery of America in 1492. Traditionally on that day, the Knights of Columbus stage a parade in Boston and in some years Native Americans hold demonstrations to protest the loss of their lands to the Europeans. In some schools, kids will be taught the words to that poem by Joaquin Miller that has the line "Sail on! Sail on! And on!" Other youngsters will probably learn the couplet "In fourteen hundred ninety-two, Columbus sailed the ocean blue." To most people, however, Halloween is a far more eagerly anticipated holiday than the day set aside to honor the purported discoverer of our continent.

There was a time when Columbus Day was celebrated in grand style in Derry and Londonderry. The year 1892 was the four hundredth anniversary of Columbus's landing on San Salvador. A massive world's fair was held in Chicago. Many locals traveled a thousand miles by rail to the Windy City for a visit to the World's Columbian Exposition. Brown Bessie, a cow from the Hood farm, was exhibited at that fair and named the best cow in the world.

In Derry and Londonderry in 1892, it was decided to center festivities on the school children. Though October 12 was the actual date of Columbus Day, we chose to celebrate it on October 21. Why? Our reasoning was that under the Julian calendar of the fifteenth century, Columbus actually discovered America on October 21, 1492. It would not be until nearly three centuries later that the calendar was "reformed." Under this new and improved Gregorian calendar, the day October 21 became October 12. We here in Derry, being a conservative bunch, decided that if October 21 was good enough for Columbus, it was good enough for us. Case closed! Today, however, Columbus Day is declared by the government to be the second Monday in October. Case closed!

On October 21, 1892, Pinkerton Academy was central to the celebration. At 9:30 in the morning the east doors opened to receive the stream of students, townspeople, and dignitaries. The assemblage was marched up the stairs by the fife-and-drum corps of Derry's chapter of the Grand Army of the Republic. They were our Civil War veterans organization and were like today's American Legion. On the walls of the chapel was hung a new twelve-by-twenty-four-foot American flag bunting. Also on display was a large portrait of Columbus and George Washington. On the west wall were the various flags that have been flown in America since 1492. On the opposite wall was a display of the flags of the world.

In the hall the audience enjoyed a series of readings and songs. Among the offerings were Mr. Moore reading "The Death and Burial of Columbus," Miss Abby Chase singing "Hail Columbia," and Miss Parsons reciting "Duties of an American Citizen."

At the Derry Village School, the grammar school students were marched out onto their play yard. There the children were directed to face west to replicate Columbus's direction of travel. A speech by school board chairman Professor Edmund Angell was followed by three cheers for the "old red, white and blue." Afterward, the children returned to their classroom, whose walls had been festooned with "evergreens, noble pines and bright alder berries" tied with patriotic-colored ribbons. The school sang the song "America" and listened to recitations and odes on the theme of Columbus and America.

At the Adams School in East Derry, students marched through the village and escorted several Civil War veterans from their homes to the Lane Road schoolhouse. I suppose they went willingly. At the school there were the usual recitations and songs. Perhaps the highlight of the occasion was a speech by Frederick Shepard, Esq., and the singing of the "Star Spangled Banner" by his wife. In 1923 the Shepards would become the grandparents of astronaut Alan B. Shepard Jr.

In Londonderry, the celebration was held at School #7 in north Londonderry. The students from the town's scattered one-room schools were joined by about fifty adults. At the appointed hour, the students were each given a small American flag and marched military-style to their seats. The martial marching music was provided by the school's own drum corps. After all the speeches and songs, the command to the drum corps was given by Orrin Stokes, who at thirteen, in 1862, had entered the Union Army as a drummer boy.

At each of the school gatherings in the two towns there were speeches, songs, recitations, and the reading of President Benjamin Harrison's proclamation in honor of Columbus. In addition, there was something else that was done at each of these celebrations: At every school there was a flag raising of the forty-four-star American flag, followed by the students reciting a newly written patriotic oath. It had been created by Baptist minister Francis Bellamy and published in the October 1892 edition of *The Youth's Companion*. The Reverend Bellamy had observed that the schoolchildren with whom he came in contact were not as patriotic as had been young people of previous generations. The author hoped that his words would be recited by every school child at every Columbus Day ceremony and inspire a nationwide rebirth of patriotic feelings.

Bellamy's wish came true. All across America his ode was spoken by millions of schoolboys and -girls. In prairie schools in Nebraska, sprawling brick schools in bustling New York City, and one-room schools throughout Nutfield, exactly the same words were offered up into the October air. The children of recent immigrants and those who were the descendants of the Pilgrim fathers all said exactly the same words that day.

On October 21, 1892, at nine in the morning the pledge by Francis Bellamy was recited for the first time in Derry, Londonderry, Windham, and the rest of the nation. As reported in the *Derry News,* the words to this oath were *"I pledge allegiance to my flag and the republic for which it stands; one nation, indivisible, with liberty and justice for all."* The words to the pledge of allegiance were altered in 1923, 1924, and 1954 to create the thirty-one word pledge we say today. In 1942, President Franklin Roosevelt gave official status to the pledge in our Flag Code. In 1943, the United States Supreme Court ruled that the recitation of the pledge of allegiance had to be voluntary and could not be compelled by federal, state, or local law.

Thornton Street under water during the Great Freshet of 1900.

26.

The Great Freshet of 1900

THE RAINS AND FLOODS OF APRIL 2007 CAUSED THE SUMP PUMP in my cellar to work for three straight weeks. Now it's May and the weatherman is still predicting precipitation. When will it end? Some meteorologists have called the April flood a once-in-a-century occurrence. Didn't they say the same thing about the floods of May 2006? Actually, according to my research, both the May 2006 or the April 2007 disaster were probably the greatest local flooding in 106 or 107 years, but I guess their estimate was close enough.

The Great Freshet of 1900 seems to have caused as much damage to our section of New Hampshire as did the great floods of 2006 and 2007. Between 1900 and 2006 we have had at least a half-dozen floods that produced washouts and disruptions to our lives. Significant floods in Derry occurred in March 1936, September 1938, June 1944, July 1948, March 1977, and April 1987.

The term *freshet* is rarely used today. By definition, it simply means a sudden flood. Usually freshets are brought about by a rapid snowmelt. During the eighteenth and nineteenth centuries, freshets were all too common in Derry. Flood-control dams built in the twentieth century have done much to alleviate inundation within our state.

The winter of 1899–1900 had been one of those "Jekyll and Hyde" seasons. A spell of mild weather was followed by frigid, cold temperatures. Up through mid-February there really hadn't been a snowstorm of any consequence. The fields and yards of Derry in February 1900 were covered with frozen brown grass and stubble.

This was in sharp contrast to the previous winter. In February 1899 the whole East Coast was hit by the legendary "blizzard of '99." That storm was so bad that it was called the "Great White Hurricane." Temperatures in Florida in February 1899 fell to a record minus two degrees and the port of New Orleans was frozen over. In New England it was reported that some sections received up to fifty inches of snow.

On February 11, 1900, the rains began to fall. For over forty-eight hours the sky was transformed into a waterfall. There are no reliable estimates regarding the volume of the precipitation, but it is likely that well over a foot of rain fell on Derry during that storm. Fortunately, there was no snow to melt or the result would have been dramatically worse. Because the ground was frozen solid, it absorbed none of the rain. Large puddles formed quickly and then the rising water followed gravity and flooded the lowlands. The rivers of Derry were soon flowing over the top of their banks and into the yards, fields, and forests. Within a few hours, all of Derry was experiencing unprecedented flooding.

Particularly hard hit was Derry Village. The normally tranquil Beaver Brook became an angry, raging torrent. Soon all the cellars in the area were filled with water and tool sheds, privies, and chicken coops were washed away or demolished. The entire Lower Village—from the school (now the site of the superintendent of schools' office) to Pinkerton Academy Hill and Hood's pasture (now the Hoodkroft Country Club)—was flooded. A lake was formed that rivaled the size of Beaver Lake. The *Derry News* described the scene in the village as "weird and remarkable." This was heralded as a "once-in-a-century" calamity.

The deluge forced a huge jam of ice down Beaver Brook and propelled it over the Chase Dam. This ice was thrown down the swollen river with such force that it ripped off the entire side of the Benjamin Chase Mill. Spectators on the river banks could now look into the three floors of the structure from cellar to attic. All the saws and planing machines were exposed as half the mill was swept downriver. The flood also ripped away thousands of board feet of lumber that were being stored in its yard.

The torrent hurled blocks of ice and debris against the stone bridge on Main Street. Soon this structure was swept away and its hewed-stone foundation and wooden beams ended up in Hood's Meadow. The Great Freshet of 1900 also destroyed the Broadway

Bridge by the West Side School (now the Marion Gerrish Community Center), the Fordway Bridge, the Highland Avenue Bridge, the Thornton Avenue Bridge, and the Adams Pond Bridge. Roads all over town were "utterly impassable." Some of the washouts were reported to be from two to ten feet deep.

The Chester and Derry Trolley was put out of service because the Maple Street power station was flooded and couldn't produce steam to generate electricity. The town of Derry went black and kerosene lamps were brought out of storage. The lack of power was not the street railroad's only problem; much of its tracks were also underwater. After the flood receded, it was revealed that the water had washed away the ground under long stretches of track, which left the rails suspended a foot above the ground.

After the storm, Broadway was a muddy bog and virtually impassable. The *Manchester Union Leader* reported that it was the worst freshet "ever known in this region." Even the oldest residents couldn't recall a worse flood!

Repairs took thousands of wagonloads of gravel and bushels of tax dollars. It was, of course, easier to fix the roads in 1900 than it was in 2006. All our roads were then gravel or dirt and not asphalt; the bridges in 1900 were mainly unmortared stone and timber and not made of cement and iron as they are now.

Just like the great floods of May 2006, the Great Freshet of 1900 caused destruction all over southern New Hampshire. Local towns such as Raymond, Fremont, Manchester, and Nashua reported major washouts. Countless bridges were damaged or destroyed. Despite the quagmire, the taxpayers in March 1900 voted against paving Broadway. The electorate also voted to retain the old road system, in which Derry was divided into thirty-four highway districts. Each district was under the management of its own road agent who hired his own workers and set his own priorities. In 1900 there was the equivalent of thirty-four different Alan Cotes managing our roads. It would not be for several years until Broadway was paved and we went to a single road agent.

The Angell Family lot, Forest Hill Cemetery.

27.
Everett Angell

THERE CAN BE NO GREATER TRAGEDY THAN THE DEATH OF A CHILD. Despite the distance of 117 years, the passing of Everett Angell in 1890 still speaks to us today. The sorrow of his parents still moves us and we share with them their pain and loss.

In 1890 the Angell family, of 4 Thornton Square, were well known in Derry Village. Their large, comfortable home was central to the town's social, intellectual, and religious life. Professor Edmund Angell and his wife, Lizzie, had moved into the house when he was appointed headmaster of Pinkerton Academy in 1876. He held this position for ten years and then became headmaster of Chester Academy. He was a member of the New Hampshire House of Representatives, chairman of the local school board, and a crusading foe in the war against alcohol.

Edmund Angell listed his religious beliefs as "the Golden Rule and the two Great Commandments," which command you to love God with all your heart and to love your neighbor as yourself. The Angells belonged to most of the fraternal organizations in town. Professor Angell was New Hampshire's first state chemist and ran a chemical laboratory and photography studio near his home. He was the chief promoter of a safe public water supply for Derry. He was the expert the state would use in cases of possible deaths by poison. He was well known as the author of annually published reports on the quality of drinking water at the grand hotels in the White Mountains. During his career he checked hundreds of one-room schools to make sure their privies weren't too near their wells or springs.

Four years earlier, Angell had patented "The Odorless Privy and Sanitary Commode." In a twenty-two page booklet, the inventor tried to explain to the public the "laws of volatilization" and why his chemical toilet was superior to the standard outdoor privy. He announced to the world that because of his superior household indoor toilet, there will be "health preserved and life saved."

His invention was fundamentally a toilet seat above a ten gallon copper container. When not in use, a lever-controlled airtight door sealed off the waste receptacle. On top of the toilet was a rubber bulb that could be pressed to activate an atomizer, which sprayed a solution of carbolic acid to disinfect and reduce odors. Angell advised the user to use the spray device immediately upon sitting on the commode.

At regular intervals, the homeowner was instructed to add sulphate of iron or copper to the holding tank to help destroy bacteria and spores. One of the biggest benefits of his commode was that it could be installed anywhere in the home. This would eliminate the need for the traditional "thunder jug" under the bed or the necessity to go outside in the freezing New Hampshire winter to use the privy. Angell claimed that because of his airtight design, the tank needed to be emptied only twice a month.

In his promotional booklet are numerous testimonials to the merits of the Angell commode. Among those who went on record praising the toilet were shoe manufacturer Rosecrans Pillsbury, of Londonderry; Doctor Henry Newell, of Derry; and General Arthur Emerson, of Chester. Mrs. Eliza Eaton, of Derry, wrote that her old privy gave off such an odor in the warm months that it was "sickening" but the new Angell toilet is "absolutely free from odor." The toilet would also help prevent deaths from many communicable diseases. In 1903, Angell invented an acetylene device that was used for illuminating houses, halls, and automobiles.

In 1890 the Angell household consisted of Edmund, age forty-two, Lizzie age forty-one and two active boys, Everett, nine and Ralph, five. Mom and Dad Angell viewed the boys as a gift from God. In appearance, the boys could not be mistaken for anything but brothers. In the photographs I have seen, they were well dressed and wore their hair short. Both were remembered as being energetic and well mannered. Everett was described as intellectually brilliant, a "favorite among his playmates and kind and generous."

He was considered by the residents of the lower village to be "a boy of promise."

On Sunday morning, March 16, 1890, young Everett woke up before the rest of the family. He quickly lit the fire in the kitchen's wood oven and in the parlor's stove. Soon the rest of the family awoke to the comforting smell and warmth of the wood fires. The Angells gathered for breakfast but Everett ate very little. Later that morning the nine-year-old began to vomit. Everyone assumed that Everett was suffering from nothing worse than a springtime bug that would likely disappear about as fast as it appeared. The usual household remedies were tried and by afternoon the boy seemed some better.

Everett Angell spent a restless night and arose on Monday morning feeling very weak. His mother had to help him get dressed. Word was sent to their neighbor Doctor David Clark requesting a house call. After an examination, Clark found that the boy's lips, throat, and tongue were swollen. The diagnosis seemed an easy one to Doc Clark. It was a severe case of tonsillitis. The parents were told it "was nothing serious." Soon Everett would be on the mend and running around like the free spirit he had always been.

The boy did not improve. That afternoon he was in considerable pain and became delirious. The doctor kept returning to the Angell home all through the day and night. The medical man was frustrated by his inability to do anything; the parents were distraught as their firstborn son became weaker and weaker. Professor Angell was a man of science but there nothing his knowledge of chemicals and physiology could do. (Remember this was happening in a world without antibiotics.) Lizzie Angell was equally frustrated, as no amount of love or soothing could keep Everett's life from ebbing away.

Somehow Dr. Clark had misdiagnosed the boy's condition. He failed to spot the classic symptoms of scarlet fever: the deep red rash that feels like sandpaper to the touch; a headache and fatigue; a swollen strawberry-colored tongue with white spots; abdominal pain; high temperature; and chills. Scarlet fever, or scarletina, was a frequently fatal illness in the nineteenth century. In literature, scarlet fever killed Beth in Louisa May Alcott's *Little Women*, caused Laura's sister Mary to go blind in *The Little House on the Prairie* series, and debilitated the little boy in *The Velveteen Rabbit*. Today the disease is easily treatable with penicillin.

The family gathered around the sickbed as little Everett's life began to slip away. In his last few minutes of consciousness, the nine-year-old boy pointed up toward his bedroom window. In a faint voice he told his parents that he could see angels coming into his room to take him to heaven. His last words were "See them up yonder." He died at 5:30 on Tuesday morning.

It was not until the neighbors were preparing the body for burial that Dr. Clark saw the black spots on the boy's arms and hands. He knew immediately that the boy had died of a "case of malignant scarlet fever." He understood how contagious the disease was and that the village was at imminent risk of it spreading. Everything that had been in contact with the boy must be burned immediately! As soon as a casket could be procured, the body was taken without ceremony to Forest Hill Cemetery. There was no time for a funeral! At four that afternoon, the parents and a few friends brought the body to the new part of the cemetery. There, amid the grief, Pastor Hiram Putnam of the Central Congregational Church offered a committal prayer. Five-year-old Ralph Angell told his sorrowing mother, "Mama, you must not cry any more. Ebby has gone to live with God."

March 20 was the date originally chosen for the public funeral. That day was traditionally called Blowing Out Day. This was the date when the sun annually climbed sufficiently high in the sky that workers in shops no longer needed to light candles or lamps in the afternoon. As the workingmen extinguished their lights, so had the life of Everett Angell been extinguished. His life had lasted only nine years, eight months, and sixteen days on earth.

For the next year the family was in deep mourning. Lizzie would dress in black and Edmund always wore a black armband. Professor Angell had a large portrait of his late son placed in the boy's former elementary school classroom. On the closing day of the school year, every one of Everett's thirty classmates was given a copy of his photograph. The children collected money so they could plant a rosebush on the grave.

Some day, if you go to Forest Hill Cemetery, walk down Angell Avenue. You can ask directions at the museum; I'll help you find it. There on a small rise is the Angell family burial lot. Here lie Professor and Mrs. Angell, Mr. and Mrs. Ralph Angell, and Everett Angell. Toward the rear of the lot are massive, rough-hewn blocks of granite that are placed to resemble a slide in a child's playground.

Inscribed on these stones are *In God's Workshop* and *Until the day dawns and the darkness disappears.*

In front of this celestial playground, commissioned by the sorrowing parents, are a pair of identical gravestones. They were made from a single rock that nature had split in half. This cleft stone had been a favorite play site for Everett and Ralph. The Angells had the stone's inner faces polished so that they could be inscribed with the family's names and dates. On the stone on the right is written *Everett R. Angell 1880–1890.* Below this, cut into the granite for all eternity, are the last words of Everett Angell, *See them up yonder.*

On his mother's grave are inscribed her last words. Lizzie, according to her son Ralph, was a very nervous woman who was always sure she'd do the wrong thing. Her last words in 1932 were *"I don't know how to die."*

28.

Bella Chapin Barrows:
So much in a lifetime

AS A HISTORICAL RESEARCHER, I SPEND HOURS EVERY DAY EXPLORING aspects of Derry's history—trying to find out when this fire took place, why that road was built, what was the town thinking when some event occurred. Frequently my mind starts to wander and I leave the task at hand and go on some unrelated bunny trail. Mid-morning last week, I left my analysis of colonial linen weaving in Nutfield and started a computer search for details of the life of a former slave. The man had been freed by my third cousin (by marriage) in Louisiana back in 1864. I knew that later in this freedman's life, he had been involved with the great educator Booker T. Washington. For an hour I searched online through Mr. Washington's papers.

After an hour or so I found the name "Isabel Chapin Barrows" mentioned in a footnote as a good friend of the great black leader. In a letter she was scolding Prof. Washington on the lack of toilets at his college. She told him that young ladies of any color shouldn't have to use bushes as a place to relieve themselves. They needed to have privies built to protect their privacy and dignity.

I vaguely remembered a "Bella Chapin" as the daughter of a Derry Civil War veteran. Could it be the same woman? The trail now veered in another direction as I stopped the search for the ex-slave and returned to the history of the town of my birth. Immediately, I decided to drop all other work and find this Barrows woman.

To myself, I mentally shouted something like "Quick Watson, the games afoot."

After a few minutes on the computer, I made the connection! Yes, this was the same person who had once lived in Derry! The more I researched Mrs. Barrows, the more amazed I became. How in all my years as a Derry historian could I have missed her? She was one of the greatest reformers in American history—an international legend in her own time. This lady did it all. Her biography was written in 1964 by Madeline Stein and went through many editions. Her story was called "So Much in a Lifetime." And she was indeed a Derry girl!

She was born in 1845 in Irasburg, Vermont, as Katherine Isabel Hayes, the daughter of Dr. Henry and Anna Hayes. The family moved to Derry around the spring of 1856, when Dr. Hayes took over the practice of Dr. Luther V. Bell, who was appointed director of McLain's Hospital. Young Isabel—called Bella by everyone—attended Pinkerton Academy for a year before transferring to the Adams Female Academy in the upper village of East Derry. This school was a pioneer in the field of women's education and was then led by Miss Emma Taylor, who would later become the benefactress of the Taylor Library of East Derry.

There were probably only a few dozen students in the Female Academy, but its small size belied its national reputation. It was known far and wide as a school that taught women to think and not just to write flowery poetry and paint pretty pictures on china plates. It prided itself on teaching its high school-aged students as though they were in college. The school demanded a commitment to excellence. Its motto was a line from Alexander Pope: "Drink deep or taste not." Students were expected to know their school subjects, not just know *about* their school subjects.

After graduation, in 1862, Bella taught in one of Derry's one-room schoolhouses. In 1863 she married William Chapin in a Derry church. He was a Congregational minister eight years her senior. Her mother died a month after the wedding and her father died the next year in Tennessee as an army doctor in the Civil War. Both parents are buried at Forest Hill Cemetery in East Derry.

The first church assignment for the Reverend William and Mrs. Chapin was to serve as missionaries in Bombay, India. It would likely have taken weeks to complete this sea voyage halfway around the world. She sadly said good-bye to her school friends. She knew that it would be years before she was back in America.

Things did not work out as planned. After only three months on the Asian subcontinent, the Reverend William Chapin died. In April 1865, Bella came back to America—a nineteen-year-old widow with no family and few prospects. She quickly had to find a way to support herself.

Because of the medical knowledge she had learned as a country doctor's daughter, she soon got a job as a bath assistant at Dr. James Jackson's Water Cure Hospital in Danville, New York. The doctor's standard cure for all of his patient's medical problems involved no medicines whatsoever. His clients were to abstain from eating meat and drinking coffee or tea. Dr. Jackson believed that all sickness could be cured by having the patient soak for hours in medicinal baths, having enemas, drinking gallons of water, and eating graham crackers.

At the Water Cure Hospital, Bella Chapin fell in love with Dr. Jackson's secretary. Samuel Barrows (1845–1909) was a master of a new writing technique called phonography. This way of writing rapidly had been recently developed by Isaac Pittman and is what we today called shorthand. Bella and Samuel were married in 1867 by the Reverend Henry Ward Beecher, who was quickly becoming America's most famous cleric. The bride and groom were both twenty-two years old.

Shortly after they were married, Bella expressed her desire to be a medical doctor, to follow in her father's footsteps. Her loving husband gave her much encouragement. She enrolled in Dr. Elizabeth Blackwell's Women's Medical College, in New York City. As a young woman, Miss Blackwell (1821–1910) had been turned down at every medical school to which she applied. Finally the faculty and students at Geneva Medical College voted to admit her, believing that her application was somebody's idea of a practical joke. They were more than a little surprised when they found out she was indeed serious about becoming a doctor. She graduated in 1849 and is credited with being the first woman physician of the modern era. With the advice of her friend Florence Nightingale, Miss Blackwell founded her New York Medical College in 1868.

Bella's studies were interrupted when her husband got a new job. He was hired to be the personal secretary to the U. S. Secretary of State William Seward. She decided her husband's career came first. In Washington, D.C., Bella settled in to be a proper housewife. Within the year, her husband took critically ill and would have to spend several months as an invalid in bed. There was no such thing as paid sick time in those days and there was no income for the Barrows family. Bella knew she needed to find paid employment. She approached the Secretary of State and told him that she had been taught shorthand by her husband and could do his job for his pay. After passing a dictation test, she got the job. She was now the first woman in our country's history to work for the State Department. She was a pioneer who led the way to the integration of the State Department. Her hiring in time would help pave the way for Madeline Albright and Condoleezza Rice to serve as Secretary of State under Presidents Clinton and Bush respectively.

After her husband's recovery, Bella decided to continue her medical studies. While her husband stayed in the United States, she boarded the steamship *Ethiopia* and set sail for Europe. In the nineteenth century, Europe was the center of the world of medicine. Virtually all of the great medical discoveries of the day were the product of researchers in England, Germany, France, and Austria. American colleges had not yet reached their preeminence in the world of science and were considered in fact rather backwater. While in Europe, Bella studied with the world's leading medical doctors at the Universities of Leipzig and Vienna. In just two years she had realized her dream and was a medical doctor. Her father's dreams, too became reality. She was now Katherine Isabel Chapin Barrows, M. D.

Returning to the United States, Bella set up practice in the nation's capital. She was now to be forever remembered as America's first woman eye surgeon. Her practice was not large, so she had considerable free time. To help supplement the family's income, she got a job as the recording stenographer for Congress. Because this had always been a "man's job," she was never referred to officially by her real name but instead was called "I.B." By means of that subterfuge, the voters wouldn't know there was a woman working in the committee rooms of Capitol Hill. Using the four hundred dollars she earned monthly as a medical doctor, congressional secretary, and professor at Howard University, she was able to put her husband through Harvard Divinity School.

After Samuel Barrows graduated, in 1871, he became a newspaper correspondent with the *New York Tribune*. He was dispatched to travel with the flamboyant general George Armstrong Custer into the American West. While with Custer, he was under fire at the Battles of Tongue River and the Big Horn, which pitted the seventh Cavalry against the Sioux. He later rode with General David Stanley in the Yellowstone expedition of 1873.

While he was with Custer during the Black Hills expedition, he sent back word of the discovery of gold. This news in the *Tribune* helped to incite a gold stampede. This ultimately resulted in the Indian reservation in the Dakotas being opened up to settlement by whites.

At the age twenty-eight, Bella left her practice to give birth to a daughter, Mabel Hayes Barrows (1873–1931), who grew up to be a famous dramatic director, dancer, and worker in the crusade for women's suffrage. Mabel would also become the wife of economics professor Henry Mussey, of Columbia University, who would later serve as editor of the reforming periodical *The Nation*.

Now that he was a father, the Reverend Samuel Barrows decided to forgo his exciting career as a reporter covering the Far West. The news of General Custer's death at the Battle of the Little Big Horn in 1876 may have played a role in his decision. Being a correspondent out west was much too dangerous for the father of a little girl. In 1876, Barrows became pastor of the First Parish Church of Dorchester, Massachusetts, and would remain there for the next four years.

In 1880, Bella and Samuel Barrows became editors of the *Christian Register*. This Unitarian monthly magazine was known worldwide for its progressive ideas on social reform. For the next sixteen years, the Barrowses were in daily contact with leaders in the drive for women's rights, temperance, peace, education, immigration reform, black civil rights, and prison reform. This was when she lectured Booker T. Washington on the need for toilets at his college. There were very few aspects of American life the Barrowes weren't working tirelessly to improve.

Their career as magazine editors ended in 1897 when Samuel Barrows was elected to the U. S. House of Representatives from Massachusetts. After a single term in Washington, he failed in his bid for reelection. The husband-and-wife team would thereafter devote their remaining years to the international crusade for prison reform. Samuel was elected American delegate to the International Prison Congress in 1895, 1900, and 1905. He was also secretary of the New York Prison Association from 1899 to 1909. He was elected president of the 1910 International Prison Congress but died before he could accept the honor.

Bella Barrows's contribution to the drive for penal reform was nearly as distinguished as that of her husband. She served as editor of the *Journal of the National Conference on Correction*, and secretary of the National Prison Association for two decades and editor of its publication. She was secretary of the Lake Mohonk Conference on black rights for seventeen years. She wrote or cowrote a number of books and magazine articles on reform subjects as well as *A Sunny Life*, a biography of Samuel June Barrows, which was published by Little, Brown and Company in 1918. She lectured all over the United States and Europe. In honor of her career as a reformer, the Republic of France made her a member of the Order of Chevaliers.

Isabel Hayes Chapin Barrows died in Croton-on-Hudson, New York, on October 25, 1913, at age sixty-eight. She is buried with her husband in the little Bullock Cemetery in the eastern township village of Georgeville, Quebec. Here for decades the family had vacationed in their compound of three log cabins on the shores of beautiful Lake Memphremagog. Their headstone is a chest-high granite post that measures just a foot square. On this rough unpolished stone, in no particular order, and in varying styles of calligraphy, are cut the names of four generations of the family. On the shaft is inscribed a simple couplet which may well serve to characterize Bella Barrows. It reads "Always herself to others giving/In duty and in beauty living."

One of Bella's friends and admirers was Madam Catherine Breshkovsky. She was a reformer in czarist Russia and is sometimes called the "little grandmother of the Russian Revolution." She wrote, "What a beautiful life Isabel's has been . . . an uninterrupted course of reasonable labor and noble actions. She has never been tired, and all she could give away she has given."

Bella Barrows's legacy of accomplishments was truly spectacular. In a lifetime of only sixty-eight years she was: a missionary to India; the first woman to work in the State Department; America's first woman eye surgeon; the first woman professor at Howard University; the first woman employee in Congress; a magazine editor; a published author; an internationally known activist in the cause of human rights; a giving friend and warm human being; a good mother and devoted wife.

During this decade we have spent much time debating politics, war, terror, and the role of America in international affairs. It should be comforting to find at least one thing everyone can agree on—that Bella Barrows led a great life; one devoted to public service for the betterment of mankind that should serve as a role model for us all. Hers was definitely a life worth living.

29.

The Great Derry Monster

I N SCOTLAND THEY HAVE NESSIE. IN VERMONT, THE AQUATIC BEAST known as Champie plies the waters of Lake Champlain. Washington state has its Bigfoot and the venerable Abominable Snowman roams the Himalayas. Here in Derry we once had our own mysterious beast. This is the tale of the Derry Monster, who terrified our citizens as it went a-stalking in our woods a century ago.

This story begins in October 1905. The location is southern Derry on that part of the Fordway Extension that's about a half mile from the Derry/Windham line. To visualize the town back then, you must understand that its population distribution was very much different from what it is today.

The Derry of 2007 has a population of about thirty-four thousand residents. This translates into a population density of nearly one thousand souls per square mile. In 1905 it was about a tenth that number. You must also realize that in 1905 the majority of our citizens worked in the sprawling Broadway shoe factories. Almost everyone who resided in Derry lived within a comfortable walking distance of Derry Depot. Once you left downtown Derry, you came to the kingdom of deep forests, open fields, and farm yards.

Today our population is distributed throughout town in a much more even way. There are now homes, businesses, and people everywhere. The hills and lowlands that used to be pastures for herds of cows and flocks of sheep are, in 2007, the site of housing developments with established neighborhoods. Where there used to be the forest primeval, there are now strip malls and apartment complexes. Need I say more?

A century ago, the area of the Fordway Extension was very sparsely populated. There were only four homes along this two-mile stretch of road, which extends from Island Pond Road and crosses to the Windham town line. In 1905 this was farm country, with open fields and endless miles of stone walls festooning rolling hills. Beyond the fields and pastures the openness came to an abrupt end at a wall of darkness created by the deep woods. This forestland seemed to extend for miles and miles to the south toward Windham and west to Londonderry. The only break in the woods was an occasional path or bog.

Farmer Joseph M. Hood, who was renting the old Montgomery farm, was the first to see the beast. There it was, standing alone by an apple tree. Hood later described it to a reporter from the *Derry News* as "a beauty with large wicked eyes." Soon afterwards, his wife saw it as she was walking in a field with her two children. She was most impressed by the animal. She told a Boston newspaper that she was surprised but not scared; the incident just happened too fast for her to have much time to be frightened.

The strange animal approached the mother and children and put its big paws over the top of a stone wall. It just stood there staring at them. She said it looked like a member of the feline family and "grinned at me like the Cheshire Cat in *Alice and Wonderland*. She told it to "shoo" and it ran away. Brave lady!

George Estes, a butcher, who lived a little way down the road, reported that one of his young heifers had come in from the field all bloodied. It had severe wounds across its back as if something had tried to catch it. He also reported some of his stock missing. A normally shy and reclusive deer was observed staying close to the Montgomery place. It appeared to be much too frightened to venture back into the woods. Some horses were reported to react with fear as they approached the forest that was the lair of the beast.

Farmhand E. F. Wright began to see the visitor quite often—and always at either dusk or dawn. He told a city reporter: "I've seen that thing, whatever it is, five or six times and I know it's some beast unknown to these parts." He said that the animal was much bigger than "a domestic cat can possibly be and I'm sure it is not a dog." One newspaper had begun to call the animal "the Terror of Rockingham County."

Children were now warned not go out alone. There was danger in Derry! Farmer Wright said, "The quicker this animal is shot, the better!" One night butcher Estes and his friend Mr. Cronin braved out after it with rifles and a hunting dog. They eventually came back with a report that they had managed to tree the beast—but it jumped and escaped into the darkness. The dog "took the trail" after the fleeing animal, baying as he ran into the thicket. In a few minutes, however, the hound returned looking "bad" and couldn't be induced to go back after the beast.

Another person who spread the tale of the beast was Miss Gustle Young, the housekeeper for Augustus Alexander. One night she was walking on a path in the woods and "saw something." In a panic, she ran to the nearest house, which was that of Dr. Harrison Alexander. He was a wealthy dentist who had practices in Europe and in South America. He was later a major benefactor to the town (Alexander-Eastman Hospital, Alexander-Carr Park). This man of science tried to quiet the terrified young woman by pooh-poohing the story. He told her that the tale of the Derry monster was simply nonsense.

Dr. Alexander would use his most soothing and professional voice to tell her that if someone brought him positive and undisputable proof of the existence of the wild thing, he would personally give that person a thousand dollars. To the good dentist, that was a sentence of throw-away words, uttered on the spur of the moment to calm the panicking Gustle Young.

Soon all over town the alleged thousand-dollar bounty was being talked about. Posses were formed to hunt down the beast who walked alone. Now that the story had made the Boston newspapers, it was easy to predict that the woods of Derry would soon be alive with the sound of gunners. Many hunters would no doubt be running after their baying packs of hunting hounds. These sportsmen might be thought of as men—aye, brave men—who were hell-bent on protecting the women and children of our town from the monster who had no name. It was also just as probable that the reward money was their chief motivating factor. The animal was not caught and Dr. Alexander kept his thousand dollars. This result, I'm sure, made both the monster and the good doctor very happy.

The animal was not seen again during the winter of 1905–1906. It is likely that he (or she) had plenty of food. Many of our farms had shut down after the Civil War and their once open fields and pastures had grown up into scrub and forest. This would be perfect habitat for small mammals such as rabbits and deer to live and flourish. Indeed, such a land—the home of Bambi and Thumper—would be the happy hunting ground for a monster such as ours.

Derry still had a number of farms with livestock that could also provide fine dining alfresco for the beast. The census of our farm animals for 1905 was: 513 horses, eight oxen, 651 cows, five sheep, seventy-five hogs, and 925 fowl. In addition, there were countless cats and dogs. There was certainly no reason for any beast of average intelligence in the town of Derry at the beginning of the twentieth century to starve.

There were, of course, skeptics on the reliability of the reports of monster sightings. Farmhand Jim Kelley said he had seen "it" and announced that the feared animal was "nothing but a bob cat which will harm nobody" and was only a danger to chickens and rabbits. Kelley was asked to explain the fact that while bob cats were tailless, the other witness reported that the monster had a long tail. He said they probably saw its "hind leg outstretched as it ran along."

In late April Amos Morse saw the animal drinking from a spring near the Montgomery farm. He ran and got his musket hoping to bag it as a trophy. He was unsuccessful because in his excitement he loaded his gun with "two charges of shot" and no powder. Later that day, he saw it again. "With shaking knees and hair standing on end, he took aim but no panther did he kill." The animal let out a low growl and fiercely glared at him. "Amos made a home run which has never been equaled by any baseball player who ever played in Derry." It was also reported that the animal chased a terrified Windham blacksmith and later a group of lumberjacks.

The last time the wild animal was seen was in the fall of 1906. Again the sighting occurred by the old Montgomery place in the southern part of town. Around five in the afternoon, William R. MacGregor and his three children were driving in his buggy when suddenly they saw it. The MacGregors were only about seventy feet from the wild thing. Mr. MacGregor later said it looked to him to be as large as a Saint Bernard! It just stood there by the side of the Montgomery barn. The four MacGregors watched as the farm's resident dog ran toward the beast. The canine barked at the animal but the beast held its ground and showed no fear. With this final sighting, the beast disappeared from Derry, never to be seen again.

No one is alive today who actually saw the beast. We have to examine the evidence from the distance of a century in time. The facts, do, however, point to a likely identity for the beast. Right from the start, the animal was described as being in the feline family. It was said to be large. It had big eyes. It didn't roar. It was always alone. It made great leaps to escape. Mrs. Hood thought it resembled a stuffed leopard she had seen on display at a Boston department store; others thought it might be a South American puma. The locals actually had a pretty good frame of reference from which to identify the animal. In the summer of 1906, a circus paid a one-day visit to Derry. One of its featured big-top acts was Madame Hall and Her Den of Performing Leopards. She had trained four of the big cats to jump through hoops.

A Boston newspaper hired an artist to draw a picture of the beast based on eyewitness testimony. It would seem to be almost a certainty that our forest visitor was a mountain lion (*Felis Concolor*). This wild animal was once king of our woods but had been locally hunted to extinction probably in the late eighteenth century. The last definite sighting of a mountain lion anywhere in New Hampshire was in 1890 and in Massachusetts in 1858. Certainly none of these cats had been seen by anyone living in Derry in 1905.

The mountain lion is known in different regions by different names. It can be called a catamount, a panther, a cougar, or a puma. It is a carnivore and an excellent hunter. Because its hind legs are longer than its forelegs, it can make prodigious leaps—sometimes up to eighteen feet in a single bound. The males are solitary creatures and live with a female only during mating season.

An adult male can be thirty inches high and fifty-four inches in length. Its tail will extend another three feet. Its eyes are larger than those of most other cats. According to the reference books, a mountain lion can weigh up to two hundred pounds. Most people are impressed when they first meet my large Maine coon cat—his imperial highness, King Elch the Most Aloof. I can imagine how much more traumatic would be a chance meeting with a cat ten times Elch's size and with perhaps the mass and bulk of a very large German Shepherd.

Scientists are still debating whether the catamount is making its way back into New England. Each year there are hundreds of reported sightings that indicate the possibility that they have indeed returned to the home turf of their ancestors. In recent years,

A newspaper drawing of the Derry Monster based on eyewitness.

its scat has been found as far south as Massachusetts. In August 2007, a horse was killed in Northern New Hampshire by an animal some think was a mountain lion. The state's fish and game experts still remain skeptical over the return of the big cats to the Granite State.

At the Squam Lake Natural Science Center, a pair of orphan cougars from Montana have been put on display. Maybe I'll pay that outdoor zoological park a visit soon, so I can see for myself what the Derry monster probably looked like.

30.
Robert Frost and the Association Hall

ON THE WAY FROM THE TRAFFIC CIRCLE TO PINKERTON ACADEMY there is a large, imposing building directly in your line of vision. It's very hard to miss. It looms down from a slight hill on the angle of land between Pinkerton Street and Main Street. This three-story structure is usually called Association Hall. It is one of only seven nineteenth-century commercial buildings that still survive in Derry. Today it is the home of an antiques shop.

In the earliest records, the lot was owned by William Choate (1785–1870), who built a small tavern and store there around 1817. It was converted into a large, Federal-style residence in 1838. This home was destroyed in a fire in 1870 when it was owned by Leonard Brickett. Tradition holds that the fire smoldered for two days in the home's partitions and the local men were unable to find a way to extinguish it. This gave the owner plenty of time to save all of the furniture and his belongings before it was finally gutted by the flames. The neighbors helped by carrying to safety the front door, the shutters on the windows and the entire piazza. All of these salvaged pieces were in time retrofitted onto other village homes. The now homeless, doorless, and porchless Mr. Brickett died soon afterward.

In 1875 the cellar hole and lot were sold to an association of local investors called the Derry Building Company. Their incorporation papers stated their purpose as "the purchase of land in Derry Village, the construction of such building or buildings thereon

Association Hall, Derry Village in 1895.

as the corporation may deem for their interest, the renting of the building and the beautification of the land." Among the leaders were the New England milk king H. P. Hood and prominent lawyer Greenleaf Bartlett. The association was funded by selling thirty-six shares of its stock at a par value of a hundred dollars each.

The company hired architect Washington F. Gregg to design the building. He had been born in Derry in 1848 and was the son of carpenter Benjamin Gregg. Its contractor was David H. Curtis of Haverhill. It seemed to be the right combination because within less than four months it arose, "phoenix like," from the ashes of the burnt-out Brickett homestead.

A grand-opening celebration was held on December 24, 1875. A huge, translucent cloth sign illuminated by lanterns from behind proclaimed the building officially Association Hall. The musical family of George F. Adams entertained the crowd. An "epicurean feast" followed the speeches and entertainment.

The building of the hall was a major triumph for Derry Village. In the upper village of East Derry, the new town hall was being built. It was a neck-and-neck race to see who would finish first. When the sawdust finally cleared, it was the Lower Village that won bragging rights. The Upper Village Hall wouldn't be dedicated until a week later, on New Year's Eve. Another plus for the people of the Lower Village was that their hall was built with private money; the Upper Village Hall used public funds and had put the town of Derry five thousand dollars in debt.

The two villages thought of themselves as being quite separate and in fact were rivals. Both villages now had a function hall where they could have fancy-dress balls and hold scientific lectures. Both had its own Congregational church, general store, and private academy (Pinkerton Academy and the Adams Female Academy respectively). Both villages had a number of very stately, federal-style homes built in the early nineteenth century.

The new Derry Village hall was a three-story building with a mansard roof in the très chic French style. The basement was designed for use by a small store or as storage. The first floor was divided into space for two more stores. On the second floor was the Association Hall, which could be rented for theatrics, lectures, dances, and political rallies. On the top floor was the Masonic lodge.

Saint Mark's Lodge of Masons first met in 1826 over Thom's Store in East Derry and later in the hall over the East Derry Store. The Masons dedicated their Association Hall temple on January 6, 1876, with state Grand Master John Bell. This was followed by a dinner for two hundred guests in the second-floor banquet room. Afterward, Dignain's Band kept them dancing to the "wee sma' hours." The building would remain their home until 1924, when the Masons built their present lodge, on Broadway. There are still Masonic emblems above the third-floor windows of Association Hall.

From 1875 to 1900, many businesses occupied the first-floor suites. Bell's Drug Store was there for many years before moving to Broadway. A number of dress shops rented space. A half-century later, Helen Brickett Poor recalled the care that Miss Marie Parsons would take with the gowns she made for her customers. "It took from fifteen to eighteen yards of silk for a gown," she said, "a good portion of which was made into ruffles and pleats with millions of stitches, all hand work."

This workmanship contrasted sharply with a cobbler who also rented space in the hall. Although Helen Poor didn't recall his name, she did remember the gossip about the artisan. A village local had brought him a beautifully tanned side of leather and hired him to craft it into a pair of custom shoes. A few weeks later, when he returned to pick up the shoes, he discovered that the shoemaker had made the shoes with the leather wrong-side out. The cobbler soon moved out of town. From 1893 to 1897 his suite served as the village post office

The hall on the second floor was a popular place for entertainment. Almost every week, village residents could pay their dimes to hear talent like comedian Comical Brown, a singer, or some out-of-town expert speaking on subjects ranging from temperance and history to natural religion. Among the luminaries who lectured there were the poet Oliver Wendell Holmes, abolitionists Parker Pillsbury and Wendell Phillips, women's rights activist Mary A. Livermore, and essayist Ralph Waldo Emerson. Within a month of its opening, "Professor" Gibson had started a dancing school.

Many decades later, Lillian Poor could still recall "the heartbreaking thrill which held me breathless during a presentation of Uncle Tom's Cabin when Eliza crossing the ice on a ten-by-fifteen-foot stage followed by the hounds, which almost, but not quite, grabbed her as she disappeared into the wings."

In the triangle in front of the hall was the village water pump. Here generations of area residents drew their water for cooking, cleaning, and drinking. Historian Harriett Chase Newell recalls a story that happened during one Independence Day. Mr. Thom, one of the village elders, was sitting on the planks that covered the well. He was probably resting with his eyes shut, enjoying the warm summer day. In the back pocket of his pants was dangling a string of firecrackers he was saving for a later time. One village youth (likely the future judge George Grinnell) snuck up behind the dozing figure and lit the firecrackers. "Mr. Thom went tearing down the street with loud exclamatory remarks that could be heard for quite a distance," remembers Mrs. Newell.

In 1900, the Ladies Benevolent Society of the Central Congregational Church purchased a half interest in the building. They used it as the church's social hall. Here they could have their meetings, May breakfasts, wedding showers, and Sunday school plays. The proceeds from their church suppers and rummage sales were used to support missionaries and to aid local charities.

In the spring of 1906, Association Hall was the site of one of the pivotal events in the history of American literature. Robert Frost had just been turned down for a position as a Derry public school teacher. The school board had rejected his application without even bothering to open his letters of recommendations. To school board chairman Wark, the applicant was just a rather shiftless and unsuccessful chicken farmer with no college degree and little promise, certainly not worthy of teaching the children of Derry.

A few days after this rejection, a very disheartened Frost approached the Reverend Charles Merriam to see if there was an opening at Pinkerton Academy. In addition to being a trustee at Pinkerton, Merriam was the pastor at the Central Congregational Church. The cleric read the letters of recommendation and discovered that Frost was a poet. Merriam was also a writer of verse; in fact, he had written the Pinkerton Hymn, which was sung at all school functions. He saw Frost as a brother poet. To help establish Frost's academic credentials in Derry Village, Merriam invited him to read one of his poems to the church's men's group. The annual spring banquet of the Men's League was to be held in Association Hall. If he was well received there, it would give him a leg up in securing a teaching job at the academy.

Robert Frost cringed at the prospect. He had never read any of his poetry in public—much less in a hall filled with the movers and shakers of Derry. Frost turned down Merriam's offer, saying that he just plain lacked the courage even to try reading aloud before an audience. The minister countered by offering to read one of Frost's poems for him. All the poet would have to do was sit there beside him and take credit. Reluctantly Frost finally agreed.

The poem the poet selected was "A Tuft of Flowers," that he had written about an experience he had while haying near Corbett's Pond in Salem. This double couplet was the first introduction of Frost to most of the town's folk.

> *I went to turn the grass once after one*
> *Who mowed it in the dew before the sun*
> *The dew was gone that made his blade so keen*
> *Before I came to view the leveled scene.*

The poem, as read by Reverend Merriam, was applauded by the crowd. Historian and mill owner John Carroll Chase was in the audience, and he was quite impressed with both the poem and the poet. Chase was the secretary of the board of trustees of Pinkerton Academy.

Trustee Chase approached Frost in private and told him in strict confidence that there was a teaching job that would soon become available at Pinkerton. The English teacher had just resigned for health reasons. A retired local minister, who had no desire to stay in the classroom, would be reluctantly filling in as substitute. Frost was hired in late March 1906 at a salary of $285 for the remainder of that school year. And the rest is history. His success in Association Hall would in time lead him to become America's favorite poet.

If the Men's League spring banquet had gone poorly perhaps Frost would have been too discouraged to seek further career advancement. Such failure might have led him to remain a chicken farmer here in Derry. He might have ended up with a job at Colonel William Pillsbury's shoe factory or Ben Chase's mill.

I try to imagine what might have happened if Frost had not succeeded in that first appearance in Association Hall. In my too active imagination I can see automobiles during the 1950s traveling on Route 28, each one speeding toward Salem or Derry. Few of the drivers turn their head to notice the small white farmhouse that needs a coat of paint and a lot of repair. Sitting in a wooden lawn chair at the edge of the untidy front lawn is an elderly man with a broad grin and a shock of white hair. He waves enthusiastically at all the cars that pass by whether or not he knows the driver. In front of the house is a small, hand-painted sign nailed to a tree. On the sign it simply says *Rob Frost—Country-Fresh Eggs*. And when he died in the 1960s, bushels of his scribbling were consigned to the Derry landfill on Fordway.

The Men's League banquet received front-page coverage from two local newspapers. For some unknown reason the reporter for the *Derry News* did not even mention Robert Frost or the Reverend Merriam's reading of the poem. The *Derry Enterprise* not only mentioned that Robert Frost was introduced by the toastmaster before his poem was read, but it also reprinted the entire poem on the front page. This was the first time this newspaper had ever published a poem on its front page! Obviously one reporter recognized greatness when he heard it; the other journalist missed a scoop about one of the literary giants in American history.

In 1921, the Central Congregational Church acquired the other half interest in the building, which was valued at three thousand dollars. The family of Alex Proctor made the donation in their late father's name. (His collection of Indian artifacts was given to the

Hood Museum at Dartmouth College.) In honor of their gift, the edifice was named Proctor Hall, but the name didn't stick. Considerable interior renovation was accomplished in 1922 with funds raised by the ladies of the church. An addition was made in 1927 to the side of the hall to house a new kitchen, a gift of the Chase family. Mr. and Mrs. Gilbert Hood donated the fire escape in 1937.

For seventy years the hall was used for thousands of church functions. Frequently it was rented out for parties and auctions. In February 1963 I can remember going to the hall for a free baked bean supper. The host was Nelson Rockefeller, the Republican primary candidate for president. The candidate was observed to eat his beans with a spoon. I still have the autograph he gave me that day.

In 1970, the Central Congregational Church built a large addition to its Crescent Street sanctuary to provide rooms for Sunday school, a daycare, and social activities. Association Hall was no longer needed by the church and was put up for sale. It was almost sold to the Derry Boys Club but the group decided to move instead into the Upper Village Hall. Soon a buyer emerged and Association Hall reverted to being a commercial building. For a while it was a used-furniture store and later a bicycle shop. Since 1996, Christa Guilmette, with her son Corey, has owned the building. Considerable restoration has been done to the structure in recent years by skilled artisan John Cook. It is currently an antiques shop and my frequent destination while on the prowl for treasures for the museum.

Top: Haying at the Hood Farm, Derry, NH. Bottom: Hood's Farm, Derry, NH

31.

The Hood farm

IF YOU WERE TO VOYAGE BACK A HUNDRED YEARS IN TIME, YOU'D find that most Derry residents were employed in the shoe industry. The Broadway section of town was home to dozens of buildings devoted to the various aspects of the manufacture of leather products. The stores, schools, churches, and clubs of West Derry were there mainly to service the shoe-factory workers and their families. The second largest employer in Derry was the H. P. Hood and Sons Dairy Company.

The Hood Company was founded in 1846 by Harvey Perley Hood (1823–1900). In 1844 he had left his hometown of Chelsea, Vermont, to seek his fortune in Boston. His capital at the time consisted of "a horse, harness, wagon and pung." He was soon employed as a driver for a bakery. He lived frugally and saved enough from his twelve-dollar-a-month salary so that in just two years he was able start his own one-man milk route near Boston. He moved to Derry Village in 1856 to take advantage of the railroad, which had been built through Derry a few years earlier. Hood was an entrepreneurial genius who had the vision to see a way to economically connect the supply of dairy products with the urban market in Massachusetts.

His first Derry home was the Murdock-White farm on the Route 28 bypass. This had been the site of the town's common field where in 1719 was planted the first potato crop in America. (The farmhouse and barn were torn down about thirty years ago by a developer, who replaced them with an apartment complex of 850 units.)

The farmers of New Hampshire were capable of producing lots and lots of milk. The towns and cities of Massachusetts consumed lots and lots of milk. With Derry as a transportation hub, milk could be loaded onto rail cars and hauled to Boston in about an hour. Hood was also the first New England milk producer to employ pasteurization, which allowed him to advertise that his product was certified as safe for children. He was also a pioneer in the use of sterilized glass milk bottles.

Some church leaders criticized him for shipping milk on Sunday and threatened to have him excommunicated. H. P. countered that "babies don't know the days of the week" and needed to be fed on the Sabbath just as much as on any other day. He also said cows needed to be milked seven days a week and that their milk would sour if not shipped to market in his refrigerated rail cars.

Each day H. P. loaded cans of milk onto a freight car at the Broadway Depot. In Charlestown, Massachusetts, the milk was sold from the door of the boxcar directly to the waiting milk peddlers. H. P. Hood's office was a desk and chair in the middle of the freight car. On the afternoon train back to Derry, he would sit in his "office" and figure out the daily receipts.

In 1858, he purchased Redfield Farm on East Broadway and renamed it Hoodkroft Farm. This would be his home for the rest of his life. (The structure is now Chen's Chinese Restaurant.) In 1880, his son Charles Harvey Hood graduated from New Hampshire State Agricultural College at Dartmouth College in Hanover, N.H. This institution is now the University of New Hampshire. He was, in fact, the only graduate that year. By 1882 H. P. had the distinction of paying the highest taxes in Derry. His tax bill was $108; in second place was the Derry National Bank at ninety-eight dollars. Shoe factory mogul Colonel William Pillsbury was in twenty-first place with taxes of fifty-two dollars.

A *Derry News* article in 1881 described his cows with the old schoolboy definition: "two hookers, two lookers, four stiff standers, four down hangers and a wiskabout." In the barn that year were sixty-eight white and red cows, black and brindled milk cows, and a huge "noble, full blooded Aryshire bull." There were four men milking a line of thirty cows. Each cow averaged eight and a half quarts of milk per day.

In 1883, H. P. Hood suffered a stroke, which caused him to be unconscious for several days. This "shock of apoplexy" forced the milk king to relinquish much of the corporation's daily business into the capable, college-trained hands of his sons. In 1888 Charles became a full partner and the company was renamed H. P. Hood and Son. In 1890, with Gilbert Hood joining the firm, it became H. P. Hood and Sons. In 1972 the company took its present name of H. P. Hood, Inc.

The business in the 1890s was still relatively small. Its rolling stock consisted of only four wagons, nine horses, and three railroad milk cars to ship the product to Boston. In 1892 the Hoods broke away from the pack and gained national recognition when one of the family's Jerseys was proclaimed the top cow in the known universe at the Chicago World's Columbian Exposition.

The firm also enjoyed a deserved reputation for its milk being pure and free of additives. The company introduced sterile glass milk bottles to Derry in 1896. A contract from 1903 indicated the determination of the Hoods to sell safe, sweet milk. That year local farmers were paid the relatively high price of twenty-nine and a half cents for each eight-and-a-half-quart "can" of milk they sold to the company. In return, the dairy farmers had to keep the milk at a temperature below 58 degrees and never allow the milk to freeze. (In 1908, the maximum temperature was reduced to forty degrees.) Empty cans had to be stored on a rack at least three feet off the floor. Any typhoid or other infectious disease had to be reported to the Hoods "at once."

By 1908 Hood milk had begun to employ even stricter standards. The government allowed up to five thousand bacteria per cubic centimeter of milk; the Hood dairy laboratory found ways to reduce the bacteria count in their milk to as low as one hundred per cubic centimeter. Each lot of milk was tested before it was sold. The specially designed "Hood Pail" allowed for all milk to be strained through absorbent cotton—both as it enters and leaves the pail.

The company around 1905 pioneered in developing and marketing special milk for infants. The Hood dairy in Derry combined its purest milk and cream with a formulated mixture of line water and milk sugars. This prepared formula was put up in sterilized six-ounce bottles and sold in eight-pack boxes.

Because of all these safeguards to assure the purity and safety of their product, Hood milk was more expensive then most other brands. The company's response to criticism over its higher price was "milk at nine cents a quart is not only cheap, but it's too cheap for the maintenance of proper precautions of absolute safety and high quality." Cheaper milk too often "barely passed inspector's tests" and was handled by men that most customers "would not allow to cross the thresholds of their homes." The Hood company became known as the "Milk Experts" and it was widely believed that "You can feel good about Hood."

After H. P. Hood's death, in 1900, his three sons, Charles, Edward, and Gilbert took over the running of the business. This second generation of Hoods were Derry-born but had been educated in private schools in Massachusetts. H. P. Hood wanted his heirs to have a better education than what Derry could offer. During most of their childhood, the three Hood boys returned to Derry only during summer vacations and holidays. When it came their turn to manage the firm, they moved the corporate headquarters from Derry to Somerville, Massachusetts. Hoodkroft Farm would be the show farm for the mighty Hood milk empire. Here their prize herds of Jerseys and Guernsey's would be kept. Each year Hood employees from through New England came to Derry for a company outing.

The Hoodkroft compound in 1906 consisted of three large houses that were used by the family and their retinue of five family servants. Several other large homes were used as boardinghouses for farm workers. Behind 116 East Broadway is a small, expertly crafted log cabin that was built for Gilbert Hood Jr. (1899–1985) as a playhouse. In 1906 Charles and Edward Hood were living in Somerville while Gilbert Sr. lived in Derry managing the Derry aspects of the business. Gilbert's salary in 1906 was three thousand dollars a year. By 1910, Gilbert had also taken up full-time residence in the Bay State.

The Hoodkroft barns at the beginning of the twentieth century were the pride of Derry Village. The main barn was three stories tall and 135 feet in length. There were numerous other farm buildings, all of which were kept in perfect repair and painted a dazzling white. The Derry Village farm in 1906 was home to about 120 dairy cows and heifers as well as fourteen horses. The barns were kept very clean and were lit by electricity. Each day the herd produced about eighteen quarts of milk; much of this was shipped to the Boston market. Four ponds supplied water to the barns. The huge main barn was destroyed in a Christmas Day fire in 1962.

In 1961, the Hoodkroft Farm was the winner of the Green Pastures award as the best farm in Rockingham County. At the time, the farm had a milking herd of 150 cows. To grow award-winning forage, farm manager Robert Martin spread two thousand tons of manure each year. His annual yield was over twelve hundred tons of hay and ensilage.

Towering over the farmyard were two large silos that were filled each year with 640 tons of ensilage. In addition to this ground-up corn and grass, hundreds of tons of hay were raised on the farm's 325 acres. The Hoods took pride in the fact that their herds were fed exclusively on fodder raised on Hoodkroft Farm. During the warm months, the cattle were brought across the street to graze on what is now the course of the Hoodkroft Golf Club. Twice a day, all traffic on Broadway was stopped while the Hood's herd was paraded to or from the pasture. This fondly-remembered traffic disruption continued until 1969, when the herd was sold at auction.

On Manning Street in West Derry was located the Hood creamery. A private railroad siding made it easy to load Hood products into its fleet of refrigerated cars and bulk milk tankers before speeding to markets in Massachusetts. It was the creamery, grain store, and icehouse that first made the firm of H. P. Hood and Sons the "milk king" of New England. Derry was the hub to which New Hampshire dairy farmers shipped their milk. From here it could be made into butter, sold locally, or routed to Boston.

Immense amounts of ice were needed to cool the various Hood products. The company built a mammoth one-hundred-by-three-hundred-foot icehouse near the shores of Hood Pond. (The back wall of the present Rollins Street tennis court is part of the foundation of this huge structure.) Workmen would cut blocks of ice on the pond when the ice was about fourteen inches thick. Each of the forty-four-inch-square blocks weighed about eight hundred pounds. In January 1906, it took eighty-five men ten days to harvest 40,000,000 pounds of crystal-clear ice. The blocks were moved to the icehouse by a steam-powered conveyer belt. The elevated ice run very much resembled the roller coaster at Canoby Lake Park. Before being grappled into the icehouse, the blocks were shaved to uniform size to aid in packing. The eleven-hundred-foot-long ice run from pond to icehouse was believed to be the longest in the country.

The creamery, grain warehouse, and storage building stood three stories tall and extended about three hundred feet in length down Manning Street. The southern part extended nearly to Broadway and was used to store sacks of grain. Its own generating plant produced electric power for the facility. Milk from Hoodkroft and other local dairy farms was brought to the Manning Street facility where it was dumped into huge vats. Each of the vats could hold up to five thousand quarts of the white liquid. Up to five hundred pounds of butter was produced here daily in 1906. Some of the hoisting equipment is displayed at the Granary of Derry building. This store/apartment building at 101-110 Manning Street was built about two decades ago and I have been told that it incorporates some of the original Hood building. The creamery building was torn down in 1963 and is now the site of the Derry Municipal Building and Court House.

In 1906, the Hood Company was producing 120,000 quarts of milk a day. This was the product of nearly two thousand farms scattered throughout New England. Today the company has sales of 2.2 billion dollars and has five thousand employees. Hood's cooperate headquarters is now in Chelsea, Massachusetts. H. P. Hood Inc. is owned by the family of CEO John Kaneb.

It has now been more than a 150 years since Harvey Hood's arrival in Derry. Although the company is no longer a Derry-based concern, its presence is still felt locally. Among the many family benefactions to the town are the Gilbert H. Hood School, the two Hood Parks, and the Hoodkroft Country Club. The Hoods also gave Derry the first Alexander-Eastman Hospital and also opened its first shopping mall. We in Derry take pride in our town being the birthplace of such a great commercial institution. It is a real Derry success story.

32.

The Chester and Derry Trolley

RECENTLY THE DERRY MUSEUM OF HISTORY PURCHASED A COPY of the program that was distributed the day of the opening of the Chester and Derry Street Railroad. Today that trolley line is just a memory. Only the most senior of our senior citizens can recall riding its Toonerville-style cars or the sound of its clanging bell.

To our citizens 109 years ago, the advent of the trolley in Chester was viewed as a milestone that would change the economic life of both Chester and Derry. Its inaugural run on September 22, 1896, was an exciting event that demanded speeches, music by a brass band, and the spectacle of fireworks.

During the last half of the nineteenth century, the town of Chester felt like "Mister Left-Out." Every town in this part of Rockingham County was on a railroad line—except the little town of Chester. A map shows Chester as an island surrounded by railroad tracks that passed through other towns. To make it even more galling, Derry, her next-door neighbor, had two different lines cutting through its territory. Even the rather diminutive, farming community of Sandown had rail service and a busy depot.

Many in Chester believed that the citizens of Sandown had in 1872 resorted to bribery to persuade the Nashua and Rochester Railroad to choose them over the far better route through Chester. Chester desperately wanted a rail link to the world. Towns that had trains were certain to prosper and grow; towns that remained trainless were left behind to stagnate. Chester had tried everything it could think of to get on the track but had no success.

The Chester and Derry Trolley approaches the West Derry Depot during the 1920s.

In 1891, the idea of a light rail train clicked in someone's mind. If not a real railroad, then why not a street railroad—a trolley? That year the New Hampshire Legislature incorporated the Chester and Derry Railroad Association. Its incorporators were the crème de la crème of the two towns. Among its stock subscribers were Derry businessmen Colonel William Pillsbury, Frederick Shepard, and *Derry News* publisher Charles Bartlett. In Chester the chief supporters were storekeeper Arthur Wilcomb and physician General Arthur Emerson.

Work on the line began in May and within five months it was completed. Its path ran from the Derry Depot on Broadway east on Route 102 toward where the rotary is today. From the traffic circle area it made a few jigs and jogs before veering to run through East Derry and by the east side of Beaver Lake. It eventually rejoined Route 102 and ended at Wilcomb's store in Chester Center.

The entire length of the track from Chester to Derry was only about seven and a half miles. This makes the C&D the shortest street railroad in the state. That distinction was lost in ten years, however, when the Uncanoonuc Incline Railroad in Goffstown was built. This mountain-climbing tourist train was only three miles long from beginning to end.

The day of the official opening of the Chester and Derry was scheduled for September 22, 1896. All of Chester was excited. Derry was less so. Chester was now going to be connected to the world;

Derry was now going to be connected to Chester. The only really obvious benefit to Derry was that the trolley would provide speedy transportation to Beaver Lake.

The *Derry News* printed the program for the grand day. The four-page handout contained several stories on the history of the trolley company and its heroic efforts to get local support. On its front page was a photograph of its fleet of cars. Most of the space, however, was filled with advertisements from local merchants; these included Nutfield Tonic, Pettee's Day Light Oil, 7-20-4 Cigars, Bell's Apothecary, and Wilcomb & Son's general store. The *Derry News's* ad said it was published every Friday with a subscription price of $1.00 per year (!). To fill in unsold ad space, the program also had stories of curfew laws in Kansas, a recipe for pickles, and a visit to Washington, D.C. by the British colonial secretary.

The big day arrived finally—and the sky was overcast and gloomy. The first electric car left Derry Depot at seven in the morning and arrived in Chester forty-five minutes later. This special car, with its dignitaries, arrived in the little town to be greeted with the ringing of church bells and the firing of a cannon salute. Among the guests on board were New Hampshire's governor and a congressman along with assorted generals and local power brokers.

After the guests de-trolleyed at Chester Center, a ceremonial line of march was formed. The Derry Brass Band led the parade to the Chester Inn. This hotel was a stately, eighteenth-century tavern that stood just north of the present-day Chester Hardware store. Its sprawling piazza and a platform in front were slated to serve as a stage for the ceremony. By this time, though, the sky was opening up with a drenching rain. Everything was hastily moved into the sanctuary of the nearby Congregational church.

The church was filled to overflowing and many spectators had to stand outside in the torrential of rain. The president of the day was storekeeper Wilcomb. He made the opening speech, proclaiming this "the greatest event in the history of Chester." He shared with the crowd his dream of the trolley bringing in new industry and sparking people to move into the rural town. He closed his oration with his hope that "in a few years we shall rival our esteemed neighbor, Derry."

Professor Cassius Campbell, of Pinkerton Academy, followed him on the platform. He was serving as the first president of the Chester and Derry Trolley Company. He declared that the crowd was made up of citizens "who believe nothing is too good for them—and that they are not too good to work with brain and muscle to secure whatever good things the progress of civilization brings within their reach." The Puritan ethic of hard work was alive and well in the minds and hearts of the citizens of Chester and Derry.

The next speaker was Congressman Cyrus Sulloway (1839–1917). He was known across the Granite State as the "tall pine of the Merrimack." At six foot, eight inches tall, with broad shoulders and a huge physique and a long, unkempt beard, he must have been an imposing figure on the platform. He said he came to Chester to mingle with the crowd and share in their celebration and not to make a speech—but of course he did so anyway. Somewhat later, Governor Busiel gave a brief talk, whose theme was the wisdom of investing in New Hampshire and not sending our money out west.

On and on went the speakers. General Charles Bartlett of Manchester said that "in these days of doubt and gloom it's good to be among people who were rejoicing." He didn't explain what the cause was of this depression; however, there was a hotly contested presidential election in progress. The voters were angry at the incumbent Democrats because the national economy had been pretty sour since 1893. In November, Republican McKinley would defeat populist Democrat William Jennings Bryan. One interesting thing I noticed when researching this article was that the 1896 presidential election map is almost exactly the opposite of that of the election of 2004: What was Republican in 1896 is Democrat now and vice versa.

The last speaker was the Honorable Aaron Whittier, who praised the trolley because of what it could do for the education of Chester's youth. He postulated that students could leave Chester in the morning; attend classes at Pinkerton Academy; and in the same day "return at night to the guardian care of their mothers." In the old days, Chester students had to board in Derry during the week and walk back to Chester for the weekends—each student would, of course, be carrying a sack of dirty clothes to be washed by his mother.

When the orations were finally over, the hotel provided a dinner for the dignitaries. The crowd of non-dignitaries was sold a meal prepared by the Chester Grange and the Women's Relief Corps.

In the afternoon, there were scheduled to be sporting events, including a five-mile bicycle race, hundred yard dash, and a baseball game between the trolley company's team and the town of Derry's team. The steady rain forced cancellation of these outdoor events. The crowd was entertained in the car barn by the Derry Brass Band.

All day the trolley gave free rides to everybody. All three cars were kept busy and traveled a distance equal to one trolley car running the entire line about seventy times. Many riders boarded in Chester, got off at the Beaver Lake stop, and got on the next trolley heading back to Chester.

In the evening, the weather cleared up enough for a fireworks display at Chester Center. An ice-cream social and dance was held at the Chester Inn. The festivities wouldn't break up until midnight.

The rolling stock of the Chester and Derry consisted of three passenger cars and a freight car, all built in Amesbury, Massachusetts. The power for the line was provided by two 250-horsepower engines. The car barn near the Derry Village rotary measured thirty by one hundred feet and the one adjoining Wilcomb's store was thirty by fifty.

Several local poets wrote verses to commemorate the day. The poet laureate of Chester, Isabelle Fitz, penned perhaps the most memorable of the poems. Hers was a fifteen stanza effort; I will share with you only its first and last:

Ring the bells with peals exultant!
Let your banners be unfurled!
Lift your voice in jubilation,—
Chester is open to the world!

******

Welcome then, electric railroad!
Chester's joy and Chester's pride!
Motor man, turn on the current—
Come, o Muse. We'll take a ride.

With that daylong celebration, the Chester and Derry Street Rail Road Company began operations. Its first printed schedule, in September 1896 had a trolley leaving Derry for Chester about every hour from 7:40 in the morning until 7:40 in the evening every day of the week. The forty-five-minute trip between the two towns cost twenty cents.

Despite the enthusiasm of the promoters, the trolley company was never a success. During its thirty-two year history, it managed never to show a profit and in fact lost money most years. The advent of the automobile finally caused it to go bankrupt. The last run of the trolley was on June 4, 1928. Bart Shepard, the father of the astronaut, was at the controls that day. After the trolley came into the barn, Bart put the brass power switch lever into his pocket and walked home to East Derry. The trolley era had officially ended in Derry.

33.

The Test

AWHILE AGO I HAD THE PRIVILEGE OF SPEAKING AT THE ROBERT Frost Farm. I guess the theme of my speech was that Derry in the Frost years (1900–1911) was not a sleepy, backwater town. We were not populated by rubes who knew little of the outside world. Derry was a vibrant community with a strong industrial base. The poet had his choice of riding on two trolley lines, shopping at a dozen stores, or deciding which flick he wanted to see in one of four places regularly showing movies in town.

Robert Frost did not teach at a normal, garden-variety high school. Pinkerton Academy was, in fact, an exclusive prep school that admitted only the brightest and the best. The student body was not by any means a cross-section of the town's youth. By and large the children of shoe workers and farmers did not go to high school: their golden school days ended when they graduated from the district's one-room schoolhouses. Most of the Pinkerton Academy graduates went on to college and employment in the professions.

Derry in the first decade of the twentieth century had eight public schools. Of these, half were rural one-room schoolhouses. Usually students stayed in these district schools until about the age of thirteen, at which time most called it quits and joined the town's labor pool. Only a few thought about going to high school. Those who did want to go on to secondary school were mainly the children of the more affluent class.

It wasn't the cost of tuition that kept the children of shoe workers from attending Pinkerton Academy. The tuition in 1900 was only fifteen dollars a year. This was equal to about eight days wages for a typical workman in a Derry factory. By 1901, the state of New Hampshire required the town to provide free tuition to any young person who was going on to high school. Many youngsters dropped out because their family needed the money they would earn. For most, their intended employment did not require education beyond the three R's; these they had no doubt mastered in grade school. There was little need for higher education for most shoe factory jobs.

In 1903 the town paid for thirty-three and a sixth pupils to attend Pinkerton. (One student dropped out during the first semester, hence the "sixth of a student.") This cost the taxpayers a total of $497.49. About 11 percent of the school-age population would enter high school and only about 5 percent would achieve the distinction of being a high school graduate.

Perhaps the greatest impediment to going to Pinkerton Academy was the admittance test. You didn't just finish your years at the rural school and seamlessly merge into the freshman class at P.A. The trustees at the academy did not accept an eighth-grade certificate of graduation as a ticket of admission to their elite school on the hill. You had to prove your worthiness to enter its ivy-covered hall. Few would rise to the level of educational mastery deemed satisfactory by the academy's trustees.

There were many critics of the grade schools in Derry. The *Derry News* published many letters that were highly critical of the teachers and of the school district. The New England milk king H. P. Hood of Derry chose to send his sons to school in Massachusetts because he didn't believe that Derry's elementary schools were up to the task of educating his heirs.

Each year on a designated Saturday in mid-June, those young people who were thinking of enrolling at Pinkerton Academy would show up for the admittance test. Each had previously submitted a certificate of graduation from his or her district school. This nervous gaggle of adolescent boys and girls consisted primarily of kids from Derry, Salem, Londonderry, Hudson, Chester, and Raymond.

The admission exam by tradition consisted of about thirty questions that would test students on their knowledge of English, geography, arithmetic, and American history. The young people were given four hours in which to complete the test. Here are the questions that were used in 1903. See how well you would do. Oh, by the way, calculators and laptop computers with spelling and grammar checkers weren't allowed. All writing was done with a nib-style pen whose point you dipped into the ink well. Students were warned that "carelessness in spelling, punctuation, or penmanship will count seriously against you."

English
1. Write sentences using correctly the possessive singular of *knife, lady, ox,* and the possessive plural of *child, leaf* and *boy.*
2. Analysis: The Indians are exceedingly skillful in shooting buffalos; they send an arrow quite through the body of a full-grown buffalo when he is in a favorable position and sufficiently near.
3. Parse these words: *send, through, he, favorable.*
4. Separate the independent and dependent clauses of the following sentences; give also the kind of dependent: A. I am not satisfied with the horse I own. B. I will finish the work when the clock strikes twelve. C. Did you ask him what he knew about the matter? D. If you are sure of the truth, you must make known the facts. E. They were so tired that they lay down to rest.
5. Write a description of the town in which you live.

Arithmetic
1. If $^3/_8$ of a yard of cloth costs $^2/_5$ of a dollar, what will $^5/_{16}$ of a yard cost?
2. The gross receipts of a railroad company are $234,100. After deducting 35 percent for working expenses and paying 6 percent interest on $2,500,000 in bonds, what sum is left for dividing among the shareholders?
3. If 5 lbs. of tea at $1.56 per lb., 5 lbs. at $1.20 and 7 lbs. at $0.60 are mixed, at what price per pound must the mixture be sold to gain 2½ percent ?
4. What is the difference between the simple and compound interest on $550 for three years at 5 percent?
5. Find the cost of wallpapering a room 10 feet, 8 inches wide, 19 feet, 4 inches long and 9 feet high, with paper 3 feet wide at 5 cents per yard, allowing 10 feet of the paper for waste?
6. Compare the area of a square and an equilateral triangle if the perimeter of each is 60 feet.

7. Simplify 3 ($^1/_2$ + $^1/_3$) − ($^1/_5$ + $^1/_6$).
8. The diagonal of a square field measures 340 yards. What will it cost to fence it at $2.00 per rod?
9. The distance between the posts of a railway telegraph is 60 yards. Find the rate of a train that passes 11 posts in 50 seconds.
10. If you buy 3 pints of milk a day, how many gallons will you buy in one common year?

Geography
1. Name the different forms of water on the earth's surface. Give an example of each.
2. In what zone do we find most of the civilized nations of the world? Why not in the others?
3. Name the states which border on the Great Lakes and give their capitals.
4. How could you go from Portland, Maine to St. Paul, Minnesota, by water?
5. Name the chief exports of Derry.
6. If you could not live in New England, in what part of this world would you like to live and why?
7. Describe the Mississippi River and tell some of the ways it is useful.
8. Name and locate 6 of the most important cities of the eastern hemisphere.
9. In what parts of the United States is coal chiefly found?
10. What two kinds of grain are most used for food? Where are they mostly grown?

American History
1. What was the Louisiana Purchase? Name 5 states and 3 cities that are located in the territory then obtained. Show some of the good results that have been obtained from it. When and by whom was the purchase made?
2. Write a careful account of either the Mexican War or the War of 1812.
3. What in your opinion are the 3 most important inventions made in this country? Tell what you can about them, naming the inventor and why you consider the invention as important.
4. Write carefully and briefly about each of the following: Monroe Doctrine, Daniel Boone, Underground Railroad,

John Brown, Emancipation Proclamation, Stamp Act, John Stark, Rough Riders, Lewis and Clark.
5. Tell where each of these places is located and why each is important in U. S. history: Quebec, Gettysburg, Yorktown, Plymouth, Jamestown, Mount Vernon, Vicksburg, Manila, Saratoga.

To pass the test a candidate had to achieve a score of at least 75 percent in each area and exhibit "reasonable proficiency in spelling, writing and reading."

Pinkerton Academy Principal George W. Bingham announced that "to the faculty of the Academy these questions seem to be fair and reasonable—certainly not too difficult" for students who have studied the accepted curriculum in common schools. Up until about 1900 Pinkerton had a preparatory year during which entering freshmen were introduced to the rigors of higher education. Around 1900, the academy abolished the prep year and now expected the district schools to prepare their students.

The school took the view that its academic function was to prepare young people so that they would be "fit for any college they wish to enter." For those of its students who chose not to go to college, Pinkerton would "prepare them for the activities of life." The trustees of the academy felt they could not lower their admission standards and remain true to their mission of providing a top-notch preparatory education.

There were fifty-two students who took this test on Saturday, June 13, 1903. Of these, only three received a passing grade. This is a failure rate of 94 percent! Nineteen of the scholars flunked so badly they were told to go back to grammar school and study for another year before re-applying. There were thirty others in the group who were allowed to retest in September in those areas in which they had failed. They could hope that if they boned-up and tried harder they might just make it into the Academy.

When the bell rang on the first day of class that year, there were a total of thirty-eight students who were judged qualified for admittance into the freshman class. Of these, only fifteen would survive the demands of the academy and go onto graduate four years later.

The editor of the *Derry News* put the blame for the high failure rate squarely on the shoulders of the Derry School Board and not the public school teachers. Editor Bartlett believed that it was not that the test was too hard but that our public schools were too soft and the public schools' curriculum was not aligned with that of the academy. He felt that the town-run schools should serve as preparatory schools for Pinkerton. He urged that the elementary school teachers and school board meet with representatives from the academy to find out what was expected at Pinkerton. The *Derry News* editor predicted that meeting the demands and requirements of Pinkerton Academy would do much to raise the standards and performance in the grade schools.

I don't know when the academy stopped requiring the passing of the test for admission to the school. It was still being administered in 1910. It was probably passé by the start of the 1920s. It wouldn't be until after the Second World War that completing high school became a rite of passage for most adolescents. It has only been in the last half-century that the kids who drop out of high school are the exception and not the rule.

It would be interesting to give the 1903 test to a group of Derry students today. I wonder how they'd do. Would their scores be better than the dismal showing the kids made 104 years ago? If anyone works out the answers to the math or English part of the test, please forward them to me via the Heritage Commission at the Derry Municipal Center. Just don't ask me if your answers are correct. I won't have a clue.

34.
The Greatest Baseball Game Ever

I'M SURE THAT EVERYBODY HAS A FAVORITE MOMENT IN SPORTS. For many it was the Red Sox victory in the 2004 World Series. For others it was watching our own Trish Dunn at the 2002 Olympics or Pinkerton's Ryan Mihalko carrying the football to the state Class L football championship in 1985. For me, it was a baseball game that happened many decades before I was born. Although I wasn't there to see it, I have relived it many times in my imagination.

In 1907, Dr. Walter Sanders thought the town of Derry needed something to liven up the lazy days of summer. In 1904 he had sponsored a baseball game that pitted the Rathbone Sisterhood of the Rebeccas against the mighty men of the Knights of Pythias. The ladies played in bloomers and the men in the "frills of feminine attire" with lace and ribbons attached to emasculate their sporting garb. The game took place on the Fourth of July at a field near the pavilion at Beaver Lake. The teams called the game after only three innings. It was a blowout. The score was 22-3 in favor of the ladies. Girls rule! The game and the Rathbone Sisters were the talk of the town for weeks.

Doc Sanders proposed a challenge baseball game between the young men of Derry and the aging men of Pinkerton Academy, class of 1880. The battleground was to be the newly built Pinkerton Oval which was (and is) in the triangle of land between East Broadway, Crescent Street, and Main Street. It was to be a classic match between old and young; the mature and the immature; the colts against the plow horses; men of the nineteenth century in sporting conflict against the boys of the twentieth.

The game was scheduled for four in the afternoon on July 10, 1907. At the appointed day and time, onto the field came the "Old-Timers" and "the Pinkerton Independents." Surrounding the field were six hundred cheering spectators. The umpire was the venerable colonel Frederick Shepard. Cheers went up when Professor Edmund Angell tottered into the infield to start the game. He had been the academy's principal back in 1880. Before the game, the Old-Timers met in a huddle; they agreed among themselves to go easy on the kids. They would let the youngsters win so as not to cause them to suffer from the scars of embarrassment for the rest of their lives.

The Pinkerton Independents were dressed in regulation base-ball uniforms and comprised athletes who were either presently playing on the Pinkerton baseball team or recent graduates. The Old-Timers wore dress shirts, dark trousers, and ties, just as though they were going for a day at the office. They were all respected local businessmen, merchants, or tradesmen. To use the politest possible terms, it might be said that many of the Old-Timers were full-bodied men. Three of the men (Abbott, Pillsbury, and Floyd) collectively weighed in at nearly half a ton.

The leader of the Old-Timers that special day was New Hamp-shire State Senator Charles Abbott. Other team members included District Judge Ernest Abbott, Dr. Walter Sanders, shoe factory owner Rosecrans Pillsbury, hotel owner William Bradford, and ice men John and Bill Madden. The player who had brought out the crowd that day, however, was the Honorable Charles Floyd. This Derry native had just been elected governor of the state of New Hampshire.

Charles M. Floyd was the first and only Derry man ever to be elected governor of the state. Though Samuel and John Bell had been chosen governor in five separate elections, they were not technically from Derry. The brothers had been born in Derry before 1827, when their section of the town was still part of Lon-donderry. The patriot Matthew Thornton was selected as the state's chief executive in 1775 but his title was president. Governor Charlie Floyd was truly from Derry.

He was born on Lane Road on July 5, 1861. As a boy, he attended the brick one-room school that stood on the land at the junction of East Derry and Lane Roads. The structure was torn down around 1886 when the town took over the Adams Female Academy and made it the new district school. Later Floyd attended Pinkerton Academy for a couple of years before dropping out, and thus completed his academic education at the age of fourteen. He found employment as a farmhand for Derry philanthropist Benjamin Adams and afterward in the Broadway shoe factory of Colonel William Pillsbury. This was not enough for Floyd; he knew he had too much promise to remain a farm or factory worker.

Starting when he was twenty years old, he clerked for two years in a hardware store in Haverhill, Massachusetts. After the death of his parents, he returned to Derry to run the family farm. In 1888 he moved to Manchester and opened an Elm Street clothing store. For the next century, Floyd's Department Store was a city institution. The Derry man became both very wealthy and very famous. He is credited with starting the shoe industry in the Queen City in 1891. For decades, he was on the board of directors of many of Manchester's financial and charitable institutions.

Floyd entered politics in 1899, when he was elected to the state Senate, and was elected to the Executive Council in 1905. The battle for the Republican gubernatorial nomination in 1906 was an old-fashioned slugfest. At the GOP convention, the two leading contenders were Derry businessman Rosecrans Pillsbury, the publisher of the *Manchester Union* and Winston Churchill, who was a well-known writer from the town of Cornish, New Hampshire (and not the future prime minister of England.) After the speeches and debates, the voting went on for nine rounds of balloting. During some counts there were more votes cast than there were actual delegates. Votes were being bought and traded like shares of stock on Wall Street; confusion and pandemonium reigned. Finally, Pillsbury dropped out and gave his votes to his old Pinkerton Academy classmate Charlie Floyd.

In the statewide election, Floyd bested Democratic candidate Nathan Jameson 40,581 to 37,672. However, because there was several minor party candidates, Floyd did not receive an actual majority of all the votes that had been cast. By constitutional law at the time, that meant the election would have to be decided by a vote of the legislature. In that Republican-controlled body, Floyd won easily, by a vote of 263–144.

Charlie Floyd was nicknamed the barefoot governor because it was said he first walked from Derry to Manchester without the benefit of shoes. Such wearing apparel was not to be wasted on mere travel; he could instead slip on a pair of shoes just before a job interview. He was a large man, standing about six feet tall and weighing more than three hundred pounds. Physically, he very much resembled his close friend President Howard Taft. He would serve only a single term as governor. He died in 1923. The former Floyd School on Highland Avenue, Derry, was named after him.

At the great baseball game of 1907, first up were the Old-Timers. Senator Abbott whacked the ball squarely into the "burdock beds" in the outfield and arrived safe on second. Next the rotund Rosecrans Pillsbury hit the horsehide sphere, but it bounced right into the pitcher's glove. The 250-pound factory owner was picked off as he ran "like an express train" toward first base. His hit, however, went into the record books as a sacrifice, which allowed Abbott to reach third. Johnny Madden next swung on the pitch "like he was trying to send the ball to Chester." Disappointingly, the ball managed to fly only as far as the shortstop. In the excitement, Abbott reached home plate. The score was 1–zip in favor of the class of 1880. Old-Timers rule!

Next the umpire yelled "Floyd up" and to the batter's box waddled the governor: a big man politically, a big man physically. His success and enjoyment of the good life were dramatically demonstrated by his fifty-four-inch waist. Before the governor could grab his bat, he was surrounded by a committee of his friends. They presented him with a special bat hewed from a thick plank in the shape of a large paddle. The hitting surface was about a foot across. The governor accepted this gift with a "smile of gratitude." It was reported that when Floyd's bat made contact with the first pitched ball, the force of his swing caused ripples to be stirred up on the surface of Beaver Lake two miles away. Unfortunately, however, the ball went high and popped into the hands of the shortstop. Floyd was thrown out at first and Madden was picked off at third. The side was retired.

The Pinkerton Independents were now up. Governor Floyd was positioned in left field, where he immediately lit up a big cigar. Not being a man to waste energy, he signaled for his aide to bring him a soapbox that he could use as a chair. Floyd would leave the comfort of his seat only when he was required to catch balls that were hit into his immediate zone. As soon as the ball was snagged and thrown into the infield, the governor would immediately return to his soapbox and resume puffing on his cigar.

At the end of the fifth inning, the score was 9–1 in favor of the Independents. Floyd and fellow members of the class of 1880 were not pleased! It was at this point that the Old-Timers decided to rescind their promise to let the youngsters win. It was time for the class of 1880 to stand up and prove they were still athletes. So what if a regulation baseball cost a dollar twenty-five and would be lost forever if it was whacked into Hood's Meadow. They were successful businessmen and could well afford to buy a replacement. The class of 1880 would try to snatch defeat from the jaws of humiliation. Losing 9–1 was not an option!

In the sixth inning, the Old-Timers had the bases loaded and Governor Floyd was at bat. With all his strength, the state's chief executive swung his mighty war club and hit the ball. The sound of cowhide against wood "could be heard for a mile." The spheroid was hit into the outfield and three of the Pinkerton Independents collided into a pile in their attempt to catch it. During the confusion, three runs were scored for the Old-Timers. Man-Mountain Floyd circled the bases, dashing like "a runaway steer." Huffing and puffing, he crossed home plate just a yard ahead of the ball. An "inside-the-park" home run for Governor Floyd and the Old-Timers! The tide had turned.

By the end of the ninth inning, the score was even at eleven runs. Some of the Old-Timers were demanding the game go into extra innings. They could smell victory; they had the mo! Most of the players, however, decided that as it was now six o'clock, it was getting too dark to continue. Many players and spectators had to catch trains and trolleys to get back home. It was voted to officially declare the game a tie that was ended on account of darkness.

As both sides congratulated each other, Dr. Sanders walked into the center of the field. From the pitcher's mound he announced that a hat would be passed around to cover the expenses of the game. Governor Floyd raised his hand and silenced the crowd with his deep baritone voice. He announced that a collection would not be necessary. He would pay all expenses from his own pocket. A mighty cheer went up through Derry Village.

The year 2007 is the hundredth anniversary of this great game. Wouldn't it be a hoot to invite Governor Lynch to Derry to stage a reenactment of the great contest of 1907? I bet there are a lot of Derry's old-timers who would love to challenge those young colts from Pinkerton Academy to a baseball game. Let's see who has the right stuff! I'll bring my own cigar, soapbox, and bat.

The white-bearded Lucien Adams sits on the front steps of his Crescent Street home surrounded by his children (l to r): attorney Edward F. Adams, astronomer Walter Adams, and teacher and nurse Helen A. Adams, circa 1904.

35.
Walter Adams

WALTER SYDNEY ADAMS WAS BORN ON DECEMBER 20, 1876, IN the mountain village of Kessab near Antioch in northern Syria, then a province of Turkey. His parents, Lucien and Dora Adams, were both missionaries for the Congregational Church. The family moved back to Derry in 1886 during a four-year break from the foreign Christian service. In Derry, Lucien was known by one and all as "Turkey Adams," though probably not to his face. During this time, Walter attended elementary school in the old two-room school that was at the site of the current school district office; from 1887–1889, he attended Pinkerton Academy. He would later prepare for college at Andover Academy.

One can imagine warm summer evenings with young Walter lying on his back on the lawn of his backyard and looking up at the canopy of stars. He must have wondered what was up there in space and whether man would ever walk on the moon. Did he ever attempt to count the stars? Did he try to guess how far they were away from Derry Village? Perhaps it was here on Crescent Street that he decided to make space his lifelong career and passion.

Decades afterward, Walter recalled how things were for a "preacher's kid" during the Victorian era in Derry. As a boy he was forced to hide his stash of dime novels out of sight in the attic. He knew that his father would throw into the fireplace any such unchristian literature he found in his son's procession. Many in Derry Village considered adventure novels the "work of the Evil One."

Young Walter Adams was an avid reader. One of his major problems, however, was figuring out what kind of literature could or couldn't be read on a Sunday afternoon. If you were caught with the "wrong kind of book," the usual punishment in his crowd was to do three uninterrupted hours of reading the Bible. Walter soon figured out that books on "the religious wars of Europe after the Reformation were suitable but the Napoleonic campaigns were outside the pale."

Among the people he remembered in Derry Village was a "little old man with a white beard." The man was a leader in the Central Congregational Church who at prayer meeting each week ended his prayer with the request that God have mercy upon "the great and wicked city of New York." How the old man knew New York was such a Sodom and Gomorrah young Walter could only guess. This old saint would reportedly arise early each morning and rush to a bedroom window that faced the meadow to the east to see if "the second coming of the Lord was at hand."

In 1886, Lucien Adams had built a house at 24 Crescent Street to serve as a dormitory for missionary children who were attending Pinkerton Academy. One piece of the granite foundation is eighteen feet long and weighs nearly four ton. This plan never succeeded and it remained a private residence.

His parents moved back to Syria in 1890 and the fourteen-year-old Walter remained here in Derry. His mother died at their mission station in 1891. His father returned to Derry in early 1895, possibly to escape the anti-Christian holocaust that was being carried out by the Turkish government.

In Derry, Lucien was frequently a supply minister in the pulpit of local churches. He was a strong supporter of the Republican Party and the move to make illegal the manufacture, sale, and drinking of all forms of alcohol. In 1899 he was the founder of the Derry Anti-Saloon League. He contributed money in Londonderry to lengthen the school year. He also donated a large bell to one of that town's one-room school houses so the kids would have no excuse to be tardy. He was always publicly critical of the Catholic Church, which he considered an enemy of religious freedom, the American way, and personal salvation.

In retirement, Lucien maintained his hatred for the Moslem leaders of Turkey who had massacred the Christian Armenians in 1896. One Sunday, Lucien Adams approached Deacon Robert Hawkins of the Central Congregational Church. Adams asked the deacon if he would offer a prayer on his behalf that morning.

Hawkins readily agreed and asked Adams what the subject of his prayer request was. The old missionary replied, "I have learned that the unspeakable Turk sultan Abdul-Hamid is dead—and I must give thanks to God for that." It is hard to imagine the deacon's response. As it turns out, the sultan hadn't died but instead had been deposed by his brother.

Teenager Walter Adams was enrolled as a freshman at Dartmouth College, where he earned his A.B. in 1898. He would later earn degrees from the universities of Chicago, Munich, Columbia, Princeton, Pomona, and Southern California.

His passion was astronomy. From 1904 to 1923 he was an astronomer at the newly built Mount Wilson Observatory in California. He later served as its director, from 1923 to 1946. Here he gained an international reputation and is still regarded as one of the legends in the science. It was during his years of administration that the two-hundred-inch telescope was installed at the Mount Palomar Observatory.

Please accept the fact that I am not a scientist; I don't really understand much of what I'm about to write in the next few paragraphs. I have tried to put into a layperson's language the research I have done and only imperfectly comprehended. I suggest the reader who is really concerned about astronomy and things like "trigonometrical parallax" to "Google" the name Walter Adams and find out for yourself.

Much of his lasting fame centered on his research of the sun and other stars. He developed the methodology to determine the distance of stars from earth through the means of stellar spectroscopy. Over his career he published more than six thousand such measurements.

Among his other achievements was discovering the presence of carbon dioxide on Venus and of trace amounts of oxygen and water vapor on Mars. This latter research led to the determination of the arid nature of the surface of Mars.

In 1925 he identified Sirius B as the first ever "white dwarf star." This kind of star is a regular star that is running out of fuel and is at the end of its life. This is what scientists predict our sun will become in about five billion years. Sirius B is roughly the size of earth but has the mass of the sun. It has gravity equal to 100,000 times that of Earth. A piece of this star stuff about the size of a pencil would weigh a ton. His calculations of its gravitational redshift were the first evidence of the validity of the theory of relativity. Adams would maintain a professional friendship with Einstein for the rest of their lives.

Adam received many awards, including seven honorary doctorates. He received medals from Britain's Royal Astronomical Society, the French Academy of Science, and the American Academy of Science. He was president of numerous learned societies and authored over three hundred papers on space.

In recognition of his lifetime accomplishments, the International Astronomical Union named a crater on the moon, a minor planet in our solar system (asteroid #3145), and a crater on Mars in his honor. Perhaps someday our great-great-grandchildren will spend their Martian vacation skiing on the Adams crater or hop a rocket ship to dine at a restaurant on Planet Adams. Perhaps Derry pride might lead us to teach our children to sing:

> Twinkle, twinkle little star,
> Now we know just who you are.
> Walter Adams is your name,
> One of Derry's claim to fame.
> In Derry town you were alive
> But now you're asteroid 3-1-4-5.

We can also try to convince our kids that the first name of the "man in the moon" is Walter.

Dr. Adams spent ten years in retirement in the warmth of California pursuing his love of golf, tennis, and bridge, surrounded by his family and reaping the great honors he earned in his long career. For forty years he was a member of the Board of the Public Library in Pasadena. When they built their new library Dr. Adams had inscribed over the main entrance this quotation from a poem by Mary C. Davies:

> Be made whole by books
> As by great spaces and the stars

His scientific papers can be found today at the Huntington and Niels Bohr Libraries.

Walter Adams continued his scientific research until suffering a stroke in the spring of 1956. He died at home on May 11, 1956, in Pasadena, at the age of seventy-nine. One obituary credits him as being the last great researcher of the pioneer age of modern astronomy. He was survived by his wife, Adeline, and sons Edmund and John.

The family honored his request to have his ashes buried in his old hometown of Derry—in the Adams lot at the Forest Hill Cemetery. There for nearly half a century he has rested with his father, grandparents, and great-grandparents under the canopy of stars that shine down brightly on East Derry Hill.

The celebration of Yom Kippur, 1908 in Derry. Local cigar manufacturer Louis Lewis is on the far left.

36.
Louis Lewis the Cigar Maker

THE TOWN OF DERRY TODAY IS HOME TO NEARLY THIRTY-FIVE thousand immigrants or descendants of immigrants who came to this country seeking a better life. Our population is made up of men and women whose ancestors came here from nearly every country. It is claimed that in 1938 President Franklin Delano Roosevelt impishly opened his speech to a convention of the Daughters of the American Revolution with the phrase "My fellow immigrants . . ."

The ethnic, racial, and cultural diversity we celebrate has added much to the quality of life in Derry. A century ago, our citizens were made up almost exclusively of just two large ethnic groups—those from the British Isles and French Canadians. Derry did have a few black families, an Oriental couple who ran a "Chinese" laundry, and an Italian family who operated a fruit store. Occasionally a man with a hurdy-gurdy and a trained monkey would perform on Broadway. There were no Chinese restaurants or pizza parlors.

In 1877 New Hampshire became the last state in America to grant Jews full political rights. In 1880 the United States had a Jewish population of about 250,000. Within the next forty years, that figure would increase to two million. Most of this immigration came from Eastern Europe—where a third of that area's population emigrated to the United States. Among the "huddled masses yearning to breathe free" were Bella and Louis Lewis. In 1903 they became the first Jewish family to settle in Derry.

According to an interview in the *Derry News*, Louis Lewis was born on April 29, 1860, in Zaslaw, Poland, the son of a wealthy distiller. In 1884 he married Bella, whose parents gave the couple a dowry of five thousand dollars. With this money and a gift of three thousand dollars from his parents, he began a lumber business. Soon this enterprise went bankrupt and Louis and Bella lost all their money. Rather than prove a burden to their parents, the young couple quietly packed and secretly arranged to sail to America.

There is no way of knowing if these recollections on why he moved to this country are the whole, unvarnished truth. It is quite possible that Louis preferred not to discuss the anti-Semitism that was a daily fact of life in the nineteenth-century Russian empire. Poland was a part of imperial Russia from 1795 to 1918. In 1881, the assassination of Czar Alexander caused the Russian government to begin rigorous, religious persecution against its Jewish citizens. Such pogroms are dramatically portrayed in the play *Fiddler on the Roof*, which centers on the village of Anatevka in Czarist Russia. Regardless of what really happened, it was certainly for the best that the Lewis family left Poland. During the Second World War, his hometown of Zaslaw was the site of a major Nazi detention camp where thousands of Jews were exterminated.

In 1888, the twenty-nine-year-old Louis and Bella arrived in the port of Boston to start a new life in America. In Bella's arms was their infant son Max. It is highly unlikely that the family name was originally Lewis. Possibly the American immigration official changed it because he couldn't spell the unfamiliar-sounding Polish name. It is also possible that the family changed their name hoping to better blend into the American culture. That very same year, my great-grandmother would also arrive by ship in Boston having left Liverpool, England, to work in the mills of New Hampshire.

For several years, Louis worked in Boston as a clothing presser. In 1892 he learned the cigar making trade. The census of 1900 indicates that both he and his wife could not write English but could speak the language. It was recorded that his native tongue was Yiddish. For a dozen years he made stogies in Chelsea, until in 1903 he decided to open his own cigar business in Derry. He took considerable pride in being the first member of his faith and heritage to live in this New Hampshire town. He became a U.S. citizen in 1906.

Bella and Louis with their two sons, fifteen-year-old Max and three-year-old Joseph moved into a small house at 9 Lawrence Street. Louis quickly built an addition to serve as a cigar manufactory. He was successful in this endeavor and hired several workers to increase his output. He publicly bragged that all of these new workers belonged to the Cigar Makers Union. The cigars were made of pure Havana filler with a Sumatra wrapper with "no flavoring or doctoring."

He manufactured two different brands of cigars—J.H.A. (ten cents each) and the Swampscott (five cents apiece). He never did say what these names meant but he guaranteed that they were made of "the best tobacco with no drugs or coloring." The J.H.A. was advertised as an after-dinner smoke; the Swampscott was for "all the time." In 1905, Louis published a statement from four local physicians (Doctors Perkins, Cogwell, Gravel, and Beckley) as to the quality of his product. These medical men testified that the cigars contained nothing "injurious to the health of those who may smoke them. And we can most cheerfully recommend them to those who enjoy good health as well as a good smoke." W. H. Benson's Cozy Corner Store on Broadway was Louis's chief outlet for his product.

The cigar manufacturer believed most earnestly in advertising. Every local newspaper carried his ads. His slogans were "In God we trust and L. Lewis's J.H.A. we smoke" and "Everybody smokes them. Do you?" He sent a box of smokes to New Hampshire Governor Charles Floyd, a Derry native. The politician sent back a polite letter of acceptance and from then on Louis advertised the cigars as "the brand governor Floyd smokes." In the local movie theaters he paid to have his slogan flashed on the screen. He gave vaudeville stage comedians free boxes of cigars if they mentioned his cigar during their routine. One of those "funny men" quipped on stage that J.H.A. stood for "Jews Have it All." In 1907, Lewis manufactured 150,000 of his fine stogies.

The Polish cigar maker tried very hard to assimilate into mainstream Derry. He joined the Derry Board of Trade, the Cigar Makers Union, the Knights of Honor, the Eagles, the Red Men, and the Knights of America. He may have wanted to join other fraternal organizations but membership would have been forbidden because of his immigrant and Jewish background.

Louis's success may have caused some envy in a certain group of Derry residents. A whispering campaign is what likely led the *Derry News* in January 1908 to include a paragraph promoting the business acumen of the Jewish people. The paper informed its readers that "they are noted for their thrift and enterprise. They always make business and as a rule succeed in the business they undertake. They are not extravagant people, but make a point to be saving and frugal till they get to the place where they are able to give and then they are noted for their wonderful generosity." The paper concluded with the hope that someday more Jews would settle here, which would be "a bonanza for Derry."

Toward the end of 1908, there were about one hundred Jews living in Derry. Most of the adults were employed in the sprawling shoe factories of Broadway. In October it was reported that there was enough support to establish a synagogue in town. The synagogue officers were Charles Tuckyner, president; Nicholas Kassian, vice president and secretary; and Barney Sainer, treasurer. Soon they also founded the Derry Hebrew Educational and Aid Society, with its clubroom in the brick Whitney block at 13 West Broadway. This is now vacant but it was, until recently, the home of Northlite Glass.

The club was established to help "deserving Hebrews" in seeking employment and to be a social and literary club in the evenings. There were fifty-five charter members, with shoe worker Simon Shamroth as chairman. Louis Lewis is listed as on the board of trustees and as its press agent. Publicity releases announced that everyone was welcome to use the clubroom and library with "no distinction between nationalities." In 1909, the association had grown so large that it had to hire the auditorium of the Odd Fellows Hall for its annual meeting. A rabbi from Boston was hired for the occasion.

On September 26, 1908—the year 5655 in the Jewish calendar—the first celebration of Yom Kippur was held in Derry. For the occasion, they rented the Knights of Pythias Hall at 45 East Broadway. The religious service lasted from eight in the morning to one in the afternoon and from six to eight in the evening and was under the direction of Rabbi F. Cohen of Boston. The next year the holiday service was conducted by Rabbi Sam Peniev, of Nashua's Temple Beth Abraham, at the home of synagogue president Joseph Cohen. The first Jewish wedding believed to have been held in Derry occurred in February 1910, when Maurice Spector married Sadie Siegel. The ceremony was followed with a dinner at the home of Mrs. Weisblat at 17 Central Street.

The Hebrew Society and Synagogue was not mentioned in the press after 1919 and may have disbanded. Louis closed his cigar factory and he and Bella got jobs as stitchers in a local shoe factory. Bella passed away around 1928 and Louis retired, sold his Lawrence Street home, and moved away from Derry. G. M. Phalan opened a cigar factory in 1909, taking over from Louis his position as Derry's cigar king. At the Abbott Block, 8 East Broadway, Phalan manufactured the Chief Cigar which retailed for ten cents apiece.

Many Jewish families remained in Derry. During the remainder of the twentieth century their numbers increased. They were our merchants, our neighbors, and our friends. For the next eighty years, members of the Jewish faith would have to travel to Manchester or Nashua to attend temple and celebrate high holidays. In 1992, the Etz Hayim Synagogue was established with Rabbi Bruce Diamond. Now at last, the Jewish families had a chance to worship in Derry, just as they did in 1908.These latter-day descendents of Bella and Louis Lewis have become an important part of the warp and weft that makes up the fabric of the community of Nutfield. L'chai-im.

The original Saint Thomas Aquinas Church and rectory are shown before the fire of 1914.

37.
The burning of Saint Thomas Aquinas Church

DERRY WAS FIRST SETTLED BY EUROPEANS IN 1719. THERE WOULD be no recognizable Catholic community within the town, however, until the mid-nineteenth century. Nutfield's founding fathers and mothers were Scotch-Irish from Ulster (Northern Ireland), a part of Great Britain which was officially a Protestant nation. Our first settlers were Presbyterian separatists who wanted to remain in isolation from the Catholics of Ireland and the Anglicans of England. They put their faith in their own kirk (church), which was subject to control from neither the Vatican in Rome nor Whitehall in London.

During the sixteenth century, England was rocked by a series of religious conflicts. Protestant king Henry VIII outlawed the Catholic Church and executed many of its adherents. Soon after his death, Britain was ruled by his daughter Mary (Bloody Mary), a Catholic. She had burned at the stake many Protestant martyrs. She was followed on the throne by her Protestant sister Elizabeth, who reinstituted the persecution of the Catholics. And on and on it went.

In New Hampshire, Roman Catholics were officially denied the rights of full citizenship after 1679. Even celebration of Christmas was outlawed as being too Catholic. In 1877, after nearly two centuries of official disenfranchisement, our Catholic men were finally allowed to hold elected state office in the Granite State. And it was not until 1968 that the state's constitution was amended by the voters to allow for non-Protestant classroom teachers in our public schools. Though this anti-Catholic teacher provision in the constitution had been ignored for generations, it still existed in fact if not practice.

During the nineteenth century, the cotton mills of our state were attracting boatloads of Irish-Catholic immigrants. The first Catholic church in New Hampshire was established in Claremont in 1822. In 1848 there were an estimated five hundred Roman Catholics in Manchester. The Irish potato famine would soon send more and more sons and daughters of the Old Sod to our shores. To service this growing church community, the Reverend William McDonald was sent to found the area's first church and parish. In 1857, the Sisters of Mercy in Manchester started the state's first parochial school.

By the time of the American Civil War, in 1865, there were just five Catholic families living in Derry. It is likely that few of these faithful attended mass on a regular basis due to the distance between Derry and Manchester, which was the site of the nearest Catholic church. In time, however, the needs of the Catholics in Derry were noticed by the Church. In June 1868 the first mass ever celebrated in Derry was held at the home of James and Margaret Madden. The priest was Father John O'Brien, the pastor of St. Joseph's Church (now Cathedral) in Manchester.

The Maddens lived in a farmhouse on Madden Road on Madden Hill in the West Derry section known today as the Seven Hills. Their house is now long gone. To date I have not been able to find a picture of the structure that was the birthplace of Derry's Catholic church.

Mr. and Mrs. Madden were both born in Ireland and settled in Derry during the 1850s. Their exact ages are difficult to determine because different records give different birth years. James Madden is listed as born in 1830, 1823 and 1825; Margaret was born in 1833, 1830 or 1822. James was a farmer; Margaret, a housewife. The couple had nine children. One grandchild, Johnny Madden, recently passed away at the age of 103 and was reportedly the oldest man in the state of New Hampshire.

After the 1868 service at the Maddens' home, the celebration of mass would occur only infrequently in Derry. In April 1870, Father William McDonald celebrated mass at the home of Daniel and Alice Owen, who also lived in the Seven Hills region. Like their neighbors the Maddens, they were natives of Ireland. Daniel listed his occupation as farm laborer. From April 1870 on, Catholic services were offered in Derry on a regular basis. The residence of John and Mary Duffy was another early mass site. Now every three months a priest from St. Anne's Church in Manchester would celebrate mass at one of the homes of the faithful or in a hired hall. In 1885, Derry officially became a mission church with services conducted every month by a priest from Manchester.

On August 15, 1888, Bishop Bradley ordained Derry as a separate parish. The Reverend Father William J. O'Connor was appointed pastor of the flock. His responsibility included a mission field that comprised Goffs Falls, Candia, Windham, Sandown, and Epping. Father O'Connor was born in Manchester in 1862 and attended the local parochial schools. In 1878 he graduated from Notre Dame University, and then did graduate work at Laval University. He was ordained a priest in 1886 and assigned as assistant rector in a Nashua parish.

During Father O'Connor's eleven years in Derry, he traveled long hours every week by horse, trolley, and train to serve his far-flung mission churches. Father O'Connor was instrumental in building a Catholic church building in Derry, Epping, and Goffs Falls. It was his responsibility to offer the sacraments as well as to administer the finances and daily needs of each of these three churches. Just to visit Epping required a horseback ride to Hubbard's Station in southern Derry, then a long trip on the Nashua and Rochester Railroad. The round-trip train ride between Derry and Epping involved nearly sixty miles of travel and alone cost the busy man several hours of his precious time. While in Epping he would conduct mass, oversee mission business, encourage the faithful, and visit the sick. Father O'Connor would have to leave Derry in the early morning and probably did not return to Broadway until after dark.

Epping ceased to be a mission church of Derry in 1898, when it became a separate parish. Goffs Falls went on its own in 1907. Such hard work nearly ruined Father O'Connor's health, and he left Derry in 1897. He died in Manchester in 1907 when he was just forty-five years old. He was replaced in Derry by Father Daniel Dunn, who served as pastor from 1897 until his death in 1920.

Under the leadership of Father O'Connor, a drive was undertaken to build a Catholic church building in Derry. While it was still a mission church in January 1887, the local believers had purchased a lot on Crystal Avenue from lumberman M. J. Horne. Their prayer was that in time they would build a real church-home on this site. In August 1888—the first month of the parish's existence—the congregation met in Smith's Hall on West Broadway. Starting in September 1888 mass was celebrated in the newly constructed Bell's Opera House on East Broadway. The time of Sunday worship services was ten in the morning.

The Derry parish was not a wealthy one. It was composed primarily of farmers, housewives, and factory workers. The Catholic population of Derry was growing rapidly however. The increasing need for workers at the Pillsbury Shoe Factory was bringing in large numbers of Irish Catholics to Derry. Starting at the end of the nineteenth century these numbers would begin to swell even more with a migration of French Canadians from the province of Quebec. Soon this ethnic group would be followed by immigrants from Eastern Europe. By 1897, the Catholic census reported sixty-five Catholic families living in Derry. Roman Catholics now represented about 10 percent of the population.

In April 1889, an additional three-quarters of an acre of land and a house were purchased from George S. Rollins on Crystal Avenue. This large four-year-old house with barn was to be used as a home for the pastor. Father O'Connor had been renting an apartment in the Jordan home in West Derry before he moved into the new rectory.

The rectory was seriously damaged by fire on July 1, 1890. The nephews of Father O'Connor had started the conflagration by playing with matches. The barn, stable, and ell of the rectory were destroyed but the main building and the church suffered only minor damage. Much of the credit to saving the building goes to the Derry Village Fire Department. These stalwart men pulled their chemical engine to the fire in just twenty minutes after the fire alarm was sounded. This quick response is remarkable because the engine was pulled to the fire by a team of men, not horses or an engine!

To raise funds to build a church, the congregation held a series of fund-raising events at Bell's Opera House. The first was a "strawberry festival" on July 1, 1887. Entertainment was provided by the schoolboys of St. Joseph's School in Manchester. One such "Catholic fair" in January 1889 sold handmade "fancy goods" and home-cooked treats. Talent shows with local performers also drew large audiences. Several times a special train was run from Manchester to bring in hundreds of paying customers. Area businessmen such as William and Rosecrans Pillsbury contributed additional funds.

Groundbreaking for the church occurred on May 1, 1889. I have not been able to determine the identity of the architect. He was not local, as he arrived every few weeks by train and left on the same day. It was reported in the *Derry News* that he was a very busy man, as he had at that time twenty-five churches in various stages of construction. The local building contractor was Ellsworth Martin. The golden cross on top of the church was installed on Friday, September 13, 1889. The church was now the tallest structure in West Derry. When construction was finally completed, the parish was about fourteen thousand dollars in debt.

The dedication of new Saint Thomas Aquinas Church was held on Thursday, November 28, 1889. The day was rainy, so crowds were smaller than anticipated. The service was conducted by Bishop Dennis Bradley and Vicar General Reverend John E. Barry. Fifteen other clergymen assisted in the service. A choir from Father O'Conner's former church in Nashua was also was in attendance. The service lasted two and a quarter hours. This religious celebration and dedication was followed by a turkey dinner in the basement hall of the church. The day's managers had to borrow 1,888 pieces of dinnerware for the banquet. Three long tables were set for 150, but only eighty bought tickets.

This 1889 church was smaller than the present Saint Thomas Aquinas building. Among its most striking features were twelve memorial stained-glass widows in the sanctuary. At the base of each was the name of its donor. These included Bishop Bradley, and local church pioneers such as John Duffy, Daniel Owen, and James Madden. One window honored the pastor's mother, Catherine O'Connor. Hanging from the ceiling was a huge chandelier of kerosene oil lamps. Flanking the altar were life-size polychrome statues of Mary and the holy infant and Christ in the pose of blessing the congregation.

A poem of dedication for the new church was written by Miss Sarah Allen of Chester:

> Our little church stands dedicated
>   To bless the future with the past.
> The little seed sown by the wayside
>   Has yielded forth its fruit at last.

Upon its graceful spire adorning,
    Our dear redeemer's cross we see;
Reminding us of him who bore it
    With pain and grief to Calvary.

Within this shrine God's peace abideth;
    A place is found to rest and pray.
Our lord says, come all ye who seek me.
    I am the truth, the light, the way.

A pastor kind to us is given
    He giveth us his watchful care,
To guide our pilgrim souls to heaven,
    Our joy and sorrow he doth share.

To some, sick bed or home of sadness
    He goeth forth in calm or storm;
Faithful to his holy calling
    His savior's mission to perform.

We thank thee, lord, for all thy mercies,
    That thou hast sent us from above
For thy dear sacraments we bless thee,
    Which makes us worthy of thy love.

Bless thou, O Lord, this sanctuary,
    Made sacred by Thy servants prayers;
Give us grace to love and serve Thee,
    Like the saint whose name it bore.

With the dedication celebration over, the church relaxed and began to concentrate on being the church home to the ever increasing Catholic community in the Derry area. As new families were brought into the fellowship, over-crowding became an increasing problem. At many masses the pews were filled to overflowing and there was beginning to be talk of building a larger sanctuary.

HOLY FIRE

The year 1914 did not start well. On January 13, a fire gutted the ten-year-old Benjamin Adams Memorial Building. Soon, however, the mood in Derry improved as sports fans followed the exploits of the "miracle Braves"—the National League's franchise in Boston.

The team went from last place in the standings in July, to winning the pennant to victory in the World Series in four straight games. Derry native George "Lefty" Tyler was one of their star pitchers. In March, Derry businessman Rosecrans Pillsbury announced his candidacy for governor of the state.

In early August, Derry was in an upbeat mood. The weather had produced a month of long, wonderfully lazy summer days. A nickel ride on the Chester and Derry trolley would bring you to the Beaver Lake pavilion. There you could rent a canoe, swim in the crystal-clear water, bowl, enjoy the zoo, dance to a live band, or play the slot machines.

In the evenings, the Derry Brass Band gave a series of free concerts at the bandstand at the corner of Broadway and Birch Street. Baseball games were being played on vacant lots all through town and Nelson's Fruit Store was selling ice cream for five cents a scoop. On August 7 the opera house at the Adams Memorial Building finally reopened with the Eagles Club Minstrel Show. William Boggle opened the gala with a brand-new song entitled "If You Can't Make a Hit at the Ball Game, You Can't Make a Hit with Me."

Much of the town talk centered on the upcoming Old Home Day at the First Parish Church. For weeks people were heard singing "Meet me at East Derry, Derry/Meet me at the fair./Don't tell me the lights are shining/Anywhere but there." On Saturday August 1, an estimated ten thousand spectators crowded the sidewalks of Broadway to watch the grand Old Home Day parade. In the lead car was New Hampshire Governor Felker riding with Derry native and former governor Charles Floyd. Behind the dignitaries marched "bands, drum corps and finely decorated floats and uniformed bodies of men." A town-wide picnic was followed by a baseball game in the afternoon and fireworks in the evening. This was pure Norman Rockwell America.

The next day, August 2, was devoted to family gatherings and church. The morning worship services at all the town's churches were filled with visitors who had returned to Derry for Come Back Day. Saint Thomas Aquinas was particularly crowded that Sunday with regulars, visitors for the gatherings, and summer boarders. During most Sundays the pews were filled anyway, but this Sabbath, Saint Thomas was packed to the point of being uncomfortable. Many of these worshippers would leave town that afternoon by buggy, flivver, trolley, or train.

Around 2:30 in the afternoon a fire broke out somewhere near the altar at Saint Thomas Aquinas Catholic Church. Much of the roof of the church was engulfed before anyone even noticed smoke coming from the building. At three o'clock, Fred Sargent saw the smoke and ran to pull the signal at firebox 57 at the corner of Rollins Street and Crystal Avenue. By the time help arrived, the flames had spread across most of the top of the church.

The Derry Fire Department quickly rushed from its Broadway station and soon call-firemen arrived from all across town. The hoses were attached to three nearby hydrants but the pressure was so low that the streams of water could not reach the top of the church. The water department's standpipe was at about the same elevation as the church so the force of water proved inadequate to spray the roof of the chapel.

The heat from the fire was so intense that it was impossible for firemen to get close to the building. All the hoses had to be aimed from the southern side, where they were shielded from the strong wind that was blowing from the southwest. A few who tried to get in through the back of the church had to flee when bricks from the chimney began to rain down on their heads.

Derry was still using antiquated "hand tub"-type fire engines and lacked the big steam-powered pumpers that could force a jet of water hundreds of feet into the air. Firemen risked their lives by leaning long wooden ladders against the side of the church and climbing up toward the roof. With one hand they held on to the ladder and with the other they hauled fire hoses to attack the flames. Despite this heroic effort, it soon became obvious that the church could not be saved. All the men's efforts were now concentrated on saving nearby buildings, which were being ignited by flying embers. The rectory next door was saved and sustained very little damage. Three other houses suffered only minor damage

Several local men, without thought to their own safety, rushed into the smoke-filled church to save what they could. From the altar they grabbed several religious statues, the tall brass candlestick holders, a small vestry organ, some altar furnishings, and whatever vestments they could bundle into their arms. Within a single hour, the church was destroyed. All that remained were portions of the charred frame and the brick foundation.

The fire consumed the new pipe organ, the fourteen bas-reliefs of the Stations of the Cross on the wall, the hymnals, the mass books and the pews. Destroyed in an hour were the elaborate altar, the dozen memorial stained glass windows, and the frescoed walls that had been painted only the decade before. Down to the ground, near the front entrance, crashed the gold cross that had been on top of the steeple. Before the fire, it had towered nearly eighty feet above Crystal Avenue, placed there on September 13, 1889.

The thirty-six-by-sixty foot church was completed just twenty-five years before at a cost of about fourteen thousand dollars and had been dedicated on November 28, 1889 before a crowd of six hundred. Originally it served a membership that was almost exclusively Irish. By the time of the fire those of French-Canadian ancestry were becoming the largest bloc of parishioners. Most of the church members worked in the area's shoe factories. This was their home church and the pride of the Catholic community. It was, for many, an outward symbol of God's presence in Derry. Now it was just a smoldering ruin.

Immediately, Father Dunn and the church leadership announced that they would rebuild. Perhaps some thought the fire was a blessing because the church had become much too small for its rapidly growing family. In 1914, the plan was to build a church that would be twice as large as the destroyed chapel. The insurance settlement would be a start but most of the cost of the new building would have to be borne by the parishioners.

The Derry Board of Selectmen offered Father Dunn the use of the Adams Memorial Building. Pastor Enslin of the First Baptist Church said the Catholics were more than welcome to use his church for their services. Father Dunn decided instead that mass would be held at Dan Casey's Scenic Movie Theater on Railroad Avenue (the site of the present Eagles Club). This building was built originally as a roller-skating rink but since 1909 was a combination movie theater and bowling alley. In 1925 it was purchased by the Eagles Club; it was destroyed by a fire in 1945.

Father Daniel Dunn scheduled masses at the movie theater for the next Sunday morning. Masses would be at seven o'clock and 8:15, with high mass at 10:15. Sunday school was at nine in the morning and confessions were heard on Saturday afternoon and evening. Weddings would be held at the rectory. Only eighteen days after the fire at Saint Thomas Aquinas, Pope Pius X (now Saint Pius X) died. This double whammy must have been one of the most discouraging blows in the history of the Catholic community of Derry.

Despite this adversity, however, the congregation stuck together with the unifying mission of rebuilding their church home.

It would take three years to raise the funds necessary to build the new Saint Thomas Aquinas Church. The parish was made up of mainly blue-collar workers. Each pledged as much as he could. Raffles, suppers, and fairs brought in the rest of the money. Finally, on November 11, 1917, the building was completed. It was dedicated by Bishop Guertin, followed by a solemn high mass conducted by Father Dunn.

The year 2007 marks the ninetieth anniversary of the building of the present Saint Thomas Aquinas church and the one hundred nineteenth birthday of the parish. In this church, thousands of our citizens have been baptized, were given their first communion, married, and had their life celebrated in a funeral mass. Think how many prayers have been offered for us and our town by the priests and church members. Thank you, Saint Thomas Aquinas church, for being a blessing to the town of Derry.

38.

The Adams Mill

AT 1:30 IN THE MORNING ON SEPTEMBER 17, 1925, A GROUP OF campers on the shores of Beaver Lake saw a reddening in the sky to the south. The five summer residents rushed half a mile through the woods and discovered that the Adams Lumber Mill was on fire. The men ran to the nearby home of Benjamin F. Adams and awakened the mill owner and his family.

A call was made to Fire Chief G. W. Hoisington, of the Derry Fire District, to send help. Adams called the station four times before the comforting sound of the fire siren could be heard shrieking in the night air. The mill owner waited with growing impatience until finally fire equipment arrived at the conflagration. By the time firefighters arrived at the scene, however, it was too late. The Adams mill was in ruins. After 205 years, the town's oldest continuously operating enterprise was gone. This was the mill that had generated enough income that Benjamin Adams would leave a bequest to the town of Derry sufficient to build the Benjamin Adams Memorial Building (the Opera House) on Broadway.

The first mill on the site had been owned by Elder David Cargill (1661–1734), who in 1719 hired contractor Robert Gilmore to construct a mill and dam. Originally it functioned as a fuller's mill. This kind of mill can be thought of as rather like a giant washing machine in which locally produced cloth was cleaned and fluffed. The town at the time was the regional center for the manufacture of high-quality linen. Cargill later erected a grist- and sawmill on his Beaver Brook property.

After 1734, the mill was owned by Squire John MacMurphy (1682–1755). He operated it until his death, at which time it passed to his son Alexander (1717–1763). The mill remained in the family until it was purchased in 1830 by Edmund Adams (1777–1858). Edmund was a veteran of the War of 1812. He had moved here from Salem, New Hampshire, and was the brother of Jacob Adams, the founder of the Adams Female Academy in East Derry.

It would seem that the Adams family had a pre-1830 connection to the mill. In 1820, an uncle of Benjamin F. Adams was killed while chopping ice from the waterwheel that powered the mill. He had made the mistake of turning on the flow of water to help free the wheel while he was still chopping ice. His leg was caught in the spinning waterwheel. His body was not discovered until several days later.

In 1849, a new mill was built by Edmund Adams's two sons—Edmund Jr. (1819–1892) and Benjamin (1824–1901). The latter gentleman would later be the donor of the Adams Memorial Building—the current home of the Derry Museum of History.

This new mill in 1850 used six hundred tons of wood a year and produced two hundred thousand board feet of lumber and one hundred thousand feet of shingles. It had two circular saws and one up-and-down saw. The two Adams brothers were the only workers at this enterprise. Their gristmill, with its two grinding stones, produced four thousand bushels of flour that year.

All of their sawing and grinding were done without the benefit of either steam or electric power. A stone dam backed up Beaver Brook. Through its headgates, the water rushed through the flume down a hundred-foot-long, stone-lined millrace and finally over a fourteen-foot waterfall. This surging water turned a three-foot-wide wooden waterwheel at twenty rpm, which was sufficient to generate forty-eight horsepower of energy. This kinetic power was adequate to power the saws and slice the timber into boards and shingles.

The mill was definitely not a year-round operation. It was dependent on the flow of water from Adams Pond. The dam would back up water until the brothers were ready to begin sawing and grinding. They would then open the sluice to send the water through the penstocks, which directed the flow to turn the waterwheel. When there was insufficient flow of water, the mill was shut down until the next spring. In 1850 through 1880, the mill operated only half a year. Because of the vagaries of New Hampshire weather, some years the mill would operate only two months; other years, the sawing might continue for six months.

Around 1875, the Adams brothers purchased a Reynolds turbine to power the sawmill. The old wooden waterwheel had been able to generate only fifteen horsepower—enough to operate just the two circular saws. The new turbine could produced forty-eight horsepower and power four saws.

The mill grew busier and busier during the last decades of the nineteenth century. Derry was enjoying an economic boom. The Pillsbury shoe factories had changed West Derry from a sleepy village to a thriving industrial complex. Huge new mills were being built. Housing for workers was springing up all over town. Broadway was being lined with stores, officers, churches, and fraternal buildings—all made of wood.

In response to this ever-increasing demand, the Adams mill expanded production. In 1870 the mill employed only the Adams brothers, who worked ten hours a day and paid themselves a per diem compensation of about a dollar twenty-five. By the time of the fire of 1925, it had grown to provide employment to eight full-time workers in addition to sundry members of the Adams family. In 1925 it was owned and operated by Benjamin F. Adams, the grandson of the first Adams to own the mill.

The fire in 1925 quickly enveloped the mill. Despite the frantic call to the Derry District fire chief, help did not arrive in time to do any good. The mill workers were forced to extinguish what flames they could by means of a bucket brigade from Adams Pond. All these efforts could do was to prevent the flames from spreading beyond the mill yard and into the forest.

It was not until 3:20 that the fire siren sounded to call the volunteer firemen to the scene. By the time the fire department's chemical and hose wagon firemen arrived, there was little left to save. The mill and one hundred thousand feet of sawed lumber were now just a smoldering ruin. The firemen remained at the scene to hose down the burning embers; they didn't return to the Broadway fire station until 6:30 that morning. There was no insurance. Benjamin Adams published a letter in the area newspapers thanking the firemen and volunteers for doing what they could.

A reporter for a Manchester newspaper interviewed Adams the next day and printed his criticism of the local fire department. The mill owner asked why the fire siren hadn't sounded until an hour after he made his frantic call for help. He also questioned why better equipment wasn't sent. The department owned a state-of-the-art fire engine that remained parked inside the Broadway firehouse instead of being dispatched to the Adams fire. He also offered a reward of five hundred dollars for information about the arsonist who set the fire. The fire chief, much to Adams's chagrin, had blamed the fire on natural causes.

Fire Chief Hoisington immediately fired off a response to Adams that was published in Derry's daily newspaper, the *Evening Record*. He wrote that he had pondered whether he should publicly answer the mill owner's questions. The chief reluctantly argued that the fire department had no legal responsibility or obligation to fight the fire on Adams Pond Road. The Adams family's home and mill were four miles outside the established boundaries of the Derry Fire District.

At this time, there was only one fire district in town and it covered only a portion of Derry. The residents and businessmen of the Broadway area were taxed to pay for fire protection only for their section of town. If you lived in most of East Derry, on the shores of Island Pond, at Cow Bell Corner, or in other outlying areas, you weren't sent a fire district tax bill. And because you weren't paying for fire protection, there was no guarantee of aid in case your house or mill caught fire. A certain and sure response by the fire department was only for those fortunate enough to reside within the legally established boundaries of the fire district. In the view of the fire chief, Ben Adams had no reason for complaint.

In 1920, the Derry Fire District had signed a contract to provide protection to Derry Village, which then dissolved its own village fire department. East Derry was the only village without organized protection, although there does seem to be an agreement in 1920 for the Derry Fire Department to provide fire protection for the immediate area around the First Parish Church. The Adams mill was well outside the area that was the legal responsibility of the West Derry Fire District.

The fire chief admitted that the fire whistle hadn't sounded until an hour after the call was received from the frustrated Ben Adams. The fire wagon and its cadre of firefighters did, however, arrive at the Adams mill only a half hour after the initial telephone call was made to the chief.

Hoisington also defended his decision to send only his chemical wagon. In 1915 the district had purchased a 100 horse power, six-cylinder LaFrance triple combination fire engine for nine thousand dollars. This mighty pumper was, at the time, the finest, most powerful engine in the state. When the call came in for aid at the Adams fire, the chief chose to keep that piece of equipment parked at the Broadway fire station. He argued in his public letter to Adams that the LaFrance fire truck "belongs in this district ... at the service of the people who bought it and with their money are supporting it." Adams and his neighbors didn't pay a tax for fire protection, so they shouldn't expect fire protection. The chief's tone seems to reflect the feeling that the burnt-out Mr. Adams should have been grateful that any service whatsoever was rendered by the Broadway fire department.

In the brouhaha over the response to the Adams mill fire, we can see clearly one of the several reasons for the creation of the East Derry Fire Department just three years later. The formation of this new fire district had nothing to do with the inability of a horse-drawn fire truck to climb the prodigious slope of East Derry Hill. It was instead a reasonable response by residents of the Upper Village to meet the obvious need for a more certain level of fire protection. Having their own fire department would prevent them from being at the mercy of the Derry Fire Department.

The East Derry Fire Department was incorporated in 1932. Its first fire station was a 1934 addition to the Upper Village Hall. A second addition was built in 1961, but soon that became too small. In 1970 a new station was build farther east on Hampstead Road. The East Derry Fire District voted to dissolve in 2005.

The Adams did not rebuild the mill, although the family remained active in the lumber business. In 1938 the state was devastated by a fall hurricane. All across New Hampshire towns were littered with millions of blown-down trees. The Depression-era government of Franklin Roosevelt mobilized to help the locals make some money from this windfall. The government offered to buy all the lumber at fixed prices. This would provide cash to the landowners and also prevent the price of timber from falling dramatically because of oversupply.

Anyone with hurricane-produced timber could bring his logs to designated sites throughout the New England region, where they would be purchased and a check issued by the federal government.

The local receiving mill was at Adams Pond, managed by Benjamin Foster Adams (1889–1969) and his son Benjamin Clark Adams (1915–2000). They erected a small sawmill near the site of the old mill. The pond was used as a holding tank while the logs waited their turn to be sliced into boards and planks. By the spring of 1939, the project proved to be too successful. The mill had to temporarily halt accepting timber; the pond was too full of logs!

There are no records of when this new Adams mill ceased operation though a date in the 1940s is likely. The mill site and house stayed in the family until the passing of Benjamin C. Adams, when it was sold to land developer Gene Chagnon.

The Adams Pond Mill is one of the town's most historic sites. All of the foundations of the 1720, 1849 and 1938 mills remain. The long raceway is perfectly preserved. Inside the cellar hole can be seen many of the rusting sheet-iron penstocks, gears, and turbines lying just where they fell during the 1925 fire. Unfortunately, a housing development has recently encroached on the area of the mill site.

39.

Hemlock Oil

EVERY COUPLE OF MONTHS I RECEIVE A MESSAGE THAT SOMEONE has found a strange-shaped bottle marked *West Derry, N.H.* I know immediately what that person is talking about. It's a patent medicine bottle for Darling's Hemlock Oil. The cure-all was manufactured in Derry for thirty years from a Birch Street factory.

The origin of the medicine company goes back to Willis F. Darling, who was born in Concord, New Hampshire, in 1871. In 1882, when he was eleven, he and his parents moved to Derry. As a young adult Willis was employed by the Colonel T. A. Edwards Oregon Indian Medicine Company. This was one of the many medicine shows that toured the country during the nineteenth century. Typically, their wagons would come into small towns and attract a crowd by offering a free show of singing, dancing, and real live Indians. At the end of each performance, a pitchman in the role of a doctor would come on stage and elaborate on the wondrous curative powers of his elixir. Among the future stars who got their start in such shows were Buster Keaton and Harry Houdini. The Kickapoo Indian Medicine Company made Derry an annual stop and used the Adams Memorial Building for its shows.

The Oregon Indian Medicine Company was headquartered in Corry, Pennsylvania, and operated for over a century manufacturing and hawking its patent medicine cure-alls. Its most popular elixir was Ka-Ton-Ka Tonic—the great Indian remedy. The recipe was supposedly given to Colonel Edwards by a tribe of friendly Indians. The manufacturer claimed it would cure "any blood disease, rheumatism or kidney complaint." The price was only fifty cents a bottle.

The exact ingredients were secret but it was claimed they included Oregon grape, mountain sage, prickly ash, and other herbs gathered by the Modoc and Hot Springs Indians. A chemical analysis later revealed that the actual ingredients were alcohol, sugar, aloe, baking soda, and food coloring.

During much of the nineteenth century, America was officially dry. The saloons were closed and temperance was expected from all good churchgoing Americans. There were, however, no social qualms about taking a swig of alcohol-laced patent medicine to cure whatever ailed you. Among the other medicines sold by the Oregon Indian Medicine Company were Indian War Paint Skin Salve, Warm Springs Consumption Cure, Indian Worm Eradicator, Snakebite Cure, and Moc-I-Tons Tonic. The latter elixir was billed as a cure for the "loss of manhood and muscle disorders." It was their most expensive product at ten dollars a bottle.

During his employment with the Oregon Medicine Company, Willis Darling learned the formulas for numerous medicinal herbal cures. He also learned the "manufacturing, packing and sales" aspect of business. By the 1890s he was manufacturing "Vegetable Oil" and other nostrums from his kitchen. His efforts were having considerable success in their sales to local stores. In 1897 he had fitted-up a full-scale laboratory in his house and was employing agents to go on the road to sell his products. The Derry Museum of History has in its archives a 1907 document that makes Morton's Store in Salamanca, New York, an official agent for the Hemlock Oil Compound Co. in exchange for the store's purchase of eighty-five dollars' worth of the Derry-made medicine.

His success soon attracted the attention of others. In 1902 Darling publicly complained that "would be imitators" were manufacturing worthless medicines that mimicked his product and the public was being deceived. Spear's Vegetable Oil even went so far as to imitate his label and the shape of his bottle. From now on, Willis Darling pledged to stop manufacturing his product in long round bottles that were easy to copy. From now on his products would be packaged in distinctively shaped bottles that were impossible to replicate. Now a customer could easily tell the fraudulent from the real thing.

The bottles are indeed truly distinctive. They measure about six inches long and are one inch square. Each is designed to hold two ounces of the dark amber liquid. Embossed on one side is HEMLOCK OIL CO. WEST DERRY, N.H. Sometime after 1907, the location designation was changed to DERRY N.H. There is a blob-top opening on the bottle that was sealed with a cork stopper. On the opposite side of the embossed label was pasted a yellow paper label with red lettering.

There must have been at least a million of these bottles made from 1902 to 1932. They certainly are tough little soldiers! I have rarely ever seen a broken Hemlock Oil bottle. Because there were so many of these nearly indestructible bottles, they are quite common today and they regularly sell on eBay and other auction sites for $5.00 apiece. The ones with the paper labels still intact are much rarer and are worth in the range of twenty-five to thirty dollars.

The earliest label identifies the bottle's contents as Hemlock Oil. Later this brand name was changed to Dar-Ling Oil. This change was likely caused by the fact that hemlock oil was a generic term for a medicine that had been used for centuries. Such commonly used product names could not be trademarked by any one company, just as no one could copyright the name "mineral water" or "spruce gum." The logo of the Hemlock Oil Co. was a cutaway of a man's head showing the location of the throat and sinus cavities. Inside the drawing is printed TRADE MARK REGISTERED, U.S. PATENT OFFICE.

Much of the space on the label was taken up with a list of what Hemlock Oil would cure. This included "headache, toothache, earaches, coughs, colds, catarrh, croup, sore throat, hoariness, catarrhal deafness, bronchitis, asthma, influenza, neuralgia, sciatics, lumbago, stiffness, backaches, gout and rheumatism." There were no directions on the label stating as to how the patient should administer the oil or what dosages should be taken. We don't even know whether Hemlock Oil was to be used straight from the bottle or diluted in water.

The label's list of afflictions that could be cured makes us believe that Hemlock Oil was used both internally and externally. The Pure Food and Drug Act of 1906 forced many pharmaceutical companies to change their manner of business. The act's more stringent regulations seem to have had an impact on Willis Darling's company in Derry. After 1906, the labels claimed that Dar-Ling Oil was a treatment only for "muscular aches and pains, strains, sprains, bruises, burns, frostbite, stings, bites of innocuous insects and wherever a liniment usually is applied." What was once a cure-all had been relegated to a liniment for external use only.

The Hemlock Oil was a major success for the Darling family. Willis employed "a good army" of agents around the country to sell his product to pharmacies and general stores. Advertisements were placed in newspapers to promote the curative powers of his product. The price was heralded as only twenty-five cents for a two-ounce bottle. This was not just a cure but also a bargain.

One of the largest advertisements by the Hemlock Oil Company centered on his competition. In 1904, Darling compared the manufacturers of imitation hemlock oil to pirate. They were "no better than the one who seizes his neighbor's ship on the high sea. Stealing is the same, whether it is in the taking of a man's purse or the robbing him of his good name. One may be the result of only a day's labor, but the other is the work of a lifetime." Darling charged that "these unprincipled swindlers" sold an inferior and worthless imitation of his hemlock oil, which was "calculated to deceive and injure the health of those who use it." The Derry man advised everyone to "shun" stores that sold phony Hemlock Oil and take the storekeepers to court as swindlers. Willis Darling called on those who had been cured by the real Hemlock Oil to join with him in "lashing these ignorant, impotent, piratical scoundrels through the earth with a whip of scorpions."

In 1904, Darling purchased a small home at 10 Birch Street and next door erected a one-story pharmaceutical laboratory and factory. This building would later serve as Dr. Paul Lipnick's dental office and is now Crystal Reflections beauty parlor. Darling painted the building brilliant yellow with bright red trim in imitation of the garish colors on the label of Hemlock Oil. A cloth awning, utilizing the same color scheme, went across the front of the building.

In 1905, the Hemlock Oil factory sold 175,000 bottles of the elixir. That year Darling also distributed ten thousand samples of his oil packaged in half-ounce bottles that were the same shape as the regular two-ounce containers. By October 1905 he boasted that he had received an order from one buyer for 115,200 bottles of his medicine. In addition to Hemlock Oil, Darling was manufacturing Darling's Hemlock Inhaler, Aristos Cough Syrup, and Aristos Corn Cure. The latter claimed to have no equal in the treatment of "hard and soft corns, warts, bunions, callusesv and ingrown nails." In 1906 his business had gone international and a Canadian customs agent visited his Birch Street laboratory to make sure everything was up to royal standards. It was, and the Canadian agent left Derry "pleased with the systematic way [Darling] was conducting his business."

Darling even challenged other medicine companies to try to equal his product. He offered one-hundred dollars to any competitor who could equal Hemlock Oil in the curing of neuralgia, rheumatism, sciatica, lumbago, stiffness, and backaches. There is no report that he had to pay off the wager.

The Hemlock Oil Company was not the only local medicine maker. Among the nostrum manufacturers in Derry was the Derry Drug Company which in 1904 was manufacturing Eagle Dyspepsia Cure, which cured Samuel Drew of the *Derry News,* who was "quite ill and in great distress" after eating "heartily of baked beans." Also around that time H. L. Benson was promoting Mi-O-Na, a cure for indigestion, and *Derry News* publisher Charles Bartlett of Derry Village was manufacturing his Beef, Wine and Iron Tonic to give users "strength and vigor" in the spring time. Derry was also the summer home of Dr. Harry Tuttle, the manufacturer of the celebrated Tuttle's Elixir.

A century ago, the pages of the *Derry News* were filled with advertisements for these and other patent medicines that boasted of curing everything from cancer to skin eruptions. Every issue had an ad for Lydia Pinkham's Vegetable Compound, Atwood's Jaundice Bitters, and Warner's Safe Kidney Cure.

In 1915, the forty-four-year-old Willis Darling decided that he should retire from his labors. The reason for his quitting the profitable business was never stated. He may have been in ill health. Both he and his wife, Alice, died within the next fifteen years. He may have chosen to retire just because the business was too stressful. Perhaps he figured he had socked away enough money and could afford to enjoy his remaining years in leisure. He, his wife, and his mother-in-law Nancy Clark, moved to Bedford, New Hampshire, where in the 1920 census they were listed as residing.

Chemist Karl Emil Felix Seeler in 1915 purchased the Hemlock Oil laboratory, factory, stock in trade, formulas, and goodwill. He was born in Leipzig, Germany, in 1868 and did his undergraduate studies at the University of Berlin. For several years Steeler worked for the German Department of Agriculture as a specialist in the sugar beet industry. He later received his Ph.D. in chemical engineering from the University of Leipzig.

After graduation, Felix Seeler was offered a position in a cane sugar factory near Havana, Cuba. He sailed to the United States and arrived at Ellis Island in New York Harbor on July 4, 1899. Before he could book passage to the West Indies, he discovered that the devastation caused by the Spanish-American War had wrought havoc with the Cuban sugar industry. Seeler decided to remain in the United States, and he became a citizen in 1904. For several years he was manager of an oil refinery in Elizabeth, New Jersey, before it was destroyed by fire. For eleven years he was employed by the Merck Company—the international pharmaceutical giant. He served as its head of their opium and morphine division.

The forty-seven-year-old chemist moved to Derry in 1915 with his American-born wife, Clara. They purchased an elegant Arts and Crafts–style home at 3 Boyd Road that had been built in 1907 by Horace Dinsmore. It is presently the residence of Douglas and Rosalind Hartly, the proprietors of JP's Highway Superette. In 1940 much of Seeler's side yard became the site of the new Christian Science church. Shortly after moving into their new home, the Seelers became the parents of their only child, Albert O. Seeler.

Dr. Seeler continued to manufacture Hemlock Oil and other toilet products until his death on January 31, 1932 at the age of sixty-three. He was buried at Forest Hill Cemetery in East Derry. His son Albert (1915–1976) would graduate from Pinkerton Academy and Harvard College (1934, B.S.; 1938, M.D.). Albert was associated with the Merck Institute for Therapeutic Research, Harvard Medical School, and the Massachusetts Institute of Technology. At MIT he was professor of medicine and later the school's medical director. In this position he supervised all of the medical research and programs. There he was a colleague of another Derry-connected academic: Professor Samuel Cate Prescott, the school's dean of science, who was the owner of the Benjamin Chase Mill in Derry Village.

40.
Anne Frasier Norton

AWHILE BACK I WAS WORKING WITH BRUCE ALGER, OF DERRY'S American Legion post, to research the service records of local veterans. In passing, he asked me about Anne Frasier Norton. Her name is listed on Derry's World War I monument as having died in the service. I told him I didn't know much about her. I was embarrassed over my ignorance and made a mental note to find out her story. What I have discovered qualifies her as a true American hero. My thanks go to her nephew Frank Galvin of Derry for helping to flesh out the story. With much help from Robin Perrin, Anne Parker, and Drew Wagner, I found her photograph in the archives of Pinkerton Academy.

Anne Frasier Norton was born in East Boston on April 10, 1892, to Charles Warren Frasier (1870–1954) and Catherine Anne Walsh (1872–1902). Her father was a steam-engine driver for the Boston Fire Department. Catherine died in 1902, leaving Charles with ten year-old Annie and her infant sister, Ethel. Charles was soon forced to retire from the fire department because of an injury. In 1907 he moved his family to the Nortonville section of Derry. He ran the Economy Market on Railroad Avenue and belonged to the Masons. The family worshiped at the Episcopal Church of the Transfiguration.

Annie—as she preferred to be called—was educated at Pinkerton Academy and graduated with the class of 1911. The class motto was "We conquer by degrees"; class colors were red and gray. While at the academy Annie had the young Robert Frost as her English instructor. At her graduation, she read the class poem

Anne Frasier Norton (1892–1918) is shown in her
1911 graduation photograph from Pinkerton Academy.

and was no doubt helped by Frost with rhyme and meter. There were twenty-two in the graduating class that June. Among those who received a diploma was the future army officer Mason Young and Edwin Asa Norton (born 1893). Edwin was the son of the developer of Nortonville and in due time Annie's husband.

Edwin Norton left Derry to attend Union College and majored in business; Annie attended Bryant and Stratton's College in Boston. At that business school she learned typing, shorthand, and accounting. After graduation the couple married and moved to Schenectady, New York, but they soon returned to New Hampshire. They lived at various times within the state in Rochester and Manchester. Edwin was a stockbroker with the firm of Norton, Clough & Co., with an office in the Amoskeag Bank Building in Manchester.

In 1916 the federal government found itself with a severe clerical shortage in the Navy. To attract more enlistees with that specialty, Congress passed the Naval Reserve Act of 1916. This new law somehow was enacted without mention of gender restriction. For the first time in U.S. history women, were allowed to enter the armed forces. Thousands of women applied to become a part of the Navy and do their bit to win the war. Among those who answered the call was Annie Frasier Norton. She enlisted in July and was made a yeoman second class on August 10, 1918. Edwin also signed up, and was sent to officer's training school at Fort Taylor, Kentucky.

The new women sailors were officially designated "Yeomen" though occasionally they were referred to in the press as "Yeomenettes." Most of these yeomen were assigned clerical duty but some became fingerprint experts, translators, camouflage designers, and recruiting agents. Only a few yeomen went "over there" to France. The vast majority were stationed within the continental United States performing valuable services for our embattled nation. Immediately at the end of the war, all women yeomen were discharged. With the exception of Navy nurses, there would be no more females in the uniformed Navy until 1942.

Sailor Annie Frasier Norton was fortunate enough to be stationed nearby. She was assigned as a clerk/stenographer to the office of the commander of the Portsmouth Navy Yard. This was a vital and active military post. Protecting the navy yard were several forts fitted out with batteries of four-inch disappearing guns plus a fleet of two destroyers and four submarines.

On October 9, 1918, Annie felt some flu-like symptoms. The initial diagnosis was the "grippe." Her condition quickly grew worse. It was now obvious that she had come down with the deadly Spanish influenza. This fast-killing disease was a pandemic. It has been estimated that 70 million people died from the Spanish flu—many times the number that were killed in the First World War. Soon Annie developed pneumonia and began to weaken. She died the morning of October 10, 1918, exactly two months after she entered the Navy. She was described as "very popular and well liked" by those with whom she served.

The contemporary newspapers reported that Anne Frasier Norton should forever be honored for the distinction of being the first woman in our nation's history to die while serving in the regular American armed forces. Up until 1917, the military was exclusively male. In the past, women could serve as volunteers with the Red Cross or Sanitary Corps but actual enlistment were barred to women. Annie Frasier Norton joined the honored list of seventy-two hundred other sailors who died in that "war to end all wars."

Her casket was carried from the Portsmouth Navy Yard to the venerable Saint John's Episcopal Church in Portsmouth. The military funeral service was read by Father Nelson Kellogg, the rector of the historic church. After the final prayers, the funeral cortège moved down Chapel Street, then on to Congress Street, and finally to the railroad station on Vaughan Street. Leading the procession were fourteen sailors with rifles and a bugler. The casket was borne by eight lady yeomen acting as both pallbearers and the guard of honor. The sides of the street were lined with civilians paying silent tribute to Yeoman Norton.

The railroad train carried the funeral participants to Woodlawn Cemetery in Everett, Massachusetts. There Anne was laid to rest alongside her mother. After the minister performed the funeral rite, the eight yeomen stood at attention while the bugler played Taps. Just before the casket was lowered into the ground, the riflemen rendered "the final honor" of firing a salute to their fallen comrade.

On March 28, 2007, Yeoman Charlotte Winter died in Boonsboro, Maryland, at the age of 109. She was the last surviving woman to have served in World War I. She outlived her former service sister Annie Norton by more than eighty-eight years. There now remain only four American veterans of the Great War.

During my time in the Army, I was fortunate to serve with many fine soldiers and officers—many of whom were women. During my tour of Vietnam I was a field medic, and in frequent contact with the ladies of the Army Medical Corps—all of whom outranked me. The other women I clearly remember are those singers and dancers who volunteered to be a part of the USO shows and risked their lives to perform for us in the middle of nowhere. I also recall a jungle clearing where I was served bacon sandwiches provided by the dedicated ladies of the Women's Christian Temperance Union.

The women in the armed forces perform a vital service in the safeguarding of our nation. We should be proud of the role our town has played in the history of women in the military and of the pioneering sacrifice of Annie Frasier Norton. Next Memorial Day, please remember her and the other women who served and are serving in our armed forces.

41.
Daylight Saving Time

MOST OF US ACCEPT THE FACT THAT IN MARCH WE HAVE TO CHANGE our clocks from standard time to daylight saving time. The TV weatherman reminds us that it's "spring ahead, fall back." Actually, the time change in March now comes about a week before the first day of spring, so I guess a better memory device would be "March forward." Daylight saving time (there is no *s* at the end of the word *saving*) seems to have been with us forever. There was a time, however, when the biannual changing of the clocks caused considerable debate here in Derry.

Daylight saving time (DST) was first proposed in a 1789 tongue-in-cheek essay by Ben Franklin. He reckoned that changing the clocks could save the people of Paris a fortune by cutting down on their use of candles. By Franklin's calculations, there would be a savings of exactly 65,050,000 pounds of candle wax. The founding father didn't push the idea too strongly because he admitted he never got up before noon anyway.

The concept of DST was filed away in the "crazy idea bin" until the First World War, when both England and her enemy Germany used the time-changing scheme as a way to save fuel. In 1916, the state of New Hampshire debated turning its clocks an hour ahead in spring. At a public hearing in Manchester, the opponents were so vocal that the idea was dropped. The federal government ignored our sentiments and instituted DST in March 1918. The wartime measure lasted only seven months, and in 1919 Congress voted to return the nation to standard time. Each state and town, however, was allowed to continue DST as a local option.

In 1920, Massachusetts adopted DST. What they do in the Bay State usually means very little to the residents of Derry; in fact, we often took pride in being different from our overtaxed neighbor to the south. In truth, however, the two states were bound together by the iron tracks of the Boston and Maine Railroad. The rail company adopted DST but didn't actually move the hands of its clocks and watches. It simply changed the scheduled running time of all of its trains so they ran exactly one hour earlier. The seven o'clock train now roared into Derry at six in the morning. Our two trolley lines also changed their timetables. This meant that if Derry didn't adopt DST, the farmers would have to bring their milk and eggs to the freight depot an hour earlier than before. Commuters would get an hour less sleep.

A mass meeting was held at the Adams Memorial building on March 22, 1921, to discuss continuing with DST. Frank McGregor, president of the Derry Board of Trade, called the meeting to order. He invited Attorney Ralph Davis to talk about a new law that was working its way through the New Hampshire Legislature. It would outlaw daylight saving time in our state. Anyone who was caught setting his clocks ahead could be rapped with a five-hundred-dollar fine! Davis explained that the proposed law was meaningless, as our state couldn't "control the acts of the Boston and Maine Railroad." He expressed his personal opposition to DST. He said he didn't want Derry to be like the city of Nashua, which had been vilified when it voted to set its clocks ahead.

A straw poll was taken at the meeting. The hundred or so citizens present told the Derry Board of Trade that they were of one mind in their opposition to the concept of DST. The overwhelming sentiment, however, was that Derry had no choice. It had to adopt daylight saving time in its stores, shoe factories, and schools to avoid mass confusion.

There were pockets of resistance of course. In April, the Reverend Irving Enslin called for a parish meeting of the First Baptist Church on Broadway. The other churches had all adopted DST. Each Sunday, when the Baptists were going to church, the members of the other churches were leaving their worship services and going home. The Baptist deacons likely feared that they would see a decrease in the size of their congregation as parishioners opted for an earlier worship time so they could have more leisure time each Sunday in Summer.

Many at this Baptist church meeting railed against DST. They said it "disregarded the home plans, the hours of meals, the hours of sleep for the children, and the general work day." Despite the congregation's dislike of the concept of daylight savings time, the members voted to hold all services, prayer meetings, and Sunday schools an hour earlier than usual. They also showed their disdain for DST by not moving the time on the tower clock. The official time for the Baptists would remain eastern standard time!

The opposition to changing the time continued for the next several decades. To add to the confusion, in March 1924 both Londonderry and Chester chose to keep their clocks set on standard time. Thus a trolley trip from Manchester to Chester would require the conductor to change his official watch three times. In November 1924, voters in Massachusetts voted to abolish daylight saving time.

By April 1929, things hadn't gotten any better. Massachusetts had again gone back to daylight saving time but Derry voted to remain on standard time. All of our Churches were scheduling their services to coincide with DST but the tower clocks were still set on standard time. The B & M Railroad was officially on standard time but the schedule was adjusted so trains ran an hour later than usual. Some individuals in Derry set their kitchen clocks to standard time while others opted for DST. By now even I'm getting confused just trying to write this article.

Many citizens viewed it as a conflict between "man's time" and "God's time." In 1936, three hundred Chester citizens signed a petition to get their town to adopt DST. That spring, most of the town's people had set their clocks an hour ahead, but the Chester town government didn't follow suit. Town Meetings and school sessions were posted to begin at a certain time that was an hour after the time on most people's watches and clocks. One local newspaper correspondent called it "Daylight Nuisance Time."

During the Second World War, the federal government again mandated daylight saving time. From 1945 to 1966 there was no national law on the subject. After 1966, it became a local option. Today DST is not observed in Arizona, Hawaii, or portions of Indiana. I remember years ago while driving through the border states hearing about the confusion caused by "fast time" and "slow time." Indiana is divided by the eastern and central time zones. For part of the year, the clocks in eastern Indiana are two hours faster than those in the western counties.

The confusion in Indiana is compounded by the fact that some areas choose to go contrary to the state law. Two counties that are adjacent to the Ohio border and three that are near the Kentucky line are officially on eastern standard time but set their clocks on DST. For years, politicians have been trying without success to sort out this state of confusion. Awhile back, gubernatorial candidate Rex Early firmly declared that "some of my friends are for putting all of Indiana on DST, some are against it—and I always try to support my friends."

Here in Derry the rift over daylight saving time is a thing of the past. The tower clock at the Baptist church is now in agreement with the time on my wristwatch. And no one seems to have complained that in the year 2007 the government has added a month to the length of DST. Some energy experts figure this action will save America ten thousand barrels of oil a day. Other experts say it won't. Here in Derry, most of us are willing to exchange an "hour of night for an hour of light." The day we turn our clocks ahead is also the day we replace the batteries in our smoke detectors.

42.

Iceboats in Derry

When I was a boy, my dad and I went once a year to Auburn to watch the iceboats on Lake Massabesic. From our viewing spot near the old icehouse, we could see dozens of the boats flying by at breakneck speed. I knew that when I got older, I would cruise the ice on one of these fantastic vehicles. That would be the ride of a lifetime!

In 1968 I got to know Benjamin H. Hallowell, of Juniper Lane in Derry. He was an authentic Boston Brahmin and gentleman-athlete. He had been an All-American hockey player at Harvard College and had taught sailing to Jackie Kennedy and Jane Fonda. He owned an iceboat and offered to take me out in the sidecar. I was excited. A boyhood dream was about to come true!

The day before the great event, he told me that if there was a good wind the next day, the iceboat would be able to fly over the ice at sixty miles per hour. He described in detail how during turns the boat would go up on one runner with the sidecar high up in the air at a 45-degree angle to the ice. In time the boat would right itself and the sidecar would come slamming down again, with a crash, onto the ice. After hearing this description, I rethought the whole thing. I chickened out! I told Ben I couldn't go for a ride—I had do finish lesson plans and correct papers. Since then I have never been given the opportunity to ride an iceboat. Just as well. I'd probably disgrace myself by backing out again.

The first iceboat I have found to be in Derry belonged to Colonel Frederick F. Shepard (1851–1931). He was a Pinkerton Academy and Bryant & Stratton Business College graduate.

Myron Smith and his ice sled at Lake Massabesic in 1928.

Although he never held political office, he served Derry in other ways. He would serve as president of the Derry National Bank, treasurer of Pinkerton Academy, treasurer of Adams Female Academy, Derry town treasurer, general manager of the Chester and Derry Trolley Company, Rockingham County auditor, and treasurer of Derry Water Works. In addition he earned an appointment as military aide to Governor John McLane and was a member of numerous local fraternal organizations. He was the grandfather of astronaut Alan B. Shepard.

In January 1890, the forty-year-old Frederick Shepard launched an iceboat on Beaver Lake. No other information has been found other than a comment in the *Derry News* that it could travel over the ice at a "very high rate of speed when there is a good breeze." The only other Derry iceboat I have been able to ferret out belonged to Myron M. Smith, of Rockingham Road. I call it an iceboat but in truth I suppose it was really an ice sled.

Myron Smith was born in Derry in 1911, the oldest son of hardware salesman James Smith and his wife, Annie. His ancestry was typical for early-twentieth-century Derry—he was half Irish, half French-Canadian. Myron is remembered as being a small, good-looking man with a likable personality.

In 1926 the Pinkerton Academy freshman decided he would build a craft the likes of which had never been seen before. The airplane had been invented just twenty-three years earlier and flying through the air was still viewed as the marvel of the age. What could come next? Young Myron Smith decided he was going to create the world's first successful propeller-driven land craft.

For the next two years the young man worked on building his Smithmobile. On May 20, 1927, Charles Lindbergh flew the *Spirit of Saint Louis* across the Atlantic to Paris. On February 20, 1928, just nine months later, the sixteen-year-old inventor was ready to unveil his creation that could cross Derry with the speed of the wind.

He had built a twenty-two-foot-long, thickly framed sled that weighed about fourteen hundred pounds. The front runners were seven inches wide. The rear runners were nine foot long; those on the front were three foot shorter. It was powered by a 165-horse-power Gnome Rotary motor. The engine turned an eight-and-a-half-foot wooden propeller that was mounted on the rear of the sled.

The passenger compartment rather resembled an upholstered roller-coaster car at Canoby Lake Park. It would be tight but the contraption could hold Smith and two friends. Control was achieved by a steering wheel that had been liberated from some automobile.

Myron had intended the craft to be a land vehicle. The law, however, prohibited his trying it on Derry's highways. He was relegated to driving the Smithmobile on the frozen expanse of Beaver Lake. On that sheet of water he achieved a speed he estimated to be at least ninety miles per hour. At that speed it must have taken him only a few seconds to cross the lake from the pavilion to Gallien's Beach. Smith claimed that on a later run on the larger Lake Massabesic, he achieved a speed of one hundred miles per hour. There is no way of knowing how he clocked his speed. Was it just a guess or did he use a stop watch to calculate the time the sled took to travel across a know distance?

Unfortunately, I have discovered nothing more about Smith's iceboat. I know that Myron continued to seek speed and adventure. In 1938 he built a large kite that he used to windsurf across the snow on skis. From 1937 to 1941 he was a leading member of the Derry Flying Club. One senior gentleman recently told me that Smith used to regularly land his plane on Hood's upper meadow (now the Hood Shopping Plaza.) The club's landing field on Ryan's Hill was usually called Smith Field.

During the Second World War, Myron Smith moved to Kansas City, where he was employed as a pilot by Trans World Airlines.

Though not in the regular service, he risked his life for the war effort. He was a civilian who flew aircraft across the vast expanse of the North Atlantic to Britain. His brother, Paul, was a fighter pilot who was awarded the French Croix de Guerre. Myron Smith died in January 1973.

43.
Ned and the Dancing Bear

EVERY TOWN IN NEW ENGLAND USED TO HAVE A STORYTELLER. During most of the twentieth century, Ned Reynolds fit that description here in Nutfield. His family had lived in Derry since before the Revolutionary War. His ancestors had belonged to the First Parish Church for seven generations. In fact, it was his great-great-great-great-grandfather who helped build the church in 1769.

Ned was born in East Derry in 1900, the son of Ernest and Lula Reynolds, and graduated from Pinkerton in 1917. He was the manager of the Agway Store in Derry and the first chief of the East Derry Fire Department. He was also a cofounder of the Derry Driving Club, which gained national fame for racing horses on Beaver Lake. He and his wife, Helen, moved to Londonderry in 1944. In 1990, at the age of ninety, he was selected as Londonderry's Citizen of the Year. He spent his last years raising vegetables and Christmas trees on his Litchfield Road farm as well as caring for his wife and his mother, who lived to the age of 102. I remember Ned as a large man with sparkling blue eyes, red suspenders, and a shock of white hair that I have been told was once auburn.

He was a man who had seen remarkable changes in Derry and Londonderry. He entered this world in the era of horse and buggies and lived long enough to see a neighbor's boy grow up to hit a golf ball on the moon. He saw our roads become highways and shopping malls replace orchards and pastures. An article in the *Derry News* noted, "Through it all he maintained his good humor and joviality." Ned died peacefully in his favorite chair in 1993. After his passing,

Charlie Doherty and Jim Comeau with the bear cub in 1906.

Madden's Restaurant in Derry hung his photograph on the wall by his favorite booth.

Recently I was chatting with store owner Grant Benson when Ned's name came up. Grant asked me if I remembered the story of Ned and the Dancing Bear. This was an exercise in storytelling that was considered Ned Reynolds's tour de force. By story's end, all but the most flinty-hearted listener would have moist eyes. I remembered some of the story but, during the span of two decades, most of the details had become vague. Grant was able to fill in pieces of the yarn I had forgotten. That sent me to the microfilm section of the Derry Public Library to find if I could flesh out the story of the bear and the boy. With that additional information, combined with the tale that Grant and I reconstructed, I can now retell the story—but nowhere near as well as did Ned Reynolds, the master storyteller.

In February 1906, James Comeau, of Derry, returned to his birthplace in Nova Scotia. He and his brother Will decided to do some hunting. Deep in the forest they killed a large black bear. Upon closer examination, they discovered that they had shot a mother bear. Close by her lifeless body they discovered two very young cubs. They brought both cubs back to their home rather than let the animals die alone in the cold Canadian forest. They tried their best to feed the twins, but one died that first day. The remaining cub seemed to enjoy all the attention being given by the Comeau family and their neighbors.

Jim Comeau decided to bring the bear back to his home in Derry. He and his sister, Augusta, were the managers of the Beaver Lake pavilion. This was Derry's chief tourist attraction, offering a sandy beach, snack bar, canoes for hire, movies, dancing, bowling, and slot machines. The twenty-eight-year-old Comeau thought a small zoo would lure in even more tourists. Derry's bear park opened twenty-four years before the first bear strutted his stuff at Clark's Trading Post in the White Mountains.

By the time the pavilion opened for the season, a pair of deer along with a flock of tame ducks and turkeys had been procured from Corbin Park in Corydon, New Hampshire. A chicken-wire fence was put up to create an enclosure. The star of the menagerie was Jack—the bear cub from Nova Scotia. It was promoted by Jim Comeau as being "tame and playful and could be safely fondled and caressed by children and ladies." The quickly growing bruin was taught tricks to amuse the spectators, such as begging for food and spinning around, which was claimed to be Jack's version of the latest Derry dance craze.

Ned Reynolds and Muffy the Cow at the 1989 Londonderry's Olde Home Day celebration. Derry News *photo.*

Among Jack's biggest fans was six-year-old Ned Reynolds. Almost every day the young boy would visit the zoo to play with his friend Jack. The animal would put his arms around the boy and they would dance together, cheek-to-cheek. In June 2007, Ned's nephew divulged to me his uncle's secret bear-training technique. A dab of honey, smeared behind Ned's ear, encouraged the bear to cuddle with the boy.

Early one morning, Mrs. Lula Reynolds heard scratching at her screen door. She was startled to find a five-foot-tall black bear demanding to be let into her home. It was Jack, who had managed to escape his enclosure and was now paying a social call on Ned. The animal walked into the kitchen and sat beside the boy at the table. Together they had a breakfast of porridge, with Ned feeling like he had just stepped into a nursery rhyme.

Young Ned was certainly the most popular kid in the area thanks to his buddy, gentle Jack. One summer's day, Mrs. Reynolds sponsored a blueberry pie eating contest. All the neighboring children and Jack sat at a long table with a pie placed in front of each. Each participant—both human and animal—wore a bib around his neck. At a signal, each contestant began to eat his pie without the use of hands. Within seconds, the winner was declared to be Jack who had finished his pie well before his rivals had reached even the half way point in the contest. The young bruin was now perceived to be a very rare animal species—a black and blue bear.

By midsummer, Jack had begun to grow and was now larger and more powerful than the boy. Ned later recalled that it was from dancing with Jack that he learned the meaning of the term "bear hug." Even though the bear was much stronger then the boy, the animal was careful never to use his strength to hurt his playmate.

Another time the staff of the Beaver Lake pavilion began to notice that they were missing tools. More and more hammers, drills, and saws vanished. Finally suspicion pointed to Jack as the thief. The staff carefully watched the animal and finally caught him stealing a workman's tool. Silently they watched to see where he was taking the pilfered item. In the tiny area behind the pins in the bowling alley was a little cubbyhole. In that small little den the cub had hidden his stolen treasures.

Toward the end of August, the Hargreaves Circus came to Derry. It was a twenty-railroad-car extravaganza. It set up its massive tent near the site of today's Parkland Hospital. Later there was a parade of spectacles down Broadway. Among its featured acts were aerialists, clowns, and performing animals. There was a five-legged "sacred cow of India," a cakewalking horse, a huge trained bear, and Fred the six-ton elephant who was billed as "Jumbo the Second."

Jim Comeau and Ernest Reynolds decided it would a treat for Jack to visit the animals at the circus. They put a gold collar on the bear and walked him across town to the circus grounds. The Derry bear caused considerable excitement among both circus workers and the customers as Comeau showed off his tricks. Soon even circus owner Thomas Hargreaves came out to admire our Jack.

The circus impresario asked Comeau if the animal was for sale. Despite being told it was not, Hargreaves kept on pressing the Derry man to name his price. Finally, Jim Comeau blurted out a dollar amount that he thought was ridiculously high. He thought that would certainly make the circus man shut up. As soon as the words were out of his mouth, Hargreaves said "Sold," reached into his wallet, and paid Comeau on the spot. The circus owner explained that because Jack was less than a year old, he would learn "many tricks." The animal was led away by his new owner and that night the circus was loaded onto the train to be hauled to performances in other towns.

Later that day, the six-year-old Ned Reynolds wandered down to the pavilion to play with his best friend. There he learned the sad truth; he would never see or dance with the bear again.

I heard Ned tell this story eighty years later. Even then he was still sad about losing his friend and angry with Jim Comeau for selling the dancing bear.

I have not been able to find out the ultimate fate of Jackie Bear. The Hargreaves Circus closed in 1907. He may have been retired to the circus's winter park in Chester, Pennsylvania, or perhaps was sold to another circus or zoo. We will likely never know.

I'm sorry that Ned Reynolds couldn't have written this story. He was a much better storyteller than I'll ever be. Recently I received a letter from Ned's son Charlie, who lives in Alaska. He sent me a shoe box filled with a dozen audiotapes of his dad's rambling conversations. I was just too nervous to play these recordings, fearing that because of their age they would self-destruct in my cassette player. Fortunately, in response to my public moaning, Steve Heffelfinger of Derry came to the rescue. He and his son have the technical expertise to convert the recordings onto CDs. Soon visitors to the Museum of Derry History can hear the voice and stories of Nutfield's greatest storyteller. I'm sure my next Derry book will mine these CDs for Ned Reynolds's stories.

44.

The Search for Buddy Stewart

A FEW YEARS AGO, LOCAL BOOK DEALER BURT BABCOCK SENT ME a query from one of his out-of-state clients. He had seen in a reference book that the great jazz singer Buddy Stewart (1922–1950) was born in Derry. Could I confirm this? I was quickly able to find online references which seemed to support that claim. When I sought confirmation from Derry's town records, however, I found nothing! Zip! Goose egg! Nada! There was no Stewart in the birth records for that time period. For the next few months I purposely tried to ignore Mr. Babcock and would cross to the other side of Broadway when I saw him coming. I didn't like to admit being a failure in such a simple research task.

About three months ago, I purchased a scrapbook of Derry newspaper clippings from the 1940s. On one little snippet of paper was printed a story saying that the great singer had been born in Derry but few knew about it because his birth name was Buddy Burns. Back to the town records I ran. Hope quickly turned to disappointment. Again there was nothing. Later, with much help from Sherry Bailey at the research desk of the Derry Public Library, I was able to find out that his actual birth name was Albert J. Byrne Jr.—a fact not found in a single reference book. With that important piece of knowledge, I was able to use about a dozen sources to craft a biography of this son of Derry.

Buddy was born in Derry on December 15, 1921, and was delivered at home by Dr. Beckley. The proud dad, Albert Sr., was a thirty-year-old shoe worker who had been born in Boston; the mother was the thirty-two-year old Mamie (Mary) O'Donnell Byrne, originally from Townsend, Massachusetts. This was the couple's fourth child and their second son. Such a large, growing brood forced the family to move from 3 Elm Street into a bigger apartment at 9 Demarest Avenue.

As a very young child, Buddy's talents as a singer were recognized by his family and neighbors. He was constantly put on stage to entertain various local civic groups. At the age of eight, he went out on the road doing songs and comedy in a vaudeville act. Around 1930 he moved with his parents to Lowell, where he graduated from high school. After winning an amateur contest in a Lowell theater, he toured New England with several musical groups. He was good enough to win top prize on the nationally broadcast radio show *Major Bowes and his Original Amateur Hour*. Around this time, he took the stage name of Buddy Stewart.

In 1940 he married singer Martha Wayne (who became, of course, Martha Stewart—but not *that* Martha Stewart). They joined Glenn Miller's band as a part of his Snowflake Quartet. In 1942, the couple starred in the jitterbug movie *Count Me In*. Buddy's career was interrupted by service in the Army Air Corps, 1942–44. He later sang with many big bands including those of Charlie Barnet, Claude Thornhill, and Charlie Parker. He is perhaps best remembered for his years as the lead singer with the legendary drummer Gene Krupa. His recording of *What's This?* with Krupa is considered to be the first recording of a bebop vocal. During his career, his show stopping tour de force was scat—the singing of wordless rhythmic vocals—but both music critics and fans also gave him high praise as a ballad singer.

The readers of *Down Beat* magazine twice (1946, 1947) selected him the country's best male band singer. The same poll chose Frank Sinatra, Peggy Lee, and Sarah Vaughan as the best non-band vocalists. That's some company to be in! Buddy's sister Beverly was also a band singer. She was married to the legendary saxophonist Stan Getz, and their daughter Beverly is a vocalist on one of his best selling recordings.

On February 1, 1950, Buddy was driving with a band through New Mexico when he stopped to help a stranded driver. He was hit and killed by an oncoming car. He was only twenty-eight years old. Two weeks later, a benefit for his wife and young son, Sean, was held at Birdland in New York City. Almost every musician in the city volunteered to perform in honor of the popular young singer. The star-studded benefit lasted over six hours with different groups or performers going on stage every twenty minutes. Among the talent who performed that night were Charlie "Bird" Parker, Dizzie Gillespie, John Coltrane, Lester Young, brother-in-law Stan Getz, Ella Fitzgerald, Harry Belafonte, and Dick Hyman.

Today, Buddy is forgotten by most. In 2006, I met an elderly lady at the Tabernacle Society at Derry's Saint Thomas Aquinas Church who still remembers him. She told me with obvious pride how eighty-years before, she had danced on stage in Derry with young Buddy Byrne.

If Buddy hadn't stopped to perform an act of kindness in 1950, he would likely have experienced decades more of musical success. Fate robbed us all of his God-given talent. The only comfort is that his singing is still available today on re-releases of the albums he recorded with Gene Krupa.

45.

Radio Days

WHEN DERRY WAS FIRST SETTLED, IN 1719, WE WERE ALMOST completely cut off from the rest of the world. The news of the death of our king in London, a war in France, or a famine in Brazil might take months to arrive in Derry. In the years before the Revolutionary War, a post rider would bring a weekly newspaper from Portsmouth to East Derry. A loud-voiced deacon would stand by an oak tree next to the First Parish Church and read the paper to the news-starved throng that had gathered around him. The deacon would read everything including the advertisements and the list of ships that came up the Piscataqua River.

In 1849 the Manchester and Lawrence Rail Road laid its tracks across Broadway. Now locals could buy the daily newspapers from the big cities. Telegraph wires enabled messages to be sent and answered on the same day. In 1880 the *Derry News* began to chronicle the big and little events in our daily life. The telephone came to town in 1882.

The invention of the radio is credited to Marconi in 1896; it was later perfected by Lee Deforest. In April 1911 James Comeau, of Derry, was sailing home on the steamship *Essex* after a winter in Florida. From somewhere off Cape Hatteras he sent a wireless telegraph to Derry. The message was received at the Norfolk, Virginia, Naval Station and transmitted by telegraph line to Manchester. From the Queen City it was delivered by Western Union to Editor William Morse of the *Derry News*. The telegram was to alert Comeau's friends as to the day he expected to arrive back in Derry.

The next year many lives would be saved on the *Titanic* thanks to such wireless telegraphy sending Morse code across the waves.

Up until 1916, Derry residents thought of radios as just something to read about in the newspaper. In that year young Everett Gordon, of 17 Crystal Avenue, Derry, began to fool around with wireless communications.

Everett Payne Gordon was born in Derry on March 29, 1896, the son of Irving and Anna Payne Gordon. After graduating from Pinkerton Academy in 1913, he worked as a leather cutter in one of the town's many shoe factories. Around 1915 he enrolled in the Eastern Radio Institute in Boston.

In June 1916 the twenty-year-old Everett was visited by Homer Ellis, a radio engineer from Boston. In the Gordon home the two men set up a "radiotelegraphic apparatus for aeronautical use." This was a device that had been designed by the Derry man. The contraption was a small (eight pound) ultra sensitive oscillator, which, they claimed, could pick up signals up to nine thousand miles away. At one in the morning, the device received a series of "numerical ciphers." The coded message began with the numbers 53830 44973 03745 33222. The engineer believed it was being sent from a French or British warship somewhere in the Atlantic. This enigmatic communication was most certainly the first radio signal ever received in Derry. Our town had joined the wireless era.

The next year saw the United States enter the First World War. Everett Gordon enlisted in the Navy and earned the rank of chief quartermaster. He spent the war as an instructor in the flying corps, teaching pilots how to use the cockpit's radio.

In 1920 the first radio station began operation in America— KDKA in Pittsburgh, Pennsylvania. Soon all over the country other stations began to come on-line. By 1922 there were about five hundred stations broadcasting to the two million American households that owned a radio.

The first radio was installed in Derry in late 1921. Within the next few months, the number grew and soon there were a dozen radios in town. Among the very first of the radio pioneers in Derry were electrician Elmer Eaton, Pinkerton Academy, Erwin Dustin in the Pillsbury Kitchettes, David Griffith of the Derry Electric Company, Walter Senter, Walter Pillsbury, Richard Low, Carl Hall, Earl Kelly, and Everett Gordon.

In those early days, it was easy to know which of your neighbors had a radio. The necessity of an outdoor antenna made radio ownership difficult to hide. Gordon's antenna was a thick copper wire that ran from the ridge of his house to a pine tree on the edge of Crystal Avenue. With his small box radio, a couple of batteries, and his antenna he was able to pick up Pittsburgh. He reported hearing a church service with a sermon preached on David and Goliath. The pipe organ in this 1922 broadcast sounded like it was being played in the next room despite the fact that it was nearly four hundred miles away.

The first anti-radio article in the *Derry News* appeared on September 15, 1922. It had been a very wet summer. The newspaper reported that some scientists were blaming the rotten weather on radios. It was said, "The waves of the air are so disturbed by radio currents it makes the rain collect in the clouds and then precipitate." The editor of the *Derry News* concluded that the area could deal "with less radio service and with a good deal less rain."

The Fox Electric Company, of Haverhill, Massachusetts, was manufacturing and selling 22.5-volt radios here at $54.75—batteries not included. This was during the era when twenty-five dollars a week was a very good wage for a fifty-five-hour week. Other prices during that time were a six-room house near Broadway for twenty-four-hundred dollars; coffee at twenty-five cents a pound; an upright, crank-powered Brunswick phonograph at Emerson's Music Store, 39 East Broadway, for $150 (or three dollars down and three dollars a week); 78 RPM records for eight-five cents each. At Hyde's Heating at 29 West Broadway, you could buy and have installed a new coal furnace for $150. Admission to the Broadway Movie Theater was a dime and a Ford touring car in 1924 could be yours for $295.

The presidential election of 1924 was the first major political event carried on radio. Broadcast locally was the Democratic political conventions in which it took 103 rounds of balloting to choose the party's standard bearer. On election eve a crowd gathered in the poolroom of the Derry Athletic Association to hear the national results on the radio. Before midnight it was clear that Republican Calvin Coolidge was the winner, with 54 percent of the vote. In Derry, "Silent Cal" Coolidge captured about two-thirds of the ballots.

During the 1930s there was hardly a house in town that didn't have a radio. For those who couldn't afford a night out, the radio was a free source of amusement. Many shut-ins attended church via the airwaves. Into our living rooms were broadcast "fireside chats" by President Roosevelt. Many Americans had panicked during the 1938 broadcast of Orson Welles's *War of the Worlds*. The horrors of the Second World War were brought home each night by Edward R. Morrow, with his signature introduction, "This is London."

The *Derry News* began to publish radio schedules in the early 1930s. No one wanted to miss *Amos n' Andy*, Hedda Hopper's *Hollywood Holiday*, the *Rudy Vallee Show* or *Just Plain Bill*. As a boy I would stay awake past my bedtime with the radio hidden underneath the bedcovers to hear *Gang Busters*, *The Green Hornet*, and *Fibber McGee and Molly*. The spoken word allowed the imagination to make the stories so real!

Around 1949, Tommy Sutton (so I've been told) bought the first television in Derry. By the mid-1950s all those wonderful radio shows and dramas had gone off the airways; in their place was music and talk radio. By 1985 most of Nutfield had access to cable TV. This mass alert system proved very helpful during the floods of 2006. Today most people listened to the radio only while driving in the car. Even that exposure to Marconi's great invention is being challenged as more and more cars are being sold with built-in televisions and CD players. What will be next?

46.

The Lyon and the Elephant

THE SPRING AND SUMMER OF 1942 WERE AMONG THE MOST depressing times in our nation's history. On December 7, 1941, the Japanese had committed a sneak attack on Pearl Harbor. Within days we went from peace to fighting a war in Europe and Asia. Each month more and more of our young men and women were donning military uniforms and leaving home for an unknown fate. Soon every issue of the *Derry News* and *Union Leader* would be reporting the names of our children who were killed, missing in action, or wounded. The hell of war had come to Derry.

Advertisements in the paper only served to heighten our wartime anxiety. A local insurance agency was encouraging us to buy insurance to protect us if enemy incendiary bombs destroyed our homes. A *Derry News* advertisement on June 30, 1942, featured a graphic drawing of an American soldier bayoneting a Japanese soldier. The caption below said, "'That's the way I like to see them' said Gen. MacArthur, when he saw the rows of dead Japs in the Admiralty Islands." This ad was intended to get us to buy more war bonds.

Husbands and wives were struggling to understand the new rationing codes. Meats and fats needed red stamps and processed foods required blue stamps. Four "sugar stamps" were necessary to purchase five pounds of sugar a month—but you could fill out O.P.A. form R-322 to apply for the privilege of buying twenty pounds of sugar for home canning. Shoes required an "airplane stamp" and gasoline purchases were dependent on how many gallons the Derry ration board decided you needed. If you had an "A" sticker on your car window, you could buy only three gallons per week. A national speed limit was set at thirty-five miles per hour and soon pleasure driving was a thing of the past.

Boy and Girl Scouts were set to the task of collecting scrap metal and planting "victory gardens." Wives were saving fats and preparing "meatless meals." Their husbands were always worrying about how to make their auto tires last or how to get to work on their limited ration of fuel. Men and women were enlisting in the services or working in war-related jobs.

In June, the Plaza Theater on Broadway was showing the movie *Rosie the Riveter*. This story centers on the housing problems near a defense plant that cause two girls and two boys to share a room. The girls live there at night and the boys bunk together in the daytime. They all fall in love and by the time the movie ends, engagements are made, broken off, and made once again. When the credits roll, all is made right and the two couples live happily ever after.

In the midst of all the depressing news and the collective zeal in stopping Hitler, Mussolini, and Tojo, the citizens of Derry had an occasional chance to relax. On the Fourth of July in 1942 there were the usual picnics and baseball games. However, with gasoline rationing, there was no big parade and fireworks were forbidden, as the explosive devices were needed for the war.

The biggest event on that Independence Day in 1942 was the appearance of the Sello Brothers Circus at the D.A.A. Field on South Avenue. This was a small circus that traveled by rail to small-town America and Canada. It would arrive in the dead of night and miraculously in the morning there would a huge tent set up in some vacant field with sideshows, wagons, and a menagerie.

The Sello Circus consisted of twenty-five acts that took their turn in the center ring. The show offered the usual collection of clowns, acrobats, and aerialists. Among the animal acts were trained elephants, horses, ponies, dogs, pigs, monkeys, goats, and baboons. There was also Dynamite the Bucking Bronco. For a few coins you could take up the challenge and try to ride him. The circus advertised it would pay a dollar for every minute you could stay on his back. For the appreciators of fine music, there was also the musical styling of Shep and His Prairie Singers.

Early on the morning of Independence Day, the children of Derry were drawn, as if by a magnet, to the circus grounds. Gangs of excited preteens were investigating every aspect of circus life. They poked their noses into areas that were, in theory, off-limits to all except circus personal. Soon a gang of boys discovered an elephant that was tethered by a chain to a stake. They began to tease the huge pachyderm by yelling at him and jabbing him with sticks.

Among the leader of the tormentors was seven-year-old Vernon Lyon, of 40 South Avenue. Before anyone could stop it, the angry elephant "reached out and grasped the young boy with his trunk." Within a second, the mighty animal lifted the screaming boy up off the ground. It then threw him down hard onto the ground and stepped on him. Quickly the trainer ran to prevent more damage, as the boy was dragged away by spectators.

Everett Tappan drove young Lyon to the Alexander-Eastman Hospital, where he was put under the care of Dr. Francis King. The boy was put onto the critical list while his injuries were evaluated. The hospital X-ray machine found he was suffering from ten broken ribs, a broken collarbone, and a punctured lung. There were also significant internal injuries. The boy remained in the hospital for well over a month. It was probably the first week of September before he was declared fit to play again with his friends. By that time however, summer vacation was over and he had to go back to school.

This is all I know of the story, as the Lyon family shortly afterward moved out of Derry. I do find later references to an elephant named Frieda in Sello's Circus dying after eating a light bulb. I believe young Vernon Lyon died in September 2003 in Florida at the age of sixty-seven. If anyone knows more about this incident, please let me know.

As far as I know, there is only one other elephant story that centers on Derry. In the 1930s, the gathering spot for men was a bench in front of a Broadway drugstore. A dozen old-timers and loafers would gather there every warm day to swap lies and complain about the weather. Since their childhood, these wry Yankees had been trained that in conversation they should avoid any emotion, speak as few words as possible, and use understatement rather than exaggeration. One day the circus came to town and set up its tent at the old D. A. A. Field on South Avenue. One of the elephants broke out of its cage and ran down Broadway at a fast trot. As it passed the drugstore, the men showed no reaction to the sight of a two-thousand-pound pachyderm running down the road toward the

Londonderry town line. Finally one broke the silence and said "Well ... It looks like Charlie's gray mare's put on a few pounds, don't ya think."

There's one pachyderm story that involves nearby Hudson, New Hampshire. I believe I read it in *Yankee Magazine* years ago but it may well be apocryphal, merely another rural legend. It seems an elephant at Benson's Wild Animal Farm had been trained by his mahout to do all kinds of tricks. It could walk upright on its hind legs while waving a flag and then execute a courtly bow to the crowd. The mighty beast was also trained to go to the center of the circus ring and sit like man on a little red stool. One day the elephant got loose and tried to escape from the zoo. In time he wandered out into the parking lot. There he spotted a bright red Volkswagen Beetle. The years of training by his master alerted his mind that it was time to spring into his act. As quick as he could, he ran toward the red car, sat down upon it, and flattened the poor little vehicle.

The Hudson story probably never happened but it does make a great tale to tell the grandkids.

47.

The Hurricane of 1938

MOST PEOPLE IN DERRY HAVE NEVER HAD THE EXPERIENCE OF living through an actual hurricane in New Hampshire. The good folks in Florida, Louisiana, and Texas get walloped annually, while our state can go for decades without being hit. Mind you, we are not complaining one bit—Katrina, you weren't no lady!

Try and remember the last time a hurricane visited Derry. Your answer is probably wrong. The year is 1960. It's a trick question. Hurricanes Gloria (1985) and Bob (1991) weren't hurricanes at all by the time they reached our little corner of the world. By definition, a hurricane must have sustained winds in excess of seventy-four miles per hour. The last true hurricane was Donna (1960), which did only relatively little damage here. Before that, there was Carol (1954), which caused considerable local flooding and wind damage. To all true New Englanders, however, the only real blow was the unnamed hurricane of 1938.

The year of the Great Hurricane was the ninth year of the Great Depression. Roosevelt was in the White House and the Red Sox had lost the pennant to the Yankees. The rumblings of the approaching world war and Adolf Hitler were scaring the hell out of many of us. Top songs that year included *A-Tisket, A-Tasket* by Ella Fitzgerald and *Bei Mir Bist du Schoen* by the Andrew Sisters. Gene Krupa led a new band featuring the crooning of Buddy Steward—of Derry, New Hampshire. The big movie of 1938 was Frank Capra's *You Can't Take It with You.*

The summer of 1938 had been cold and wet. Starting on September 18, it rained four straight days in the Merrimack Valley. The

Young Bob Richardson in front of the Hood Farm after the 1938 hurricane.

streams and rivers were running at nearly flood level. One weatherman said that if this had been snow rather than rain, the area would have been "buried to a depth of 10 feet."

In 1938 there were no weather satellites or radar to give us warning of an approaching storm. The National Weather Service did, however, take notice of a severe tropical depression that was forming off the coast of Africa. By September 16, when the storm reached the Cape Verde Islands, it had strengthened into a full-fledged hurricane. By September 19 it had been classified as a category-five storm—the highest level of danger. Hurricanes with that degree of intensity have sustained winds over 155 miles per hour and storm surges of more than eighteen feet. The path of the storm appeared to be aiming straight for New England!

The experts at the government weather center, however, were sure there was no danger to mainland America. There was a large area of low pressure just off the eastern coast that they "knew" would divert the storm to the northeast. In meteorological history, this is what always happened. There hadn't been a single hurricane to hit New England since 1869. Only one government forecaster in September 1938 had developed a model that predicted this storm would track north and not northeast. His superiors overruled him. The official forecast was for "cloudy skies and gusty winds."

The experts were horribly wrong. The storm did not curve out to sea; the hurricane instead headed due north. To make matters worse, the swirling hurricane was moving at an unprecedented forward speed of seventy miles per hour. There was almost no time to warn the population! At 3:30 on the afternoon of September 21, the storm slammed into Long Island. The hurricane was huge. It measured five hundred miles across with a fifty-mile-wide eye. The wind gusts were over 180 miles per hour with sustained winds of up to 150 miles per hour. One group of storm survivors in Rhode Island remembered seeing a "40-foot fog bank rolling toward the beach" and at the last possible moment they realized it wasn't fog—it was a wall of water.

The destruction in southern New England was catastrophic. Whole summer communities were swept away without leaving a trace. In Napatree Point, in Rhode Island, forty-two summer homes, the yacht club, and seventeen residents were swept away by a storm surge and "never seen again." At Misquamicut Beach five hundred homes were washed into the Atlantic Ocean. There were at least one hundred killed in the town of Westerly, Rhode Island, alone. Many families who managed to survive did so only by clinging to floating roofs and trees. On an island in Narraganset Bay, a school was swept away killing seven of the ten grade-school children. Many of the bodies were recovered wearing only their shoes and stocks— the fierce winds had stripped them of their other clothing.

Because the hurricane struck at the time of the highest possible tides, the entire costal region experienced flooding. Much of the city of Providence was under fourteen feet of water. In Connecticut, some homes two miles inland were flooded. The Connecticut River was swollen so much that it was neck deep more than a mile from its normal banks.

As the hurricane moved north, it still retained much of its power. At the Blue Hill Observatory, near Boston, there were wind gusts of 186 miles per hour. On Mount Washington, the winds measured 163 miles per hour. It is estimated that the total rainfall for September 21 was between ten and seventeen inches in much of southern and central New England.

Shortly after four in the afternoon, the storm hit our state, with its center passing near the New Hampshire-Vermont border. Locally, its fury was first felt in Salem. The gale-force winds caused considerable panic at the Rockingham Racetrack when the massive cupola blew off the grandstand. This was followed by the race announcer's stand being "bowled over." During the sixth race, spectators witnessed the entire roof of a stable being lifted from its base. A groom and an exerciser were sent to the hospital for treatment.

About five o'clock, Derry began to feel the full might of the winds. The *Derry News* reported that "trees a century old, fell right and left before the might of the wind, carrying down power, light and telephone lines and causing untold damage to roofs, chimneys, windows and other property." The streets were deserted, as most of our citizens remained in their homes or businesses, afraid to venture out because of the danger of flying debris. Some were in near panic because of the sudden fury. All were praying for the winds to calm and the rains to stop. There were likely very few atheists in the path of the storm. For hours and hours, all that could be heard were the high-pitched howl of the wind and the sounds of destruction.

Almost immediately after the winds began, the town went dark. Electric power was cut as the storm sheared off hundreds of poles. Kerosene lamps were dusted off and forgotten stashes of candles were found tucked away in drawers. Telephones went dead and radios went silent. The men, women, and children of Derry felt completely alone and isolated; there was no way of knowing the fate of the outside world. All they could know with any certainty was what they could see from their windows. As the darkness of night fell, all they could hear were the breaking of trees and the whining of the wind.

Throughout the hurricane, emergency workers were the only ones to venture onto the streets. Derry's firemen and police were rushing from one emergency to the next. Volunteer electricians were sent to secure downed power lines. Members of the American Legion and the Boy Scouts spent the long night trying to remove debris from streets and directing traffic. One area of special concern was Broadway. This main artery was closed a number of times because of barriers caused by pieces of wood and shingles ripped from area buildings. Firemen in the middle of the storm had to climb on the roof of Ganem's Market to secure its signs so they wouldn't be blown into the street. The emergency room of the Alexander-Eastman Hospital was filled with victims of the storm.

The winds finally slowed around midnight. The next morning, at early light, the weary Derry residents slowly began to leave their homes to survey the damage. The streets were littered with lawn furniture, trees, signs, bricks from chimneys, and parts of roofs. Trees were uprooted, blocking roads and driveways.

The initial count was 450 trees downed by the storm. This estimate would prove very conservative. The thickly forested Hood's Grove, between Lenox Road and Mount Pleasant Street, was nearly flattened. (This would later become the site of the Hood School.) Although every section of town suffered damage, particularly hard hit was the area of West Broadway, Nortonville, and High Street. Most of the boats on Beaver Lake had been ripped off their moorings and were dashed against the western shore of the lake.

Without electric power, many businesses could not function. Ice cream melted in the drugstore soda fountains; gasoline couldn't be sold at filling stations that used modern automatic pumps. A couple of gas stations that still used the old-fashioned hand pumps did a land-office business. The presses of the *Derry News* were also without power, so the editor had to make arrangements to have the paper printed in Manchester. Predictably, the next edition had advertisements for home-repair loans from the First National Bank, and the Bartlett & Shepard Insurance Company was offering to sell windstorm insurance for the next blow.

All over town there were reports of barns and sheds being flattened; and many houses experienced considerable structural damage. Through Herculean efforts by the linemen of the Public Service Company, the power was restored to Broadway after only forty-eight hours of darkness. At exactly 5:40 on Friday afternoon, the lights of Broadway came back on. The movie theater had a sell-out crowd that night. Much of the rest of the town, however, would continue to be without power for nearly a week. It would also take a long time before the familiar wild songbirds returned to Derry.

Derry was very fortunate to escape the storm without incurring a single death. The greatest material loss was to the Anna Rogers home, near the site of today's Hidden Valley Golf Course. This massive house connected right onto the barn and may have had the longest ridgepole in the state. A fire broke out in the middle of the storm and gutted the building.

Edna Clark was vacationing in North Weare, New Hampshire, when the hurricane struck. She and three other women were standing on a bridge watching the surging water when a nearby dam gave way. A wall of water rushed downstream and overturned the bridge. The four women were thrown into the Piscataqua River and swept away to their deaths. Miss Clark had grown up in what is now the Pinkerton Tavern Restaurant.

The hurricane of 1938 will stand as one of the greatest natural disasters ever to hit our country. In New England and Long Island there were nearly six hundred people killed, thirty-five hundred injured, and seventy-five thousand buildings damaged or destroyed. In New Hampshire, an estimated sixty thousand people were made homeless after the storm and thirteen died. The hurricane did about $12 million in damage to our state. This estimate is, of course, in 1938 dollars; today it would be calculated into a loss measuring in the billions. It took an estimated million man-days of labor just to clean up the debris.

For years afterward, the damage done to Derry's trees and forest was quite noticeable. Adams Pond was filled with thousands of logs that were waiting their turn in the sawmill under the federal government's plan to purchase wind-fallen trees. In our state it was estimated that two billion feet of usable timber was felled by the storm. In 1939 local poet Josie Shackett published in the *Derry News* a poem entitled "In Memory of Our Beautiful Trees." It closes this way:

> Our maple tree the wind cut down
>> And O! We loved it so
> For Father planted it one day.
>> And watched it grow and grow.
>
> So this dear tree has memories
>> Intrusted to our care,
> And I'd be happy could I but see
>> That old tree standing there.

48.

Cigar Box John

WHEN I WAS YOUNGER AND THINNER, I SPENT A YEAR AS A MEDIC with a combat unit bobbing around the delta region of Vietnam. It was only by the grace of God, dumb luck, and Sergeant Betts that I survived my year in 'Nam. On many occasions I lived in tents, bunkers, and Quonset huts. Frequently I drove my deuce-and-a-half truck over pontoon bridges. All that time I never realized that the modern Quonset hut and the pontoon bridge were the designs of Captain John Laycock of Derry, New Hampshire.

John Noble Laycock was born in Methuen, Massachusetts, in 1892 and attended the U.S. Naval Academy. At Annapolis he played lacrosse and as student-commander led his men to "win the colors" as best midshipman company of the academy. After graduation in 1914, he served as a lieutenant (jg) during the U.S. invasion of Vera Cruz, Mexico. In 1917 he graduated from Rensselaer Polytechnic Institute with a degree in engineering.

After the First World War, he became a commander in the Civil Engineer Corps and helped run many of our navy yards, including Philadelphia, Charleston, and Newport. In 1920 he supervised the construction of the massive dirigible hangar at Cape May, New Jersey. In 1927, President Hoover sent Lieutenant Commander Laycock to Haiti. There he was director of municipal engineering for the city of Port-au-Prince. The president of Haiti later appointed Laycock as public works administrator for the entire country. He served in this post from 1928 to 1931. For this service he was decorated with the Order of Honor by the Republic of Haiti.

Captain John Laycock (right) shows his cigar box model of a pontoon bridge to Admiral Ben Moreell in 1945.

Upon returning to the United States, Laycock held command positions at the Boston and Portsmouth Navy Yards. In 1934 he purchased a house at 79 East Broadway as a permanent home for his wife, Mildred, and their two sons, Robert and John Jr. Mrs. Laycock was the sister of Senator William Cole, of Derry. In 1938, Laycock was appointed war plans officer in the Bureau of Yards and Docks in Washington, D.C. In 1941 he was in charge of planning for the Navy Seabees and is considered one of their founders.

The clouds of war were darkening over the skies of America. It was obvious that the nation would soon be fighting a war in both Europe and Asia. Laycock's task was to see that we were prepared to win. He knew that when war broke out, we would immediately need a navy yard in Europe. Among Laycock's principal supporters and confidants for advance preparedness were Prime Minster Winston Churchill, President Franklin Roosevelt, and Roosevelt's chief adviser, Harry Hopkins.

Laycock redesigned the lowly Quonset hut to make it a more practical, all-purpose structure. Prior to the actual start of the war, he arranged for massive quantities of these prefabricated structures to be shipped secretly to a site in Londonderry, Northern Ireland.

Laycock knew there was not a sufficient supply of timber in Ireland for construction of his new navy yard; also, the Irish climate demanded weather-resistant structures that could be built quickly. A week without rain in Northern Ireland was considered a drought by most of its residents.

On February 6, 1942, in Londonderry, Northern Ireland, the navy yard was operational. A team of three hundred Laycock-trained technicians had already assembled the Quonset huts, so within twenty-five days America had a functioning Navy base able to refit and repair any class of ship that could make port. This was America's first and largest naval station in the European theater and a major convoy staging area.

Just before the war, a naval engineer had toyed with the idea of utilizing steel boxes as floating platforms. The chief problem was that they capsized when a load was put on their front and there seemed no practical way to link the hollow boxes to create a stable platform. Captain Laycock took on the task of solving the problem.

In 1939, while vacationing at Beaver Lake, Laycock began secretly experimenting with cigar boxes joined together with strips of wood. Here in Derry, he solved all the design problems of the proposed pontoon devices. Soon America was manufacturing thousands of pontoons. Each unit weighed twenty-eight hundred pounds and measured five feet by seven feet by five feet. Each could support a weight of seventy-five tons. From then on, throughout the Navy, Laycock was known as "Cigar Box John."

The Laycock-designed pontoon first proved its value during the invasion of Sicily. The island's lack of port facilities, entrenched defenders, and shallow water made conventional landings impossible. The pontoons served as an artificial causeway onto which troops and cargo could be quickly brought to the beachhead. The pontoons were later instrumental in the Allies' successes during the Normandy invasion and in the Pacific campaign. Over the years John Laycock's "cigar-boxes" were used as wharves, piers, barges, platforms for floating cranes, ice breakers, and even aircraft landing fields. When powered by a small engine, they could even function as tugboats.

For his development of the pontoon, Quonsets huts, self-contained power plants, oil-fog generators, and numerous other devices, Laycock was one of the first Americans to be awarded the Legion of Merit. His award citation mentions that the pontoon "has been employed with gratifying results by both Army and Navy in practically every advanced base movement throughout the world." He later received a second Legion of Merit for his "remarkable engineering skill and organizational ability."

Captain Laycock retired from the Navy in 1945 and moved permanently to Derry. Here he wrote a book entitled *Unemployment Unlimited*. This economic treatise contained methods to rid the nation of economic depressions. He proposed to free us "from the apron-strings of the socialistic-nurse-maid and from the petty restraints and destruction of initiative that goes with them." A second edition of the book was published by the Cole-Noble Co. of Derry, N.H. Unfortunately, I did not do all that well in my college economic classes and am unable objectively to analyze his ideas. The book remains unread (by me) on the shelves of the library of the Derry Museum of History.

John Noble Laycock died of cancer on February 3, 1967, at the Alexander-Eastman Hospital. He was seventy-four years old. His funeral was held at the Central Congregational Church. He is buried at the Pine Grove Cemetery in Salem. His wife, Mildred Cole Laycock, passed away in 1972.

Few Americans can lay claim to having contributed as much to our success in the Second World War as John Noble Laycock. Watch the national news tonight. I bet during the segment on the war in Iraq, you'll be able to spot a newly constructed pontoon bridge at Tikrit or Quonset huts serving our troops in the form of barracks, hospitals hangars and supply depots. Captain John Laycock: a real American hero.

My thanks to Captain Raymond J. Brown, U.S. Coast Guard (ret.), for his help in researching this article.

49.
Walter Borowski, Hero

FROM THE TIME OF THE ORIGINAL NUTFIELD SETTLEMENTS IN 1719 to the present day, our sons and daughters have gone off to fight in a dozen wars. Of these conflicts, none was harder fought than the Second World War. From Iwo Jima to Normandy, our men and women gave their all to protect hearth and home from the evils of despotism. These soldiers had all-American names like Broderick, Daprato, Feinauer, Pelletier, Grady, Alexander, Langelier, Pillsbury, Shepard, Gross, and Sing. Each of their lives is worthy of its own chapter in this book. Space, however, allows me to chronicle just one soldier's story. I have chosen to write about Walter Borowski, to let him represent the courage of those who survived both the Great Depression and the Great War to become what we now call the "greatest generation."

One dictionary tells us that a hero is "a man of distinguished courage or ability, admired for his brave deeds." I would like to tack on this addendum: "Every hero will always deny that he is a hero." Walter Borowski is a man who fits both parts of our definition. Walter's heroism during World War II cannot be denied. But when asked about it, he'll say his brother Eugene, who died during the D-Day push, and the military nurses who worked amidst unbelievable blood and gore were heroes. "Not me," Walter has told me several times. "I'm no hero; I came home alive."

His parents, Alexander (1879–1960) and Amelia Jakubowski Borowski (1883–1974), emigrated from that part of imperial Russia that we now call Poland. In 1907 they sailed from Bremen, Germany, on the North German Lloyd passenger ship *Barbarossa*. This was a

Sargent Walter Borowski, U.S. Army Ranger

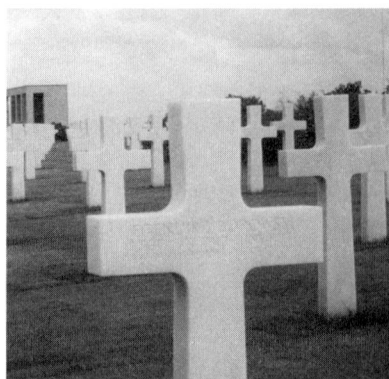

Grave of Sargent Jerry Borowski, Normandy American Cemetery, Colleville-sur-Mer, France

large, luxurious cruise ship that was 526 feet long and capable of speeds up to fifteen knots. It was likely that Alex and Amelia didn't have a fancy stateroom; no doubt they were crowded into the barrack like rooms of steerage class. During the First World War the *Barbarossa* was seized by the American government and renamed the USS *Mercury*. From 1917 to 1919 it was credited with sixteen trips across the Atlantic as a troop carrier. After the war, it was sold into private hands and then sold for scrap in 1928.

It took thirteen days for the Borowskis to cross the Atlantic and arrive at the Port of New York on November 25, 1907. At Ellis Island, all their information was taken down by government clerks. Alex was recorded as being a twenty-eight-year-old farm laborer; Amelia was listed as eighteen years old. Her actual age was twenty-four. She had no listed profession but was recorded as literate. Neither of the Borowskis could speak English. Their ultimate destination was listed as Manchester, New York. After hours of waiting in lines, they were checked by an Ellis Island physician and judged healthy enough to enter America.

After clearing the inspectors, they managed to find a train to the correct Manchester. They soon moved to Pleasant Street in Manchester, New Hampshire, where several of their relatives were already living. Soon they started to grow their own family. The firstborn was Frank in 1912. In time there would be a dozen in the family with seven daughters and three sons. Walter Borowski was born in

Manchester on January 5, 1920. The census officially records his first name as Vladisla the Polish version of Walter.

In 1922 the Borowski family bought a small farmhouse at 81 High Street. Amelia remained at home as a housewife while Alex worked in the local shoe factories. Alongside the house were a large vegetable garden and barn. This kitchen garden was not planted for recreation; it was a necessity to feed the many hungry mouths in the family. They also raised pigs, chickens, and cows. By the time he was ten years old, Walter was being hired out with the family horse to plow gardens for neighbors.

They were a family of very modest means, but it's doubtful that the children knew they were living in poverty. Their clothes were usually hand-me-downs but they were always kept clean, neat, and well mended; Amelia insisted on that. Not until after 1930 could they afford the luxury of a radio. The parents, while proud to be American, were also proud of their Polish heritage and the kids were taught to speak Polish and even some Russian.

When Walter was six, he entered the first grade at the West Side School, which is now the town's community center. For junior high school, he attended the Oak Street School. In 1933 he became the first member of his family to enter high school. Although he felt awkward wearing hand-me-downs he was told by his mother to walk tall. She told him over and over "keep your head up. You're not just another dumb Pollack."

At Pinkerton Academy, Walter was a very good student and president of the Future Farmers of America. He gained a school-wide reputation for always keeping up his hand in the classroom to ask questions. Young Walter wanted desperately to learn and to justify his mother's faith in him. He was frequently a judge at poultry shows at the University of New Hampshire and even made a speech at the St. Louis Livestock Show.

Even though he was a gifted athlete, Walter didn't earn any letters in high school; he always had to work after school. Upon graduation, he wanted to go on to college, but with a family of ten children, this was just not possible.

After graduating with the class of 1937, Walter had to forgo any future educational plans to earn money to help out the family. His unemployed father went to work for the federally funded WPA. Frank, the oldest son, worked long hours in area shoe factories and was considered a skilled employee. His brother Eugene joined the

Civilian Conservation Corps on the Yale River for a dollar a day. His name at birth was actually Egeniurz but everyone called him Jerry. After deductions, Jerry's monthly pay was only twelve dollars. Walter worked at the KlevBros Shoe Factory in Derry and at Holland's Cleaners, where he earned seventeen cents an hour. In time Walter found better employment outside of town at the New Boston Drill Press Company in the tool-and-die division.

In 1939 Adolf Hitler forced Europe into war. Many in America prayed that the bloodshed would end before our country was brought into the conflict. Despite these prayers, the war clouds were soon drifting over Fortress America. Young men around the country were enlisting in the Army, Navy, Marines, and Coast Guard.

Among the very first to enlist in Derry was the twenty-three-year-old Jerry Borowski. He was, in everyone's opinion, quite a man. He had quit school right after grammar school to work in Derry's shoe factories and as a landscaper; the family needed the income to feed the large family. As one of the older children, he willingly assumed the role of "big brother" for his younger siblings. His kid-brother Walter later recalled that "if anyone tried to pick on me, they'd have to come through Jerry first." Jerry gained considerable local notoriety as a boxer under the ring name of the "Blond Tiger." Frequently, touring carnivals and circuses that showed up in Derry offered a challenge to all comers. If you could stay in the ring with their boxer for three rounds, you would win ten dollars. Jerry usually walked away with the purse. He would eventually be the Golden Gloves champion of New England. Walter idolized his brother, saying, "He was all man with more courage than Carter had liver pills—no one had a bad word about Jerry."

At the time of his enlistment, on October 14, 1940, Jerry Borowski stood five feet ten inches tall and weighed 152 pounds. After Army basic training he was assigned to the medical corps but quickly decided he wanted to be where the action was. He applied for a transfer to the paratroopers. He went through jump training in Alliance, Nebraska, and broke his ankle there. Staff Sergeant Borowski arrived in Ireland in December 1943 as a member of the 507th Parachute Infantry Regiment attached to the 82nd Airborne Division. While there he broke his ankle again during a practice jump. In March 1944 his regiment was moved secretly to Nottingham, England, to prepare for the D-Day invasion.

On December 7, 1941, the Japanese Imperial Air Force attacked the American naval base at Pearl Harbor. We were at war! On February 18, 1942, Walter Borowski enlisted in the Army intending to follow his brother into the paratroopers. At induction Walter was twenty-two years old, nearly six feet tall with blond hair and blue eyes. Old photographs show an intense, handsome young man with piercing eyes and movie-star good looks.

After basic training, Walter tried to get accepted into the paratroopers. Because he weighed 181 pounds, though, the Army decided he was just too heavy. While at training maneuvers in Needles, California, he heard about a new Army outfit called the Rangers. It was to be an American version of the legendary Commandos of the British military. It would comprise hand-picked elite soldiers—the toughest of the tough and the best of the best. A normal infantry division consisted of thirty-seven officers and 857 enlisted men; the Rangers were intended to be a small, fast-moving outfit of just twenty-seven officers and 484 men. It was also an understood but unspoken fact that many Rangers would not survive to come home again. Their avowed purpose was to go in harm's way and in battle live up to their motto, "Rangers lead the way." Walter later said, "We were so tough we had the Marines shine our boots."

Historically, the first fully American Rangers group was formed in New Hampshire by Robert Rogers in 1756. It was the most famous fighting force during the French and Indian War. Rogers's standing orders for irregular warfare are still taught to modern-day Rangers. Rogers lived in Derry during his boyhood and his father is buried at Forest Hill Cemetery in East Derry. His lieutenants were John and William Stark, who were born on the slopes of Ryan's Hill in Derry.

A grueling physical test was administered to the men who applied for the 1943 version of the Rangers. Many soldiers felt the call to be Rangers but few were chosen. At his post, Walter Borowski scored in first place. By train he was transported to Camp Forrest, Tennessee, where in April 1943 the Second Rangers Battalion was activated. On this eighty-five-thousand acre sandy pine barren the Rangers were trained in an isolated tent city. They were given shabby secondhand uniforms because their training would be so hard that the brass saw no sense in wasting new ones. To get a shower meant hiking a mile to where non-Rangers were housed in regular wooden barracks. The food was usually cold and not up to even Army standards.

Although Walter Borowski was in great physical shape, nothing could have prepared him for the Rangers' training demands. During the first week he went through a "shake down march." Wearing full battle gear, including rifles and full packs, the men had to complete a three-mile hike in just thirty-seven minutes, then a five-mile march in one hour, and finally a nine-mile march in two hours. Some of these marches were carried out in torrential rain and others in Tennessee's unforgiving searing sun. The Rangers were not allowed to have any water until they completed their hike. Soon the length of the "speed marches" increased to twenty-five miles. Oftentimes the men were made to move at six miles an hour and one Ranger training company claimed to have marched fifteen miles in just two hours! Those who couldn't keep up were washed out of the program.

Quickly Walter lost a few pounds and after a few weeks he wrote to his sister Celia that the hard work made him feel "swell." Training included hours and hours of calisthenics and having teams of six men lift fifteen-foot-long telephone poles. One exercise all the Rangers remember was the "sawdust pit." A forty-foot-square three-and-a-half-foot-deep pit was dug; the sides were made of logs and the bottom had a thin cushion of tick-infested sawdust. Gangs of Rangers were ordered into the pit and told to fight until there was only one man standing. Walter recalled that this activity had to be stopped as "too many men were having their arms broken." The enlisted men had little respect for their officers because while the EMs marched, the officers rode alongside in jeeps drinking water out of their canteens. While the men exercised, the brass watched.

In June, 1943, Major James Rudder took command. He led by example and did everything with his men. When they marched, he marched. He immediately brought in better food, wooden barracks, showers, and brand-new uniforms. He treated his trainees as men, not animals. In one training exercise he had the men form up in lines facing each other, about twenty-five feet apart. Each man held his rifle with its bayonet affixed. On command, the weapons were thrown back and forth from soldier to soldier as quickly as possible. As the exercise continued, the speed of the throws was faster and faster. This taught the Rangers-in-training concentration and agility. Remarkably, only a single soldier suffered a bayonet wound.

Tarzan-type rope swings were set up across wide, swift-moving rivers. There were classes on killing with knives, demolition, and night fighting. Frequently, training would cease for the day at two in the morning with the bugle sounding reveille at 5:45. If anyone complained about the harshness of the training, the standard reply was "You volunteered."

Half the soldiers who started Ranger training were not there at the end to graduate. Many quit and others were asked to leave; most of the washouts were good men who just didn't have what it took to be a Ranger. As Walter Borowski remembered, "It was too harsh; they overdid it and showed no mercy—especially on the city boys." Despite the brutality of the training, Walter held only the highest respect for his commanding officer and called Colonel Rudder "my buddy." But of Camp Forrest, Walter still retained a definite dislike, calling the whole state of Tennessee "a hell of a place to be."

After Camp Forrest, the Rangers were sent for further training at Fort Pierce, Florida; Fort Dix, New Jersey; and Camp Richie, Maryland. Only after all that were they declared fit to be sent to the European theater as Rangers. Out of 1,024 men and sixty-two officers who began the training in April, there were only 488 men and twenty-five officers in the program in November. At 1700 hours on November 23, 1943, the luxury liner the *Queen Elizabeth* left New York's Pier 90 on the way to England. On board were fifteen thousand servicemen and -women including Corporal Walter Borowski and his band of 513 brothers of "Rudder's Rangers." During the voyage, the Rangers were detailed as the military police for the ship; it was thought "Rudder's boys" were too tough to allow any breach of discipline. And they were!

After an eight-day voyage, the Rangers were delivered to Scotland, where they were billeted in private homes. There and later in England they were given further training with the British commandoes. On their first Christmas away from home, the Rangers hosted a party for seven hundred English children complete with American cartoons, a Christmas tree, and Santa Claus. The men saved candy, cookies, and fruit from the rations and care packages to give the war-deprived children a taste of American love. Walter remembered that the kids were eating out of trash cans and "followed the Rangers everywhere we went" hoping for handouts.

None of the Rangers knew officially why they were in England and why they were climbing over and over again up the two-hundred-foot-tall White Cliffs of Dover. Only the top brass knew their mission and they weren't telling. Unbeknownst to Walter Borowski, he was part of a plan that was the best-kept secret of World War ll. If the Germans found out that the Rangers were being trained to climb cliffs, then German General Rommel might figure out that the invasion was to be at Normandy and not Calais; the element of surprise would be lost and many more thousands of our soldiers would be killed.

By 1944, Germany had pretty much lost the war for the sea and for the air; now was the time for the Allies to reclaim the land. Operation Overlord, as conceived by General Marshall and commanded by General Eisenhower, consisted of an invasion of France via the beaches of Normandy. The D-Day invasion was to include an initial flotilla of 6,939 boats from eight different navies. On board would be 176,000 men. Overhead support would be provided by 11, 590 aircraft.

On D-Day there were to be one Canadian, two American, and two British beaches. Each of these landing zones would be difficult to take but the American beaches, code named Omaha and Utah, would be particularly challenging. On top of the hundred-foot cliffs at Pointe du Hoc on Omaha Beach was a Germany artillery battery of 155 mm guns with a range of over fourteen miles. Unless these guns could be silenced, the American landing force would be decimated. Supreme Commander Eisenhower felt sure that successes on D-Day hinged on those cliffs being scaled and the guns destroyed. The Rangers would have to lead the way and the rest of the American army would follow.

This was the task of the Second Ranger Battalion; this is for what they had been secretly trained. And this is what they will be forever remembered—they will always be Rudder's Rangers—the boys of Pointe du Hoc. General George Marshall told Rudder just before the assault, "Never has any commander been given a more desperate mission." Under Admiral Sir James "Blinky" Hall, the British Intelligence Office was considered the best in the free world. Its assessment of the assault on Pointe du Hoc was that "three old women with brooms could keep the Rangers from scaling the cliffs." In response Colonel Rudder told his superiors just five words: "The Rangers will do it."

The Germans realized that Omaha Beach would be a likely landing site by Allied invaders. To protect against such an attack, they had installed thirty-seven hundred dragon-teeth obstacles that would rip the bottoms out of boats that tried to land at high tide. They also laid ten thousand mines just offshore. On the cliffs of Pointe du Hoc were trenches, bunkers, and cement pill boxes that concealed eighty-five German machine guns. Historian Samuel Eliot Morrison described the German defense on Omaha Beach as "the best imitation of hell for an invading force that American troops had encountered anywhere."

The Second Rangers were divided into two groups. Abel, Baker, and Charlie Companies along with the Fifth Rangers and First and Twenty-ninth Infantry Divisions were to land on Omaha Beach. The hardest assignment was to be given to Dog, Easy, and Fox Companies. They had the honor of being the first Americans to land on D-Day. They were the 225 men who would scale the cliff at Point du Hoc.

On June 5 at 4:30 in the afternoon, Walter Borowski and the men of Fox Company, Second Rangers were loaded onto the SS *Ben-My-Chree* to sail toward France. Twelve miles from shore the men were loaded onto ten landing craft and four DUKWS; each could hold about a few dozen men. Silence was maintained as they headed toward the Normandy coast in total darkness. The men sat on benches and when they got close to shore, their boat's front would lower and they were trained to run like hell to meet their fate. Walter recalled that it "was a bad, rainy day, a miserable, windy day. The sea was grayish-green and the wind was blowing." In Borowski's words, "Everyone and his brother was seasick."

Immediately on that D-Day morning, everything began to go wrong. One boat immediately sank in the rough seas, drowning twenty soldiers. The British pilots got confused and headed for the wrong drop-off point. The Brits corrected their course, but now they were forced to sail four kilometers diagonal to the coast. The element of surprise was lost. They were twenty minutes late at the start of their assault and the cover of darkness had turned into the light of dawn. The flotilla of Ranger boats was spotted by the Germans, who set off flares to warn that an invasion was under way. Now a hail of machine-gun and 20 mm cannon fire rained down at the Rangers. It would be after 7:00 in the morning when the Rangers were ready to attack the beach at Pointe du Hoc.

The landing craft let off the men of Easy and Fox Companies in water that was about chest deep. As the Rangers ran for shore, all hell broke loose. Machine-gun rounds whizzed through the air like swarms of angry yellow jackets. The surface of the sea was pock marked by doughnut-shaped craters made by incoming rockets. The water turned red with blood as the men were cut down as they ran for shore. Bodies were floating everywhere. The sandy beach was only about five feet wide before it hit the perpendicular cliffs of Pointe du Hoc. There was almost no protection from the rain of death. For a moment, it seemed like the invasion was certain to fail.

Immediately as each team of Rangers scrambled out of the Higgins boats, they fired off their rockets. These missiles were designed to carry a three-quarter-inch rope and grappling hooks to the top of the cliff. This was their route to the top. Most of the hooks, however, failed to catch and only four grapples stuck firmly into the rocky cliff top. Using just these four ropes, the squads began to climb like monkeys to the top of the cliff.

Much of the success in placing these climbing ropes is credited to Walter Borowski.

The rockets for Borowski's team misfired and his men had no choice but to scramble for cover in a small cave at the base of the cliff. Walter assessed the problem. He rationalized that he had just two choices: he could turn around and swim the twenty-eight miles back to England or he could find a way to climb the cliff. He and his buddy mortar specialist John Cripps grabbed four sets of spare rockets and ran toward the beach. All around them the water was churning as machine-gun bullets were aimed at the two men. When they got through the water and onto the sand, they fired their rockets. The rockets worked and the grapples caught. This allowed his squad to complete its mission. For that act of heroism Walter Borowski and John Cripps were awarded the Silver Star.

Climbing hand over hand up a hundred foot perpendicular cliff by rope is not easy on the best of days. On D-Day, the ropes had a greasy feeling as they were saturated with mud, rain and blood, and this made them extremely difficult to hold on to. In addition, climbers had the distraction of German soldiers firing at them with rifles and machine guns. Other threats included Germans who were trying to cut their ropes and heaving rocks and hand grenades. In addition, the Rangers had to climb the cliff in full battle gear with bandoliers of ammunition, grenades, and their weapons. Walter Borowski had to achieve this climb carrying three heavy weapons that weighed him down. Beginning the climb he crossed himself, and then started pulling himself up hand over hand.

Forty years later, on June 6, 1984, President Ronald Reagan spoke at the anniversary of the Ranger's assault on the Pointe du Hoc. His speech that day was certainly among the most stirring of the twentieth century. In describing the climb, the President said, "The Rangers looked up and saw the enemy soldiers—[at] the edge of the cliffs shooting down at them with machine guns and throwing grenades. And the American Rangers began to climb. They shot rope ladders over the face of these cliffs and began to pull themselves up. When one Ranger fell, another would take his place. When one rope was cut, a Ranger would grab another and begin his climb again. They climbed, shot back, and held their footing. Soon, one by one, the Rangers pulled themselves over the top, and in seizing the firm land at the top of these cliffs, they began to seize back the continent of Europe. Two hundred and twenty-five came here. After two days of fighting, only ninety could still bear arms . . . . These are the boys of Pointe du Hoc. These are the men who took the cliffs. These are the champions who helped free a continent."

The first Ranger was reported on top of the cliff five minutes after the start of the assault. Within a half hour, all the Rangers had gotten to the top of Pointe du Hoc. They had accomplished the impossible. On the cliff, Colonel Rudder immediately established his command post. At 7:25 Rudder sent the code word "Tilt" to headquarters, which meant the first of the Rangers were on the cliff; at 7:45 he sent the message "Praise the Lord," meaning every Ranger who had survived the assault, made it to the top.

At the top, the men quickly discovered that the big German guns were gone. Because of Allied bombing the Germans had decided to hide the cannons. They had replaced them with telephone poles so their absence wouldn't be noticed. Immediately, bands of Rangers began searching for the big guns. They were found just a thousand yards inland ready to fire at Utah beach. Using hand grenades and their rifle butts, they made the 155 mm howitzers unusable. If the Rangers had not made their assault, these weapons could have been quickly sighted on Omaha and Utah Beaches and used to kill thousands of American soldiers. The Rangers had accomplished their mission. They had led the way.

The Rangers now had to direct their efforts at securing the area and capturing the cement pill box fortification. Rudder sent word to his superiors that he had suffered heavy casualties and needed relief. A simple message came back: "No reinforcements available." The Rangers were on their own and surrounded by the enemy.

The scene on the top of Pointe du Hoc was one of chaos, and each Ranger's life depended on working with his brother Rangers. The men had to leapfrog to move forward. The first Ranger would run through enemy fire while the other Rangers covered him with their rifle fire until he found cover. This action would be repeated again and again until the Rangers were together. Walter spent the next forty-eight hours "throwing grenades into German bunkers, fighting hand-to-hand, and keeping [his] head down."

By now Colonel Rudder had less than a hundred men still fit for duty. They had no food or water and had to repulse wave after wave of German counterattacks. For nearly forty-eight hours the Rangers were virtually alone except for a few stragglers from the 506th Parachute Infantry Division to give them support. (This parachute outfit was later made famous in the book and television series *Band of Brothers*.) In time, they were running out of grenades, mortar rounds, and bullets. They were sometimes reduced to using captured German weapons to fight off enemy attacks. They had gone more than three days without sleep or food and still they fought; they were Rangers. It would not be until nearly noon on June 8 that the Rangers were reinforced. During their time at Pointe du Hoc, they suffered about 70 percent casualties. This was truly the "Longest Day" any of the survivors of this band of heroes would ever experience.

At some point in the battle, Walter Borowski was shot in the wrist by a German sniper, but he was determined to keep on fighting; he was a Ranger. He had earned his first Purple Heart. Out of 225 Rangers, he was one of only about seventy-five who were still standing at battle's end on day three. When I asked him, "Were you scared?" he gently replied, "I was and so was everybody else. I was just glad I was wearing my brown pants that morning."

After the Rangers were finally relieved, Walter tried finding his big brother. Staff Sergeant Jerry Borowski was with the 507th Parachute Infantry Division and on D-Day he had been dropped behind German lines. His division had suffered some of the worse casualties in the invasion. There were 2,499 killed out of the 6,603 who had landed. After a few days of searching, Walter learned that his brother had been killed in combat on June 7. Jerry is buried in the Normandy American Cemetery at Colleville-sur-Mer, France, in Plot P, Row 28, Grave 28—a piece of Europe that will be forever Derry. He was survived by his wife, Norma, and their infant daughter Dawn. The "rage and fury" Walter felt over the death of his brother would remain with him for the rest of the war.

The last year of the war for Walter "Whitey" Borowski was one battle after another. A number of times he was promoted to sergeant for his platoon but soon his Derry joie de vivre would get him busted down to private again. Walter always knew when the Rangers were going into combat because he would be called into his C.O.'s billet. There he would be given his sergeant's stripes again. Whitey was the man they needed to be in charge when the shooting began.

Each man in the Rangers had a military specialty, such as medic, radio operator, explosives. Walter Borowski was his platoon's sniper, and was assigned an arsenal of weapons. He always carried a .45-caliber pistol on his hip. Slung over his shoulder was a .45-caliber Thompson submachine gun. This fearsome weapon was capable of firing up to seven hundred rounds a minute and had a recoil kick like a Missouri mule. Also on his shoulder was his .30-caliber 1903 Springfield sniper's rifle. With its telescopic scope he could hit his target at three hundred yards. Frequently his outfit was trapped by Germans firing from church towers or windows. It was Walter's task to neutralize this danger so his men could continue in their march to Berlin.

On August 1944 the Rangers took part in the battle for the port city of Brest, France. The town was a major Allied objective because it was home to a pack of German submarines. It was rough fighting that continued for weeks. On September 3, Walter's luck ran out. During the attack on Hill 63 his leg and shoulder were ripped apart by German bullets. He had earned his second Purple Heart. He was evacuated to the 216 General Hospital in Coventry, England, where it took many stitches to close his wounds. After the operation, his nurse told him he had a visitor. His brother Staff Sergeant Frank Borowski (1912–1967) came to his bedside. He was the mess sergeant for the hospital. That night Walter had what he described as the best steak dinner he had ever eaten.

After a couple of months in rehabilitation, Walter requested to be sent back to his outfit. He had earned a posting well behind the fray but said "I still had a job to do." He returned to the Rangers in November, just in time to take part in the Battle of Castle Hill. On Hill 400 his company took a horrible beating. Walter remembered his squad running up the hill "like a bunch of Indians." There was absolutely no cover from the rain of German machine-gun fire. All around him his friends were dying. Walter managed to carry some of the wounded to safety. "Why wasn't I killed?" he asked me. "I guess I just happened to get lucky that day."

During the battle it began to snow, and the temperature fell to minus 20 degrees. The Rangers fought like hell and captured the hill. They held the top for fifty-six hours despite the weather, five German counterattacks, and round-the-clock shelling. At the end of the battle about 450 German soldiers were dead. The Rangers had suffered twenty-six men killed, eighty-six wounded, twenty injured, and four missing in action.

As the war was ending in Europe, the Rangers were used in a variety of ways. When the Rangers came close to German death camps, Walter said he could smell the odor of death and he knew why he was fighting the Germans. He was stationed at Grafenwohr Concentration Camp, near Pilsen, Czechoslovakia. Here were held thousands of displaced people from all over Central Europe. Walter Borowski quickly became invaluable to the American commander. He was fluent in Polish and could get by in Russian, knew some German, and a little French. There would have been chaos in the camp without Walter's linguistic skills. With his assistance, the refugees even organized a concert that was performed before an appreciative General Patten. For his contribution to this humanitarian mission, he was awarded a Bronze Star.

On May 8, 1945, the war ended in the West. Many soldiers remained in Europe to help keep the peace and restore normalcy. Thousands more were put on boats and shipped to the Pacific theater to battle Japan. The Rangers stayed in Europe until October 16· when General Omar Bradley singled out the Rangers by allowing them to go home together as a unit. Other outfits complained and demanded the same privilege but Bradley would not be moved. The Rangers had fought so hard, had lost so many men and had accomplished so much that they earned the honor. They had arrived in Europe together, they would go home together.

The Rangers sailed across the Atlantic on the former luxury liner the SS *America*. Four days later they landed in Newport News,

Virginia. There was no parade, no speeches, no ceremonies. The colors were retired and the men were given a ticket to return home. Their war was over; mission accomplished. The Rangers had led the way.

On October 23, 1945, the Second Ranger Battalion was officially disbanded. Its flag and honors were filed away in an Army warehouse until they would be needed again. In 1974 the Second Ranger Battalion was reactivated and in 1984 it became the Second Battalion, seventy-fifth Ranger Regiment, headquartered at Fort Lewis, Washington. They have seen service in Desert Storm, Somalia, Kosovo, Afghanistan, and Iraq.

After the war, Walter Borowski returned to Derry. He had seen enough of the world and wanted to remain here for the rest of his life. Shortly after his return, he paid a visit to Charlie Doherty's blacksmith shop on Wall Street; this had always been a local hangout. Charlie asked Walter if being in the Rangers had changed him in any way. Walter didn't feel the need to answer the question with words; he just bent over and grabbed with his two hands the heavy iron anvil that was sitting in the middle of the smithy. Without struggling or groaning, he lifted the anvil over Doherty's head. After repeating this feat ten times, he gently put it back on its stand.

In February 1946, Walter Borowski was King of the Derry Winter Carnival. All the newspaper photographs show him handsome in his tuxedo with his queen Theresa Bourassa. He dismissed his Hollywood good looks or his war record as the reason he was selected for the honor. As he explained it, he was the only man in Derry who was single, available, and actually owned a tux.

In time Walter married the beautiful Helen Glod (1918–1988). During the war she was an Army nurse and had been a champion swimmer. The couple bought a little home on land directly across from Walter's parents on High Street. There they raised two sons and two daughters. Walter didn't take advantage of the G.I. Education Bill; he had to work. He coached the area children in baseball and was a volunteer in the police and fire departments. He was a leader in the town's horseshoe league. He became a foreman at the KlevBros Shoe Factory and later worked in the crystal room at the Western Electric Company in Andover, Massachusetts. He retired in 1985 at the age of 65.

Since retirement, Walter has spent much of his time working in his gardens. Each year he prays for an early spring, a mild summer, and a late frost. It is believed that he gives away many more bushels of vegetables then he eats. For years he attended Ranger reunions and hosted his war buddies in Derry. Those activities have ceased in recent years as he finds it increasingly difficult to get around. He still belongs to the American Legion and Veterans of Foreign Wars.

Walker is a modest man who is not given to telling people about his military service and those horrible days in France. He never sat his children down to tell them about his service with the Army Rangers. He couldn't show them his war souvenirs such as the Luger pistol and Nazi flag he had captured; they were stolen while he was in England. His Silver Star, Purple Hearts, Bronze Star, and the rack of other medals were stolen from his house during a break-in during the 1950s.

All Walter now has from the war are his memories and those he keeps to himself. Real heroes never have a need to brag. They know what they did. Few in his family or circle of friends knew the complete story of his wartime experiences. Walter recently told me that "unless you were there, you can't even begin to imagine what it was like," and if you were there, it is hard to talk about it because for some things there just aren't the words.

There are now very few living members of Fox Company, Second Army Rangers Battalion. So many, too many, of these warriors did not return from Europe. It has now been 63 years since they scaled the cliffs of Pointe du Hoc. Most of those who somehow survived D-Day and the battle for Castle Hill eventually married and raised children. In the fullness of time they passed on to their final rest. Perhaps four members of Fox Company are still alive. In Derry we are privileged to have Walter Borowski, one of these proud warriors, as our neighbor and friend.

Few have honored the memory of the fighting men and women better than the British poet Laurence Binyon. His 1914 poem *Ode to Remembrance* could have been written with the Second Rangers, Fox Company in mind.

> They went with songs to the battle, they were young.
> Straight of limb, true of eye, steady and aglow,
> They were staunch to the end against odds uncounted,
> They fell with their faces to the foes.

Thank you for your service, Walter. If you're not a hero, I don't know who is. As President Bill Clinton said at Pointe du Hoc on the occasion of the fiftieth anniversary of your climb up the cliffs: "We are the children of your sacrifice. We are the sons and daughters you saved from tyranny." And near the grave of your brother Jerry he later said: "They struggled in war that we might struggle in peace."

Firemen battle the Chelmsford Shoe Factory fire on May 6, 1960.

50.

The Great Chelmsford Fire

Among the most common questions I'm asked at the Derry Museum of History is "Do you have anything on the Chelmsford fire?" The answer is, "Yes, we certainly do." To these individuals, the great fire of 1960 is an event etched forever in their minds and can be recalled as clearly as the death of President Kennedy or the events of September 11, 2001.

In 1887, South Avenue became the site of the new Woodbury Shoe Factory, which had been built by a group of local businessmen. On May 17, 1915, a fire destroyed the four-story building. The loss of this industry and its hundreds of jobs was a potential economic calamity. To avoid a local economic depression, investors from Derry rebuilt the one-hundred-fifty by two-hundred-fifty-foot wood-frame factory within the year. The fire had brought about a greater awareness of the need for better firefighting equipment to protect stores and factories. In 1915, all we had were ancient horse-drawn hand-tub fire engines. Within months, the town had the most modern self-propelled fire truck and pumper in the state.

The building remained a part of the Woodbury Shoe Company empire until the Great Depression. Around 1931, it changed owners and became the Chelmsford Shoe Company. This was a vibrant economic concern and employed 295 workers. Its four-story South Avenue factory had a total floor space of thirty thousand square feet.

On Friday, May 6, 1960, the shoe factory horn sounded at four o'clock to mark the end of the workday. Quickly the employees streamed out of the building. Each was certainly looking forward to the weekend; Sunday was Mother's Day.

Many of the workers planned on treating Mom to a restaurant meal that weekend. The Oxen Yoke Restaurant on Broadway was advertising Chicken in the Ruff with french fries and fried dough for a dollar. For about twice that amount you could have a "feast fit for a Queen" at the Chanticleer Restaurant on Route 28, where Wal-Mart is now located.

Some families would probably take in a movie. Derry's Plaza Theater was showing *Goliath and the Barbarian*. The Manchester Drive-In was offering *Never So Few* with Frank Sinatra. At Newberry's department store on East Broadway you could buy Mother a parakeet and cage for $4.99. For those who wanted to eat at home, the A & P was offering ground beef at two pounds for seventy-nine cents and the First National store was selling chuck roast at forty-five cents a pound.

Many of the workers lived within walking distance of the factory, in one of the numerous three-decker apartment buildings in the South Avenue area. Others commuted from Manchester. Those workers who drove home would have heard on their car radio the details of the Soviet shooting down of an American U2 spy plane. Eisenhower was in the White House, Khrushchev was in the Kremlin, and the cold war was at its zenith. Castro had just taken over in Cuba and we were on speaking terms with Iran, Iraq, and Syria.

For those who dialed in the music stations, the number one song that week was *Cathy's Clown*, by the Everly Brothers. Also in the top 10 was *Sink the Bismarck* (Johnny Horton), *Stuck on You* (Elvis), and *Let the Little Girl Dance* (Billy Bland). Editor Vin Bartimo, of the *Derry News,* however, was predicting that rock 'n' roll was on the way out and that Bing Crosby and Perry Como would rise again to the top of the charts. Rap was something you did to make your presence known at the front door.

The sports news that week was depressing. During May and June, the Red Sox had won ten games and lost thirty-six. Now, after losing ten games in a row, the local press was savaging our Bosox, and owner Tom Yawkey responded by threatening to move the Sox out of Boston.

No one knows the actual cause of the Chelmsford Shoe Factory fire. It has been speculated that it started in the rear of the building in a pile of empty shoe boxes that contained highly flammable rubber cement and solvent residue. An eyewitness said he saw flames leaping from a transformer on the loading dock on the south side of the factory. Regardless of where or how it began, of course, the effect was the same. With brutal speed, flames shot up the elevator shaft and spread to the upper floors. The factory's sprinkler system quickly proved inadequate and the flames burst unchecked onto the roof. Soon the sparks and embers were being picked up on strong breezes and scattered through the area. At 4:08 in the afternoon, the first alarm was sounded at Fire Station Number One on Broadway. By now black smoke was shrouding much of West Derry. The smell of burning rubber was everywhere.

The first hero to emerge from this tragedy was Dominic Acorace (1906–1985), a shoe shop foreman. He was the one who first the fire department to report the fire (Hemlock 2-2556). When he saw the extent of the fire, he took on the responsibility of making sure no one was still in the building. The fifty-three-year-old man ran though every floor in the huge, sprawling building and down every aisle looking for workers. The smoke and flames trapped him on the third floor and he had to exit the building via the fire escape.

Within only a few minutes, the entire building was a rolling swell of flames. A steady twenty-five-miles-per hour wind sent out red tongues of fire in every direction. From the Chelmsford Shoe Factory a plume of black smoke now extended hundreds of feet into the air. The stench of burning leather was spreading through the downtown.

Among the first to arrive at the scene were *Derry News* photographer Dan Fitzgerald, Judge George Grinnell, and Attorney Ed Bureau. The trio raced through the neighborhood pounding on doors to alert residents to evacuate immediately. They helped move some cars out of harm's way. With little thought to their personal danger, they tried to stomp out the spreading flames with their feet. Fitzgerald "forgot his newspaper instincts" and missed his chance to capture many dramatic photographs—choosing instead to try and save lives. Photographs could come later.

Most of the tenement dwellers escaped with only the clothes on their backs. One female shoe worker ran back into her apartment determined to rescue a picture of her mother on her living room wall. When she tried to pull it down, she discovered the wall was "red hot and untouchable." She would have to be nearly dragged from the burning building.

As soon as he arrived at the scene, Fire Chief Harvey Cote realized that all of downtown Derry was in immediate peril. At that time, the Derry Fire Department consisted of a chief and his two part-time assistants. The town's only fire station was the one on Broadway, which had been opened in 1899. (This building is now the Fire Hall, Restaurant and Pub.) There were also five permanent engine drivers who worked shifts so that there were always two in the ready at the station. In addition, there was a call force of twenty-five firemen. The fleet of trucks consisted of a 750-gallon-per-minute and two five-hundred-gallon-per-minute pumpers.

Chief Cote issued an immediate general alarm to all firemen in Derry. The first unit to respond was a fire engine from East Derry. The *Derry News* reported that these firemen "performed in a manner far beyond the call of duty." They were soon joined by equipment from Londonderry and Grenier Air Force Base.

When it became obvious that the fire was spreading, Chief Cote extended the call to all fire companies within a twenty-mile radius. Inside of an hour, equipment and men rolled in from Manchester, Salem, Windham, and Chester, and from the Massachusetts cities of Merrimack, Andover, and Lawrence. In total, a dozen fire departments with hundreds of firefighters battled the Chelmsford fire.

Water was the chief weapon with which they hoped to quell the hungry flames. Fire hydrants were few and far between in Derry in the year 1960. Because so much water was being drawn from the water pipes, the streams aimed at the fire became very feeble. They increased the water pressure by hooking up the pumpers in relay. Three pumpers were employed to suck water from Beaver Brook on Birch Street. At one time there were a total of nineteen pumpers supplying twenty-five fire hoses.

To prevent looting and to control the crowds, the National Guard was ordered in by Governor Wesley Powell. Derry was placed under martial law. More than two hundred Guardsmen from the First Howitzer Battalion, 172 Field Artillery, commanded by Major General Frank McSwiney, arrived in Derry by six o'clock. The area was sealed off, and had the appearance of an armed camp. To many veterans, it reminded them of scenes they had witnessed in wartime Europe.

Within twenty-five minutes of the first fire call, the Chelmsford Shoe Factory was leveled and beyond saving. The first stand by the firemen was an attempt to save a row of three six-family triple-decker tenements. Despite the obvious danger, the Derry firemen laid hoses from a hydrant directly in front of the factory to shoot a stream of water at the three-story buildings. Within only a few minutes, the roaring flames from the factory leaped over their heads and set the tenements ablaze. This eruption happened so quickly that the firemen had to instantly abandon their hoses and run for their lives.

There was little the men could do. One by one the South Avenue buildings ignited and went up in flames. The men were forced to fight a war of containment. They decided to concentrate their efforts on a large apartment building on Railroad Avenue. Directly behind this tenement were six large oil-storage tanks owned by the Holmes and Wheeler Company and the Wells Oil Company. If the fire got to them, a massive explosion would rock Derry and Londonderry and the whole of Broadway would be lost in a massive conflagration. A curtain of water was spread across the immediate area. The fire incinerated most of the wooden tenements on Railroad Avenue but the oil tanks and Broadway were spared.

The Red Cross secured sleeping quarters for the homeless in the American Legion Hall. The Salvation Army arranged for Air Force cots to be set up in the VFW hall. All of these groups worked tirelessly to do what they could. There were dozens of families who lost everything except their lives and the clothing on their backs. A Salvation Army canteen truck was brought in from Lawrence to feed the firemen and the displaced. Pinkerton Academy opened its auditorium and kitchen to help the needy. Goundrey's Funeral Home of Salem and Peabody Funeral Home of Derry used their vehicles to transport the injured to the hospital. The local Boy Scouts were "Johnny-on-the-spot," doing every task that was asked of them. Local churches opened to provide a refuge, counseling, and a place for prayer. Traffic control was placed in the hands of the volunteers from the New Hampshire Motor Vehicle Department.

The linemen of the Public Service Co. had the highly dangerous job of shutting off the power to the burning buildings. They also had to quickly string temporary electric lines to provide emergency power to the firemen and rescue workers. To many, it was an absolute miracle that some of these electricians weren't killed as they climbed ladders in the middle of the smoke and flames.

The telephone linemen also put their lives in danger. The flames had burned the telephone wires and melted the lead connectors. This had the effect of shutting down telephone service throughout the town. Communications had to be reestablished to allow emergency messages to be sent. The arcing electricity kept telephone workers Frank Galvin, Phil Palmer, Charlie Matson, and Roger Nutting from getting anywhere near the switches. Finally, in desperation, they threw a clothesline around the switches and with all their strength closed the circuit. Derry was again connected to the rest of the world.

At seven o'clock, the fire was declared under control. All through the night, however, teams of firemen were kept at the scene to wet down the smoldering ashes in anticipation of secondary outbreaks of fire.

The next day, the Derry town fathers began to assess the damages. The Chelmsford Shoe Factory was a total loss. This cost the town nearly three hundred jobs. The Fieldside convenience store was no more. There were a total of thirteen homes and tenement buildings gutted. Two hundred people were now homeless. This represented a total of fifty-seven families devastated by the fire. Many other buildings were damaged and six automobiles were ruined. The total loss was estimated to be upwards of two million dollars in 1960 dollars. This, of course, doesn't take into consideration the irreplaceable personal items that were incinerated. Who can put a price on the family photograph album, a son's baseball mitt, a daughter's doll house or those collections of love letters tied up with a ribbon? Many homeowners also reported that they lost the gifts they had just purchased for Mother's Day.

The greatest financial loss fell to Lewis C. Apkaker, of Andover Massachusetts, and Louis Gallant of Brookline, Massachusetts, the owners of the factory. Their loss was estimated to be more than $150,000. Albert Gallant saw two of his South Avenue tenements destroyed in the fire.

One of the miracles was that not a single life was lost. There were, however, thirty-seven firemen who had to receive emergency medical aid. Fortunately, only two required hospitalization: Deputy Chief Edward McGrail, of Manchester who had a burn on his face, and Deputy Chief Frank "Babe" Houle of Derry, who suffered smoke inhalation. Both men were released from the Alexander-Eastman Hospital after only a few days. John Rider (1891–1965), an auxiliary police officer, was hospitalized after collapsing while directing traffic.

Martial law had to remain in force for nearly a week due to the increased pedestrian and automobile traffic downtown. The

Derry News reported that "a million cars bumper to bumper are esti-mated to have crawled through town in the last ninety-six hours." Broadway merchants complained of losing business because there was too much traffic and no vacant parking spaces. A number of minor traffic accidents were reported.

Henry L. Dion (1917–1992) who had been president of the local shoe workers union (AFL-CIO) since 1948, met with Governor Powell and Director of Employment Security Benjamin Adams, of Derry, to help coordinate the relief activity. The federal govern-ment declared Derry an official disaster area. Dion and Adams set up an office in the Adams Memorial Building to assist the burned out workers in finding employment. The owners of the Chelmsford Shoe Company were given office space in the First National Bank building to pay out back wages and assist in filling out paperwork. The Federal Small Business Administration also had an office at the Adams Building. Senator John F. Kennedy, of Massachusetts, offered his help in securing federal aid.

The local Red Cross, under the direction of Fred Manning, organized clothing drives for the burned-out families and found housing for the homeless. That organization pledged to contribute fifty thousand dollars in rehabilitation work. Selectman Frank Buckley and bank president Walter Tewksbury ran the Derry Disaster Fund Committee. Within a month they raised more than fifteen thousand dollars. The local A & P and the First National both gave food certificates to every fire victim. The Sweet Adelines choral group put on a show at the Grinnell School to raise funds for the needy.

Local mailmen, including Arnold Keith and Lee Burdick, brought a collection can with them as they walked their routes. Our younger citizens, such as Skip Buffum, Gail Mannarini, and Richard Bonner, canvassed their neighborhoods to collect money to help the unfortunate.

A few years before the fire, the town had been given the old KlevBros Shoe Company building on Maple Street. The only restriction the Kleven brothers had placed on the gift was that the building not be sold or rented to another shoe company. Why should the KlevBros Company want a rival shoe factory in Derry, competing for the same customers and workers? Since that time the building had sat empty while vandals broke an estimated fif-teen hundred windowpanes. After the fire, the Klevens saw that the workers of the former Chelmsford Shoe Company needed jobs, so the brothers encouraged the town to rent the derelict factory to anyone—including another shoe company. Derry Development Inc. helped raise thirty-five thousand dollars to make it suitable for a new shoe factory to start operating and soon Jodi Shoe Company was providing jobs for the unemployed.

As soon as the fire was over, the *Derry News* was filled with advertisements offering employment to the former Chelmsford shoe workers. In 1960, the shoe industry in New England was still fairly prosperous. The Derry men and women were known to be highly skilled leather workers. Many would be hired at the new KlevBros and Derry Shoe companies, which had built modern buildings on Manchester Road. Initially there was a persistent fear that there would be a mass migration of unemployed shoe workers from Derry. In fact, very few Chelmsford Shoe Company workers actually left us to take up residence in other towns and states.

At the time of the fire, the *Derry News* was located on Birch Street, only a few hundred feet from the blaze. The three phones in its office were bombarded with hundreds of calls from reporters and worried citizens. As a service, the newsroom was kept open all weekend. Its press run of three thousand copies of the *Derry News* was quickly sold out. Journalists were kept busy reporting the story, which was sent out to the world via the UP and AP news services. Photographs taken by its staff were rushed to Boston to be shown on television news programs and printed in newspapers all over the eastern seaboard. In addition to journalistic responsibilities, two members of the newspaper staff had to be positioned on top of the newspaper's building to extinguish flaming material that was being carried by the wind and landing on their flat roof.

In October 1960, the remaining debris was hauled away by a Massachusetts salvage firm. The area's economy was changing. Unlike after the 1915 fire, this time the shoe factory would not be rebuilt. Cheap shoes made overseas would soon sound the death knell for the leather industry in New England. In 1989, the last of Derry's shoe factories closed. Soon buildings, where once hundreds of millions of shoes had been crafted, would be retrofitted into space for other commercial ventures or be torn down. Our last surviving shoemaker was Barry, the Continental Cobbler, on Merchants Row, who retired in May 2007. Regrettably, Derry is now totally shoe worker-free. This is in dramatic contrast to Derry in

1915 when three out of every five of our men, women, and children worked in our shoe factories.

The great Chelmsford fire is now forty-seven years in the past. There is little that remains in Derry to remind us of that tragic day in 1960. On the site of the factory is now a neat row of town houses called the Chelmsford-Hardy Place. I wonder how many of those who live in those neat little homes know the origin of their development's name.

This was not the only great fire in Derry that year. On August 19, 1960, the pavilion at Beaver Lake burned to the ground in a late-night fire. It had been built in 1896 by the Chester and Derry Trolley Company as a destination to encourage the buying of trolley tickets on weekends. Inside the pavilion were a dance hall, bathing suit changing rooms, bowling alleys, a snack bar, and even a number of one-armed-bandit slot machines. The first pavilion building had burned down in 1915 and was rebuilt within a few months.

The reviewing stand for the Shepard parade, June 9, 1962. The four men giving honors to the American flag are (l to r) Commander Shepard; his father, Col. Alan B. Shepard Sr.; the astronaut's father-in-law, Russell Brewer; and congressman Perkins Bass. Sullivan photo.

51.

The Parade That Just Happened

IN THE LAST FORTY YEARS, THE POPULATION OF DERRY HAS GROWN by about 400 percent. Each year the number of us who were in Derry before the opening of Interstate Highway Route 93 grows smaller and smaller. There may be only a couple of thousand area residents now who can remember the 1961 "parade that just happened" that was in honor of Derry's great hero Alan Shepard.

Back in 1961, we had much reason to be proud; the astronaut was one of us. Admiral Alan Bartlett Shepard Jr. was in fact the descendant of five generations of Derry men and women. His great-great-grandparents William B. (1779–1867) and Lucy Shepard (1782–1862) and great-grandparents William (1816–1893) and Rosina Shepard (1817–1886) first arrived here around 1859. His grandparents Colonel Frederick (1851–1931) and Annie Bartlett Shepard (1861–1944) were quite prominent in the business and social life of the town. Frederick was always called Fritz and Annie was known as Nanze. She was a leader in the Molly Reid chapter of the Daughters of the American Revolution and in the First Parish church. She was very active in politics, although in 1917, she had been opposed to giving women the right to vote. She was the first woman elected president of the New Hampshire Republican Club.

Frederick Shepard was president of the Derry National Bank for forty-nine years, treasurer of the Derry Savings Bank for twenty-five years, treasure of Pinkerton Academy, and president of the New Hampshire Society of Colonial Wars. He was head of the Derry Water Works, 1890–1907; superintendent of the Derry Sewer

Company, 1901–1915; treasurer of the Derry Electric Company, 1892–1897; president of the Derry Building Association when it constructed several local shoe factories and hundreds of houses in West Derry, 1885–1915; general manager of the Chester and Derry Trolley Company, 1897–1927. In addition, he served as treasurer of the town of Derry for sixteen years; Rockingham County Auditor, twenty-five years; and was military aide-de-camp during the Russo-Japanese Peace Conference in 1905. The week before his passing, Frederick had announced the merger of the town's two banks to form the First National Bank, with himself as president.

He and Annie lived in the largest house in town and employed a maid and a butler. Their mansion on East Derry Hill was a Victorian fantasy that even boasted of a large formal ballroom on the second floor that had hosted a reception for President Taft in 1912.

Alan's parents were Alan Bartlett (1891–1973) and Pauline Renza Emerson Shepard (1900–1993). This well-known couple were always called Bart and Renza Shepard. She was the daughter of a prominent shoe factory owner and grew up in the Edwardian mansion directly across from the Shepard estate. She was active in the DAR, the Derry Garden Club, and the Christian Science Church.

Colonel Bart Shepard was a graduate of Pinkerton Academy (1909) and Dartmouth College (1913). He and his two brothers served as combat officers during the First World War. He was associated with his father's bank but lost that position during the Great Depression. Later he took over as president of Shepard and Bartlett Insurance Company and succeeded his father as treasurer of Pinkerton Academy. Together they would hold that academy office for eighty-three years. During the Second World War, he was in charge of the manpower division of the Massachusetts local and state draft boards. He played the organ at the First Parish Church for more than fifty years.

Bart and Renza Shepard were definitely the elite of Derry. They had the nicest house, the fanciest car, and the best clothes. They had a summer cottage on Big Island Pond despite the fact that Beaver Lake was practically in their backyard. Soon after they were married, they built an elegant Colonial Revival home just to the south of Fritz and Nanze Shepard's mansion. Just off the parlor, Bart had installed a huge organ with a separate room to house its forest of pipes.

Renza was extremely social and very approachable. Bart, in contrast, was perceived as rather cold and standoffish. He sported a neatly trimmed, distinguished mustache and wore a suit and tie even when he was home on weekends. He was also known to be quite frugal. Every weekday, precisely at noon, he would leave the office of his Broadway insurance company and walk to White's Restaurant. His lunch every day, all year-round, was the thirty-five-cent special—a grilled cheese sandwich with a slice of tomato. Restaurant owner George Katsakiores remembers that during the 1940s and 1950s, he never sat in a booth but instead would take a stool exactly in the center of the counter. There he would sit, ramrod straight, as was appropriate for a man of his military rank.

Alan was born in an upper room at the Shepard house on East Derry Road. He was brought up in a wealthy household but his stern father expected that his son would learn the work ethic. If the boy wanted a bicycle, he would have to earn the money himself by doing farm chores and having a paper route. He attended the nearby Adams School. This was the former Adams Female Academy which had been built in 1824. He was a precocious student who completed the six years of the school in just five years. He attended junior high at the Oak Street School and graduated from Pinkerton Academy with the class of 1940.

Alan Shepard earned his Bachelor of Science degree from the U. S. Naval Academy in 1944; this was a year ahead of schedule because the Navy needed ensigns for the war effort. He served during the Second World War aboard the destroyer USS *Cogwell* in the Pacific theatre. He earned his pilot's wings in 1947 and served several tours on aircraft carriers. In 1950 he attended test pilot school at Patuxent River, Maryland. There he proved that he really did have "the right stuff." In 1959, the newly created National Aeronautics and Space Administration (NASA) sent out invitations to the 110 top test pilots in America to join the space program.

On April 9, 1959, word spread through Derry that Alan Shepard was one of the seven selected for astronaut training. We were nearly speechless! We all knew him. He wasn't just a name. He was born in Derry in 1923. He was Bart and Renza Shepard's kid who had gone to Adams School, Oak Street School, and Pinkerton Academy. He was that skinny boy with the big grin who loved sailing and flying. The chances of actually being chosen to be the first man in space was statistically only one in seven, but the local bets were on Alan making the cut.

All America waited for NASA to make the choice. Would it be Alan? Or John Glenn? Gus Grissom? In the meantime, the Soviet Union had blasted cosmonaut Yuri Gagarin into obit and by twenty-three days robbed America of the glory of putting the first man into space.

Our American flight, however, would be different. The Soviets had kept their flight secret until it was finished; ours was flown in full view of the world. Gagarin had just gone along for the ride; the American would be able to maneuver his spacecraft. The *Derry News* in April 1961 speculated that only God and the Shepard family knew who would eventually get the nod. Finally, on May 2—only three days before the scheduled launch—the choice was announced. America's first astronaut would be . . . Commander Alan B. Shepard Jr., U.S. Navy, of East Derry, New Hampshire.

Immediately after the announcement, a town wide celebration was planned. A committee of the town's political, social, and civic leaders met at the summer cottage of Mildred DiMarzio on Beaver Lake. It was decided to decorate Broadway and have a parade. The chairman was selectman Al Johnson. Mrs. DiMarzio and Mrs. Gil Boroski were in charge of finding ways to honor Mr. and Mrs. Shepard as the parents of the astronaut. The problem was that it was impossible to actually schedule a parade, as space launches were always subject to delays. The idea was to plan for a parade and that was all. They would just let it happen. When Alan went up, we would have a parade and the participants and crowds would come. Any real planning would have to wait until just hours before the launch.

Soon Derry was awash with reporters from all over the world. A sign on Al's Food Center proclaimed Derry to be Space Town USA. For days, camera crews were set up in front of the Shepard home on East Derry Road. On April 25 a test rocket carrying a dummy astronaut was blown up in flight; just three days later another test rocket was also destroyed. Alan later recalled thinking while sitting in his capsule that the contract to build his Redstone rocket had been awarded to the lowest bidder.

Despite this realization, the Derry native was ready to be blasted into space. On the day of the launch, delay followed delay. In desperation, Shepard told the technicians to fix all the problems and "light this candle." No one was a 100 percent sure the rocket wouldn't explode into a ball of fire. Would Derry have a day of jubilation or mourning? Our children were excited and couldn't imagine anything but success; the adults were worried, as they knew of the dangers of space flight.

Finally, at 9:34 in the morning on May 5, 1961 at Cape Canaveral, Florida, the Redstone rocket fired Alan and his spacecraft, Freedom 7, into space. Everything went, in his words, "A-OK!" The rocket blasted Alan 116 miles into space. In 15 minutes, 28 seconds, his capsule landed 303 miles down range from Cape Canaveral. America had entered into the space age! Church bells sounded throughout Derry. The siren on the Broadway fire station was sounded a dozen times to tell the town that "our boy's in space"—and 15 minutes, 28 seconds later, it sounded again to announce his safe return to earth.

All over town, we watched the launch on television. The entire student body and faculty at Pinkerton Academy crowded into the chapel. All eyes were glued on a single small black-and-white television set. A jerry-rigged antenna was extended from the third floor room to improve reception. As one Pinkerton student said, as the school's bell pealed 147 times in celebration, "Man, am I proud!"

All over town, county, and state the word went out: "Come to Derry when the fire siren sounds—there's going to be a hell of a parade." My mother and I drove to pick up Dad at the Chase Mill in Derry Village and sped on to Broadway. I remember exactly where I watched the parade. Forty-six years ago, on May 5, 1961, I stood for hours at the traffic lights on the corner of Broadway and Crystal Avenue.

The street was blocked off. The crowds were huge and growing with every minute. I was a fifteen-year-old country boy who had never seen that many people in my life. On the sidelines, vendors were selling balloons, hot dogs, and candy. Local merchant Art Margolis was selling T-shirts on which was printed: DERRY N.H. SPACE TOWN USA. He prophesied that some day he might have to print new shirts announcing Derry to be "Moon Town USA." His prediction of Alan's future came true in 1971, when Alan did walk on the moon.

The fire siren signaled the start of the parade. Leading the procession was a detachment of Derry policemen carrying the American flag. Immediately after came a bright red convertible carrying the beaming Mr. and Mrs. Alan B. Shepard Sr. On the side of the car was a hand-written sign proclaiming them to be "America and Derry's #1 Mother and Father." The cheering for Bart and Renza Shepard was huge and could probably be heard in Manchester. The couple was followed by an antique car bearing the astronaut's cousin, District Court Judge George Grinnell. Overhead an airplane buzzed the crowd at an elevation estimated to be just about one hundred feet over Broadway.

For an hour, the parade worked its way down Broadway. There in his official automobile was New Hampshire's governor Wesley Powell waving to the throng. Miss America Nancy Anne Fleming had been making an appearance nearby in Massachusetts, so she came to help Derry celebrate with Miss New Hampshire, Drina Bouchard. Both the Army and the Air Force sent marching units with bands. Pinkerton Academy, Hood School, and Salem's Woodbury High School also sent their marching bands. Town and county officials rode or marched; local businesses improvised floats with space motifs. The American Legion, Veterans of Foreign Wars, their auxiliaries, took part as did the Grange and Welcome Wagon. Many Boy and Girl Scouts, the Cubs, and Brownies marched in their school clothes as they didn't have time to change into their uniforms. Toward the end of the parade were the equestrians. Bringing up the rear came the fire trucks with their sirens blaring. The fire engines represented Derry, East Derry, Hudson, Salem, Nashua, and Manchester.

After the parade, the celebrations went on. Broadway remained crowded with locals and tourists until well after midnight. All the local clubs "were taxed to capacity." Space-themed parties were held in private homes throughout the town. City newspapers said "there would be dancing in the streets" but in truth the Broadway throngs made it too crowded for such goings-on. The *Derry News* wrote that in downtown Derry there was no room "except in the space above" and that "gravity forbade" taking advantage of it. The last recorded event was an impromptu conga-line that snaked down the middle of Broadway at midnight. Music was provided by a strolling band from Manchester.

The Boston newspapers reported that a "Roman Holiday Orgy" occurred in Derry after Alan was blasted off into space. In truth, there was little rioting in the town. This may be, in part, because a large delegation of night-stick-carrying state troopers had been sent to Derry to maintain order. There were only three groups of brawlers brought before the district court and they were the result of "private arguments" and had nothing to do with the space launch.

When the day finally drew to a close, it was said that though it hadn't really been Derry's largest parade—the 1946 V-J Day parade held that record—it was our most exuberant and most spontaneous. Regardless, Derry really knew how to throw a party! It was too bad that astronaut Shepard had to miss it. The selectmen declared that the fifth of May each year would always be Alan Shepard Day in Derry. Cinco de Mayo is for other towns. The New Hampshire Legislature decided that Derry would be legally known as Space Town.

Other news stories that week were pushed onto the inner pages of newspapers. All that America wanted to read about was America's success in space. That day many people probably missed the story that President Kennedy announced that he was considering sending U.S. soldiers into South Vietnam. Also that day, congress raised the minimum wage from one dollar to a dollar and twenty-five cents an hour. On any other day, those two stories would have been reported with front-page headlines but not on May 5, 1961. On that day, from California to Maine and from Coos to the sea, the lead story was Alan Shepard and the Derry celebration.

On June 9, 1962, there was a second Alan B. Shepard Jr. parade in Derry. This time the astronaut was in attendance. Thousands lined the sidewalks of Crystal Avenue and Broadway to view our hero. Later that week he set off the dynamite charge to begin construction of I-93, which when it opened a year later received its official designation as the Alan B. Shepard Highway.

After 1963, Alan was grounded from flying because of dizzy spells, the result of Ménière's syndrome. An operation in 1969 restored him to flight status. On February 5, 1971, at the age of forty-seven, he became the fifth person to walk on the moon. This lunar visit of thirty-three and a half hours is perhaps best remembered for Alan Shepard hitting a golf ball with a makeshift club. In the moon's gravity, which is one-sixth that of Earth Derry, the ball went "for miles and miles and miles." On April 5, 1971, he returned to Derry for the third Shepard parade.

Shepard was given the rank of rear admiral and retired from the Navy on August 1, 1974. He spent the rest of his life managing his business ventures, writing, and doing charity work. In 1971 he served as American ambassador to the United Nations. A high school in Illinois (1971) and a Navy supply ship (2006) were named for him. In Derry, in addition to the highway, a building at Pinkerton Academy (1963) and the Derry Post Office (2001) were named in his honor. The Derry Museum of History, at 29 West Broadway, in 2007 opened a room that is devoted exclusively to the admiral's life and career. His space capsule Freedom 7 is on exhibit at Annapolis.

Alan B. Shepard Jr. died in California from leukemia on July 21, 1998, at the age of seventy-four. Just five weeks later, Louise, his beloved wife of fifty-three years, passed away. They were survived by three daughters and six grandchildren. Alan and Louise were both cremated and their ashes were scattered at the Big Sur. Their daughters have placed a memorial stone for their parents in the Forest Hill Cemetery in East Derry, where it is surrounded by gravestones of five generations of the family. It is a simple flat granite stone with an inscription that reads:

LOVE IS ETERNAL
R. Adm. Alan Bartlett Shepard Jr.
U.S. Navy
America's first man in space
1998
His Loving Wife
Louise Brewer Shepard
1998

52.
Sin Town

RECENTLY I WAS GOING THROUGH A FAMILY SCRAPBOOK WHEN I came across an envelope of brittle newspaper clippings my late mother had put away. The articles all centered on the Great Derry Shame and Scandal of 1967. Here in these yellowing pages of newsprint was the account of a real brouhaha. Staid old Derry was being compared to Sodom and Gomorrah.

This incident in our history has since turned into a story that is only whispered. Now only our older residents can remember the substance of those shocking accusations of 1967. To most modern, newly arrived residents, the story is probably considered more myth than reality. I will now relay the basic facts of the story for those residents so they can understand the depth of Derry's depravity.

Forty years ago Derry made the front pages of dozens of newspapers across the state, and it wasn't because of Alan Shepard or Robert Frost. We were being bandied about as "sin city" and another Peyton Place. For those readers below the age of fifty, a word of explanation is in order. *Peyton Place* was an international bestselling novel depicting the sensual affairs of a fictitious New Hampshire town. It was written in 1956 by Manchester native Grace Metalious and sold eight million copies. It was later made into a movie and then a weekly television show. At the time, I was only eleven years old and not allowed to read the novel—but I did anyway.

In October 1967 the *Manchester Union Leader* sent Arthur C. Egan Jr. to Broadway to see what dirt he could dig up on Derry. Previously he had been employed by the paper to find information in support of Teamsters President Jimmy Hoffa. Egan was later used as an investigative reporter to ferret out scandalous stories involving the Ted Kennedy tragedy at Chappaquiddick.

In 1967, Derry had a population of only ten thousand residents. This is less than a third the size of our town in 2007. We still had just one traffic light and no malls. The Hood cows sauntered across Broadway twice a day as they went between barn and pasture. The town hall was the Adams Memorial Building, where a three-man board of selectmen reigned over Derry. The police chief earned sixty-five hundred dollars a year and voters at Town Meeting still decided the town's budget. The *Derry News* was published from a Birch Street address and contained letters nearly every week on the need for a Derry bypass and the reasons for and against merging the two fire departments.

In that year Lyndon Johnson was still president. The two top records were *Respect* (Aretha Franklin) and *Light My Fire* (The Doors). John and Bill's Diner was Derry's favorite place to be and Vietnam was not.

Mr. Egan, the investigative reporter, spent "many hours" in lunchrooms, groceries, and stops. There he struck up conversations with customers and merchants, the young and the old, to find out what Derry was really like. He queried them about a wide range of subjects. All this information he forged into a series of three articles that ran on the front page of the *Manchester Union Leader*. The headline, as read by its hundred thousand readers, proclaimed "Derry—where the action is."

The focus of the first article was Derry's police department. Egan chronicled how the last police chief had left his wife and four children and run off with another man's wife. Beginning with this fact, the reporter then listed peccadilloes of other members of the force. All of the charges were unsubstantiated by any real proof. They were based only upon those conversations with his lunchroom and street-corner contacts. Maybe the stories were God's truth; maybe they were lies or exaggerations.

According to the reporter's confidants, the local police didn't spend much actual time protecting the public. Instead, it would appear that our men in blue were spending most of their duty time with other men's wives or taking naps at a taxi office. The patrol cars could frequently be seen driving to a remote sandpit for assignations with girlfriends. One officer was accused (by an unnamed source) of confining his "dating activities only to young high school girls."

There were stories told to the reporter of teenagers being roughed up by patrolmen. There were also tales told of how one gang of youngsters put a water hose through a window of the police station. They turned on the nozzle and soaked the officer on duty. The boys were quickly apprehended by the drenched officer but were released when they threatened to tell the public "where you were last night and what you were doing."

There was one story reported of a twenty-one-year-old ex-con who was dubbed the "king of Broadway." He and his gang were allowed to "get away with anything he wants." The informants claimed certain members of the police force gave him protection from prosecution. These officers feared that the punk knew too much about their love lives.

The reporter told his eager readers that one man was "framed on a narcotics charge" because a policeman's girlfriend "wanted it that way." Egan reported that a selectman who was present when these accusations were made "seemed to hang his head with shame."

Selectmen William Boyce, Emile Bienvenue, and Harold DiPietro all admitted to reporter Egan that there had been some concerns about the morals of the last police chief. That, however, had been fixed with his resignation. On the other charges, though, they said there was absolutely no proof. They invited the public to bring to the selectmen their complaints—if they had any. The town fathers even promised as much confidentiality as the laws allowed.

After exposing the sins of the constabulary, Egan went after the general morality of the citizens. One unnamed women reportedly told him, "Peyton Place has to take a back seat to Derry, believe me."

To the readers of the *Union Leader*, the town of Derry was presented as the gambling capital of this section of the state. The press was told about a home on Crystal Avenue that had been in the betting business for more than two decades. Wages on horse races could be made at a Broadway news store and a downtown barbershop. An automobile sales room was the site of roulette and card and dice games. One bookie made daily rounds to the shoe factories to pick up bets on the "numbers game." According to his sources, there was fourteen hundred dollars bet every day in Derry.

To further enlighten his readers about the debauchery of the town, reporter Egan devoted considerable column space to sex.

Derry was presented as a town known "far and wide for its loose morals." One unnamed woman told him that she and her husband belonged to a wife-swapping "key club." She claimed that she took part only because of her fear of losing her husband if she didn't.

On Beaver Lake, according to a teenage boy, there was a cottage owned by a mother-daughter team who threw wild parties where "anything goes." The price of admission was a bottle of booze. The youngster also alleged there was a store in Derry where fifteen-year-olds could buy liquor if they were willing to pay a 50 percent premium. When Egan asked the teenager if sex occurred at these parties, the young person looked incredulously at the reporter and said, "Man, are you square? Of course it does . . . if you don't know how, you'll get taught in a hurry."

On and on went the accusations as reported by Egan. Derry's reputation was being tried in the court of public opinion. It didn't seem to matter that not a single one of these allegations could be substantiated. Some said that all Egan did was to put into the newspaper every bad thing he heard from every malcontent he met. There was no way to tell truth from fiction or to gauge the number of sinners in our town of ten thousand. The only good thing he said about Derry was that he believed no drugs were being used by our kids.

The first to publicly defend the honor of the town was the *Derry News*. Publisher and Editor Conrad Quimby published an editorial entitled "Come Now Mr. Egan, We're Not All That Bad." The newsman conceded that an investigation of the police force was probably in order—but believed the rest of the attacks were a "playboy fantasy" and that the articles were a disgrace to the field of journalism. Quimby wrote that just because the Manchester paper said Derry was "sick" didn't make it so.

Some residents believed the stories. Other felt that the *Union Leader* was printing those articles only as a way to sell more newspapers—and if this was true, it certainly succeeded. Newsstand sales of the Manchester paper did increase in Derry. Most of our citizens felt they had to know the particulars of how outsiders were trashing their town or perhaps to find out what their neighbors were up to.

In our churches, sermons were preached on the exposé of Derry. One pastor told his flock from the pulpit, "I truly pity him [Egan] that he must wallow so in the misery of others, blow it up beyond proportion and use it only to fill a column of newsprint."

The Reverend Daniel Courter, of Calvary Baptist Church, took the position that we are all sinners and that all people "should fall on their knees before God, confess the burdens of sin and claim God's forgiveness."

The selectmen on October 23, 1967, started to talk of hiring a lawyer. The three town fathers were angry. They were ready to take the *Union Leader* to court for besmirching the good reputation of Derry. The board felt that it was time to defend our honor and reputation.

The substance of the Derry story was reported all over the state. Human nature being what is, many people enjoyed these juicy bits of gossip. A couple of newspapers, however, printed editorials in defense of Derry. Their general consensus was that Derry was no better or worse than the average New England town. Derry, they felt, had a population made up of both saints and sinners and all shades in between. Quimby spoke for most in Derry when he said, "No town in our recollection has ever been so journalistically disemboweled as it was Derry's ill fortune to experience last week—but we withstood the onslaught well, gaining a sense of unity that can move mountains if we wish."

The end of the Loeb press's attack on Derry came because of the near certainty of a successful lawsuit for libel. The articles had made a number of scurrilous accusations against two sisters in town. Though Egan didn't use their actual names, he called them by their nicknames—"the Gold Dust Twins."

In small-town Derry, everyone and his brother knew who the Gold Dust Twins were. All their lives the strikingly beautiful Lewis twins had been called by that nickname. The pair even considered that the term was bestowed "favorably and with affection." The original Gold Dust Twins were two cartoon children who appeared in national advertisements for the popular Fairbanks brand of soap. Mrs. Millie Lewis DiMarzio (1923–1981) was a local real estate agent; Mrs. May Lewis Casten (1923–2004) was a columnist for the *Derry News*. Both ladies volunteered their time to serve on many local boards and committees. They justifiably felt that their honor had been forever stained by yellow journalism.

The two young women hired a prominent Manchester lawyer to file a four-hundred-thousand-dollar libel suit against publisher William Loeb and the Union Leader Corporation. The twins charged that the stories were published with a "wanton disregard of whether they were true or false" and had caused great harm to their reputations. The stories "made them objects of public ridicule, disgrace and scandal." Mr. Loeb in reply said that he would answer their charges in court.

The twins never did have their day in court. Bill Loeb wisely decided to settle the case out of court. He publicly apologized to the two women with a letter published in the various editions of the *Union Leader* and the *Sunday News*. He admitted, "Your righteous indignation at the false linking of your lives with the moral aberrations reportedly prevalent in Derry is certainly justified." Loeb further called the attacks on the women "rumor mongering" and said he regretted the airing of these completely false charges. I'm not privy to the particulars of the secret financial settlement between Loeb and the Gold Dust Twins. It is remembered, however, that Mrs. Casten for years enjoyed showing off an expensive mink coat she said was bought with Bill Loeb's money. She would later be elected to the town council, and served as the last mayor of Derry.

With the Loeb apology, the attacks on our town came to an end. Derry reverted to being a small town with all the usual small-town problems. Was there any truth to the dirt dug up by Egan? Perhaps a few of the charges were on the mark. Probably our police department did need reorganization back then. Chief Ed Garone has since run the force without public scandal for the last umpteen years. But most of what was told to the reporter was likely just idle gossip, exaggeration, or rumor. Adults and teenagers have always been eager to talk about what they "know" to be true—and too frequently it ain't.

Editor Conrad Quimby, after most of the dust had settled, reflected on five things Derry learned from these attacks. He said in an editorial that we now know "the danger of wagging an evil tongue; the elements that make good and bad journalism; the difference between fact and fiction; how to sell newspapers; and the remaining need to do some house keeping where we know dirt had accumulated for many years."

It has now been over forty years since the front page of the Manchester *Union Leader* called Derry a regular "Peyton Place" and that we should be called "Sin Town." We now have a pretty good relationship with that big city newspaper. Now, I think that's progress we can all applaud!

53.

The Eclipse

MOST PEOPLE WHO HAVE HAD OCCASION TO USE THE DERRY Public Library are familiar with Sherry Bailey. She's the petite reference librarian and master of the help desk. She is a kind, soothing voice for the informationally frazzled, a certain comfort in times of need. She and her coworkers Jack Robillard, Susan Brown, Cheryl Stockman, and Tim Sheehan labor without complaint to serve as my guides down the paths of the information superhighways and byways.

During much of March 2006 Sherry was missing from her desk and sorely missed. The explanation for her absence is that she and her friend Kerry Shetline took a trip to North Africa in pursuit of knowledge. Kerry is the host/creator of skyviewcafe.com, a very popular site that daily receives thousands of hits from fellow astronomy aficionados. The two locals decided to yield to the temptation of their passion (for things heavenly) and view the March 29 total eclipse. The best viewing spot was in the desert country of Libya.

Sherry and Kerry spent a week touring historical sites in Egypt before flying on to Libya. From their airport they were caravaned eighty kilometers into the sandy waste of the Sahara Desert. Finally, at the end of a temporary one-lane road, they reached their destination. It was a city of more than a thousand tents that had been set up in the desert to accommodate the foreign tourists and scientists who had come to view the grand celestial event. The only sign of civilization in that flat sand barren was oil-drilling rigs profiled against the horizon. At night the temperature fell to forty

The eclipse in Derry, August 31, 1932. Allen photo.

degrees in their canvas tents. During the day it got hot. This remote area had been chosen by eclipse experts because it was free from light pollution, would have the longest view of totality, and have the greatest likelihood of a cloud-free sky.

In midday on March 29 the eclipse began. The desert started to feel cooler, and the horizon took on a strange burnt orange glow. The darkness of the blacked-out sun lasted only four minutes and fourteen seconds. A thousand cameras and camcorders snapped into action recording the sun's corona, the diamond ring effect, and Baily's Beads. Glorious! The experience was priceless—or almost so. Using my calculator, I figure it cost Sherry and Kerry about $39.37 for every second they watched the celestial event in North Africa. Kerry thinks it was worth it; Sherry is still deciding.

Here in Derry we've had partial eclipses of the sun in 1972, 1984, and 1994. The last total eclipse occurred here on August 31, 1932. On that day, a 104-mile-wide path of darkness cut across New England and stretched from the province of Quebec to Kennebunkport, Maine. The totality of darkness lasted only one minute and forty-four seconds. One town in Massachusetts reported that when the darkness descended, the "cows headed for the barn and chickens began to roost."

Visiting in Derry in August 1932 was Dr. Walter Adams, the head of the Pasadena, California Mount Wilson Observatory. He was a Pinkerton Academy graduate and world famous astronomer. He and his team had set up cameras in several places in New Hampshire to record the event on film for the Smithsonian Institution. His uncle Benjamin Adams was the donor of the Adams Memorial Building. This building is, of course, the home of the Derry Museum of History.

In Derry the eclipse was accepted with stoic appreciation for the workings of nature. Nobody seemed to get all that excited. Local photographer Charles Allen took a picture of the event and sold it around town for a nickel a copy.

The businessmen of Chester took a different view. They saw the eclipse as an opportunity to improve their business market share. Chester J. Wilcomb advertised that his Cloverfarm Store at Chester Center would be having a five-day eclipse sale. He further publicized the fact that he would give away dark-colored glass to allow for easy viewing of the eclipse. He created this optical prophylactic by the time-honored technique of using a smoking candle to make a soot-covered piece of window glass. Some local stores sold official eclipse spectacles made of dark-colored cellophane set into a cardboard frame. (Today we know such eclipse-viewing devices to be very, very dangerous. A medically approved solar or welder's filter glass is recommended to help protect the spectator from eye damage.)

The publicity seemed to have worked well for the businessmen of Chester. It was estimated that seven hundred automobiles made it to the little hill town to see the great eclipse. Wilson's Market did a land-office business selling ice-cream cones. Bell Hill Candy

Kitchen quickly sold out its entire stock of sweets. Lots of people bought postcards and wrote notes to their friends about being in Chester for the eclipse. Many locals set up roadside farm stands and did the best business of the entire year. As a welcoming gesture, Mr. Wilcomb put benches and seats outside his Cloverfarm Store; he also hung posters on his storefront to educate spectators on what to watch for during the eclipse. The stone wall of the cemetery was covered with spectators and the sides of the road became an automobile parking lot for half a mile in all directions from Chester Center. Since that summer day in 1932, the town of Chester has been a lot more quiet.

The next total eclipse of the sun is scheduled to visit Derry in the year 2035. I will then be in my ninetieth year. I fully anticipate that on that day I will be standing on a hilltop in Chester with an ice-cream cone in one hand and a soot-covered piece of glass in the other. I hope you'll make plans to join me. Driving to Chester is a damn sight cheaper than flying to Libya. And besides, I don't like Mu'ammar Gadhafi all that much anyway.

Bibliography

Belknap, Jeremy. *The History of New Hampshire.* 3 vols. Boston: Bradford and Read, 1812.

Brinkley, Douglas. *The Boys of Pointe du Hoc.* New York: HarperCollins Co., 2005.

Browne, George Waldo *Early Records of Londonderry, Windham and Derry N.H. 1719–1745.* [Proprietor's records] Manchester, N.H.: John B. Clarke Co., 1911.

Browne, George Waldo. *Early Records of Londonderry, Windham and Derry, N.H. 1719–1762.* [Town Clerk's records] Manchester N.H.: John B. Clarke Co., 1908.

Browne, George Waldo and Daniel Gage Annis. *Vital Records of Londonderry, New Hampshire.* Manchester, N.H.: The Granite State Publishing Company, 1914.

Clarke, John B. *The Northwood Murder.* Manchester, N.H.: Mirror and Farmer Publishing Co., 1872.

Cummings, O.R. *Trolleys to Beaver Lake.* Forty Fort, PA: Harold E. Cox, 1990.

Daniel, Jere R. *Colonial New Hampshire.* Millwood, N.Y.: KTO Press, 1981.

Derry Historic Research Committee. *From Turnpike to Interstate.* Canaan, N.H.: Phoenix Publishing, 1977.

Forsaith, Carl Cheswell. *Pinkerton Academy 1814–1964.* Derry, N. H.: Edward O. Hatch, 1965.

Gebler, Carlo. *The Siege of Derry.* Boston: Little, Brown, 2005.

Laycock, John Noble. *Employment Unlimited.* Derry, N.H.: Cole-Noble Co., 1945.

Levassseur, Auguste, translated by Alan R. Hoffman. *Lafayette in America in 1824 and 1825.* Manchester, N.H.: Lafayette Press, 1906.

Londonderry Historical Society. *Early Londonderry Tidbits and Historical Sketches.* 4 vols. N.P.: 1962, 1968, 1972.

Morrison, Leonard. *The History of Windham in New Hampshire.* Boston: Cupples. Upham & Co. 1883.

Newell, Harriett Chase. *Houses of Derry Village N. H.* Littleton, N.H.:
    The Courier Printing Co. 1951.
Newell, Harriett Chase. *Houses of the Double Range and East Derry,
    N.H.* Littleton, N.H.: The Courier Printing Co. 1954.
Newell, Harriett Chase. *Houses of the English Range and Beaver Lake
    Derry, N.H.* Littleton, N.H.: The Courier Printing Co. 1959.
Newell, Harriett Chase. *Houses of West Derry New Hampshire.*
    Littleton, N.H.: The Courier Printing Co., 1963.
Newell, Harriett Chase. *In Retrospect.* Littleton, N.H.: The Courier
    Printing Co., 1968.
Newell, Harriett Newell. *Outlying Districts of Derry New Hampshire.*
    Littleton, N.H.: The Courier Printing Co., 1965.
Newell, Harriett Chase. *Through the Years with Central Congregational
    Church Derry Village, N.H.* Littleton, N.H.: The Courier Printing
    Co., 1972.
Parker, Rev. Edward L. *The History of Londonderry.* Boston: Perkins
    and Whipple 1851.
Schmidtchen, Ferne F., editor for Town History Committee. *The
    History of Londonderry,* Vol.3. Somersworth, N.H.: New England
    History Press, 1977.
Stern, Madeline B. *So much in a Lifetime, the story of Dr. Isabel
    Barrows.* New York: Julian Messner, 1964.
Stearns, Ezra S. *Genealogical and Family History of the State of New
    Hampshire.* 4 vols. New York: Lewis Publishing Co., 1908.
Upton, Richard Francis. *Revolutionary New Hampshire.* Hanover,
    N.H.: Dartmouth College, 1936.
Willey, George F. *Willey's Book of Nutfield.* Derry Depot, N.H.:
    N.P.,1895.

Newspapers
Most of the information and stories of daily life in Nutfield
was gleaned from years of researching the local newspapers.
Unfortunately scrapbooks frequently contain clippings without dates
or the names of the newspaper from which they were cut.
Derry (NH) *News*: 1880 to present
Derry (N.H.) *Serviceman:* 1944-1946
Evening Record, Derry, N.H.:1919-1933
Exeter (N.H.) *News-Letter:* 1831-1880
Londonderry (N.H.) *Times*: 1866-1882
New Hampshire Gazette, Portsmouth, N.H.: 1756-1831

The Derry (N.H.) *Star.* 1958-1971
Union Leader, Manchester, N.H.1967

Manuscripts, public documents, collections, etc.
Annual Reports, Town of Derry, N.H.1836 to present
Derry Public Library. Their most helpful staff is eager to assist in
    finding items in their New Hampshire room. Many of the area's
    newspapers are contained in their microfilm collection.
Heritage Commission, Town of Derry, N.H. Within its collections
    are a large, varied collection of documents, scrapbooks, books,
    diaries, photographs and newspapers relating to the history of
    the Nutfield towns.
New Hampshire Historical Society, Concord, N.H. It houses the state's
    greatest collection of books, maps and manuscripts relating to
    the history of New Hampshire. Its genealogical and town history
    collection is outstanding.
New Hampshire State Library, Concord, N.H. It has a vast collection
    of historical newspapers on microfilm.
New Hampshire State Archives, Concord, N.H. Within its collections
    of well over a million documents are files relating to all aspects
    of Nutfield's history.
Town Clerk's records of the Nutfield towns of Derry, Londonderry
    and Windham 1722 to present. The earliest volumes are at the
    state achieves, Concord, N.H. Much of the 18th century material
    has been transcribed by George Waldo Brown and published in
    3 volumes.
Pillsbury Family Archives. The collections of several members of this
    venerable family contain much information on the early life of
    William and Leonard Pillsbury.
Provincial and State Papers. These 34 volumes were printed by the
    state during the 19th century and contain a wealth of official
    documents from the 17th and 18th century. Many local Libraries
    have the complete set.
Reports to the Legislature- 19th and 20th century printed reports by
    various state department including railroads, trolleys, schools
    and agriculture. A complete set is at the State Library.
Taylor Library, East Derry has a fine collection of local items
    including manuscripts on the Adams Female Academy.

Index

A & P store, 335
Abbott, Charles, 137, 234
Abbott, Ernest, 234
Abbott, sheriff, 147, 149
Acorace, Dominic, 331
Adam, Lucien, 238 241
Adam's School, 182
Adams Female Academy, 73-74, 195, 262,
Adams Memorial Building, 128, 257, 261, 278, 335
Adams Mill, 261-266
Adams Pond, 262, 265-266, 306
Adams, Benjamin, 235, 261-263, 266, 335, 355
Adams, Dora, 239
Adams, Edmund, 262
Adams, Edward F., 239
Adams, George F., 208
Adams, Helen, 155, 238
Adams, Jacob, 262
Adams, Samuel, 80
Adams, Walter, 238-243, 355
Adams, William, 82-84
Aghadowney, 4-6
Agway Store, 285
Aiken, James, 30-39, 83
Al's Food Center, 341
Alexander-Eastman Hospital, 299, 304
Alexander, Harrison, 204
Alexander, Randall, 6
Allen, Charles, 354-355
Allen, Sarah, 256
Allison, Samuel, 6
American Legion, 304, 333, 344
American Revolution, 30-39, 40-54

Amoskeag, 14-16
Anderson, Allen, 6
Anderson, James 6
Angell Family, 188-193
Angell, Edmund, 182, 189-193, 234
Angell, Everett, 189-193
Angell, Lizzie, 189-193
Angell, Ralph, 190, 192-193
Anti-war, 135-136
Apkaker, Lewis C. 334
Apples, 143
Aristos, 270
Association Hall, 145, 172, 207-213,
Association Test, 38-39, 47-48
Atkin family, 34, 37
Babcock, Bert, 290
Back peddlers, 104
Bailey, Sherry, 290, 353-354
Bannister, Zilpah Polly Grant, 73-74
Barnett, John, 6
Barr, Gabriel, 111
Barrington Beggars, 90-94
Barrington, N.H., 90-91
Barrows, Isabel Hayes Chapin, 194-200
Barrows, Mabel Hayes, 198
Barrows, Samuel, 196-199
Barry the Continental Cobbler, 336
Bartlett, Charles, 167, 171, 222-224, 232, 271
Bartlett, Greenleaf, 208
Bartlett, Nathaniel, 117- 118, 120-121
Baseball, 233 -237
Bass, Perkins, 338
Bears, 95-99, 285-289

Beaver Lake Pavilion, 257, 286-288, 337

Beaver Lake, 285, 309

Belknap, Jeremy, 95

Bell Hill Candy, 355

Bell, Charles, 117

Bell, John, 42, 44, 209, 234

Bell, Louis, 154

Bell, Luther V. 154, 195

Bell, Samuel, 234

Bell, Samuel, 75

Bell's Opera house, 164-166, 254

Bellamy, Francis, 183

Benson, Grant, 286

Benson, H. L., 271

Benson, W. H., 247

Benson's Hardware, 168

Benson's Wild Animal Farm, 300

Betts, Doyle R., 307

Bienvenue, Emile, 349

Bingham, George, 146, 231

Blackwell, Elizabeth, 196

Bleeding, 24

Blistering, 93

Blowing-out day, 192

Bonner, Richard, 335

Boroski, Gil, 341

Borowski family, 311-313, 316, 323, 325

Borowski, Jerry, 312-314, 322-323

Borowski, Walter, 311-327

Bouchard, Drina, 344

Bourassa, Theresa, 325

Boy Scouts, 304, 333, 344

Boy's Club, 213

Boyce, William, 349

Boyd, William, 5

Bradford, Frank, 147

Bradford, William, 234

Brewer, Russell, 338

Brickett, Leonard, 207

Broadway, 62-63, 79, 124-129, 134, 140-151, 167-172,

Brown, Raymond J. 310

Brown, Susan, 353

Brown, Winifred, 16

Brownies, 344

Buckley, Frank, 335

Buckley, Raymond, 135

Buckley, Rita, 135

Buffum, Skip, 335

Burdick, Gladys, 16

Burdick, Lee, 335

Bureau, Ed, 331

Burnham, John, 83

Burnside, Thomas, 109 -111

Byrne, Albert J. 290

Byrne, Mamie, 290

Caesar, 23-26

Caleb Stark, 75

Campbell, Cassius, 223

Candia, 176

Capital punishment, 179-180

Cargill, David, 261

Carr, John, 12

Casey, Dan, 259

Casten, May, 351-352

Catholics, 250-260

Central Congregational Church, 210, 212-213, 240, 310

Chagnon, Gene, 266

Chanticleer Restaurant, 330

Chapin, Bella, see Isabel Hayes Barrows

Chapin, William, 195-196

Chase Mill, 186, 272

Chase, John Carroll, 211-212

Chelmsford-Hardy Place, 337

Chelmsford Shoe factory, 328-337

Chen's Restaurant, 72, 216

Chester and Derry Trolley, 187

Chester, 84, 221-226, 279, 355-356

Child labor, 126

Choate, William, 80, 83, 207

Chrispeen family, 102-106

Chrispeen Farm, 100

Christian Science church, 272
Churchill, Winston, 235
Cigars, 246-249
Circus, 205, 288-289, 297-300
Citizens Building Assoc. 127
Civil War, 123-124, 131-133, 138,
    152-155
Clark, David, 191-192
Clark, Edna, 305
Clark, James, 6
Clark, John, 84
Clark, Matthew, 8
Clark, Nancy, 271
Clement, Coburn shoe factory, 125
Clement, Erskine & Co. 125
Clendinon, Archibald, 6
Coburn & Fuller shoe factory,
    125-126
Cochran, John, 96, 108-109
Cohen, Joseph, 248
Colbath, Jeremiah, 93-94
Colby, George A., 169
Cole, William, 308
Columbus Day, 181-183
Comeau, Augusta, 286
Comeau, James, 286-288, 293
Comeau, Will, 286
Concord, 33
Cook, John, 213
Cosgrove, Alice, 19
Cote, Alan, 187
Cote, Harvey, 331-332
Courter, Daniel, 351
Craig family, 101-102
Crime, 101-107, 173-180
Crowell, Peter, 97
Cub Scouts, 344
Cummings, Anne, 32
Currier and Boyd shoe Factory, 123,
    125
Curtis, David H., 208
D.A.A. Field, 299
Dana, Daniel, 74

Daniels, Jere, 30
Dark Day, 118-119
Dar-Ling Oil, 269
Darling, Willis E. 267-271
Davidson, William, 158
Davis, Ralph, 278
Daylight Saving Time, 277-280
D-Day, 318-323
Derby, Elias Haskett, 71-72
Derry-Londonderry split , 77-85
Derry Athletic Assoc. 295
Derry Board of Trade, 247, 278
Derry Brass Band, 223, 257
Derry Building Co. 207-208
Derry Depot, *see* Broadway
Derry Driving Club, 285
Derry Drug Co. 271
Derry Enterprise, 212
Derry Fire Dept., 258-259, 261-265,
    332
Derry Flying Club, 283
Derry Museum of History, 262, 268,
    346
Derry News, 63, 107, 117-118, 120
    128, 136, 150, 159, 166-167, 171-
    172, 186, 212, 223, 228, 231-232,
    245, 247-248, 271, 285, 293, 295-
    296, 305, 331-332, 335-336, 344,
    348, 350-352
Derry Shoe Co. 127, 336
Derry Village Fire Dept. 254
Derry Village, 78, 114-115, 152-155,
    189-193
Derry, 3 villages, 167
Derry, Northern Ireland, 1-9, 85,
    308-309
Derryfield, 16
Devil, 65
Diamond Bruce, 249
Dickey, Joseph, 81
DiMarzio, Mildred, 342, 351-352
Dion, Henry L., 335
DiPietro, Harold, 349

Doe, Charles, 178
Doherty, Charlie, 325
Downs, Benjamin, 115-116
Downs, Mary, 115-116
Dracut, 6, 15
Drew, Samuel, 271
Duffy, John, 253, 255
Duffy, Mary, 253
Dunn, Daniel, 253, 259
Dunn, Trish, 233
Dustin, Erwin, 294
Eagles Club, 247, 257, 259
East Derry Fire Dept. 265, 285
East Derry Meeting House, *see* First
    Parish Church
East Derry succession, 85
East Derry, 21-26, 41
Eastman, Benjamin, 102
Eaton, Eliza, 190
Eaton, Elmer, 294
Eclipse, 353-356
Eels, 16, 20
Egan, Arthur C. 347-352
Elch, 206
Elections, 295
Elephant, 299-300
Ellis, Homer, 294
Emerson, Arthur, 190, 222-223
Emerson, Charles S., 129
Emerson's Music Store, 295
English Range, 32
Enslin, Irving, 278
Escumbuit, 12
Estes, George, 203
Etz Hayim Synagogue, 249
Evans, Benjamin, 176-177
Evans, family, 173-174,177
Evans, Franklin, 173-180
Evans, James, 36, 176
Exeter, 49-52, 178-179
Ezekiel, 14-15, 20
Ezekiel's Pond, 14, 16
Farm animals, 203

Fire Department, 167-172
Fire house, 172
Fire, 134, 167-172, 218, 254, 256-259,
    261-266, 328-337
First Baptist church, 136-137, 142,
    169, 171, 278-280,
First National Store, 335
First Parish Church, 8, 12, 41-43, 46,
    76, 80-82, 157-159, 257, 293, 340
Fisher, Ebenezer, 83
Fisher, John, 98
Fitz, Isabelle, 225
Fitzgerald, Dan, 331
Fleming, Nancy Anne, 344
Flood, 185-187
Floyd, Charles, 234-237, 247, 257
Forest Hill Cemetery, 29, 54, 89, 195,
    192-193, 195, 243, 272, 315
Franklin, Ben, 277
Frasier, Charles Warren, 273
French and Indian War, 41, 108
French, Samuel, 89
French-Canadian, 259
Frost, Robert, 17, 210-212, 227,
    273-274
Fulton, Robert, 50, 157
Gage, Billy R., 79
Gage, William Washington, 113-114
Gallant, Albert, 334
Gallant, Louis, 334
Galvin, Frank, 334
Gambling, 349
Ganem's Market, 304
Garone, Ed, 352
Garrison, 13
Getz, Beverly, 291
Getz, Stan, 291
Gilchrest, David, 87-88
Gilcreast, Daniel, 98-99
Gilmore, Robert, 261
Girl Scouts, 344
Gold Dust Twins, 351-352
Gordon, Anna Payne, 294

Gordon, Everett Payne, 294-295
Gordon, Irving, 294
Gould, Albert, 68
Goundrey's Funeral Home, 333
Granary of Derry, 220
Grand Army of the Republic, 128
Grange, 344
Gregg, Benjamin, 208
Gregg, James, 13
Gregg, James, 6
Gregg, Lucinda, 9
Gregg, Washington F., 208
Griffith, David, 294
Grinnell School, 335
Grinnell, George, 210, 331
Guilmette, Christa, 213
Guilmette, Cory, 213
Gypsies, 94
Hall, Carl, 294
Hallowell, Benjamin, 281
Ham, Marilyn, 113
Hamblett, Otis, 13
Hargreaves Circus, 288-289
Hartly, Douglas, 272
Hartly, Rosalind, 272
Haverley's Minstrels, 164-166
Hawkins, Robert, 240-241
Hayes, Anna, 195
Hayes, Henry, 195
Hebrew Society, 248
Heffelfinger, Steve, 289
Hell, 61-63
Hemlock Oil, 267-272
Hidden Valley Golf Course, 305
Historical society, 9
Hogg, Joseph, 157
Hoisington, G.W., 261, 264-265
Holland family, 42-43
Holland Family, 54
Holland, Jane, 42, 52-54
Holland, John 52-54
Holland, Stephen 22-26, 33-35, 40-54
Holland's Cleaners, 314

Holmes and Wheeler Co. 333
Holmes, Richard, 357
Holmes, William, 4
Hood farm, 181, 214-220, 302
Hood School, 305
Hood, Charles Harvey, 216, 218
Hood, Charles, 218
Hood, Gilbert, 213, 217-218
Hood, Harvey, P. 72, 171, 208,
    215-218
Hood, Joseph M., 203
Hoodkroft Golf Club, 219
Hoodkroft, see Hood farm
Horse Hill, 21-26, 41, 63, 65-67
Hotel Bradford, 146-148, 172
Houle, Frank, 334
Hudson, 300
Hume, Patricia W., 16
Humphrey, William, 27-29
Humphrey, Willie, 6
Hurricane, 301-306
Hyde's Heading, 295
Ice, 219
Iceboats, 281-284
Indians, 11-17
Irish, 259
Jackson, Lemuel, 157
James, MacGregor, 13
Jewish faith, 243-249
John Moor, 48
Johnson, Al, 342
Jones Hotel, 170
Josselyn, Mr. 96-97
JP's Superette, 272
Kassian, Nicholas, 248
Katsakiores, George, 341
Keith, Arnold, 335
Kelly, Earl, 294
Kelly, Jim, 203
Kerry, John, 8
Kilrea, 27-29
Kingston, 15
KlevBros Shoe Co. 314, 325, 335-336

Knights of Pythias, 233
L. H. Pillsbury & Son, 134-135
Ladies Benevolent Society, 210
Lafayette Spring, 72 -73
Lafayette, Marquis de, 71-75
Lambert's Cornet Band, 171
Langdon, John 51
Langdon, Woodbury, 51
Law and Order Society, 146-147
Lawyer, 55 -59
Laycock family, 308
Laycock, John Noble, 307-310
Laycock, Mildred Cole, 308, 310
Leathers Family, 90-94
Lewis, Bella, 245-245
Lewis, Joseph, 246
Lewis, Louis, 244-249
Lewis, Max, 246
Livermore, Samuel, 54 -55
Loeb, William, 351-352
Londonderry-Derry split, 77-85
Londonderry Turnpike, 78
Londonderry, Northern Ireland, see
    Derry, Northern Ireland
Lovering, Georgianna, 177-178, 180
Lovering, Harold, 113
Lovering, Nellie, 113
Low, Richard, 294
Lowell, 88
Lurvey, Cora, 115
Lutwyche, Edward Goldstone, 35-36
Lyon, Mary, 73
Lyon, Vernon, 299-300
MacGregor, Alexander, 109-110
MacGregor, David, 110
MacGregor, James, 3-9,12, 17, 54,
    110, 157
MacGregor, Susan, 109-110
MacGregor, William R., 205
Mack, Robert, 18, 79, 85
Mack, Wallace, 129
MacMurphy, Alexander, 262
MacMurphy, John, 262

Madden, James, 252, 255
Madden, John, 157,234, 236, 252
Madden, Margaret, 252
Madden, William, 234
Madden's Restaurant, 286
Magnet Printing Co., 148
Manchester Fire Department, 170
Manchester Union, 143
Manchester, 15, 16, 33,
Mannarini, Gail, 335
Margolis, Art, 343
Marriage, 108-116
Martin, Ellsworth, 255
Masons, 209
Matson, Charlie, 334
May, Henry, 171
McDonald, William, 252
McGrail, Edward, 334
McGregor, Frank, 278
McKeen, James, 6, 28-29
McMurphy, Abby, 89
McMurphy, Alexander, 101 -102
McMurphy, Archibald, 14
McMurphy, Elizabeth, 14
McMurphy, Henry, 88-89
McMurphy, James, 88-89
McMurphy, Sally, 87-89
Medicine, 93
Meevers, Frank, 31
Melvin, Richard, 88
Men's League, 211-212
Merriam, Charles, 211
Merrick, R.R., 169
Merrill, Lillian, 114-115
Methodist Church, 159
Mihalko, Ryan, 233
Milk, 215-220
Mills, Eliza, 175-176
Mills, Mary,175
Mills, Nancy, 175-176, 180
Mills, Stephen, 175-176
Miltimore, John, 80, 83
Minstrel shows, 163-166, 257

Mitchell, John, 6
Monster, 201-2006
Montgomery farm, 202-204
Moor, Robert, 48-49
Moore, Robert, 157
Morrison, Jane, 7
Morrison, John, 6,7,83
Morse, Amos, 204
Morse, William, 293
Movies, 138
Murder, 101-107, 173-180
Murdock-White farm, 215
Mussey, Henry, 198
Names, 96
Nancy's Meadow, 180
Nashua, 33
Native Americans, *see* Indians
Navy, 275-276
Nesmith, James, 6
New Hampshire Gazette, 158-159
Newell, Harriett Chase, 210
Newell, Henry, 190
Newell, John P. 154-155
Northumberland, 110-111
Northwood, 177 -178
Norton, Anne Frasier, 273-276
Norton, Edwin Asa, 274-275
Noyes, John, 103
Nutfield Colony, 6-8, 11-20, 22, 27,
    78-79
Nutting, Roger, 334
O'Brien, John, 252
O'Connor, William J., 253-256
Oak Street School, 341
Odd Fellows, 169, 172
Old Home Day, 257
Oregon Indian Medicine Co. 267-268
Owen, Alice, 252
Owen, Daniel, 252, 255
Oxen Yoke Restaurant, 330
Palmer, Phil, 334
Parade, 154-155, 338-246
Parker, Anne, 273

Parker, Edward, 31, 71, 112
Parsons, Marie, 209
Passaconaway, 11
Pattern Murdock White Farm, 18 -19
Patterson, Robert, 82 -83
Patterson, Thomas, 83
Payne, Nelson, 147, 149-150
Peabody Funeral Home, 333
Peavey, Gardner, 174
Perrin, Robin, 273
Phalan, G.M., 249
Philippine Insurrection, 136
Pillsbury Family, 122-151
Pillsbury Guard, 127
Pillsbury Shoe Company, 125-129
Pillsbury, Ambrose Burnside, 135
Pillsbury, Ann, 130
Pillsbury, Everett, 135
Pillsbury, Frederick, 144, 147, 149
Pillsbury, John, 137
Pillsbury, Josiah, 134
Pillsbury, Lavinia, 123, 130-131
Pillsbury, Leonard, 63, 123-124, 130-
    139, 140-151
Pillsbury, Martha, 128
Pillsbury, Parker, 130
Pillsbury, Rosecrans, 97, 128-129,
    142-151, 190, 234-236, 255, 257
Pillsbury, Stephen, 123, 130-131
Pillsbury, Walter, 139, 234, 294
Pillsbury, William, 122-129, 134, 141-
    151, 169, 172, 216, 222, 255
Pinkerton Academy, 74, 154-155, 182,
    195, 211-212, 223, 227-237, 239
    -240, 273-274, 282, 294, 313, 333,
    340, 343
Pinkerton George, 160
Pinkerton Tavern Restaurant, 87, 305
Pinkerton, James, 87-88, 99
Pinkerton, John, 83
Plaza Theater, 298, 330
Pledge of Allegiance, 183
Politics, 150

Poor, Helen Brickett, 209 -210
Poor, William W. 150
Porter, John, 79-84
Portsmouth, 8, 33, 44-45
Potatoes, 10, 17-20
Prentice, family, 59
Prentice, John, 55
Prentice, Ruth, 57
Prentice, Tabitha, 58
Presbyterian, 4, 78, 111, 141-142
Prescott, Samuel Cate, 272
Proctor, Alex, 16, 212
Prohibition, see temperance
Public Service Co. 333
Putnam, Hiram, 146
Quebec, 41
Quimby, Conrad, 350-352
Radio, 293-296
Rail road, 62-63
Railroad, 160, 221-222, 278, 293
Rangers, 315-327
Raymond, Carrie, 114
Rebeccas, 233
Red Cross, 333
Red Men, 247
Redfield's Tavern, 72, 74-75
Reid, Abraham, 51
Reid, David, 87
Reid, George, 109
Reid, George, 39, 42, 43, 44
Reid, Mary (Molly), 108-109
Reid, Sarah, see Sally McMurphy
Reynolds, Ernest, 285, 287
Reynolds, Lula, 285, 287
Reynolds, Ned, 285-289
Richard, Bob, 302
Rider, John, 334
Roach, Harriett E. 113-114
Robillard, Jack, 353
Roger's Rangers, 41
Rogers, Robert, 12, 42-43, 315
Rollins & Smith's general store, 171
Rollins, George F. 164-166

Rollins, George S., 254
Ryan's Hill, 15
Sainer, Barney, 248
Saint Thomas Aquinas Church, 250-260, 292
Salvation Army, 333
Sanders, Walter, 233-234, 237
Sawmill, 97
Scarlet fever, 191
Scenic Movie Theater, 259
Schools, 227-232
Scipio, 23-26
Scotch-Irish, 1-9, 109, 112
Scott, Kenneth, 31,
Seeler, Albert O., 272
Seeler, Clara, 272
Seeler, Emil Felix, 271-272
Sefton, Charles, 114-115
Sello Bros. Circus, 298-299
Senter, Walter, 294
Shackett, Josie, 306
Shamroth, Simon, 248
Sheehan, Tim, 353
Sheep, 105-107
Shepard and Bartlett Insurance Co., 340
Shepard family, 339-341
Shepard, Alan B., 226, 338-346
Shepard, Frederick F., 281-282
Shepard, Frederick, 182, 222
Shetline, Kerry, 353-354
Shivaree, 112-115
Shoe making, 122-129
Shoes, 148
Siegel, Sadie, 248
Simpson family, 159
Slaves, 23-26, 157-159
Smith Hall, 254
Smith, Alden Bradford, 172
Smith, Annie, 282
Smith, Frank, 115
Smith, James, 282
Smith, Myron M., 282-284

Smith, Paul, 284
Smith, Thomas, 12
Smyth, Frederick, 160-161
Sons of Union Veterans, 127
Spanish-American War, 135
Spanish flu, 275
Spector, Maurice, 248
Sports, 233-237, 281-284
St. Luke's Methodist church, 146
Stark, Archibald, 13
Stark, James, 13
Stark, John, 8, 12-13, 39, 42, 47, 49,
    109-110, 315
Stark, William, 16, 49, 315
Steele, Thomas, 6, 27-29, 109
Sterrett, James, 6
Stewart, Buddy, 290-292
Stewart, Flora, 156-162
Stewart, George, 159-160
Stewart, Isaiah, 159
Stewart, John, 6
Stewart, Martha, 291
Stewart, Salona, 159-161
Stinson, John, 42, 51,
Stinson, Mary Hogg, 42
Stockman, Cheryl, 353
Stokes, Orrin, 183
Sullivan, John, 39
Sullivan, John, 52-53
Sulloway, Cyrus, 224
Sutton, Thomas, 296
Sutton's Barber Shop, 171
Sweet Adelines, 335
Tabernacle Society, 292
Tappan, Everett, 299
Tavern, 41-42
Taylor Library, 71
Taylor, Emma, 195
Telephone, 293
Television, 296
Temperance, 62, 137-138, 141-151,
    161, 240,
Tenney, David, 81

Tewksbury, Walter, 335
Thom, Isaac, 159-160
Thom, James, 159, 79, 81, 83-84
Thom's Tavern, 63
Thornton, Matthew, 24, 39, 42, 44, 47,
    60-62, 109, 234
Thyng, Adie, 147
Thyng, Ralph, 147 -149
Toilets, 189-190
Trolley, 221-226, 279, 337
Tsienneto, 12
Tucker Alanson, 79 -82, 84
Tuckyner, Charles, 248
Tuttle, Harry, 271
Tyler, George, 257
Ulster 1-9
Union Leader, 187, 347-352
Upper Meadow, 21-22, 26
Upper Village Hall, 19, 209
Upper Village, 78
Upper Village, see East Derry
Vance, William, 45
Veterans of Foreign Wars, 333, 344
Vietnam, 276
Vietnam, 307
Wagner, Drew, 273
Wallace, Thomas, 158
Walsh, Catherine Anne, 273
Washington, Booker T. 198
Watkins, Mother, 67-68
Watts, Nathan, 114
Weir, Robert, 6
Welcome Wagon, 344
Wells Oil Co., 333
Wentworth, John, 32-39, 44, 47, 48,
    110-111
West Derry, see Broadway
West Running Brook, 13, 17
Wheelwright, John, 11
White, Carolyn Murdock, 18-19
White's Restaurant, 341
Whittier, Aaron, 224

Whittier, John Greenleaf, 4, 90-92, 119, 131-132

Wilcomb, Arthur, 222

Wilcomb, Chester J., 355-356

Willey, George Franklyn, 31

Wilson, Henry, 93 -94

Wilson, James, 96-97

Wilson, Mary, 96

Wilson, Rachel, 111

Wilson's Market, 355

Windham, 78, 84, 98, 118, 159

Winter, 128

Witch Hazel, 68-70

 Witch, 67-70

Women, 144

Woodburn, Mary, *see* Mary Reid

Woodbury Shoe Factory, 127

World War I, 275-276, 307

World War II, 283-284, 297-298, 308-309, 311-327

Wright, E.F., 203

Yellow Day, 117-121

Young, Gustle, 203-204

Young, Mason, 274

About the Author

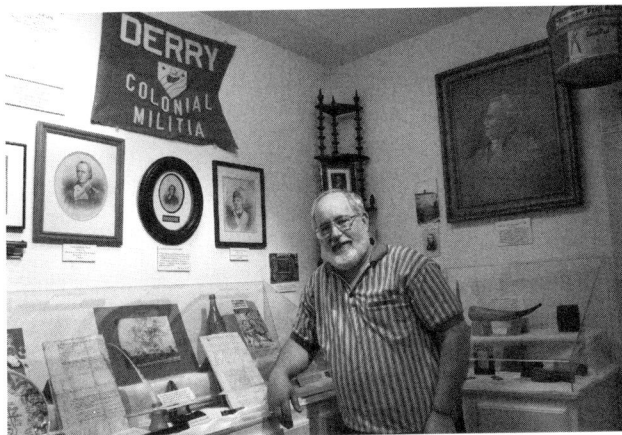

RICHARD HOLMES WAS BORN ON SEPTEMBER 6, 1945, IN DERRY, NEW Hampshire. He is the son of the late John B. and Marjorie Andrews Holmes. He attended the local schools in Sandown, New Hampshire and graduated from Sanborn Seminary (1963). He received a bachelor's degree in Education from Keene State College in 1963 and his master's degree in history from Rivier College in 1980. He served with the U.S. Army in Viet Nam (1969–1970) as a medic with a combat battalion.

In 1970 he married Carol Martineau and the couple moved to Derry. They are proud to be the parents of John B. Holmes III and Leah K. Gonzalez, and grandparents to Jacob Holmes and Christopher Gonzalez.

Since 1985 Richard has been a member of the Derry Heritage Commission and its chairman since 1995. In 2003 he founded the Derry Museum of History. Since 2004 he has been a regular columnist for the *Derry News* and a frequent contributor to the *Nutfield News*, the *Lawrence Eagle Tribune* and the *Manchester Union Leader*.

In 2007, Richard Holmes received an Award of Merit from the American Association for State and Local History (AASLH), the most prestigious recognition for achievement in the preservation and interpretation of state and local history.

Nutfield Rambles is his fifth published volume on local history. He is a trustee of the Frost Farm state historical site in Derry.